W9-DDY-819

PSYCHOSOMATIC MEDICINE: THEORY, PHYSIOLOGY, AND PRACTICE

Volume I

International Universities Press
Stress and Health Series
Leo Goldberger, Ph.D.
Editor

Monograph 1

Psychosomatic Medicine: Theory, Physiology, and Practice

Volume I

Edited by

Stanley Cheren, M.D.

International Universities Press, Inc.
Madison   Connecticut

Library of Congress Cataloging-in-Publication Data

Psychosomatic medicine : theory, physiology, and practice / edited by
   Stanley Cheren.
      p. cm.—(Stress and health series ; monograph 1-2)
   Includes bibliographies and index.
   ISBN 0-8236-5725-6 (v. 1)—ISBN 0-8236-5726-4 (v. 2)
      1. Medicine, Psychosomatic. 2. Psychophysiology. I. Cheren,
Stanley. II. Series.
      [DNLM: 1. Psychophysiologic Disorders. W1 ST799K monograph 1-2 /
WM 90 P9752]
   RC49.P823 1989
   616.08—dc 19
   DNLM/DLC
   for Library of Congress   89-1669
                                                                     CIP

Manufactured in the United States of America

Contents
Volume I

Contents
Volume II

Contributors to Volumes I and II

Charles Spencer Adler, M.D., F.A.P.A., Chief, Division of
Psychiatry, Rose Medical Center, Denver, Colorado
Sheila Morrissey Adler, Ph.D., Clinical and Developmental
Psychology, Denver, Colorado
Stanley Cheren, M.D., Associate Professor, Division of Psychiatry,
Boston University School of Medicine, Boston, Massachusetts
Christopher L. Coe, Ph.D., Assistant Professor, Laboratory of
Developmental Psychobiology, Department of Psychiatry and
Behavioral Science, Stanford University School of Medicine,
Stanford, California
Lewis M. Cohen, M.D., Assistant Professor of Psychiatry, University
of Massachusetts Medical School; Director, Psychiatric
Consultation-Liaison Service, University of Massachusetts
Medical Center, Amherst, Massachusetts
Rosine DeBray, Ph.D., Professor of Psychology, Institut de
Psychosomatique, Hôpital de la Poterne des Peupliers, Paris,
France
Glen Elliott, Ph.D., M.D., Research Physician, Department of
Psychiatry and Behavioral Sciences, Stanford University
Medical Center, Stanford University School of Medicine,
Stanford, California
Noble A. Endicott, M.D., Assistant Clinical Professor of Psychiatry,
Department of Psychiatry, Mt. Sinai School of Medicine, New
York, New York
Fawzy I. Fawzy, M.D., Assistant Professor of Psychiatry,
Department of Psychiatry and Biobehavioral Sciences, School
of Medicine, University of California, Los Angeles; Chief of
Consultation-Liaison Psychiatry, UCLA Neuropsychiatric
Institute, California

ix

Kenneth K. Kidd, Ph.D., Associate Professor of Human Genetics and Psychiatry, Yale University School of Medicine, New Haven, Connecticut

Chase Patterson Kimball, M.D., Professor of Psychiatry and Medicine, Division of Bilogical Sciences, University of Chicago, Chicago, Illinois

Peter H. Knapp, M.D., Professor of Psychiatry, Director of Psychosomatic Services, Boston University School of Medicine, Boston, Massachusetts

Erwin K. Koranyi, M.D., Professor of Psychiatry, Health Sciences Faculty of the University of Ottawa; Director of Education, Royal Ottawa Hospital, Ottawa, Ontario, Canada

Seymour Levine, Ph.D., Department of Psychiatry and Behavioral Sciences, Stanford University School of Medicine, Stanford, California

Harold Levitan, M.D., Allen Memorial Institute, Montreal, Quebec, Canada

Fernando Lolas, M.D., Associate Professor, Psychophysiology Unit, Department of Physiology and Biophysics, Faculty of Medicine, University of Chile, Santiago, Chile

Pierre Marty, M.D., Chief Physician, Institut de Psychosomatique, Hôpital de la Poterne des Peupliers, Paris, France

Lois A. Morton, M.D., Ph.D., Postdoctoral Fellow in Psychiatry, Veterans Administration Hospital, West Haven, Connecticut, and Yale University School of Medicine, New Haven, Connecticut

Ranan H. Rimón, M.D., Professor of Psychiatry, Department of Psychiatry, University of Helsinki, Helsinki, Finland

Malcolm P. Rogers, M.D., Assistant Professor of Psychiatry, Harvard Medical School; Assistant Director of the Psychiatry Division, Brigham and Women's Hospital, Boston, Massachusetts

H. S. Sandhu, M.D., Assistant Professor in Psychiatry, Boston University Medical Center; Director, Psychiatric Consultation-Liaison Service, University Hospital, Boston, Massachusetts

Gary E. Schwartz, Ph.D., Professor of Psychology and Psychiatry, Yale University School of Medicine, New Haven, Connecticut

Samir Stephanos, M.D., Professor of Psychiatry; Head Department of Psychosomatic Medicine, University of Ulm, Ulm, West Germany

J. Peter Strang, M.D., Assistant Professor of Psychiatry, Boston
    University School of Medicine; Associate Director,
    Consultation-Liaison Service, Boston City Hospital, Boston,
    Massachusetts
Albert J. Stunkard, M.D., Professor of Psychiatry, University of
    Pennsylvania School of Medicine, Philadelphia, Pennsylvania
Michael von Rad, M.D., Professor of Psychiatry, Psychosomatic
    Clinic, University of Heidelberg, Heidelberg, West Germany
Thomas A. Wadden, Ph.D., Assistant Professor of Psychology in
    Psychiatry, University of Pennysylvania School of Medicine,
    Philadelphia, Pennsylvania
Herbert Weiner, M.D., Professor of Psychiatry, Department of
    Psychiatry and Biobehavioral Sciences, School of Medicine,
    University of California, Los Angeles, California; Chief of
    Behavioral Medicine, UCLA Neuropsychiatric Institute;
    Member, Brain Research Institute

Introduction

The purpose of this two-volume text is to present a comprehensive and detailed compilation of the latest thinking on the subject of psychosomatic medicine. I have taken several steps to assure these ends and to avoid diluting the result. One is that I have chosen to limit the sources of material to those areas that have demonstrated theoretical power, explanatory force, and clinical utility. A second is that I have gathered together authors who are prepared to search through and assess the evidence for and against the many complicated issues operating in this area. A third is that these authors have presented their material from a critical and questioning position with a clear appreciation that the field is an open and evolving one, yet there is much that is known and must be accounted for in any valid conceptualization. The epoch of theory based upon beliefs supported by convoluted reasoning rather than evidence is long past.

The text is organized around three areas of psychosomatic endeavor: psychodynamic psychiatry, psychophysiological research, and biobehavioral approaches.

The reason for choosing these three areas is that each functions according to a shared dedication to scientific rules of public presentation of ideas for scrutiny and evaluation by peers. Each adheres to principles governing the validation and documentation of sources from which hypotheses are drawn, complete definition of materials and methods, honest and undistorted reporting of results, and rational discussion of conclusions in an open forum.

These safeguards against doctrinaire and unsupported distortion of fact, against the misrepresentation of opinion as verified observation, and against cultish adherence to powerful leadership or emotionally appealing concepts have produced tremendous expansion in our understanding of mind-body relationships in health and disease. Nonetheless, they have not produced a consensus.

There are deep divisions between ideological factions within the field. The psychodynamic and behaviorist groups vie with each other for exclusive rights to the "truth," for academic leadership positions, and for access to patients. The researchers divide into clinical and basic groups which then shun each other. The different camps, sometimes in various combinations, present their material at different meetings and in different journals. This state of affairs is usual in any scientific field and in every other area of medicine. Therefore I do not raise it as a criticism, but I do pose it as a problem for those who wish to see the field as a whole and in depth. The many and varied locations in which the findings are reported are not encompassed in a single place, which makes it difficult for any but the most devoted student of the field to bridge all of the divisions and to maintain an overview of the current state of thinking.

This text puts together the most current work from all of these fields under one cover without diluting the individuality of the points of view held by each. Advances in the psychodynamic study of the individual contribute to our grasp of the specific areas of emotional vulnerability that place susceptible patients at risk at particular times in their lives. These advances focus on the content of mentation and subjective experience as well as the relationship of these qualities of mental life to the expression of disease. Psychophysiological research has vastly increased our knowledge of the mechanisms by which the psychosomatic unit functions. Endocrinology, genetics, and immunology have made particularly impressive contributions. Biobehavioral techniques have added speed, specificity, and access to the arsenal of interventions available for psychologically unsophisticated or resistant patients. Each of these three areas deserves a full measure of attention, without the necessity of vying for space or for center stage. This volume accomplishes just that—it gives an evenhanded presentation of all of the major positions, explores their interrelationships, and avoids their competing with one another in any way that devalues any of them.

Section 1 on theoretical considerations starts the book because there is a logic to progressing from the general to the particular, which is especially relevant for psychosomatic medicine. Its relevance lies in the fact that there have been many widely differing meanings applied to the term "psychosomatic." It is necessary first to comprehend the variety of theoretical issues in order to make sense of those considerations that determine a narrow or a broad definition. I personally favor a narrow definition of what constitutes a psychosomatic condition. Several of the other contributors use a much broader definition. Clarifying these distinctions requires considerable explanation. This is thus one of the tasks of the theoretical section—to study the range of definitions of the term "psychosomatic," so that psychosomatic phenomena are clearly distinguishable from nonpsychosomatic phenomena.

The above considerations do not limit the use of the term *psychosomatic* to only the classical conditions. Indeed, they question the accuracy of assigning certain of the classical conditions to the area of psychosomatic medicine, extend the area to others, and according to a systematic argument for inclusion, bring in new conditions. Some of the authors argue convincingly for the psychosomatic nature of a variety of illness patterns not usually considered psychosomatic. What is distinctive about this volume is its emphasis on a clear definition of psychosomatic process, explicit justification of that definition, and the presentation of evidence supporting the inclusion of any specific entity.

This section also addresses questions of how psychosomatic concepts have arisen, where they have taken us and where we have yet to go. Finally, several of the key concepts of current interest are taken up in specific chapters. They include the relationship of the expression of psychosomatic illness to reality issues of life-change stress and situational triggers, and to the complicated area of the psychological peculiarities of vulnerable patients. Throughout this section, the emphasis is on the evidence for and against various positions.

Section 2 deals with advances in psychophysiological research and is organized according to processes, both physiological (immune, endocrine, and genetic regulation) and psychological (deeply embedded in physiology, as in stress regulation). The evolution of major forward leaps in our understanding has dictated this format—they are the areas in which the richest material has been emerging.

Section 3 on psychosomatic conditions not only reviews and updates the status of our knowledge of specific psychosomatic illnesses but searches out the roles of psychosomatic processes in various illnesses. Chapters in this section vary in their definition of a psychosomatic illness in precisely the way that the theoretical section indicates that they may be expected to. Some make no distinction between a psychosomatic element in any illness state, while others distinguish between specific diseases that require a particular psychological element for the illness to become manifest and the wider body of diseases affected by psychological factors but which do not necessarily require a psychological factor to transform the disease potential into an illness state. These are the two general forms of the definition of psychosomatic disease, the broad and the narrow. Thus, this section reviews what many consider as psychosomatic illness and extends that to investigate the possible roles of psychosomatic processes in many conditions. This dual task is necessary since it reflects one of the theoretical problems of the field. It cannot possibly be entirely exhaustive since the number of conditions to be included would vary with the definition used. And, since comprehensiveness could not be a goal in organizing this section, I aimed to present areas that are representative of the several major viewpoints in the field and to present them in sufficient depth and detail as to reflect accurately the current thinking.

The organization of the above section follows several different formats. This is because the relevant conditions are sometimes within the same organ system, dictating an organization by systems (e.g., endocrine, gastrointestinal, cardiovascular, connective tissue), and sometimes within a common physiologic process, dictating a process format (e.g., allergic processes, appetite regulation).

Section 4 on clinical practice considers whom to treat, how to get him to treatment, and the factors that affect the choices and conduct of the treatment. The division into psychodynamic and biobehavioral considerations follows my opinion that all of what has thus far been shown to be of value is subsumed under these two approaches. Patients with psychosomatic conditions have special characteristics, some shared with all seriously ill persons and some peculiar to themselves. These affect the conduct of treatment in a variety of ways which we have grown to appreciate increasingly in recent years. The relevant characteristics fall broadly into the area of primitive character vulnerabilities, which are addressed in the theoretical section and readdressed in the clinical section from the standpoint of their influence on the nature and course of treatment. Their impact on psychodynamic and on biobehavioral treatments is enormously important.

The book does not try to address the question of the relative merits of psychodynamic versus biobehavioral approaches. Rather, it takes the position that both have considerable scientific support and a substantial history of clinical evidence. Furthermore, both are the favorite, most highly represented, approaches to the psychosomatic patient. The clinical literature in this field centers on these two approaches, with far less emphasis on any other approach. The contributors to these sections present the material that has been collected by both psychodynamic and behavioral clinical work.

The overall goal is to present an inclusiveness and detail that puts the field in focus for all of us.

Stanley Cheren, M.D.

Section 1.
THEORETICAL
CONSIDERATIONS

1.
An Integrative Model of Health, Disease, and Illness

HERBERT WEINER, M.D., and
FAWZY I. FAWZY, M.D.

For many years Western medical theory, research, and practice have been guided by three traditional models—biomedical, psychological, and psychosomatic. They have served us well in our efforts to understand and treat physical disease and mental illness but in other ways have hindered these endeavors. We shall discuss several variations of these models and their contributions to medical knowledge. We shall then attempt to integrate three models in order to overcome their respective limitations.

TRADITIONAL MODELS

THE BIOMEDICAL MODEL

The biomedical model is the oldest and most venerated in Western medicine. It is materialistic and mechanistic: it views man as a machine—a physical being surrounded by a physical environment. In this view, disease is an entity invading organs in the body, altering their structure and function; it can only

9

be understood in biophysical or biochemical terms (de Duve, 1975). It focuses on the single, proximal—pathological, biochemical, immunological, physiological, structural, and genetic—cause of disease.

This model defines health as the absence of a disease and ascribes illness to disease; illness does not come about by any other means. It has a restricted view of biology as the science of cells, not of life. It pays little attention to the interaction of persons with their social, economic, and cultural environments in the development of disease or the impact of disease on the social and economic life of patients, their families and communities.

The biomedical model has its roots deep in the history of medical research on the body, its physical perturbations, and in anatomy, pathological anatomy and the infectious diseases. Thus it has appeared in many forms over the years. The earliest of these is the infectious disease model which we owe to Pasteur, and then to Koch who discovered the link between *Mycobacterium tuberculosis* and the disease "tuberculosis." Koch contributed significantly to the view that disease is a single entity, linearly caused by a single, proximal agent. He isolated a virulent acid-fast tubercle bacillus from a patient and injected large quantities into the inguinal region of a normal guinea pig. Although little or no reaction was apparent for two weeks, enlarged lymph nodes then developed adjacent to the site of the injection. Later, the infection progressed along the lymph channels and slowly became widespread. He recovered the bacterium after the death of the animal.

The circumstances under which Koch conducted his experiments are not the usual ones in which tuberculosis develops in human populations. Not only are exposure levels to the bacterium lower, but the route of infection is different. A whole host of other factors—genetic, immunological, and nutritional—play roles in determining whether or not tuberculosis will develop and major anatomical disturbances occur. Koch contributed to the view, still held by many, that disease has only one cause that is both necessary and sufficient. He failed to realize that one may have tuberculosis and not be ill. Further, he did not understand that a specific disease agent (e.g., the spirochete of syphilis) may manifest itself in a wide variety of symptoms and lesions. Even viruses, specifically the hepatitis B virus, have been linked to a variety of outcomes: no disease, a carrier state, mild forms of the disease, acute or chronic liver disease, or hepatic carcinoma.

We owe the second biomedical model to Virchow—which holds that disease is the product of material defects in the cells of organs in the body. He believed that the defect was singular and directly caused by a specific aberration. Later, disease was also defined in molecular terms, e.g., the absence of or structural changes in an enzyme. Virchow put forward the idea that disease should be sought in one particular organ. His data were obtained from the examination of cadavers; therefore, he was not able to discern other factors which we have since learned to recognize—the interaction or lack of it between a molecular defect and a drug, or the fact that a peptic duodenal ulcer, a disease, is the product of a variety of factors which may be associated in a variety of combinations in different persons. Peptic ulcer may be anteceded by burns, brain injury, and other diseases. Other antecedents of peptic duodenal ulcer include gastrinomas, extensive resection of the small intestine, alcoholic cirrhosis of the liver, chronic renal failure, chronic obstructive lung disease, or a syndrome of limb tremors, congenital nystagmus, and a disturbance of consciousness similar to narcolepsy.

The third example of the biomedical model is the curative one that is based on the infectious disease and cellular pathological models. We owe it to Ehrlich. It asserts that when we know the singular pathogenic cause of a disease, we can develop and implement a cure by developing a "magic bullet." The successful treatment of bacterial diseases and specific vitamin deficiencies has contributed to the credibility of this model. The curative model reinforces the molecular-cellular view of disease by ignoring the contributions of social and environmental factors to disease, other than nutritional deficiencies, toxins and germs. Despite its successes, it ignores such issues as the timing of the onset and choice of diseases and the role of the physician in treatment. In focusing on defining disease by its end-product, it ignores the fact that a lesion may come about in a variety of ways. It is historic in its approach (Weiner, 1977, 1978).

The fourth biomedical model is the diagnostic one of disease, which draws attention to the "recognition and palliation of symptoms to the characterization of a specific disease in which etiology and pathogenesis are known and treatment is rational and specific" (Kety, 1974, p. 959). Kety recognized that though earlier models spoke of the cause of disease, their adherents tended to treat symptoms without any real attention to cause. He sought to refocus attention on the cause of the disease entity. However, diseases are not uniform entities and they have no single causes, even when they are known.

As with all ideal constructs—paradigms—which have a pervasive impact upon the intellectual activity of an era, the various biomedical models have had marked consequences for both medical education and practice. The student-physician learns to view anatomical, physiological, biochemical, and other biological systems as existing in one of two discontinuous states—"normal" or "abnormal," "healthy" or "unhealthy." Therefore, as stated before, he comes to think of health as the absence of disease.

This traditional approach to medicine has major consequences for patients because there are patients who have symptoms without empirically detectable deviations from biological norms; they do not have anatomical lesions or biochemical variations in blood samples. Other patients manifest these deviations without symptoms. In the first case, physicians tend to label the patient as "uninteresting," "a malingerer," or as having a "functional" ("nonorganic") disturbance. In the second case, the physician may prescribe premature or incorrect treatment, which then leads to iatrogenic disease (Steel, Gertman, Crescenzi, and Anderson, 1981; Jahnigen, Hannon, Laxson, and LaForce, 1982).

THE PSYCHOLOGICAL MODEL

The psychological model also has its roots in history. Interestingly, each of the four biomedical models discussed above has had psychiatric supporters or detractors. Nineteenth century and late twentieth century psychiatry believed psychiatric illnesses to be diseases of the brain. This conception was reinforced in the early 1900s by Noguchi's discovery that the spirochete *T. pallidum* that resided in the brain was causally related to paretic neurosyphilis. The disease was then treated according to the infectious disease model without consideration of the fact that the spirochete, in its tertiary phase, causes a variety of diseases of which paretic neurosyphilis is only one. In addition, paresis is a highly variable disease: we still have no satisfactory explanation for its diversity except that its variable symptomatology is in some way related to the interaction of the spirochete with the host's "personality." This model also does not consider that the disease syphilis came about by the patient's sexual actions.

The biomedical model of psychiatric illness also led psychiatry to search for a single, proximal and linear *physical* cause: candidates for such solitary causes have included bacterial, molecular, enzymatic, viral, and metabolic agents or avitaminoses. In another guise, the model has been used to explain most psychiatric disease and symptoms in terms of a specific *psychological* conflict. Freud's initial explanation that hysteria was rooted in unconscious sexual conflict or memory has the earmarks of the infectious disease model. The disease hysteria is seen as a uniform entity—its single, proximal cause is the conflict that cannot be contained. It is disguised as a symptom and is a product of an alteration in kind by the mechanism of "conversion."

The great contribution of the psychological model to the practice of medicine lies in the fact that it began to focus attention on the psychological aspects of illness and disease. However, like the biomedical models and the medically oriented psychological models upon which it was based, Freud's initial approach to diseases such as hysteria was also mechanistic and tended to promote the idea of single, proximal, linear causes.

Later, he changed his mind: psychological symptoms were multifactorial and could not be separated from the person's history. Freud thus introduced a historical approach to our understanding of illness and disease. Furthermore, he clearly indicated that persons had illnesses and that their conflicts were not independent entities. The psychological model of illness and disease is of a totally different nature than is physical disease. Psychiatric illnesses cannot be located in structural alterations of the brain, but are to be found in a psychic apparatus—not an organ or system—which is the product of its owner's past experience and is the seat of conflict. Therefore, disease is not merely the product of a structural alteration. Even when a patient has diabetes mellitus, epilepsy, or another disorder he may have profound psychological reactions to it: he may not comply with treatment; he may become profoundly sad or depressed about his state; and the complications of these diseases may alter his relationship to his family or make it impossible for him to work.

An integrated medicine must do equal justice to our understanding of the etiology and mechanisms of disease as to our knowledge of sick persons. It must also come to grips with defining the main subject matter that it treats—health, illness, disease.

THE PSYCHOSOMATIC MODEL

The psychosomatic model attempted to bridge the psychological and biomedical models. Initially, its proponents introduced the role of personality variables and psychological conflicts into the study of physical diseases (Dunbar, 1943; Alexander, 1950). They emphasized the pathogenic role of emotion in physical disease and asked the critical question of why one person falls ill with one disease and not another. They also postulated that psychological conflicts alone did not determine the choice of the disease—additional factors played a role in its choice. The contributions of psychosomatic medicine were to provide a multifactorial theory of some diseases (Dongier, Wittkower, Stephens-Newsham, and Hoffman, 1956; Weiner, Thaler, Reiser, and Mirsky, 1957). This model tried to understand the historical antecedents, etiology, and the context of disease onet, rather than its pathological anatomy and physiology.

However, the attempt to integrate psychology and physiology foundered on the indissoluble mind-brain-body problem. Psychosomatic medicine and its proponents also critically eschewed the social, ecological, and cultural factors for personal ones in disease. It also remained silent about two additional questions: (1) why is every disease heterogeneous in nature? and (2) what is the nature of health and illness, not only disease?

SIMILARITIES IN THE THREE TRADITIONAL MODELS

Similarities among the biomedical, psychological, and psychosomatic models do not end here. Due to the basic paradigms upon which they are based and the nature of the sample upon which they draw, all of the models tend to (1) take a linear, nonrecursive view of the health-disease process; (2) define health similarly; (3) ignore normal and pre-illness or pre-disease conditions; and (4) focus on the most advanced cases in which successful treatment is least likely. They also ignore the fact that most persons are ill, not diseased.

The psychosomatic model does take into account multiple or interactive causes of disease, but still views the pathogenic link between emotion and structural change in a linear fashion. Recursive interactions between causes and diseases and between diseases and causes have been given little or no attention by any of the traditional models. In addition, diseases not only result from behavior but may also affect societies and their economies.

As the result of these traditional views, medicine is organized into two health care delivery systems that stem directly from the biomedical and psychological models of disease. We have clinics and specialists for patients with "pure" bodily diseases—for bodies or body parts without minds, and other clinics for disembodied minds. The result is that one aspect or the other of sick persons is neglected or wrongly diagnosed. The fact is that inaccurate diagnosis, unnecessary treatment, and careless or unfeeling transactions between patients and their physicians may prolong illness or disease, or produce iatrogenic disease.

Such a dual conceptualization of "health" and the organization of medicine leaves little room for research on health or on the prevention of illness and disease.

TOWARD AN INTEGRATIVE MODEL

The foregoing statements do not minimize the advances in our understanding of human disease which have resulted from the use of the models described. They have been discussed here in order to put them into perspective, and to identify their attributes and drawbacks—in short, to clarify the questions that need to be addressed before an integration of their points of view is attempted. For the reasons stated, the limitations of the biomedical, psychological, and psychosomatic models have recently been pointed out (Dubos, 1959, 1965; Brock, 1972; Brody, 1973; Moss, 1973; Engelhardt and Spicker, 1975; Fabrega, 1975; Rasmussen, 1975; McKeown, 1976; Eisenberg, 1977; Engel, 1977; Weiner, 1977, 1978, 1983; von Uexküll, 1979; Ader, 1980; Coulehan, 1980). A number of alternatives have been proposed, most of which attempt to avoid the inadequacies of previous models.

We will suggest an integrative model to bring together current knowledge of the subject matter of medicine. According to the integrative model, health is not defined in absolute terms—as the absence of disease—but rather, as a successful psychobiological adaptation to the environment. Disease is defined as an impairment of or interference with some component of a person's structure or function. Disease is not the sole cause of illness. Illness also stems from a person's inability to adapt to environmental situations of many different types, and to disease: it results from a discrepancy between the adaptive capacities of persons and the demands placed upon them. This adaptive failure leads to illness or ill-health. Illness is a signal that a person's survival in a particular environment, or as a result of disease, is threatened. In this model, treatment is designed to improve or correct the adaptive failure, not to pursue the elusive ideal of cure—to achieve some undefined state of health.

The integrative point of view is inclusive. It differs from the traditional view that a disease is a discrete entity that the physician must first diagnose. Having done so, he then deduces the pathogenic agent or anatomical lesion which gives rise to it. In this view, the correlation between the agent or lesion and the symptoms and signs is sufficient to account for the disease. However, the correlation between symptoms and lesions is by no means a tight one. Furthermore, a person may even be predisposed to a disease and not be ill. He can have a disease and be healthy, or have a disease and not be ill. Moreover, he can be ill without a disease—but he can never be both healthy and ill.

THE VARIABLE NATURE OF DISEASE AND ILLNESS

Even in the laboratory, the production of disease in animals is marked by variability—multiple factors are involved (Ader, 1980). When persons at risk for a disease are exposed to the same changes in their lives only some develop the disease (Weiner et al., 1957). To compound the matter further, the factors associated with the initiation of illness and disease are often, if not always, different from those that sustain them. For example, the maladaptive physiological adjustments to high blood pressure levels which sustain elevated levels are different from the physiological factors which initiate them (Weiner, 1979b).

Thus, ". . . the integrative point of view attempts to account for the multiple factors that protect against, and are responsible for the predisposition to, initiation, maintenance, and variable natural history of illness and disease and their consequences for the ill person, his family, the society in which he lives and its economy and structure" (Weiner, 1981b). The multiple interacting factors are genetic, bacterial, immunological, nutritional, developmental, psychological, behavioral, and social.

The integrative point of view is process—not structure —oriented. It seeks to account for the paradox of having symptoms with or without the presence of anatomical lesions or physiological deviations. It views illness and disease as a breakdown in biological adaptation, which may or may not lead to anatomical lesions. The breakdown may occur at a variety of levels of biological organization from the psychological to the immunological; it may take many forms and lead to the same disease through quite different pathways.

MULTIPLE FACTORS IN THE MAINTENANCE OF HEALTH

Many factors contribute to health—genetic, immunological, psychological, and social. Health is also maintained by good nutrition, adequate sanitation, and stable political conditions.

GENETIC FACTORS

Certain genes (HLA-DW2, -DRW2, -B5, -B7, and A-11 alleles) have been linked to decreased susceptibility to juvenile-onset diabetes (Notkins, 1979). Paradoxically, the HLA-B5 allele has also been associated with increased risk of certain types of peptic duodenal ulcer (Rotter, Rimoin, Gursky, and Samloff, 1977). Simple links such as this between genetic deficiencies and disease are rare. Most diseases seem to be divisible into subforms, each of which is the product of a variety of genetic and nongenetic predisposing factors.

Genetically determined defects in protein structure may even protect some persons against a specific disease. Other defects, although not protective, may not manifest as disease.

There are 18 different forms of glucose-6-phosphate dehydro-
genase (G-6-PD) deficiency. Only three of these have been correlated with disease. Each variant is the product of a distinctive
change in the structure of the enzyme, in which a single amino
acid is substituted for the customary one at a single position in
its polypeptide chains. The deficiency is due to the presence of
the structurally abnormal enzyme in red blood cells. Two enzyme variants only express themselves in certain situations—one
when the person ingests specific drugs, another on exposure
to fava beans. A third enzyme variant is associated with achronic
hemolytic anemia without the apparent intervention of environmental factors. The remaining forms of defect in the enzyme exist in persons without being manifested as disease; the
person with the deficiency remains in perfect health. In fact,
one aberration (an increase in G-6-PD production in sickle cell
anemia) may correct or compensate for another genetic deficiency (a G-6-PD deficiency). Interaction between two genetic
defects may cancel each other out; two diseases may be conducive to health in the same person. Structural variations in
enzymes—a marker of disease—are not necessarily expressed
in disease. Quantitative variations in enzyme levels are also seen
in healthy persons. Elevated levels of the pepsinogen isoenzyme
(PG-I) are found in persons with peptic duodenal ulcer. Rotter
and colleagues have demonstrated that they are inherited traits
(Rotter, Sones, Richardson, Rimoin, and Samloff, 1977; Rotter,
Sones, Samloff, Richardson, Gursky, Walsh, and Rimoin, 1979).
Enhanced PG-I levels are not invariably associated with peptic
duodenal ulcer; only 42 percent of those with it have the disease.
Rotter and Rimoin (1977) have shown that raised PG-I levels
account for about 25 percent of the etiological variance in this
form of duodenal ulcer disease. Other genetic factors also play
a role in this disease. They include blood type (O), the absence
of the blood group antigens ABO in saliva and gastric juice, the
presence of HLA-B5 in white men (Sievers, 1959; Hanley, 1964;
Vesely, Kubichova, and Dvorakova, 1968; Marcus, 1969; Rotter
et al., 1977). Other nongenetic factors that are associated with

peptic duodenal ulcer have been reviewed by Sturdevant (1979) and Weiner (1977).

These data suggest that a person may be predisposed to a disease but not be ill. They also raise the question of why some subjects with raised PG-I levels develop a disease such as peptic duodenal ulcer and others do not. There are no answers to this question at this point in time. There are many other examples of persons predisposed to a disease and not ill (Weiner, 1979a).

IMMUNOLOGICAL FACTORS

The immune system is the major protective system against infectious agents. However, as a result of its agency it is possible for a person to have a disease and not be ill. The hepatitis B virus is "carried" by millions of persons around the world. Some carriers may show certain symptoms of subclinical disease manifested by mild biochemical abnormalities of liver function tests. Yet most will never develop any of the diseases associated with the virus. The carrier state and the ability of carriers to transmit the disease is, in part, genetically determined (Blumberg, 1977).

The virus-host relationship may be influenced by factors other than genetic or immunological ones. The Epstein-Barr virus is related to different disease states, or to no disease at all in different locations throughout the world. The key explanatory factor would appear to be the presence or absence of mosquitos (de-Thé, Geser, Day, Tukei, Williams, Beri, Smith, Dean, Bornkamm, Feorino, and Henle, 1978), whose sting in and of itself appears to lower the immune response to the virus.[1]

The role of developmental and experiential factors in the immunological response cannot be overlooked either. Immunological tolerance can be imparted to mammalian embryos by injecting them with antigens from another strain (Medawar and Medawar, 1977; Ader, 1980). After birth they are tolerant to repeated challenge by this antigen. Furthermore, the age at which a young organism is exposed to a virus may play an

[1]Ballieu, R.: Personal communication.

important part in the effect that virus will have on the organism (Hotchin and Buckley, 1977).

PSYCHOLOGICAL FACTORS

Health, illness, and disease are in part determined by psychological factors. For example, women whose sera contained rheumatoid factors (RF) and had rheumatoid arthritis scored on the MMPI in some ways similar to and in some ways different from their sisters whose sera contained RF but did not have rheumatoid arthritis, and different from other sisters without RF in their sera who were also free from the disease (Solomon and Moos, 1965; Moos and Solomon, 1965a,b). The first set of well-sisters were functioning well in their daily lives, the arthritic sisters were not.

Another factor in adaptation may be psychological maturity (age-appropriate adaptive patterns of coping with the environment and of defending against personal distress and problems), which seems to be associated with health (Vaillant, 1977). Distress and discontent characterized those in a group of socially and economically similar persons who repetitively became sick, especially when increased demands were placed upon them or increasing difficulties in their relationships with others occurred. Healthy subjects in this cohort, on the other hand, were in tune with their environments (Hinkle, 1974). Learning and practicing good health habits are conducive to good health even when other signs of potential disease are manifest. Belloc and Breslow (1972) reported that persons practicing seven personal health-related behaviors (sleeping about eight hours per night; eating breakfast; not eating between meals; maintaining the appropriate weight; participating actively in reasonably intense physical activity, drinking moderately; never smoking) were likely to be in good health. This finding held true even with controls for age, gender, and economic status. Breslow and Enstrom (1980) found an inverse relationship between the practice of the seven behaviors and age-adjusted mortality in men versus women: Male followers of all seven health practices had a mortality rate of only 28 percent for men following zero to three health practices; in female followers the comparable rate was 43 percent of women "nonfollowers."

SOCIAL AND CULTURAL FACTORS

The effects of social factors on health, disease, and illness are many and varied. Stable societies impose a minimum of adaptive tasks on their members. Tradition and stability protect persons against myocardial infarction, for example. Even immigration to another country is less conducive to coronary artery disease, if the immigrant preserves his traditional way of life in the new country (Marmot and Syme, 1976).

The incidence and prevalence of ischemic heart disease and death due to myocardial infarction (M.I.) is unevenly distributed both within and between various European countries, for reasons that are not completely understood (Stallones, 1980), social stability and traditional customs, normal blood pressure levels and diet are some of the factors involved (Marmot and Syme, 1976). Conversely, poverty, social and familial discord, and a dangerous, unpredictable environment, are conducive to raised blood pressure (Harburg, Erfurt, Hauenstein, Chape, Schull, and Schork, 1973).

THE NATURE OF ILLNESS

We now come to the problem of illness. To recapitulate: Most persons who seek out physicians' ministrations are ill but do not have a disease; they complain. The best estimate of those who are ill is 50 to 70 percent of any physician's panel. They suffer pains in the head, back, gut or limbs. They are unhappy, irritable, and discontented with their lot. They vomit, have menstrual cramps, and are tired. They sleep poorly, drink too much alcohol, drive cars too fast, and take drugs. They destroy their family lives, undereat, overeat, binge-eat, or fail at their jobs. They fear disease or are preoccupied with their bodies. Some of these symptoms or symptomatic behaviors are the products of disease, but most are not. A structural or infectious disease model cannot explain such complaints.

As we study these individuals we discover that their ills are the product of their situation in life, expressed in diverse ways. They are discontented, bitter, or disappointed by their fate. The demands placed upon them by poverty, work, spouses, or children are overwhelming for them. They do not know how to manage; they appeal to others for advice, friendship, help, and succor. Having nowhere to turn, they seek out the physician.

Failure to discriminate between illness and disease leads daily to serious consequences for patients. Persons do feel ill without having discernible, identifiable changes in function or structure in organ systems. The mechanisms of the body seem unperturbed. Because of the traditional manner of defining disease in terms of structural changes and physiological perturbations, persons in ill-health are not tolerated by physicians. Yet, the evidence is persuasive that ill-health is related to an interaction of persons with their environments. Ill-health in turn may make persons susceptible to a variety of diseases.

MULTIPLE FACTORS IN ADAPTATION BREAKDOWN AND DISEASE

We next follow the line of argument that (1) all disease is multiply determined; (2) the characteristics of the disease and its course are specified by the host and by his transaction with the environment in which he lives; and (3) the antecedents of disease and illness are many and varied and may be genetic, developmental, nutritional, immunological, psychological, and sociocultural.

GENETIC RISK FACTORS

Genes play a role in a wide variety of diseases. However, their expression is not always invariant for a particular disease. Even diseases in which they play a predominant role are heterogeneous; they exemplify genetic variation. For example, the chromosomal abnormality, Turner's syndrome, in both its XO and the XO/XX mosaic variety, may be expressed in primary anorexia nervosa or in mild mental deficiency (Kron, Katz, Gorzynski, and Weiner, 1977). However, most patients with anorexia nervosa do not have the syndrome in either variety. Some women develop it after they stop taking the oral contraceptive "pill" (Fries and Nillius, 1973). *Per contra* taking the "pill" has been associated with the development of high blood pressure and thromboembolic disease in women with other predispositions. In addition, patients with hereditary agammaglobulinemia are particularly prone to rheumatoid arthritis, repeated infection, or cancer. Although rheumatoid factors (RF) are not detectable in the serum of these patients, they can be detected in the serum of most other patients with rheumatoid arthritis (Kellgren and Ball, 1959; Strober, Glaese, and Waldmann, 1971–1972). In some forms of anorexia nervosa, peptic duodenal ulcer and rheumatoid arthritis, specific X-linked or simple autosomal dominant genetic defects appear. However, in most diseases, genetic heterogeneity is the rule. A particular clinical disorder generally exists as a number of subforms with different genetic and nongenetic predisposing factors, which are shaped by a variety of initiating mechanisms into a particular anatomical lesion.

VIRAL FACTORS

Diseases produced by viruses also demonstrate the oversimplifications which can arise when the traditional biomedical model is employed. Lymphocytic choriomeningitis is a disease which, although incited by a virus, is characterized by the invasion of the meninges by a profusion of lymphocytes. However, the virus does not appear in the brain or the meninges; it is the immunological response to the presence of the virus elsewhere in the body that produces the main lesion in the brain. Multiple factors are at work in the production of the disease.

If the lymphocytic choriomeningitis virus is first injected into a pregnant animal and later into its offspring, lymphocytes do not invade their meninges; or when newborn mice are infected with the scrapie virus, a latent period of one year occurs before it manifests itself as disease. However, when they reach 18 months, high titers of the virus can be found in their brains and spleens. If mice are injected at four days or older, the virus replicates immediately and kills 70 to 100 percent by the age of ten months (Hotchin and Buckley, 1977). These two examples illustrate a developmental principle—the kind of lesion produced by a virus depends on the age at which the animal is injected with it. Developmental factors in part account for the nonlinear nature of some virus diseases.

PSYCHOLOGICAL AND SOCIAL FACTORS

No single factor in the human environment is inevitably or invariably associated with *one* disease. Nor does everyone in a population exposed to a particular psychosocial situation fall ill. However, certain environmental factors are indeed associated with the increased probability of a variety of diseases, or of mortality. People respond individually to environmental change, challenge, migration, work, marriage, friendship, parenthood, divorce, and so on. Some show greater adaptability and ingenuity than others. Some rise to the challenge; others are defeated by it. Adaptive (and maladaptive) solutions to change and challenge are many and varied because, in part, they mean different things to different people. Virtually every disease and a shorter life span are associated with poverty and low socioeconomic status (Weiner, 1981a). These diseases include essential hypertension, ischemic heart disease (in the United Kingdom), obesity (in women in the United States), premature delivery, social and nutritional deprivation, infant mortality, tuberculosis, cancer of the cervix in women, alcoholism, and drug abuse (Syme and Berkman, 1976; Weiner, 1981b). Single, divorced, and widowed persons are more susceptible to a wide variety of diseases, illnesses and causes of death than are married persons (National Center for Health Statistics, 1970). Persons who are socially or culturally mobile tend to have an increased prevalence rate of ischemic heart disease, depressive moods, sarcoidosis, lung cancer, and the complications of pregnancy (Hinkle, 1974; Syme and Berkman, 1976). Obesity can predispose to a number of diseases including high blood pressure, ischemic heart disease, diabetes mellitus, cholelithiasis, gout, osteoarthritis, the Pickwickian and sleep apnea syndromes, as well as carcinoma of the breast, and uterine endometrium in women (Wynder, Escher, and Mantel, 1966; Mirra, Cole, and MacMahon, 1971; De Waard, 1975). Obesity is associated with the effects of rapid sociocultural change or with migration. It may also result from increases in dietary fat intake and lack of exercise in adult life, which may raise serum cholesterol levels and account for the association between obesity and increase of prevalence of ischemic heart disease (Marmot, Syme, Kagan, Kato, Cohen, and Belsky, 1975; Marmot and Syme, 1975; Syme and Berkman, 1976; Ostfeld, 1979).

Metabolic changes have been associated with a range of psychosocial events. Kasl and Cobb (1970) found elevated blood pressures in men who had lost their jobs. Anticipated plant shutdown was associated with increased serum uric acid (SUA) levels (Kasl, Cobb, and Brooks, 1968). The more personal the anguish associated with the loss of employment, the higher were the SUA levels. Upon reemployment, both SUA and serum cholesterol levels returned to normal. Saxena (1980) discovered involuntary unemployment to be linked with a rise in type IIA Fredericksen lipids, a fall in high density lipoproteins, the increased smoking of cigarettes, and use of alcohol and carbohydrates.

Bereavement that is not properly coped with is the setting in which a variety of different diseases begin (Schmale, 1958;

Engel, 1968). They are cancer (LeShan, 1966; Kissen, 1967; Bahnson, 1969), tuberculosis (Day, 1951), diabetes mellitus (Hinkle and Wolf, 1952), lymphomas and leukemias (Greene, 1954), juvenile diabetes mellitus (Stein and Charles, 1971), heart failure (Perlman, Ferguson, Bergum, Isenberg, and Hammarsten, 1971), ulcerative and granulomatous colitis, Graves' disease, and disseminated lupus erythematosus. Premature separation places animals at high risk for disease in later life, and produces alterations in behavior and in the physiology and biochemistry of the brain and other bodily systems (Ackerman, 1981; Hofer, 1981; Weiner, 1981b).

However, just as hepatitis B virus is associated with a variety of diseases, bereavement *per se* is not the sole determinant of their nature. Bereavement may elicit a specific disease only in those otherwise predisposed to it. In other persons, a loss produces no disease, but does produce appropriate grief and sorrow which eventually resolve.

Good evidence exists that the same environmental challenges do not result in the same psychological or physiological changes in man. Frankenhaeuser (1979) has demonstrated one reason for this: different persons will interpret the same circumstance differently. Conversely, diverse environmental conditions can evoke the same neuroendocrine responses because they have the same meanings for different persons (Frankenhaeuser, 1975a,b; Mason, 1971).

The same physiological responses occur to different contingencies; novelty, change, ambiguity, challenge, and anticipation all act as stimuli for catecholamine turnover and excretion. However, the same increases can occur when persons are understimulated as when they are overstimulated. The key factor is a *change* in the level of stimulation, not in the direction of the stimulus (Frankenhaeuser, Nordheden, Myrsten, and Post, 1971). Individual differences in hormone patterns depend on the manner in which the task is performed, or whether the person succeeds or fails.

These findings are instructive but do not explain why some persons develop one disease and not another, or how environmental events set off a chain of psychobiological events that culminate in illness or disease. Two alternative answers to these questions exist. We can arrive at the first by using viral diseases as a model (Blumberg, 1977). That is, several factors determine which form of disease a person will develop—the age at time of initial challenge, the variable nature of the challenge (e.g., the antigenic properties of the virus or the psychological meaning of the challenge to the person), the capacity of the host to recognize and respond immunologically, humorally, and/or psychologically, and the timing and persistence of the response to the challenge. Similarly, psychobiological responses in man in frightening situations are individual. They also depend on age, experience, and success and failure at performing the appropriate behavioral programs. Novelty and ambiguity elicit greater responses than routine performances. The roles assigned to men in a situation of danger determine the physiological responses—the responsible leader has greater ones. Finally, coping-defensive maneuvers when successful dampen hormone responses.

The second alternative is that some common psychobiological denominator exists that links the many different socioenvironmental factors and reduces or increases the incidence and prevalence of many different diseases. Although some conditions and diseases are clearly related to each other (e.g., smoking, obesity, diabetes mellitus and ischemic heart disease; obesity and high blood pressure), many are not. The nature, etiology, and pathogenesis of many diseases and conditions are very different, yet they covary with specific socioeconomic or environmental situations that do not define the specific diseases, illnesses, or conditions.

Syme (1979) has suggested that low or high socioeconomic status, urban or rural living, industrialization, job loss, immigration, social mobility, divorce, widowhood, bereavement, and other life changes, obesity, and smoking are all responsible for diminishing the resistance of the host to disease. While all of these increase the vulnerability to disease, other factors intervene to determine its specific nature.

Syme (1979) has raised two other questions that are critical to our understanding of health, illness, and disease: (1) Why do only certain persons become ill when exposed to socio-environmental conditions or personal situations? and (2) Why do those who are susceptible develop one disease and not another? These seemingly separate questions are actually closely linked. The partial answers to them is that persons differ in their genetic make-up and past experiences, which allows them to resist, or makes them succumb to, the impact of change, migration, poverty, job loss or dissatisfaction, and bereavement.

Human beings are not passive witnesses of events and experiences. They cognitively appraise and interpret them. An event may have shared or idiosyncratic meanings for different people (Lazarus, 1966) as a result of past experiences. On the other hand, preexisting behavioral programs do not exist for dealing with novel or ambiguous situations. Social factors, like genetic or viral ones, play a role in the inception and maintenance of disease; they do so in a manner analogous to physical agents, by producing (psychological) responses in a person which are signaled, if at all, by distress, fear, anxiety, apprehension, and so on. Such events and situations may have portentous, trivial, or challenging meanings. If portentous or challenging, they generate adaptive coping devices which may result in flight from, or meeting and overcoming the challenging event, or defeat. Successful coping is more likely when the person possesses personal qualities such as intelligence, problem-solving ability, past experience in mastering the event and having information about it (Hamburg and Adams, 1967; Cullen, 1980), the capacity to use information, support or advice from others, self-reliance and self-confidence, realism and hopefulness in the face of challenge, and the fortitude to face it if the odds are not overwhelming.

There are many persons who are less adaptable or have fewer skills of this kind; they include children, the mentally defective or impaired, those who have lost a spouse, the lonely, and the elderly. For various reasons these tend to lack the education, information, knowledge, social supports, and interpersonal skills to cope with events and solve the problems which arise from such events.

Other persons who fall ill share a group of psychological characteristics described by Ruesch (1948), Marty and de M'Uzan (1963), McDougall (1974), and Nemiah and Sifneos (1970). Ruesch, in particular, stressed the age-inappropriate behavioral and psychological characteristics of adult patients that made them particularly unadapted to and unable to cope with their environments. These characteristics include impaired or arrested social learning, a reliance on imitating others, a tendency to express thought and feeling in direct physical action, dependence on others, passivity, childlike ways of thinking, lofty and unrealistic aspirations, difficulties in assimilating and integrating life experiences, a reliance on securing love and affection from other persons, and above all else, an inability to master changes in their lives or to learn new techniques for overcoming challenge or the deprivation of their wishes. The other writers have focused on psychological ("alexithymic") characteristics of patients—an incapacity to apperceive their own emotions and feelings as indicators of personal distress or to solve problems through constructive imagination, and focus on concrete specifics rather than the meaning and significance of events in their lives.

In some persons helplessness, hopelessness, and giving up result from their failure to master events (Engel, 1968); an adaptive failure ensues. In others, the response to change or challenge may be excessive. The more a person possesses the characteristics described by Ruesch, the more likely he will require assistance and the stronger is the influence of the social field upon him (Bettelheim and Janowitz, 1964). Hence, events alone do not produce disease in a linear fashion. They do so in interaction with the meaning they have for the person, his ability to cope with events and their meaning, and his adaptive capacities.

Our understanding of the differences between those who fall ill or develop a disease and those who do not is enhanced when the psychological differences between the two groups are specified; they in turn are determined by genetic endowment, personal history, nutrition, education, and learning—the product of an "average expectable environment" (Hartmann, 1958). Psychological maturity and adaptive capacity are psychobiological concepts that define man's transactions with and adaptation to his ever-changing social, economic, political, human, and nonhuman environment and assure his health.

Illness and disease viewed from both a physiological or psychological perspective are adaptive failures at several levels of biological organization, programmed by numerous factors. Once disease and illness present themselves, they become experiences with which the person again must cope. All that has been said to this point also applies to coping with disease and illness and its associated symptoms and signs. However, additional adaptive tasks are imposed on the sick person by the specific nature of the disease and its meaning (Weiner, 1983). Other factors that determine individual responses are whether the disease comes on abruptly or gradually, is treatable or not, carries with it a special stigma or not, requires hospitalization, special technical procedures or surgery, or is welcome or not. The role of response of the caring professional person is critical in the patient's successful adaptation, or not, to his disease. Much has been written about the positive and negative therapeutic effects of the doctor-patient relationship and its conscious and unconscious aspects. The physician who disregards his role in this very powerful and important relationship does so at the patient's peril.

The successful adaptation of a patient to his disease is also a function of his previous ability to cope with disease, and with those who tended him during it. However, additional factors must be considered in the patient's responses to disease: for example, the disease or its symptoms may acquire a very individual meaning; the metabolic and physiological alterations of the disease or the drugs used to treat it may impair cerebral metabolism and function, thereby altering the patient's perception, memory, or problem-solving ability and, therefore, his ability to cope with his environment. Elderly persons and children have fewer coping abilities and strategies than those in other stages of their lives; they require very special care in the strange environment of the hospital and help in adapting to disease.

We have begun to answer Syme's first question—why only certain persons fall ill when exposed to the same socio-environmental conditions. However, we have not answered the second—why the susceptible develop one disease and not another.

THE SPECIFICATION OF DISEASE: DISTURBANCES IN REGULATION

We know little about the manner in which sociocultural and personal factors (e.g., poverty and bereavement) specify a particular disease. We do not know whether they first produce an illness state (without an identifiable disease) characterized by symptoms such as headache, undue fatigue, backache, "nerves," depression, irritability, vomiting, and indigestion (Morrell, 1978), which heighten susceptibility to disease; or whether they influence the development and specification of identifiable disease in a more direct manner. We also know little about how poverty, job loss, and bereavement are mediated (presumably by changes in diet, habits, and psychological adaptation) to set off a chain of events leading to structural and functional changes which we recognize as the specific disease.

Nonetheless, we do know that a number of different diseases and conditions are anteceded or characterized by a variety of disturbances in communication between cells (Rubenstein, 1980) and that these disturbances can alter the usual manner by which physiological processes are regulated (Weiner, 1977). We can no longer merely look for increases or decreases in some function or substance in the body that seems to account for the disease. Rather, we look for dynamic disturbances in the interaction between cells, which may lead—not invariably, it must be emphasized—to symptoms, disability, or structural change.

Disturbances in physiological regulation come about in several ways: (1) when the receptor of a cell is preempted by some foreign substance that binds to it and displaces the usual mediator; for example, the cholera toxin binds to intestinal cells to produce a massive loss of electrolytes and water; (2) when the receptor is absent or diminished and thus unavailable or less available to the mediator; for example, obese persons with adult onset diabetes mellitus have fewer insulin receptors; (3) when the receptor is present in increased numbers or is excessively "sensitive" to its mediator; and (4) when the mediator is absent or diminished, or its access to the receptor is blocked, as in some forms of paralysis agitans where dopamine is depleted or a neuroleptic binds to its receptor.

Regulatory disturbances can occur in virtually any system of the human body. Such disturbances or their impact have been documented in the cardiovascular, immune, pulmonary, and gastrointestinal systems (Weiner, 1983, reviews some of the literature on regulatory disturbance in these systems and its role in the generation of disease states). However, these disturbances are not invariant: nine different regulatory disturbances have been described in subforms of peptic duodenal ulcer disease. The nine regulatory disturbances in gastric function have been identified in peptic duodenal ulcer after onset. Prior to the development of this disease, at least two different forms of peptic ulcer disease exist, as already outlined. Similarly, it would appear that in order to develop essential hypertension in one of its forms, excessive responses of heart rate and systolic blood pressure to stimuli must be present. The point is that man is more programmed psychobiologically to develop a specific disease, although for each disease subform the program differs: psychobiological heterogeneity in the subforms of a particular disease have been demonstrated (Julius, Randall, Esler, Kashima, Ellis, and Bennet, 1975; Vollhardt, Ackerman, Grayzel, and Barland, 1982).

FACTORS THAT SUSTAIN OR MODIFY
THE COURSE OF DISEASE

We know less about factors sustaining disease than about their pathophysiology. However, some evidence about this topic is beginning to accumulate. The factors which incite high blood pressure in animals, for example, are different from those that sustain it. One set of brainstem and hypothalamic mechanisms participates in the maintenance of the experimental elevation of blood pressure levels (Chalmers, 1975; Ganten, Schelling, and Ganten, 1977; and Weiner, 1977), another in the initiation of such levels.

In some cases of human hypertension, secondary physiological adaptations to the elevation of blood pressure consist of a diminution in the sensitivity of the arterial baroreceptors (Korner, West, Shaw, and Uther, 1974), structural increases in resistance to regional blood flow (Folkow and Hallback, 1977), and changes in cardiac performance (Frohlich, Tarazi, and Dustan, 1971).

Changes in other systems accompany essential hypertension and probably play a role in sustaining it. For example, the plasma concentration of aldosterone rises with age in essential hypertension, while in normotensive persons it declines (Genest, Koiw, and Kuchel, 1977). Plasma renin activity increases markedly during the development of the malignant phase of hypertensive disease and renal failure. Renal dynamics change in a complex way in a subform of borderline hypertension in which an increased activity of the sympathetic nervous system (probably coupled with decreased parasympathetic activity) occurs. The renal blood flow is reduced due to reversible intrarenal vasoconstriction to diminish the excretion of sodium and water (Hollenberg and Adams, 1976; Brown, Fraser, Lever, Morton, and Rubinson, 1977). The rise in blood pressure should normally cause an increased excretion of sodium and water; at first it does occur but later it does not, in this form of hypertension. Therefore, a progressive resetting of the relationship of blood pressure to sodium and water excretion—a regulatory disturbance—is produced. Progressive renal changes ensue, which account for the change from borderline hypertension to essential hypertension. In short, the kidney maintains the blood pressure increases that were initiated elsewhere by a fall in renal blood flow and renin, and a rise in total and renal vascular resistance (Brown et al., 1977).

Psychological changes are also associated with essential hypertension. Patients in the borderline phase of the disease demonstrate aggressive tendencies which they feel are dangerous and produce anxiety in them (Safar, Kamieniecka, Levenson, Dimitriu, and Pauleau, 1978). They have fewer fantasies but a variety of psychophysiological symptoms and signs of anxiety. In the later phase of sustained hypertension these symptoms and signs vanish as anxiety disappears. The hostility can still be inferred, but patients do not apperceive it.

In clinical and more systematic studies, evidence has been found to support the notion that changes in patients' lives influence the progression of essential hypertension and its various complications (Reiser, Brust, and Ferris, 1951; Reiser, Rosenbaum, and Ferris, 1951; Aagaard and Kristensen, in press a,b). Within a period of six months after the beginning of one study, disease progression was accelerated by job loss or retirement, especially in patients 50 years or older. In a period of the next 18 months, the signs and symptoms of hypertension were most likely to be enhanced by discord in the family that elicited anger and rage.

Secondary metabolic alterations occur in many chronic diseases or after weight loss. They consist of a nonspecific depression of the thyroid hormone, triiodothyronine (T3), the production of reverse T3 with secondary effects on the metabolism of several steroid hormones (cortisol, estradiol, and testosterone).

Patients successfully treated for Graves' disease with antithyroid medication or thyroid surgery may show persistent metabolic alterations and psychological deficits and maladaptations (Ruesch, Christiansen, Patterson, Dewees, and Jacobson,

1947), which place them at risk for recurrences and chronic disability.

Noncompliance to treatment is one of the major behavioral contributors to the maintenance of disease. While some patients will not comply for reasons which are unique to their life situation, many will not do so because of recent or more remote experiences with improper or inadequate medical care. The noncompliant patient may eschew all further help, and resort to inexpert or self-treatment, or help from untrained or unscrupulous persons.

Failure to appreciate adequately the patient's psychological responses to illness and disease may lead to his or her chronic invalidism: chronic symptomatology is the rule in the case of injuries sustained at work, which are compensated for. Society, therefore, encourages the maintenance of symptoms that are only directly related to the industrial accident or illness. Some societies, of course, sustain certain diseases by stigmatizing their hosts—especially the mentally ill or defective, the handicapped, and the old person—and by providing inadequate care, or insufficient funds for their education, nutrition, housing, and medical care.

We have presented a few selected examples of the factors which sustain disease and which may have to be corrected before adequate treatment can be achieved. These examples direct attention to the variety of other factors in the treatment of disease in addition to its pathophysiological changes. Medicine is dedicated exclusively to the "cure" of this pathophysiology, which is the outcome of many antecedent factors. For some persons and some diseases and illnesses a more mundane, but still valid and realistic goal is to help the patient achieve his optimal functioning despite disease or illness, to assist him to live with illness, to relieve suffering, or to help the patient die in dignity.

SUMMARY AND CONCLUSIONS

The integrative approach to health, illness, and disease does not attempt to discard the deep insights that molecular and cell biology, biochemical genetics, virology, bacteriology, immunology, biochemistry, and physiology have provided us. These revelations have been clinically useful, enlightening, and intellectually satisfying. They approach with the medical scientists' ideal goal—the explication of the mechanisms of disease couched in molecular and cellular terms. An eventual hope is to reduce further these mechanisms to atomic or subatomic terms.

The integrative approach seeks to broaden the biological basis of medicine by incorporating behavioral, developmental, and evolutionary knowledge in our understanding of health, illness, and disease.

To summarize:

1. In every population a pool of persons exists who, by virtue of their genetic endowment, personal characteristics, and the social environment, remain well.

2. In the same population there is a pool of persons who, by virtue of their genetic endowment and personal characteristics, may be predisposed to disease but remain well. Additional factors are required to induce disease.

3. Various social factors—migration, job loss or dissatisfaction, poverty, nutritional deprivation, bereavement, and loss of social supports—may occur to produce a state of adaptive breakdown, manifested by ill-health but not necessarily by disease.

4. The age a person is exposed to infection, the route of infection, nutritional deprivation, poverty, bereavement, and migration may determine the time of onset, course, and natural history of the disease.

5. The same inciting agent, be it genetic, infectious, pharmacological, or social, may give rise to several different disease forms.

6. The adaptive response of the organism—at an immunological, physiological, and psychological level—may vary quantitatively and qualitatively. Disease is a consequence of adaptive failure.

7. The variable adaptive responses (e.g., an immunological

response) determine in part the form in which the disease is expressed.

8. The ultimate form of the disease is determined by disturbances in regulation and communication between cells and organs.

9. Disease may be transmitted vertically and horizontally in several ways.

10. The society, culture, economy, family, and sick person are in turn influenced by illness and disease.

The integrative approach attempts to impress on the practitioner and the investigator the multifactorial, nonlinear nature of disease and illness etiology, maintenance, and treatment. It also tries to divert medicine from its tendency to classify, diagnose, study, and treat disease after onset, and from its efforts only to reverse material defects (traditionally believed to have single causes) in organs, cells or subcellular structures. Finally, this chapter points out that a comprehensive and broad approach to health and disease can and must incorporate our knowledge of the roles of social and psychological factors at every stage of illness and disease.

References

Aagaard, J., & Kristensen, B. O. (in press a), A clinical and sociomedical prospective investigation of patients with essential hypertension. I. Clinical characteristics, social factors, life events and symptoms. *J. Hum. Stress.*
———— ———— (in press b), A clinical and sociomedical prospective investigation of patients with essential hypertension. II. Determinants for disease symptoms and disease aggravation. *J. Hum. Stress.*
Ackerman, S. H. (1981), Premature weaning, thermoregulation, and the occurrence of gastric pathology. In: *Brain, Behavior and Bodily Disease*, Vol. 59, ed. H. Weiner, M. A. Hofer, & A. J. Stunkard. New York: Raven Press, pp. 67–86.
Ader, R. (1980), Psychosomatic and psychoimmunologic research. *Psychosom. Med.*, 42:307–321.
Alexander, F. (1950), *Psychosomatic Medicine*. New York: Norton.

Bahnson, C. B. (1969), Psychophysiological complementarity in malignancies; past work and future vistas. *Ann. N.Y. Acad. Sci.*, 164:319–334.

Belloc, N. B., & Breslow, L. (1972), Relationship of physical health status and health practices. *Prev. Med.*, 1:409–421.

Bettelheim, B., & Janowitz, M. (1964), *Social Change and Prejudice*. New York: Free Press.

Blumberg, B. S. (1977), Australia antigen and the biology of hepatitis B. *Science*, 197:17–25.

Breslow, L., & Enstrom, J. E. (1980), Persistence of health habits and their relationship to mortality. *Prev. Med.*, 9:469–483.

Brock, J. F. (1972), Nature, nurture, and stress in health and disease. *Lancet*, 1:701–704.

Brody, H. (1973), The systems view of man: Implications for medicine, science and ethics. *Perspect. Biol. Med.*, 17:71–92.

Brown, J. J., Fraser, R., Lever, A. F., Morton, J. J., & Rubinson, J. I. S. (1977), Mechanisms in hypertension: A personal view. In: *Hypertension*, ed. J. Genest, E. Koiw, & O. Kuchel. New York: McGraw-Hill, pp. 529–548.

Chalmers, J. P. (1975), Brain amines and models of experimental hypertension. *Cir. Res.*, 36:469–480.

Coulehan, J. L. (1980), Human illness: Cases, models and paradigms. *Pharos*, 43:2–8.

Cullen, J. (1980), Coping and health. In: *Coping and Health*, ed. S. Levine & H. Ursin. New York: Plenum, pp. 295–322.

Day, G. (1951), The psychosomatic approach to pulmonary tuberculosis. *Lancet*, 1:1025–1028.

de Duve, C. (1975), Exploring cells with a centrifuge. *Science*, 189:186–194.

de-Thé, G., Geser, A., Day, N. E., Tukei, P. M., Williams, E. H., Beri, D. P., Smith, P. G., Dean, A. G., Bornkamm, G. W., Feorino, P., & Henle, W. (1978), Epidemiological evidence for causal relationship between Epstein-Barr virus and Burkitt's lymphoma from Ugandan prospective study. *Nature* (London), 274:756.

De Waard, F. (1975), Breast cancer incidence and nutritional status with particular reference to body weight. *Cancer Res.*, 35:3351–3356.

Dongier, M. E. D., Wittkower, L., Stephens-Newsham, L., & Hoffman, M. M. (1956), Psychophysiological studies in thyroid function. *Psychosom. Med.*, 18:310–323.

Dubos, R. (1959), *Mirage of Health*. New York: Harper.

———— (1965), *Man Adapting*. New Haven: Yale University Press.

Dunbar, H. F. (1943), *Psychosomatic Diagnosis*. New York: Hoeber.

Eisenberg, L. (1977), Psychiatry and society: A sociobiological analysis. *New Engl. J. Med.*, 296:903–910.

Engel, G. L. (1968), A life setting conducive to illness: The giving-up, given-up complex. *Ann. Intern. Med.*, 69:293–300.

—— (1977), The need for a new medical model: A challenge for biomedicine. *Science*, 196:129–136.

Engelhardt, H. T., Jr., & Spicker, S. F. (1975), *Evaluation and Explanation in the Biomedical Sciences*. Boston: Reidel, pp. 126–139.

Fabrega, H. (1975), The need for an ethnomedical science. *Science*, 189:969–975.

Folkow, B. U. G., & Hallbäck, M. I. L. (1977), Physiopathology of spontaneous hypertension in rats. In: *Hypertension*, ed. J. Genest, E. Koiw, & O. Kuchel. New York: McGraw-Hill, pp. 507–529.

Frankenhaeuser, M. (1975a), Experimental approaches to the study of catecholamines and emotion. In: *Emotions—Their Parameters and Measurement*, ed. L. Levi. New York: Raven Press.

—— (1975b), Sympathetic-adrenomedullary activity, behavior and the psychosocial environment. In: *Research in Psychophysiology*, ed. P. H. Venables & M. J. Christie. New York: Wiley, pp. 71–94.

—— (1979), Psychoneuroendocrine approaches to the study of stressful person-environment transactions. In: *Selye's Guide to Stress Research*, ed. H. Selye. New York: Van Nostrand Reinhold, pp. 46–70.

—— Nordheden, B., Myrsten, A. L., & Post, B. (1971), Psychophysiological reactions to understimulation and overstimulation. *Acta Psychol.*, 35:298–308.

Fries, H., & Nillius, S. J. (1973), Dieting, anorexia nervosa and amenorrhoea after oral contraceptive treatment. *Acta Psychiat. Scand.*, 49:669–679.

Frohlich, E. D., Tarazi, R. C., & Dustan, H. P. (1971), Clinical-physiological correlation in the development of hypertensive heart disease. *Circulation*, 44:446–455.

Ganten, D., Schelling, P., & Ganten, U. (1977), Tissue isorenins. In: *Hypertension*, ed. J. Genest, E. Koiw, & O. Kuchel. New York: McGraw-Hill, pp. 240–255.

Genest, J., Koiw, E., & Kuchel, O., eds. (1977), *Hypertension*. New York: McGraw-Hill.

Greene, W. A., Jr. (1954), Psychological factors and reticuloendothelial disease: I. Preliminary observations on a group of males with lymphomas and leukemias. *Psychosom. Med.*, 16:220–230.

Hamburg, D. A., & Adams, J. E. (1967), A perspective on coping behavior. *Arch. Gen. Psychiat.*, 17:277–284.

Hanley, W. B. (1964), Hereditary aspects of duodenal ulceration: Serum pepsinogen level in relation to ABO blood group and salivary ABH secretor status. *Brit. Med. J.*, 1(5388):936–940.

Harburg, E., Erfurt, J. C., Hauenstein, L. S., Chape, C., Schull, W. J., & Schork, M. A. (1973), Socio-ecological stress, suppressed hostility, skin color, and Black-White male blood pressure: Detroit. *Psychosom. Med.*, 35:276–296.

Hartmann, H. (1958), *Ego Psychology and the Problem of Adaptation*. New York: International Universities Press.

Hinkle, Jr., L. E. (1974), The effect of exposure to culture change, social change, and changes in interpersonal relationships on health. In: *Stressful Life Events*, ed. B. S. Dohrenwend & B. P. Dohrenwend. New York: Wiley.

——— Wolf, S. (1952), A summary of experimental evidence relating life stress to diabetes mellitus. *J. Mt. Sinai Hosp.*, 19:537–570.

Hofer, M. A. (1981), Toward a developmental basis for disease predisposition: The effects of early maternal separation on brain, behavior and cardiovascular system. In: *Brain, Behavior and Bodily Disease*, Vol. 59, ed. H. Weiner, M. A. Hofer, & A. J. Stunkard. New York: Raven Press.

Hollenberg, N. K., & Adams, D. F. (1976), The renal circulation in hypertensive disease. *Amer. J. Med.*, 50:773–784.

Hotchin, J., & Buckley, R. (1977), Latent form of scrapie virus: A new factor in slow-virus disease. *Science*, 196:668–671.

Jahnigen, D., Hannon, C., Laxson, L., & LaForce, F. M. (1982), Iatrogenic disease in hospitalized elderly veterans. *J. Amer. Geriat. Soc.*, 30:387–390.

Julius, S., Randall, O. S., Esler, M. D., Kashima, T., Ellis, C. N., & Bennet, J. (1978), Altered cardiac responsiveness and regulation in the normal cardiac output of borderline hypertension. *Circ. Res.*, 36-37 (Suppl. 1):I-199–207.

Kasl, S. V., & Cobb, S. (1970), Blood pressure changes in men undergoing job loss: A preliminary report. *Psychosom. Med.*, 32:19–38.

——— ——— Brooks, G. W. (1968), Changes in serum uric acid and cholesterol levels in men undergoing job loss. *J. Amer. Med. Assn.*, 206:1500.

Kellgren, J. H., & Ball, J. (1959), Clinical significance of the rheumatoid serum factor. *Brit. Med. J.*, 1:523.

Kety, S. S. (1974), From rationalization to reason. *Amer. J. Psychiat.*, 131:957–963.

Kissen, D. M. (1967), Psychological factors, personality, and lung cancer in men aged 55-64. *Brit. J. Med. Psychol.*, 40:29–43.

Korner, P. I., West, M. J., Shaw, J., & Uther, J. B. (1974), "Steady-state" properties of baroreceptor-heart rate reflex in essential hypertension in man. *Clin. Exp. Pharmacol. Physiol.*, 1:65–76.

Kron, L., Katz, J. L., Gorzynski, G., & Weiner, H. (1977), Anorexia nervosa and gonadal dysgenesis: Further evidence of a relationship. *Arch. Gen. Psychiat.*, 34:332–335.

Lazarus, R. S. (1966), *Psychological Stress and the Coping Process*. New York: McGraw-Hill.

LeShan, L. I. (1966), An emotional life-history pattern associated with neoplastic disease. *Ann. N.Y. Acad. Sci.*, 125:780–793.

Marcus, D. M. (1969), The ABO and Lewis blood-group system. *New Eng. J. Med.*, 280:994–1006.

Marmot, M. G., & Syme, S. L. (1975), Acculturation and coronary heart disease in Japanese-Americans. *Amer. J. Epidemiol.*, 104:225–247.

——— ——— Kagan, A., Kato, H., Cohen, J. B., & Belsky, J. (1975), Epidemiologic studies of coronary heart disease and stroke in Japanese men living in Japan, Hawaii and California: Prevalence of coronary and hypertensive heart disease and associated risk factors. *Amer. J. Epidemiol.*, 102:514–525.

Marty, P., & de M'Uzan, M. (1963), La pensée opératoire. *Rev. Franc. Psychanal.*, 27:Suppl. 1345.

Mason, J. (1971), A re-evaluation of the concept of "non-specificity" in stress research. *J. Psychiat. Res.*, 8:323–333.

McDougall, J. (1974), The psychosoma and the psychoanalytic process. *Internat. Rev. Psychoanal.*, 1:437.

McKeown, T. J. (1976), *The Role of Medicine: Dream, Mirage or Nemesis*. London: Nuffield Provincial Trusts.

Medawar, P. B., & Medawar, J. S. (1977), *The Life Science*. New York: Harper & Row.

Mirra, A. P., Cole, P., & MacMahon, B. (1971), Breast cancer in an area of high parity: Sao Paulo, Brazil. *Cancer Res.*, 31:77–83.

Moos, R. H., & Solomon, G. F. (1965a), Psychologic comparisons between women with rheumatoid arthritis and their nonarthritic sisters. I. Personality test and interview rating data. *Psychosom. Med.*, 27:135–149.

——— ——— (1965b), Psychologic comparisons between women with rheumatoid arthritis and their non-arthritic sisters. II. Content analysis of interviews. *Psychosom. Med.*, 27:150–164.

Morrell, D. C. (1978), The epidemiological imperative for primary care. In: *Primary Health Care in Industrialized Nations*, Vol. 310. New York: New York Academy of Sciences, pp. 2–10.

Moss, G. E. (1973), *Illness, Immunity and Social Interaction*. New York: Wiley.

National Center for Health Statistics, *Mortality from Selected Causes by Marital Status* (1970), Vital and Health Statistics, Series 20, No. 8A and B. U.S. Dept. of Health, Education and Welfare.

Nemiah, J. C., & Sifneos, P. E. (1970), Affect and fantasy in patients with psychosomatic disorders. In: *Modern Trends in Psychosomatic Medicine*, Vol. 2, ed. O. W. Hill. London: Butterworths, pp. 26–34.

Notkins, A. L. (1979), The causes of diabetes. *Sci. Amer.*, 241:62–73.

Ostfeld, A. (1979), The role of stress in hypertension. *J. Hum. Stress*, 5:20.

Perlman, L. V., Ferguson, S., Bergum, K., Isenberg, E. L., & Hammarsten, J. F. (1971), Precipitation of congestive heart failure: Social and emotional factors. *Ann. Intern. Med.*, 75:1–7.

Rasmussen, H. (1975), Medical education: Revolution or reaction. *Pharos*, 38:53–57.

Reiser, M. F., Brust, A. A., & Ferris, E. B. (1951), Life situations, emotions and the course of patients with arterial hypertension. *Psychosom. Med.*, 13:133–139.

——— Rosenbaum, M., & Ferris, E. B. (1951), Psychologic mechanisms in malignant hypertension. *Psychosom. Med.*, 13:147–159.

Rotter, J. I., & Rimoin, D. L. (1977), Peptic ulcer disease—a heterogeneous group of disorders? *Gastroenterol.*, 73:604–607.

——— ——— Gursky, J. M., & Samloff, I. M. (1977), The genetics of peptic ulcer disease—segregation of serum group I pepsinogen concentrations in families with peptic ulcer disease. *Clin. Res.*, 25:114A.

——— Sones, J. Q., Richardson, C. T., Rimoin, D. L., & Samloff, I. M. (1977), The genetics of peptic ulcer disease—segregation of serum group I pepsinogen concentrations in families with peptic ulcer disease. *Clin. Res.*, 25:325A.

——— ——— Samloff, I. M., Richardson, C. T., Gursky, J. M., Walsh, J. H., & Rimoin, D. L. (1979), Duodenal-ulcer disease associated with elevated serum pepsinogen I: An inherited autosomal dominant disorder. *New Engl. J. Med.*, 300:63–66.

Rubenstein, E. (1980), Diseases caused by impaired communication among cells. *Sci. Amer.*, 242:102–121.

Ruesch, J. (1948), The infantile personality: The core problem of psychosomatic medicine. *Psychosom. Med.*, 10:133–144.

——— Christiansen, C., Patterson, L. C., Dewees, S., & Jacobson, A. (1947), Psychological invalidism in thyroidectomized patients. *Psychosom. Med.*, 9:77-01.

Safar, M. E., Kamieniecka, H. A., Levenson, J. A., Dimitriu, V. M., & Pauleau, N. F. (1978), Hemodynamic factors and Rorschach testing in borderline and sustained hypertension. *Psychosom. Med.*, 40:620–630.

Saxena, K. (1980), Physiological effects of job loss. Presented at the annual meeting of the International Society for the Prevention of Stress.

Schmale, Jr., A. H. (1958), Relation of separation and depression to disease: I. A report on a hospitalized medical population. *Psychosom. Med.*, 20:259–277.

Sievers, M. L. (1959), Hereditary aspects of gastric secretory function: Race and ABO blood groups in relationship to acid and pepsin production. *Amer. J. Med.*, 27:246–255.

Solomon, G. F., & Moos, R. J. (1965), The relationship of personality to the presence of rheumatoid factor in asymptomatic relatives of patients with rheumatoid arthritis. *Psychosom. Med.*, 27:350–360.

Stallones, R. A. (1980), The rise and fall of ischemic heart disease. *Sci. Amer.*, 243:53–59.

Steel, K., Gertman, P. M., Crescenzi, C., & Anderson, J. (1981), Iatrogenic illness on a general medical service at a university hospital. *New Eng. J. Med.*, 304:638–642.

Stein, S. P., & Charles, E. (1971), Emotional factors in juvenile diabetes mellitus: A study of early life experience of adolescent diabetics. *Amer. J. Psychiat.*, 128:700–704.

Strober, W., Glaese, R. M., & Waldmann, T. A. (1971–1972), Immunologic deficiency diseases. *Bull. Rheum. Dis.*, 22:686.

Sturdevant, R. A. L. (1979), The role of stress in peptic ulcer disease. *J. Hum. Stress*, 5:29–30.

Syme, S. L. (1979), The role of stress in hypertension. *J. Hum. Stress*, 5:10–11.

—— Berkman, L. F. (1976), Social class, susceptibility and sickness. *Amer. J. Epidemiol.*, 104:1–8.

Vaillant, G. (1977), *Adaptation to Life*. Boston: Little, Brown.

Vesely, K. T., Kubichova, K. T., Dvorakova, M. (1968), Clinical and characteristics differentiating types of peptic ulcer. *Gut*, 9:57–61.

Vollhardt, B. O., Ackerman, S. H., Grayzel, A. I., & Barland, P. (1982), Psychologically distinguishable groups of rheumatoid arthritis patients: A controlled single blind study. *Psychosom. Med.*, 44:353–360.

von Uexküll, T., ed. (1979), *Lehrbuch der Psychosomatischen Medizin*. Munich: Urban & Schwarzenberg.

Weiner, H. (1977), *Psychobiology and Human Disease*. New York: Elsevier-North Holland.

—— (1978), The illusion of simplicity: The medical model revisited. *Amer. J. Psychiat.*, 135(Suppl.):27–33.

—— (1979a), Psychobiological markers of disease. In: *Psychiatric Clinics of North America*, ed. C. P. Kimball. Philadelphia: Saunders, pp. 227–242.

—— (1979b), *Psychobiology of Essential Hypertension. Monographs in Psychobiology and Disease*, Vol. 1. New York: Elsevier North-Holland.

—— (1981a), Brain, behavior and bodily disease: A summary. In: *Brain, Behavior and Bodily Disease*, ed. H. Weiner, M. A. Hofer, & A. J. Stunkard. New York: Raven Press.

—— (1981b), Social and psychological factors in disease. In: *Human Behavior*, ed. W. R. Gove. Tennessee: Lexington Books of Heath.

—— (1983), Health, illness, and disease: An integrative approach. In: *Expanding Definitions and Models of Health*, ed. M. Lipkin & A. Etzioni. New York: Rockefeller Press.

—— Thaler, M., Reiser, M. F., & Mirsky, I. A. (1957), Etiology of duodenal ulcer. I. Relation of specific psychological characteristics to rate of gastric secretion (serum pepsinogen). *Psychosom. Med.*, 19:1–10.

Wynder, E. L., Escher, G. C., & Mantel, N. A. (1966), An epidemiological investigation of cancer of the endometrium. *Cancer*, 19:489–520.

2.

Stress and Illness

GLEN ELLIOTT, PH.D., M.D.

The concept that environmental stress can affect health probably dates back to the ancients, but the nineteenth century ideal of scientists in pursuit of physical causes for disease tended to minimize the role of agents that could not be seen and quantified. Thus, the current intense public and scientific interest in stress and health can be dated to shortly before World War II. Stress research was the foundation of psychosomatic medicine, a field that has as its basic assumption the belief that psychological factors can powerfully affect a person's health. Thus, it seems especially appropriate to include in a book about psychosomatic medicine a chapter that reviews some of the available evidence for connections between stress and certain types of physical and mental disorders.

Over the past 30 years, popular opinion has heartily endorsed the idea that stress, whether it be linked to a natural disaster, type of employment or kind of life style, can make people more vulnerable to disease. In response to this notion, large amounts of money are spent each year trying either to avoid or to learn how to cope with stress. There is nearly always at least one best-selling book purporting to reveal how to reduce stressful aspects of their life and thus prevent the development of illnesses ranging from insomnia, depression or anxiety to hypertension, heart attacks, and even cancer. The medical profession is also involved; three of the most widely prescribed drugs in the United States—diazepam (Valium), chlordiazepoxide (Librium), and cimetidine (Tagamet)—are all used mainly for problems thought to be stress related.

The initial upsurge of public interest in stress largely paralleled early scientific inquiries. In studying how the brain regulates the rest of the body, scientists such as Walter Cannon, Hans Selye, and John Mason discovered that exposing animals to severe physical or psychological trauma somehow could indirectly impair the function of a wide array of physiological systems and could even lead to death. Clinical observations by Stewart Wolf, Franz Alexander, Arthur Mirsky, and others strongly suggested that similar changes could occur in persons facing major life disruptions, thus contributing to the development of certain types of physical disease. Starting from these relatively limited beginnings, the concept of stress and disease has broadened markedly over time to include an astonishing variety both of stressors and of mental and physical disorders.

Stress research deservedly has numerous detractors. Many early studies of stress and illness were severely flawed, and problems in methodology continue to plague the field. Connections between specific types of stress and certain kinds of diseases generally have not held up, and the degree of risk associated with exposure to a stressor typically has been lower than originally thought. Most questions about how a stressor can produce dysfunction in a specific part of the body remain unanswered.

Even so, an impressive array of competent research now supports the belief that people whose lives are disrupted have an increased risk of subsequently becoming physically or mentally ill. Such disruptions usually are sudden and adverse, or at least demand a change in attitude or behavior, as occurs with job loss, bereavement, moving to a new location, or marriage. Associated disorders range from minor to major, including colds, infections, bronchial asthma, hypertension, peptic ulcers, heart attacks, cancer, depression, schizophrenia, and alcoholism.

As a whole, the evidence for a connection between stress and illness is compelling. Fortunately, advances in the neurosciences, psychology, social sciences, and many other fields have begun to provide the tools needed to gain a better understanding of the mechanisms that create that connection and of ways in which adverse health consequences can be avoided. This chapter begins with a description of one useful perspective from which to view the stress field, then discusses some of the literature on specific physical and mental disorders.

EVOLUTION OF STRESS DEFINITIONS

After 35 years, no one has formulated a completely satisfactory definition of stress, and no ready solution is at hand. It is easy to reach a consensus on major sources of stress that produce profound, possibly lethal effects. But where does one stop? Some definitions are too broad, such as any stimulus, or even a lack of stimulus. Others require some sort of physiological or psychological reaction, thus making a priori assumptions about the effects of stress. Still others go even further, requiring a loss of mental or physical function to distinguish stressors from nonstressors.

Walter Cannon (1935) conducted some of the first systematic studies of effects of stress on the body. His concept of stress, analogous to that used in physics, was that of physical or emotional stimuli which, if sufficiently severe, could strain animals or people beyond their adaptive limits. This emphasis on strain, especially physical strain, was maintained by Hans Selye, who played a major role in popularizing the idea of a link between stress and physical disease.

Selye discovered that a wide array of noxious stimuli produced in animals what appeared to be a nonspecific physical response, which he named the General Adaptation Syndrome. Selye (1975) identified three stages to this syndrome: "(1) an alarm reaction, in which adaptation has not yet been acquired; (2) the stage of resistance, in which adaptation is optimal; and (3) the stage of exhaustion, in which the acquired adaptation is lost again" (p. 10). Impressed with what seemed to be a universal response, Selye proposed that "stress" should refer to that response, rather than to the stimuli producing it, which he called "stressors" (Selye, 1950). His hypothesis that both physical and emotional stressors could produce readily identifiable physiological changes gave strong impetus to psychosomatic research.

Although it has historical importance, Selye's postulate of a single, nonspecific physiological response to stressors is no longer tenable. His original findings may, in part, have resulted from his using stressors that were all noxious and alarming to the animals he studied. Thus, Mason (1971) found that rapidly rising environmental temperatures produced the expected brisk response in adrenal corticosteroid secretion in monkeys; but a slow increase of temperature, which did not produce alarm, suppressed steroid secretion instead of elevating it. In addition, technological advances now make it possible to measure a large array of hormonal and physiological responses to a stressor, and there is evidence that patterns of hormonal response can be quite specific to the stressor applied (Mason, 1974). In an interesting demonstration of such specificity in humans, Dimsdale and Moss (1980) compared the effects of public speaking and moderate physical exercise on plasma concentrations of the catecholamines epinephrine and norepinephrine. The increase in norepinephrine is much more pronounced during exercise but increase in epinephrine is much greater during speaking.

Stress research on human beings typically involves studies of stressors that are much less severe than those used in animal studies and usually cannot include the use of extensive physiological or biochemical tests. As a result, clinical research has tended to emphasize stressors that are likely to produce psychological, rather than physiological, responses. Experimental stimuli such as mild electric shock, noise, or unpleasant films, and such natural events as bereavement, physical illness, or traumatic experiences, are all apt to create strong emotions of fear, sadness, and anger. One important consequence of using such stressors in research is recognition of the importance of an individual perceiving a stimulus as stressful (Lazarus, 1966; Glass, 1977; Burchfield, 1979).

In many ways, the lack of a clear definition of the term epitomizes both the frustration and the fascination of studying stress and highlights the complexity of the concept. One problem of defining stress is its relevance to many branches of science, each with its own needs and interests. Over the years, definitions of stress have increasingly derived from the specific concerns of the investigator. As a result, efforts to compare definitions have produced inconsistent and contradictory results. For example, imagine that researchers studying a group of hostages just released after a long period of captivity were able to ask them about their experience and also measure several hormones known to be elevated during severe stress. It is likely that some of the hostages would report that they were extremely angry and sad, yet show no hormonal changes; others might deny that they had been especially affected, yet have marked hormonal responses; and still others might display both emotional and biochemical reactions, or neither. Suppose these hypothetical researchers want to study the short- and long-term sequelae of this event, comparing those for whom it was especially stressful with those for whom it was not. Is it meaningful to say that captivity was a stressor for some but not for all? If so, who was stressed: those with hormonal responses? those with psychological symptoms? only those with both biological and psychological reactions? Deciding who to define as stressed well may be one of the key determinants of the results of any subsequent study.

In addition, the historical interest in linking stress and illness has resulted in a tendency to arbitrarily associate stressors with adverse events and stress with negative outcomes, thus encouraging a tendency to label both as "bad." Such an emphasis on the negative aspects of stress ignores potentially desirable effects, including increased physical stamina, more effective coping styles, or stronger social ties. Thus, "stress-induced disease" now refers to a large but poorly defined group of undesirable biological, psychological, and social outcomes; and "stress" often is used as if it were a causal explanation for such outcomes, leaving unanswered key questions about underlying physiological and psychological mechanisms.

A FRAMEWORK FOR THE CONCEPT OF STRESS

Several years ago, the National Academy of Sciences' Institute of Medicine convened an interdisciplinary group of scientists and clinicians to survey the state of stress research (Elliott and Eisdorfer, 1982). As part of its task, the committee examined existing definitions of stress and concluded that none was completely adequate (Dohrenwend, Pearlin, Clayton, Hamburg, Riley, Rose, and Dohrenwend, 1982). As one possible synthesis of the variety of definitions, they suggested a framework from which to view the effects of the environment on an individual, identifying three major elements: the environmental activator, the reaction to that activator, and the resulting consequence—a series they called the x-y-z sequence (see Figure 1).

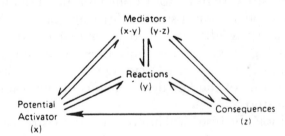

Descriptors:
Organizational Level
Intensity
Quantity
Temporal Pattern
Evaluative Quality (for Consequences only)

Figure 1. An idealized framework for interactions between the individual and the environment.
From Elliott and Eisdorfer, 1982. Reprinted by permission.

Because such a framework helps greatly in clarifying interrelationships between stress and disease, it seems useful to describe it in some detail.

ACTIVATORS

An *activator* must be defined somewhat circularly. It is an internal and external environmental event or condition that alters one's physical and psychological state. Examples of activators include being hit, having a bad tooth cavity, receiving a raise, getting kissed, and many other daily events to which everyone is exposed. In fact, an activator may even involve the absence of a stimulus, rather than its presence, for example, if someone fails to get the promotion they have been expecting or if a persistent headache suddenly goes away. Once identified, it can be characterized in several ways, including intensity, quantity, temporal pattern, and organizational complexity. The last refers to the part of the body upon which it acts, which can range from a single enzyme through organ systems to psychological states.

The concept of "potential" activators is one way around the circularity of the definition. A *potential activator* is an event or condition for which the likelihood of its being an activator can be calculated empirically under certain known circumstances. Thus, a potential activator can be defined independently of its actual effects on a specific individual. For example, loss of a spouse might be defined as a potential activator. Relevant factors in determining its chances of being an activator might include, among others, the ages of both members of the couple, how long they were married, the quality of their relationship, the suddenness of the loss, and the financial status of the survivor. The actual importance of each of these factors would have to be determined empirically.

Clearly, many activators will have little or no impact on an individual, and therefore are relatively uninteresting. Thus, it seems reasonable to define as stressors that subset of activators which are sufficiently intense or frequent to produce significant physical or psychosocial reactions. This definition is compatible with most that were mentioned earlier and has the same *post hoc* quality that they do. However, use of clearly defined potential stressors could go a long way toward encouraging systematic attention to the specific aspects of a situation or event that make it stressful.

One useful way of subdividing stressors is according to their duration, which may be thought of as four broad types (Cohen, Horowitz, Lazarus, Moos, Robins, Rose, and Rutter, 1982):

1. *Acute stressors*, which are time-limited (running into a wall, waiting to take a difficult test, being startled)
2. *Stressor sequences*, which involve a series of events flowing from some initiating event (losing a job, getting a divorce, having a bad accident)
3. *Chronic intermittent stressors*, in which an event happens repeatedly with intervening remission (job layoff, rheumatoid flare-up, discord with in-laws)
4. *Chronic stressors*, which are unremitting and long-lasting (marital discord, stressful work setting, permanent disability)

REACTIONS

Even the simplest activators can produce a variety of biological and psychosocial *reactions* in an individual, many of them minor and hard to detect. For example, hearing an unexpected knock on the door can produce an immediate increase in heart rate, blood pressure, and respiration; increased vigilance; fear, and curiosity. As with activators, reactions can be characterized reasonably precisely with such descriptors as intensity, quantity, temporal pattern, and organizational level. Thus the amount and duration of increase in heart rate from hearing the unexpected knock would be quite different from that following a mile run. Patterns of reactions may be especially important in determining the consequences they produce; but they also are particularly difficult to determine, because of the resources needed to make multiple measurements simultaneously.

Temporal sequencing of reactions over time also may be important. For example, hitting one's thumb with a hammer first may produce surprise, followed rapidly by pain, followed by anger or disgust. Similarly, at first encounter, an uncontrollable situation may produce relatively little anxiety and autonomic hyperactivity, but subsequent repetitions may produce increasingly greater reactions.

A great deal of basic research has focused on the *x-y*, or activator-to-reaction part of the sequence, so that a substantial body of information already is available to predict what types of reactions might result from specific types of potential stressors. What remains to be established in nearly all cases is which of these reactions, alone or in combination, produce major consequences.

CONSEQUENCES

At times, it can be difficult to distinguish between consequences and the reactions that produce them. In general, reactions are the transient responses to specific activators, and *consequences* are the more prolonged or cumulative effects of those reactions. Naturally, only some consequences are at all relevant to an individual's health. Consequences can occur at all levels of structural complexity. They can be biological, as occurs with stress ulcers following a major physical injury; psychological, for example, when someone becomes psychotic following chronic amphetamine ingestion; or sociological, as frequently occurs following a divorce with radical changes in work patterns and social support networks. They also can differ in intensity, quantity, and temporal pattern.

Unlike activators and reactions, consequences also can be evaluated qualitatively. It is reasonable to decide whether a consequence is desirable or undesirable, based on some social or personal standard. As documented throughout this chapter, physical and mental disorders appear to be one type of consequence of exposure to stressors that most people would consider to be undesirable. There is an unfortunate tendency to label stressors as "bad" because of this association. However, stressors also may lead to positive consequences that should not be ignored. For example, joggers know that strenuous physical exercise can build stamina and increase strength, as well as tear ligaments and create fatigue. Reserving evaluative labels only for consequences can help to avoid some logical inconsistencies in the stress field, for example, an effort to distinguish stressors from challenges on the basis of the consequences to the individual.

MEDIATORS

Even the idealized x-y-z sequence of activator-to-reaction-to-consequence must occur in the context of a specific individual. Under certain extreme conditions, the characteristics of that individual may be irrelevant. For example, an intravenous injection of a large dose of curare would paralyze any animal, producing respiratory arrest and death. Usually, however, the individual plays a much more important role. The concept of a potential activator explicitly acknowledges that it may produce no reaction in one person, only a mild reaction in another, and an extreme reaction with major consequences in a third. Of course, similar results also can occur for a single individual over time. Thus, naloxone, a narcotic antagonist, produces no reactions in someone not addicted to narcotics; but it precipitates all the signs and symptoms of withdrawal when given to an addict. *Mediators* are the characteristics of the individual that produce such differences by modifying the x-y and y-z steps.

There are many types of mediators, which can work independently or in unison. For example, impaired hearing may prevent someone from hearing a shouted warning, or a preexisting paranoia may lend dark meaning to otherwise innocuous whispers. Social and other environmental factors also can be mediators. Someone with adequate social supports may handle a job loss with far fewer reactions and consequences than would someone who lacked them. Likewise, the effects of having a car stall depend greatly on where and in what kind of weather.

DYNAMIC INTERACTIONS

A static description of each separate component of the x-y-z sequence fails to capture a crucial aspect—their *dynamic interaction*. In reality, people continuously encounter large numbers of potential activators, even as they are experiencing the reactions and consequences produced by previous activators. Thus, each part of the sequence continually alters and is altered by the others. Mediators help to specify each x-y-z sequence but also change as a result of the cumulative effects of past reactions and consequences. Suppose, for example, that eating fatty foods produced a chronic elevation in cholesterol, which resulted in plaque formation in a cardiac artery. That consequence then becomes a modifier that may greatly enhance the probability of a cardiac arrhythmia, and possibly death, as a reaction and consequence to an otherwise innocuous potential stressor of intense anger.

STRESS AS A RISK FACTOR

As mentioned earlier, a persistent problem with stress research has been the tendency of some to consider stress as the "cause" of a particular illness. Such a statement often arises in common parlance, when someone explains that his peptic ulcer was "caused" by his job. Similarly, a depressed patient may be able to identify a specific event as the "cause" of her depression. Using the x-y-z nomenclature, such statements refer to an x-z association, where the event or situation is the stressor and the ulcer or depression is the consequence. What is missing in such a formulation is the reactions, or real causes. Although the identification of such reactions is desirable, well defined x-z associations also can be of value in predicting whether a particular stressor is a risk factor of a specific consequence.

Risk-factor analyses have been increasingly important to the medical profession over the past decade. One of the most influential efforts to identify people at unusually high risk of developing a particular disease is the Framingham study of coronary heart disease (Dawber, 1980). This prospective study of a large population measured associations between various behavioral, physiological, and genetic factors and the subsequent development of heart attacks or sudden coronary death. Some individuals, for example those who had high blood pressure and smoked cigarettes, had a much greater risk of developing coronary heart disease than did those lacking such traits. These traits, or risk factors, can be used to identify persons who are likely to have heart disease, even when there is no known cause for the association. Thus, a heavy cigarette smoker is at increased risk for having a heart attack (x-z), even though the intervening steps (x-y, y-z) are unknown.

Risk factors, then, are characteristics associated with individuals who are more likely than others without such traits to subsequently develop an illness. Thus, risk factors must be present before the disease, rather than be signs or symptoms of it. For example, angina cannot be a risk factor of heart disease, because it results from it. However, this does not mean that a risk factor must cause the disease, either directly or indirectly. Thus, some initially argued, incorrectly, that the association between smoking and heart disease merely reflected the fact that people at risk for heart disease also are likely to smoke, possibly as a reflection of some personality trait. The test of etiology involves decreasing the incidence of the risk factor or blocking the behavioral or physiological reactions it produces. If the risk factor is a causal agent, such interventions should decrease disease rates. Such has been the case with cigarette smoking; quitting results in a decline in mortality from both lung cancer and heart disease (U.S. Department of Health, Education, and Welfare, 1979).

Risk-factor analyses are an appropriate and important part of stress research. As described in the next section of this chapter, considerable work in this area already has been done. However, the results of such studies should not be overestimated. The utility of risk factors for identifying persons who may be especially apt to develop a particular disorder depends entirely on the strength of the association, which typically is rather low in studies of stress. This means that some individuals with the risk factor will develop the disease, but many more will not. The real value of such research may lay more in suggesting useful directions in the study of underlying mechanisms connecting stressors to illness and in encouraging efforts to modify the risk factors as a means of trying to decrease the disease incidence.

To date, few investigators have attempted to make precise estimates of the quantity of stressful life events that increase the risk for a specific illness. Orth-Gomer and Ahlbom (1980) provide an example of such research in their retrospective study of exposure to chronically stressful conditions as a risk factor for heart disease. They looked at three groups of male Swedish workers: those who recently had had a heart attack or developed angina; healthy controls; and those without known heart disease, matched with the first group for such risk factors as hypertension, high cholesterol, and smoking habits. Comparing reports of chronically stressful events during the previous five years, the investigators found that the recent heart attack victims were significantly more likely than either of the other groups to report having experienced one or more periods of great stress lasting at least six months. The occurrence of such stressful periods was associated with a sixfold greater risk of having a heart attack or angina when healthy subjects were used as controls, and a threefold greater risk when controls were matched for other risk factors.

STRESSFUL EVENTS AS GENERAL RISK FACTORS OF DISEASE

One type of stress research looks at broad, nonspecific associations between a variety of minor to severe life stressors and minor to major illnesses. Such research, which has used both major natural or man-made disasters and more routine daily stressful events, has done much to attract popular attention to this area.

Studies of disasters have the advantage of providing a readily definable, major stressor to which a number of people have been exposed. For example, Fritz and Marks (1954) interviewed a sample population in rural Arkansas after a severe tornado had struck that area; 90 percent reported that they had experienced acute emotional, physical, or psychosomatic consequences. Similarly, Terr (1979) worked with a group of 26 normal children who had been kidnapped and terrorized but were physically unharmed; even 5 months later, 19 had major personality changes, 14 continued to reenact the kidnapping in unconscious and compulsive ways, and 8 were doing more poorly in school.

Although major disasters are not a common experience for most people, less catastrophic and more common major life events, for example, bereavement, marriage and retirement, are also associated with adverse changes in health (Holmes and Masuda, 1974; Rahe and Arthur, 1978; Levi, Frankenhaeuser, and Gardell, 1982; Ricks and Dohrenwend, 1983). Typically, these studies follow the model suggested initially by Holmes and Rahe (1967), who examined the accumulation during specific time periods of specific types of predefined major life events in relation to the subsequent development of various mental and physical disorders. Studies indicate that certain types of life events, for example, bereavement, are greater risk factors of disease than are others such as a vacation; also, events appear to be additive, at least to some extent. Even a relatively milder stressor such as the loss of a job has been reported to be a risk factor of such problems as high blood pressure, upset stomachs, swollen joints, anxiety, depression, and suicide (Cobb and Kasl, 1977). Although knowledge of such studies is widespread, awareness of their inherent limitations is not (Dohrenwend et al., 1982). Briefly, they should be viewed as supporting evidence of a connection between stress and illness, not as proof of the magnitude and nature of such an association.

Antonovsky (1979) has suggested a quite different approach to stress and disease, which looks at the positive aspects of health and coping. The author argues that because stress is so common the odd fact is the number of people who seldom get ill. He believes that certain factors, for example, a view of the world as having meaning, are protective—a concept he calls "salu-dogenosis." As with other studies mentioned in this section, his research has been on relatively nonspecific changes in health.

THE RELATIONSHIP BETWEEN STRESS AND PHYSICAL AND MENTAL DISORDERS

This section examines research evidence connecting stress with major physical and mental illnesses. It draws heavily upon one of the panel reports of the Institute of Medicine's study on stress (Bunney, Shapiro, Ader, Davis, Herd, Kopin, Jr., Krieger, Matthysse, Stunkard, Weissman, and Wyatt, 1982). Only major disorders with which stress has been associated are described, but such research offers an accurate picture of the field, both in terms of what is known and of what remains to be learned.

Discussion of each of the disorders typically is subdivided into two parts: (1) the role of stress as a risk factor in the development of illness; and (2) stress as a factor in the perpet-uation of disease. As will become clear, these two types of re-search usually are distinct, involving different methodological approaches.

PEPTIC ULCER DISEASE

Peptic ulcer disease was among the first identified stress-related diseases and has been one of the most intensively stud-ied, thus perhaps earning its place as the first to be discussed here. Several well-designed studies document associations of stress with both the onset and the perpetuation of peptic ulcers. Nonetheless, as emphasized by a group of experts in a general review of the field, the links connecting emotional processes to pathological changes in the stomach have yet to be identified (Wolf, Almy, Bachrach, Spiro, Sturdevant, and Weiner, 1979). In fact, a fascinating aspect of this disease is that its prevalence continues in a downward spiral that began several years ago, despite what many believe to be increasingly stressful times. This fact strongly accentuates the need to recognize many factors other than stress that affect the course of the disorders discussed.

There is strong evidence of an association between certain chronically stressful situations and peptic ulcer disease. The first description of this effect was that men in supervisory jobs had a higher disease prevalence than did executives or craftsmen (Dunn and Cobb, 1962). Subsequently, Cobb and Rose (1973) found that air traffic controllers were almost twice as likely to have peptic ulcers as were civilian copilots, and that the incidence of ulcers was higher among air controllers working at high-stress control centers than among those at low-stress centers. This research was, in part, the basis for disputes over working conditions that ended in the air traffic controller strike several years ago.

Research on the role of psychological factors in the perpetuation of peptic ulcer disease is found mainly in the older literature. Those studies identified ulcer patients as oral-dependent characters for whom vacillating between active/seeking and passive/yielding behaviors exacerbated preexisting ulcers (Weisman, 1956). In the best of this research, Weiner, Thaler, Reiser, and Mirsky (1957) did a double-blind prospective study of military inductees, measuring serum pepsinogen and obtaining psychological profiles. They found that a profile of major, unresolved conflicts over dependency and oral gratification reliably identified high pepsinogen secretors and predicted those at risk for developing ulcers during training. Because only high secretors developed ulcers, the combined measures were even better predictors than either alone.

Recent advances in psychological and physiological techniques argue strongly for replication and extension of the studies cited. Multivariate analyses of potential risk factors may be especially productive. For example, Sturdevant (1976) identified more than 20 potential risk factors, including biological markers, disease states, and past and current dietary habits. The potential role of emotional states was demonstrated long ago in elegant studies of patients with gastric fistulas (Wolf and Wolff, 1943; Engel, Reichsman, and Siegal, 1956). For example, anger and hostility increase acidity; depression and withdrawal decrease it. It should be possible to build on these observations in searching for mechanisms that can produce the gastric changes seen in ulcers. A starting point might be Engel's (1975) hypothesis that ulcer patients become more symptomatic after stressful life events involving loss because their dependency needs are frustrated.

OTHER GASTROINTESTINAL DISORDERS

Most other research on stress and gastrointestinal disorders is outdated, even when interesting. For example, the classic studies of ulcerative colitis identified a constellation of psychosocial influences that seemed to affect the course of the disease but could not produce it (Engel, 1954, 1955). Early speculations about the possible involvement of the immune system can only now be studied. Even less is known about a variety of other gastrointestinal disorders, including esophageal spasm, various diarrheal states, and "spastic colon." All seem likely to be problems for which an understanding of the role of emotional stress might offer useful clues to more efficacious treatment approaches.

MYOCARDIAL INFARCTION

The type A behavior pattern has commanded a large share of the research effort in studies of stress-related risk factors of atherosclerosis. People exhibiting type A behavior are unusually aggressive, competitive, and work-oriented, with a constant sense of urgency (Friedman and Rosenman, 1959). Persons with such traits have a much higher incidence of heart attacks than do type B individuals (Rosenman, 1978). Unfortunately, this fascinating finding has little clinical value. The prevalence of type A is high, especially among males in the Western culture, and many never get heart disease. Also, it still is unclear whether decreasing one's type A behavior can reduce the risk of heart disease, despite some promising pilot studies (Rahe, O'Neil, Hagan, and Arthur, 1975; Rosenman, 1978). Furthermore, widespread reduction of such behavior might have adverse socioeconomic consequences of decreasing productivity and pressure to achieve.

Rarely, extreme stressors may disrupt previously healthy cardiac tissue (Cebelin and Hirsch, 1980); stressors usually affect heart function only if it is already damaged. However, given preexisting cardiac pathology, psychosocial stressors such as bereavement, loss of prestige, and loss of employment have been identified as risk factors of heart attacks (Kavanagh and Shepard, 1973). For example, a six-month prospective study of new widowers found that those who felt depressed, hopeless, and helpless had an excess mortality from myocardial infarctions of 67 percent compared with populations statistics for that age group (Parkes, Benjamin, and Fitzgerald, 1969). Major changes in living arrangements or occupation, and discrepancies between the culture of origin and the current cultural milieu, also are substantial risk factors (Syme, 1975).

Once again, the x-y and y-z steps connecting psychosocial stressors and atherosclerosis are unknown. Some reactions and consequences to type A behaviors have been proposed, but almost all remain controversial. Among them are elevated blood cholesterol, triglycerides, and glucocorticoids; increased insulin response to glucose; greater lability and magnitude of blood pressure and catecholamine responses to time-demand tasks; and increased severity of coronary artery lesions (Rosenman, 1978). Until relatively recently, the autonomic nervous system was thought to be the major pathway through which stress could affect the cardiovascular system (Lown, DeSilva, and Lenson, 1978), but the identification of direct pathways between the brain and the heart suggests that other mechanisms also may be involved (Cohen and Cabot, 1979).

Sudden Cardiac Death

Interest in a connection between stress and sudden cardiac death grew out of the suggestion that, under some conditions, people seem literally to have been scared to death (Engel, 1971). The disorder is defined primarily by the rapidity—from minutes to hours—in which death occurs. Most people who die of sudden cardiac death apparently do so as a result of defects in the heart's electrical system that cause dysrhythmias. Usually, studies of stressors as risk factors have not distinguished sudden cardiac death from other heart attacks. Still, Friedman, Manwaring, Rosenman, Donlon, Ortega, and Grube (1973) found that an unexpectedly large proportion of type A individuals who had heart attacks died of sudden cardiac death.

Retrospective studies of sudden cardiac death are consistent with acutely stressful life events as a risk factor. For example, interviews of the relatives of sudden cardiac death victims or survivors of heart attacks showed that victims and survivors both underwent substantial life changes during the six months before the event; but, those who died underwent more changes than those who survived (Rahe, Romo, Bennett, and Siltanen, 1974). The types of life events were unremarkable, although the victims tended to have increased problems at home and work and in relating to family and friends.

The few, small prospective studies of stress and sudden cardiac death tend to support the above research. Thus, Theorell and Rahe (1975) collected charts of patients who had survived a heart attack and were then followed as outpatients; half had died from a second attack and the rest had survived at least six years. Without knowing the patient's final outcome, the investigators scored the records for life events at six-month intervals. They found that only the patients who died had marked accumulation of stressful events, which peaked during the year before death. Given the structure of the study, it is quite possible that the accumulation of life events reflected a deteriorating medical status in the dying patients. If so, these events would be a result of the disease process, rather than a risk factor. In another study, Wolf (1969) found ten recent heart attack victims who were markedly depressed on initial examination, and by the end of four years, eight of them had died from sudden cardiac death and two had committed suicide. As mentioned earlier, in the Parkes et al. (1969) study of recent widowers, most of the excess heart attacks were sudden cardiac deaths.

Most investigators believe that the association between stressors and sudden cardiac death arises from the production of arrhythmias in a diseased heart. In support of this view, Lown, Verrier, and Rabinowitz (1977) have shown that an emotionally disturbing interview can produce arrhythmias in patients recovering from a heart attack. Verrier, Calvert, and Lown (1975) demonstrated a connection between the brain and the heart's electrical system by using aversive conditioning to lower a dog's cardiac threshold to electrical dysfunction and increase its sensitivity to catecholamine effects. An imbalance between the parasympathetic and sympathetic nervous systems has been postulated as one method of producing arrhythmias in damaged heart tissue (Dimsdale, 1977).

HYPERTENSION

It is generally assumed that the association between stress and hypertension is well established and thoroughly understood. Actually, there is still much to learn about the role of stress in this disorder. For example, clinical evidence that stressors are a risk factor of hypertension are unconvincing. Hypertensive individuals have been characterized as uncommunicative, withdrawn, and anxious to avoid even appropriate confrontations. Alexander (1950) hypothesized that, because they could not confront others with their anger, hypertensives directed their anger inward, thus producing high blood pressure. However, Kalis, Harris, Sokolow, and Carpenter (1957) later proposed that the observed behaviors actually helped the hypertensive to minimize situations in which rage reactions occur. In support of this latter hypothesis, Weiner, Singer, and Reiser (1962) showed that hypertensives tend to avoid involvement. Similarly, when hypertensives and normotensives viewed movies of a "good" and "bad" interaction between a doctor and a patient, the former were less likely to perceive obvious conflicts (Sapira, Scheib, Moriarty, and Shapiro, 1971). In addition, a study by Shapiro, Miller, King, Gincherean, and Fitzgibbon (1980) indicates that young, mild hypertensives have perception and performance abnormalities consistent with central nervous system impairment—again consistent with withdrawal as beneficial.

Epidemiological studies have repeatedly confirmed an x-z association between stressful psychosocial events and hypertension (Weiner, 1970; Henry and Stephens, 1977). For example, some initial retrospective studies revealed that major traumatic events such as natural disasters or wars increase the incidence of hypertension (Graham, 1945; Ruskin, Beard, and Shaffer, 1948). Examining less severe stressors, Reiser, Brust, Ferris, Shapiro, Baker, and Ransohoff (1951a) asked subjects about life events, including seemingly minor ones that were especially significant to them; they found that the natural history of hypertension for a given subject closely correlated with temporally related life events. These and other studies of hypertension all suffer from the fact that they are retrospective and used observers who knew which subjects were hypertensive. As a result, it is impossible to tell whether the observers unconsciously biased their results by examining with special care the periods preceding the onset of hypertension, until an event was uncovered.

Psychosocial stressors also can be used to produce hypertension in animals. Some stressors, such as a loud noise, produce only temporary increases in blood pressure (Farris, Yeakel, and Medoff, 1945); others, including avoidance conditioning in monkeys (Benson, Herd, Morse, and Kelleher, 1969) and social crowding in mice (Henry, Stephens, and Santisteban, 1975), lead to sustained hypertension. These latter stressors create continuous threat and uncertainty, which seem to be key factors in their effects on blood pressure. However, the relevant reactions produced by such a state remain unknown. Recent progress in tracing brain pathways involved in blood pressure changes offers promise of a much more extensive understanding of potential mechanisms (Nathan, Tucker, Severini, and Reis, 1978).

Work also is being done on clarifying the x-y-z sequence of stressors in hypertension of human beings. Investigators have identified a number of physical and psychological stressors that can elevate blood pressure (Shapiro, 1961; Brod, 1963). It is also now possible to continuously monitor blood pressure in freely moving subjects. Using such tools, it has been possible to show that blood pressure responses are exaggerated both in hypertensives and normotensives with a family history of hypertension (Shapiro, 1960). However, the observed differences are transient, and it is unclear how such changes contribute to the etiology and perpetuation of hypertension (Reiser, Rosenbaum, and Ferris, 1951b). Obviously, biofeedback and relaxation techniques that can lower blood pressure also are relevant to understanding the psychological and physiological mechanisms that can modulate cardiovascular responses, but almost nothing is known about them as yet (Schwartz, Shapiro, Redmond, Ferguson, Ragland, and Weiss, 1979).

IMMUNE DISORDERS

Until recently, common scientific wisdom held that the immune system functioned independently of psychosocial factors. However, there is now good evidence to refute that belief. Like the rest of the body, the immune system seems to be subject to at least some control by the brain (Ader, 1981). The discovery of a connection between the brain and the immune system raises questions about how stressors might affect immune function. Such questions are particularly important because of the known or suspected role of the immune system in many major physical disorders, including some forms of cancer.

Clinical studies have long suggested an association between stressors and several immune-related disorders, especially rheumatoid arthritis (Solomon and Amkraut, 1981). Retrospective studies identified rebellious, aggressive, and highly self-controlled women as being at particular risk of developing rheumatoid arthritis (Bourestom and Howard, 1965). For predisposed individuals, separation from a love object may help to precipitate an arthritic attack (Heisel, 1972). The reactions that such stressors produce and how they lead to the consequence of arthritis are unknown. In this instance, part of the delay in progress arises from lack of information about the disease; at present, investigators even remain uncertain as to whether the disease begins in connective tissue or in its vasculature.

Stressors also have been shown to enhance an individual's vulnerability to infectious diseases such as streptococcal infections (Meyer and Haggerty, 1962) and respiratory infections (Jacobs, Spelken, Norman, and Anderson, 1970). In addition, they can delay recovery from such self-limiting illnesses as mononucleosis (Greenfield, Roessler, and Crosley, 1959) or influenza (Imboden, Canter, and Cluff, 1961). Again, most of the data are limited by the use of retrospective designs. However, the stressors clearly are neither necessary nor sufficient for developing an infection; rather, as with other disorders, they are a risk factor when combined with other pathogenic stimuli and host factors.

As noted earlier, investigators have begun to identify ways in which stressors can affect the immune system. For example, bereavement has been shown to depress lymphocyte function independently of its effects on hormonal responses (Bartrop, Lazarus, Luckhurst, Kiloh, and Penny, 1977), a finding that Schleifer, Keller, Camerino, Thornton, and Stein (1983) confirmed in a small, prospective study of spouses of women with metastatic breast cancer. Once again there is evidence to suggest that a combination of high life event scores plus an unsuccessful coping response are especially potent in depressing immunological defenses (Greene, Betts, Ochitill, Iker, and Douglas, 1978).

A large body of research in animals also confirms the influence stressors can have on infectious diseases. Much of this work has examined in detail the effects of inoculating animals with certain bacteria or viruses in close conjunction with exposing them to such stressors as fighting, avoidance conditioning, physical restraint, or social crowding. Friedman, Ader, and Glasgow (1965) found that neither exposure to a stressor nor inoculation with coxsackie B virus could induce disease in adult mice, but their appropriately timed combination could do so. Apparently, careful attention to the animal, infectious agent and stressor makes it possible to either decrease (Marsh, Lavender, Chang, and Rasmussen, 1963) or increase (Levine, Strebel, Wenk, and Harman, 1962) the risk of infection. Particularly intriguing is recent evidence that immune responses in animals can be conditioned to respond to a purely psychological stressor, strongly suggesting the presence of unidentified mechanisms connecting the brain to the immune system (Cohen, Ader, Green, and Borbjerg, 1979).

CANCER

Most research on the causes of cancer attempts to identify physical agents such as asbestos or cigarette "tars" as risk factors. Among other known predisposing factors are familial susceptibility, immune deficiency, congenital defects, and aging. The possibility that certain stressors also are risk factors is an intriguing one that has proven to be especially difficult to prove or disprove.

One of the thorniest problems in stress-related cancer research concerns the period—as long as 20 years—that can elapse between the time a cancer begins to grow and the time it is diagnosed clinically. Even prospective studies have no way of demonstrating that exposure to a stressor preceded the onset of the cancer (Fox, 1978). As a result, most stress-related risk factor studies of cancer focus on chronic stressors present from early childhood. Useful research on acute stressors has necessarily been confined to examining associations between them and the detection or course of cancer.

In an early review of chronic psychosocial conditions as risk factors of cancer, LeShan and Worthington (1956) concluded that individuals with cancer are more likely than controls to report having felt isolated, deserted, and lonely as children. This conclusion is consistent with the results of several subsequent retrospective studies of different types of cancer (Kissen, 1963; Schmale and Iker, 1971). More recent prospective studies are also in general agreement with this view. Thus, Horne and Picard (1979) reported that a perceived lack of closeness to parents during childhood was a risk factor of lung cancer, as did Thomas, Duszynski, and Shaffer (1979) in a study of Johns Hopkins medical students who developed cancers of any type. In the latter study, a reported lack of closeness with parents, particularly with fathers, was also a risk factor of subsequent hospitalization for mental illness and suicide, but not of continued ill-health, hypertension, or heart attack.

Data about other personality characteristics as risk factors of cancer are less consistent. Thus, depending on the study, cancer patients may be seen as extroverted and emotional (Hagnell, 1966), introverted (McCoy, 1976), depressed (Bielauskas, Shekell, and Garron, 1979), or surprisingly unaffected by high levels of stress (Thomas et al., 1979). It still is unclear whether this represents random variations or is a result of inadequate attention to the specific characteristics of the individuals studied, the stressors, and the types of cancer.

Early research identified recent major losses as a risk factor of having cancer diagnosed, initially in leukemia and lymphoma (Greene and Miller, 1958) and later in other types of cancer (Kissen, 1963; LeShan, 1966). This work emphasized helplessness as the key stressor; however, all utilized patients whose cancer already had been diagnosed. In a study that at least avoided the problem of subjects knowing their diagnosis,

Schmale and Iker (1971) interviewed women about to undergo biopsy for cervical cancer; they too found an increased incidence of feelings of helplessness. Using a similar design, Horne and Picard (1979) interviewed patients awaiting diagnosis of a lung lesion found on x-ray; in their study, recent major loss, job instability, and lack of plans for the future were the three identifiable risk factors of being diagnosed as having cancer. Nonetheless, as noted earlier, even with the latter studies one cannot exclude the possibility that occult disease affected the subjects' psychological state and reported life events. If confirmed, these risk factors still might be useful as indicators of persons for whom efforts to identify a cancer should be especially vigorous.

As one possible instance of the pitfalls of considering stressors as bad, patients who report being especially stressed appear to survive longer than others who are less stressed. Early studies of breast cancer (Bacon, Renneker, and Cutler, 1952) and lymphoma and leukemia (Blumberg, 1954) found an association between greater hostility and longer survival. Derogatis, Abeloff, and Melisaratos (1979) confirmed that, among women with metastatic breast cancer, long-term survivors were more likely than short-term ones to report not only symptoms of hostility but also of alienation, depression, anxiety, guilt, and poor attitudes about their physicians. Rogentine, van Kammen, Fox, Docherty, Rosenblatt, Boyd, and Bunney (1979) obtained similar results with patients with malignant melanoma; on the average, those with high levels of psychological distress relapsed one year later than those who reported experiencing less distress.

None of the above research is compelling in the strength of its conclusions. However, combined with increasing interest in connections between cancer, the immune system, and effects of stress, further research in this area is warranted. Future study of the association of acute stressors with both the diagnosis and course of cancer seems especially promising for clinical use as risk factors as well as in discovering new ways that the body can combat cancer.

HYPERTHYROIDISM

Another of the early subjects of psychosomatic research, hyperthyroidism has long been reported anecdotally to develop in some individuals shortly after a frightening or otherwise stressful event (Weiner, 1978). Systematic studies also supported such an association. For example, Bennett and Cambor (1961) did a retrospective, uncontrolled study of life events patients experienced at the time they developed hyperthyroidism. They found that 82 percent of women but only 28 percent of men reported that they had just lost or might soon lose a significant relationship or felt unable to provide the care that others were demanding; in contrast, 72 percent of men and only 18 percent of women described being made recently to feel less self-sufficient, usually because of a job loss, illness, or submission to someone else. It would be of great interest to know whether these results would hold up with a more rigorous methodology, and whether changes in social expectations of men and women might alter the distribution of reported major life events. It also would be useful to learn how the effects of such acute stressors interact with individual character styles, because early studies described hyperthyroid patients as being insecure, self-demanding, and often unconsciously dependent on one person (Ham, Alexander, and Carmichael, 1951).

Interest in psychosomatic aspects of hyperthyroidism had largely waned before assays were available for many of the hormones that regulate thyroid function and before the relevance of genetic predisposition and of the immune system was established. Renewed attempts to learn what changes in thyroid function occur with certain types of stressors, especially in individuals already genetically at risk for hyperthyroidism, might be extremely productive.

BRONCHIAL ASTHMA

Bronchial asthma is a third disorder that was of early interest to psychosomatic medicine. It seems clear that acute stressors can precipitate asthmatic attacks in susceptible individuals. The clearest evidence probably comes from learning experiments. For example, Luparello, Lyons, Bleeker, and McFadden, Jr. (1968) showed that asthmatics would develop severe broncho-constriction if they thought they were exposed to a substance to which they were previously allergic, even if it actually was harmless. In addition, there is good evidence that asthmatics can learn to alter their airway resistance voluntarily (Feldman, 1976), and that both biofeedback techniques and hypnosis can be of value in managing recurrent asthma (Knapp, 1977).

In addition, there are strong suggestions that the interaction between an asthmatic child and his or her parents is also im-portant. For example, studies have shown that chronically asth-matic children often improve when away from their parents. Thus, Purcell, Brady, Chai, Muser, Molk, Gordon, and Means (1969) found that, when skilled caretakers replaced parents who were on vacation, about half of the children improved markedly. One possible explanation for such an effect is that the usual interactions between the parents and child frequently produced acute stressors that precipitated asthmatic attacks. As at least one test of this hypothesis, Liebman, Minuchin, and Baker (1974), showed, in a small sample of children, family therapy could be used successfully to treat severe, chronic asthma.

To date, neither psychological nor physiological reactions to acute stressors have been identified as possible causes of bronchial asthma. An early psvchoanalytic formulation postu-lated that asthma was a "repressed cry for mother," reflecting her rejection of the child (French and Alexander, 1941). How-ever, later studies suggested that such mothers were actually "engulfing," rather than rejecting (Abramson, 1954), or pos-sibly even both controlling and rejecting (Jacobs, Anderson, Eisman, Muller, and Friedman, 1967). Whatever the behavior of the mother, no one knows what kinds of reactions it produces in the child and how that leads to an asthmatic attack. Naturally, such inquiries eventually must examine physiological mecha-nisms as well. Once again, rapidly expanding knowledge about the effects of the immune and nervous systems on lung function should facilitate such research. Part of the inconsistencies of the older studies may arise from the existence of several, still poorly differentiated types of asthma that have different etiologies and underlying pathology, only some of which may result from underlying pathologies that are susceptible to the effects of psychosocial stressors (Weiner, 1977). Thus, more precise characterization of asthma subtypes also is needed.

DEPRESSION

Common experience indicates that adverse life events can produce feelings of depression and sadness. Thus, it is not surprising that investigators have been interested in clarifying the association between stressors and the onset of a clinical depression. However, the fact that depression and other mental disorders greatly alter the way people think and behave makes such research even more difficult in some ways than studies of stress and physical disorders (Dohrenwend et al., 1982). Great care must be taken to ensure that the stressful events being studied are not the result of the mental disorder itself. For example, suppose an individual sought treatment for depression shortly after losing his job. Does this indicate that job loss is a risk factor of depression? Or did early, subclinical symptoms of depression interfere with job performance and jeopardize his job? Despite these and other methodological problems, interesting and useful research has been done.

Relatively few studies have attempted to identify chronic stressors that may be risk factors of depression. Two large epidemiological studies using modern diagnostic methods found that low social class was a risk factor (Brown and Harris, 1978; Weissman and Myers, 1978). However, the latter study confirmed this relationship only for people who were depressed at the time of the study; when they estimated lifetime incidences in depression, they found no such correlation with social class. Neither the significance of this discrepancy nor the specific aspects of low social class that are associated with depression has been settled.

Other types of stressors do appear to be risk factors of depression in at least some people. For example, individuals who remain for years in a living situation that they view as threatening are at increased risk (Brown and Harris, 1978), as are those who live in a family that frequently expresses intense, hostile, and critical emotions (Vaughn and Leff, 1976). Rates of depression in women, especially young wives and mothers, are two to three times those in men (Weissman and Klerman, 1977). The relevance of stressors to this large and consistent difference is unknown. It is possible that women either are more stressed than men or are more sensitive to stressors (Dohrenwend, Krasnoff, Askenasy, and Dohrenwend, 1978); however, some researchers have found no such differences (Uhlenhuth, Lipman, Balter, and Stern, 1974). Little attention has yet been given to the possibility that major stressors for women result from the absence of desired events, which can produce boredom, discouragement, and frustration.

An area of particular interest has been parent loss during childhood as a risk factor of adult depression. This idea seems to be intuitively appealing to many, and a substantial amount of research has been done. Yet, a critical review of more than 20 controlled studies concluded that the evidence was far from compelling (Crook and Eliot, 1980). The inconclusiveness of the research arises largely from controversies about what types of controls are needed. All of the studies have been retrospective, and it is impossible to prove that adequate consideration has been given to the major changes that have occurred in this century in general socioeconomic status, parental age, death rates, and divorce rates—only a few of the factors that might influence the probability of a child losing a parent.

Despite the limitations of existing studies, recent findings suggest that at least some types of childhood bereavement are associated with depression in adults (Brown and Harris, 1978; Dohrenwend and deFigueiredo, 1983). One such association might relate to the cause of the parent's death. For example, if death resulted from suicide or alcoholism, then the child might have been exposed to a variety of genetic and environmental influences which themselves predispose to depression, either independently or in conjunction with the early bereavement. Hopefully, longitudinal, prospective studies will be conducted to resolve the debate and examine in more detail aspects of growing up in a disturbed family that may be risk factors of subsequent mental disorder.

Most studies of depression have examined the hypothesis that acute life events can precipitate an episode of depression (Paykel, 1982). In general, the results support the hypothesis. For example, both Brown, Sklair, Harris, and Birley (1973) and Paykel, Myers, Dienelt, Klerman, Lindenthal, and Pepper (1969) looked at incidence of life events in recently depressed individuals and in the general public. They found that depressed patients reported a substantial accumulation of life events just before they became depressed, which controls did not report. Similar differences were found in a comparison of life events preceding an episode of depression with those preceding an episode of schizophrenia (Rabkin, 1980). The occurrence of undesirable life events also appears to be a risk factor for relapse in patients who have recovered from a depression (Paykel and Tanner, 1976). However, the incidence of life events prior to an episode of anxiety seems to be comparable to that for depression (Uhlenhuth and Paykel, 1973).

So far, efforts to identify specific types of life events that are especially strong risk factors of depression have not been fruitful; nor does there seem to be any pattern of life events with specific subtypes of depression (Brown, Ni-Bhrolchain, and Harris, 1979). A relative preponderance of events preceding an episode of depression does seem to entail a loss of other persons or threats to self-esteem, especially in relation to a spouse. Also, many, but not all, of the other life events that occur frequently are unwanted or produce negative feelings. As mentioned earlier, however, such life events are problematic as risk factors because they may represent early consequences associated with a depression that already has begun.

Suicide is depression's most dramatic and fatal manifestation. Intense, adverse, or threatening life events are known to be risk factors of suicide and attempted suicide, but there seems to be little specificity or predictive value (Paykel, 1976). One recurrent theme is that the actual or threatened loss of a meaningful relationship can be especially dangerous. Much of the large variability seen in most studies may reflect inadequate attention to the importance of individual characteristics that make people more or less vulnerable to considering suicide. For example, studies suggest that people who attempt suicide but fail have a high incidence of personality disorders and tend to be impulsive and chronically angry; in contrast, those who successfully kill themselves are more apt to have been diagnosed at some time as having a major mental disorder such as depression, schizophrenia, and alcoholism (Hankoff, 1976). In one effort to distinguish such individual vulnerabilities from more general risk factors, Pokorny and Kaplan (1976) compared depressed suicide victims with comparably depressed but nonsuicidal controls from similar socioeconomic backgrounds; based on records obtained from the hospitalization preceding the suicide, subjects were more likely than controls to score high on a "defenseless score" that assessed feelings of guilt and inferiority, anxiety, depressed mood, and suicidal ideation.

Schizophrenia

Schizophrenia has been relatively intractable to stress research. Unlike depression, its connections to stress have been neither intuitively obvious nor easily demonstrable. However, some interesting findings about the disorder have emerged from stress-related studies, particularly with respect to the potential impact of the family setting, which may be a common denominator for several of the observed associations between stressors and schizophrenia. Thus, of a large number of environmental factors studied, only lower socioeconomic status and sustained exposure to disordered family relationships have consistently appeared as risk factors for developing schizophrenia. However, it is unlikely that these two factors are mutually exclusive. For example, families of lower socioeconomic class have an increased likelihood of being disrupted because of an absent father. Furthermore, associations between acute stressors and schizophrenia, which seem to be small at best, are likely to be affected substantially by the home setting in which they occur.

Lower socioeconomic status is associated with a much higher incidence of schizophrenia (Kohn, 1973). A variety of hypotheses about this association have been proffered, including downward social drift, downward genetic drift, and negative impact of poverty. Yet none has suggested innovative ways of treating the disorder or of understanding its origins. In addition, lower socioeconomic status as a risk factor is extremely nonspecific, being associated with a number of adverse personal, social, and economic consequences.

Some intriguing research has examined the effects of certain types of chronically disordered family relationships on the development and course of schizophrenia. Although far from conclusive, such studies suggest that schizophrenics are more likely than nonschizophrenics to have been raised in families with poor and inappropriate patterns of communication, deviant or atypical role structures, and a consistently negative affective environment (Goldstein and Rodnick, 1975). For example, a five-year, prospective study of adolescents found that deviant communication patterns within the family and parental expression of negative feelings toward the subject were independent and additive risk factors of developing schizophrenia (Doane, West, Goldstein, Rodnick, and Jones, 1981). Disordered family relationships also appear to be a risk factor of relapse in schizophrenics whose symptoms have remitted. Especially disruptive are what have been called "high expressed emotion" homes, in which other members of the family are overintrusive and highly critical of the schizophrenic. Brown, Birley, and Wing (1972) found that the relapse rate for schizophrenic patients returning to such homes is over 50 percent; in comparison, the relapse rate of patients going to a low expressed emotion home, where family members are less involved and less critical, is only 13 percent. Thus, not surprisingly, the same factors that promote the development of schizophrenia may also exacerbate it.

It is completely unclear whether stressful life events are risk factors for the onset of a schizophrenic episode (Rabkin, 1980; Dohrenwend and Egri, 1981). Overall, the evidence for such an association is far less convincing than it is for depression. In two well conducted studies, Brown and Birley (1968) and Jacobs and Myers (1976) independently found that schizophrenics reported much higher rates of life events in the weeks prior to the onset of an episode. Most of the reported events were ones that might well have occurred as a result of early symptoms of the disorder, suggesting that schizophrenics may merely be prone to getting themselves into stressful situations, even very early in their illness (Fontana, Marcus, Noel, and Rakusin, 1972). However, Brown and Birley (1968) found that, even looking only at events clearly independent of the course of illness, 46 percent of schizophrenic subjects experienced such an event during the three weeks before the onset of an episode, compared with only 12 percent for controls. A study of community-based schizophrenics being treated with antipsychotics reported a similar build-up of independent events in the period just prior to relapse (Leff, Hirsch, Gaind, Rohde, and Stevens, 1973).

Some schizophrenics do seem to experience severe life stressors just before the onset or recurrence of their disorder, but such events clearly are not of major importance for the majority. Still, it is possible that the peculiar thought processes and disturbed perceptions that characterize schizophrenia make such individuals more likely to react idiosyncratically to seemingly minor stressors (Dohrenwend and Egri, 1981). This hypothesis is supported by a report that found that chronic schizophrenics had much greater stressful responses to daily living than did normal controls, with acute schizophrenics having intermediate amounts (Serban, 1975). Perhaps, as with cancer, the major effect of a stressful event is to precipitate a visit to a medical professional, where diagnosis or rehospitalization occurs, with no real change in the patient's condition. If so, a better understanding of how such events lead to rehospitalization might be of great help to clinicians trying to help patients maintain themselves in the community.

BIOLOGICAL MARKERS OF STRESS VULNERABILITY

For a variety of reasons, relatively little attention has been paid to the possibility of identifying individuals who are especially vulnerable to stress. Such an approach might be of great help in increasing the specificity of predictions about the type of illness a stressor is a risk factor for in a particular case. Two examples of work in which biological markers were used should illustrate the potential utility of this approach.

As mentioned earlier, Weiner et al. (1957) found that psychological profiles of military inductees predicted the subsequent development of peptic ulcers only when the subjects also had a high serum pepsinogen concentration. The study itself needs to be replicated, especially with the more recent suggestion that only pepsinogen I is a risk factor of peptic ulcer disease (Rotter, Petersen, Samloff, McConnell, Ellis, Spence, and Rimoin, 1979). However, if the finding remains strong, it suggests a clear way of excluding from studies of psychological factors those subjects who are unlikely to develop ulcers under any conditions.

In a novel study of overall risk for mental illness, Buchsbaum, Coursey, and Murphy (1976) measured platelet monoamine oxidase (MAO) activity in college student volunteers and obtained personal and family information about mental disorders from subjects whose MAO activities were in the top or bottom 10 percent. For families of subjects with low MAO activities, the suicide or attempted suicide rate was eight times higher than for families of those with high MAO. The researchers later measured cortical averaged evoked potentials in these same subjects (Haier, Buchsbaum, and Murphy, 1980),

classifying them either as augmenters who increased their responses to repeated presentations of evoked potentials or as
reducers who decreased their responses. They found that augmenters with low MAO activity and reducers with high MAO
both had a markedly increased risk of receiving a diagnosis of
major depression sometime during the 18 months after the
biological measures were made.

CONCLUSION

Even a brief survey of studies linking stress to certain physical and mental disorders provides a flavor of both the weaknesses and strengths of the stress field. Taken together, existing
research overwhelmingly confirms that a variety of disruptive
life events are risk factors for disease. However, the associations
are almost uniformly weak and nonspecific. The literature itself
is extraordinarily uneven. For some disorders, the most recent
research is decades old and clearly outdated; elegantly designed
animal studies may be juxtaposed with unsatisfactory anecdotal
clinical reports; and it is often difficult to imagine how different
parts of the field are ever going to be able to work together on
common projects. And yet, despite the apparent deficiencies,
there also is exciting promise of major advances in understanding how the brain and body work together.

The early research on stress and physical illness suggested
a way of understanding such varied disorders as peptic ulcers,
hypertension, and bronchial asthma; and both the public and
many scientists responded with enthusiasm. However, those
early studies were unequal to the careful scrutiny that the scientific and medical community gave them. Confusion and dis-
trust grew as major findings could not be replicated and as
stressors thought to be disease-specific were found to be equally
relevant to other, unrelated disorders. Perhaps of equal importance, the research generated increasingly difficult questions. How is it that stressors affect some people but not others?

What makes a stressor produce changes in a particular physical system of an individual and an entirely different one in another? How are psychological stressors turned into multiple physical reactions?

Most of these questions were beyond available technology 30 years ago, and many still are too complex for existing methodologies. However, technological and theoretical limitations are changing at an incredible pace. Just in the past few years, the biological sciences have developed a much more detailed understanding of the array of substances and systems through which the brain monitors and regulates the rest of the body. In many ways, the extent and precision of such controls go far beyond the claims of early stress researchers. Similarly, the social and psychological sciences have refined their research methodologies in ways that can overcome many of the flaws on which the early stress studies foundered.

In the early 1900s, stress researchers were at the vanguard of many aspects of physiological and psychological research. Now, the stress field is but one aspect of an enormous endeavor to gain increasingly precise knowledge about the human body and brain. Other chapters in this book document the progress being made in psychosomatic medicine. The link may not always be obvious, but nearly all of their lines of inquiry were started by stress researchers. It will be fascinating to see how over the next few years scientists utilize the fruits of such inquiries to once again nurture the stress field.

References

Abramson, H. A. (1954), Evaluation of maternal rejection theory in allergy. *Ann. Allergy*, 12:129–140.

Ader, R., ed. (1981), *Psychoneuroimmunology*. New York: Academic Press.

Alexander, F. (1950), *Psychosomatic Medicine, Its Principles and Applications*. New York: Norton.

Antonovsky, A. (1979), *Health, Stress, and Coping*. San Francisco: Jossey-Bass.

Bacon, C. L., Renneker, R., & Cutler, M. (1952), A psychosomatic survey of cancer of the breast. *Psychosom. Med.*, 14:453–460.

Bartrop, R. W., Lazarus, L., Luckhurst, E., Kiloh, L. G., & Penny, R. (1977), Depressed lymphocyte function after bereavement. *Lancet*, 1:834–836.

Bennett, A. W., & Cambor, C. G. (1961), Clinical study of hyperthyroidism. *Arch. Gen. Psychiat.*, 4:160–165.

Benson, H., Herd, J. A., Morse, W. H., & Kelleher, R. T. (1969), Behavioral induction of arterial hypertension and its reversal. *Amer. J. Physiol.*, 217:30–34.

Bielauskas, L., Shekell, R., & Garron, D. (1979), Psychological depression and cancer mortality. Presented at the 35th annual meeting of the American Psychosomatic Society.

Blumberg, E. M. (1954), Results of psychological testing of cancer patients. In: *The Psychological Variables in Human Cancer*, ed. J. A. Gingerelli & F. J. Kirkner. Berkeley: University of California Press.

Bourestom, N. C., & Howard, M. T. (1965), Personality characteristics of three disability groups. *Arch. Phys. Med. Rehabil.*, 46:626–632.

Brod, J. (1963), Haemodynamic basis of acute pressor reactions and hypertension. *Brit. Heart J.*, 25:227–245.

Brown, G. W., & Birley, J. L. T. (1968), Crises and life changes and the onset of schizophrenia. *J. Health Soc. Behav.*, 9:203–214.

——— ——— Wing, J. K. (1972), Influence of family life on the course of schizophrenic disorders: A replication. *Brit. J. Psychiat.*, 121:241–258.

——— Harris, T. (1978), *Social Origins of Depression: A Study of Psychiatric Disorder in Women*. London: Tavistock.

——— Ni-Bhrolchain, M., & Harris, T. O. (1979), Psychotic and neurotic depression: Part 3, Aetiological and background factors. *J. Affect. Disord.*, 1:195–211.

——— Sklair, F., Harris, T. O., & Birley, J. L. T. (1973), Life events and psychiatric disorders. Part I: Some methodological issues. *Psychol. Med.*, 3:74–87.

Buchsbaum, M. S., Coursey, R. D., & Murphy, D. L. (1976), The biochemical-high-risk paradigm: Behavioral and familial correlates of low platelet monoamine oxidase activity. *Science*, 194:339–341.

Bunney, W., Jr., Shapiro, A., Ader, R., Davis, J., Herd, A., Kopin, I. J., Jr., Krieger, D., Matthysse, S., Stunkard, A., Weissman, M., & Wyatt, R. J. (1982), Panel report on stress and illness. In: *Stress and Human Health: Analysis and Implications of Research*, ed. G. R. Elliott & C. Eisdorfer. New York: Springer, pp. 255–337.

Burchfield, S. R. (1979), The stress response: A new perspective. *Psychosom. Med.*, 41:661–672.

Cannon, W. B. (1935), Stresses and strains of homeostasis. *Amer. J. Med. Sci.*, 189:1–14.

Cebelin, M. S., & Hirsch, C. S. (1980), Human stress cardiomyopathy—myocardial lesions in victims of homicidal assaults without internal injuries. *Hum. Pathol.*, 11:123–132.

Cobb, S., & Kasl, S. V. (1977), *Termination: The Consequences of Job Loss*. DHEW (NIOSH), Publ. No. 77-224. Washington, DC: U.S. Government Printing Office.

—— Rose, R. M. (1973), Hypertension, peptic ulcer, and diabetes in air traffic controllers. *J. Amer. Med. Assoc.*, 224:489–492.

Cohen, D. H., & Cabot, J. B. (1979), Toward a cardiovascular neurobiology. *Trends Neurosci.*, 2:273–276.

Cohen, F., Horowitz, M. J., Lazarus, R. S., Moos, R. H., Robins, L. N., Rose, R. M., & Rutter, M. (1982), Panel report on psychosocial assets and modifiers of stress. In: *Stress and Human Health: Analysis and Implications of Research*, ed. G. R. Elliott & C. Eisdorfer. New York: Springer, pp. 147–188.

Cohen, N., Ader, R., Green, N., & Borbjerg, D. (1979), Conditioned suppression of a thymus-independent antibody response. *Psychosom. Med.*, 41:487–491.

Crook, T., & Eliot, J. (1980), Parental death during childhood and adult depression: A critical review of the literature. *Psychol. Bull.*, 87:252–259.

Dawber, T. (1980), *The Framingham Study: Epidemiology of Atherosclerotic Disease*. Cambridge, MA: Harvard University Press.

Derogatis, L. R., Abeloff, M. D., & Melisaratos, N. (1979), Psychological coping mechanisms and survival time in metastatic breast cancer. *J. Amer. Med. Assn.*, 242:1504–1508.

Dimsdale, J. E. (1977), Emotional causes of sudden death. *Amer. J. Psychiat.*, 134:1361–1366.

—— Moss, J. (1980), Plasma catecholamines in stress and exercise. *J. Amer. Med. Assn.*, 243:340–342.

Doane, J. A., West, K. L., Goldstein, M. J., Rodnick, E. H., & Jones, J. E. (1981), Parental communication deviance and affective style as predictors of subsequent schizophrenia spectrum disorders in vulnerable adolescents. *Arch. Gen. Psychiat.*, 38:679–698.

Dohrenwend, B. P., & deFigueiredo, J. M. (1983), Remote and recent life events and psychopathology. In: *Origins of Psychopathology: Problems in Research and Public Policy*, ed. D. L. Ricks & B. S. Dohrenwend. New York: Cambridge University Press.

—— Egri, G. (1981), Recent stressful life events and episodes of schizophrenia. *Schiz. Bull.*, 7:12–23.

—— Krasnoff, L., Askenasy, A. R., & Dohrenwend, B. P. (1978), Exemplification of a method for scaling life events: The PERI life events scale. *J. Health Soc. Behav.*, 19:205–229.

—— Pearlin, L., Clayton, P., Hamburg, B., Riley, M., Rose, R. M., & Dohrenwend, B. (1982), Report on stress and life events. In: *Stress and Human*

Health: Analysis and Implications of Research, ed. G. R. Elliott & C. Eisdorfer. New York: Springer, pp. 55–80.

Dunn, J. P., & Cobb, S. (1962), Frequency of peptic ulcer among executives, craftsmen, and foremen. *J. Occup. Med.*, 4:343–348.

Elliott, G. R., & Eisdorfer, C., eds. (1982), *Stress and Human Health: Analysis and Implications of Research*. New York: Springer.

Engel, G. L. (1954), Studies of ulcerative colitis. II. The nature of the somatic processes and the adequacy of psychosomatic hypotheses. *Amer. J. Med.*, 16:416–433.

——— (1955), Studies of ulcerative colitis. III. The nature of the psychologic processes. *Amer. J. Med.*, 19:231–256.

——— (1971), Sudden and rapid death during psychological stress: Folk lore or folk wisdom? *Ann. Intern. Med.*, 74:771–782.

——— (1975), Psychological aspects of gastrointestinal disorders. In: *American Handbook of Psychiatry*, Vol. 4, ed. M. F. Reiser. New York: Basic Books, pp. 653–692.

——— Reichsman, F., & Segal, H. L. (1956), A study of an infant with a gastric fistula. I. Behavior and the rate of total hydrochloric acid secretion. *Psychosom. Med.*, 18:374–398.

Farris, E. J., Yeakel, E. H., & Medoff, H. S. (1945), Development of hypertension in emotional gray Norway rats after air blasting. *Amer. J. Physiol.*, 144:331–333.

Feldman, G. M. (1976), Effect of biofeedback training on respiratory resistance of asthmatic children. *Psychosom. Med.*, 38:27–34.

Fontana, A. F., Marcus, J. L., Noel, B., & Rakusin, J. M. (1972), Prehospitalization coping styles of psychiatric patients: The goal-directedness of life events. *J. Nerv. & Ment. Dis.*, 155:311–321.

Fox, B. H. (1978), Premorbid psychological factors as related to cancer incidence. *J. Behav. Med.*, 1:45–133.

French, T. M., & Alexander, F. (1941), Psychogenic factors in bronchial asthma. *Psychosom. Med. Monogr.*, 4:2–94.

Friedman, M., Manwaring, J. H., Rosenman, R. H., Donlon, G., Ortega, P., & Grube, S. M. (1973), Instantaneous and sudden deaths: Clinical and pathological differentiation in coronary artery disease. *J. Amer. Med. Assn.*, 225:1319–1328.

——— Rosenman, R. H. (1959), Association of specific overt behavior pattern with blood and cardiovascular findings. *J. Amer. Med. Assn.*, 169:1286–1296.

Friedman, S. B., Ader, R., & Glasgow, L. A. (1965), Effects of psychological stress in adult mice inoculated with Coxsackie B viruses. *Psychosom. Med.*, 27:361–368.

Fritz, C. E., & Marks, E. S. (1954), The NORC studies of human behavior in disaster. *J. Social Issues*, 10:26–41.

Glass, D. C. (1977), *Behavior Patterns, Stress, and Coronary Disease*. New York: Wiley.

Goldstein, M. J., & Rodnick, E. H. (1975), The family's contribution to the etiology of schizophrenia: Current status. *Schiz. Bull.*, 14:48–63.

Graham, J. D. P. (1945), High blood pressure after battle. *Lancet*, 1:239–240.

Greene, W. A., Jr., Betts, R. F., Ochitill, H. N., Iker, H. P., & Douglas, R. G. (1978), Psychosocial factors and immunity: Preliminary report. *Psychosom. Med.*, 40:87.

—————— Miller, G. (1958), Psychological factors and reticuloendothelial disease. *Psychosom. Med.*, 20:124–144.

Greenfield, N. S., Roessler, R., & Crosley, A. P., Jr. (1959), Ego strength and length of recovery from infectious mononucleosis. *J. Nerv. & Ment. Dis.*, 128:125–128.

Hagnell, O. (1966), The premorbid personality of persons who develop cancer in a total population investigated in 1947 and 1957. *Ann. N.Y. Acad. Sci.*, 125:846–855.

Haier, R. J., Buchsbaum, M. S., & Murphy, D. L. (1980), An 18-month followup of students biologically at risk for psychiatric problems. *Schiz. Bull.*, 6:334–337.

Ham, G. C., Alexander, F., & Carmichael, H. T. (1951), A psychosomatic theory of thyrotoxicosis. *Psychosom. Med.*, 13:18–35.

Hankoff, L. D. (1976), Categories of attempted suicide: A longitudinal study. *Amer. J. Public Health*, 66:558–563.

Heisel, J. S. (1972), Life changes as etiologic factors in juvenile rheumatoid arthritis. *J. Psychosom. Res.*, 16:411–420.

Henry, J. P., & Stephens, P. M. (1977), *Stress, Health, and the Social Environment*. New York: Springer-Verlag.

—————— Stephens, P. M., & Santisteban, G. A. (1975), A model of psychosocial hypertension showing reversibility and progression of cardiovascular complications. *Circ. Res.*, 36:156–164.

Holmes, T. H., & Masuda, M. (1974), Life change and illness susceptibility. In: *Stressful Life Events: Their Nature and Effects*, ed. B. S. Dohrenwend & B. P. Dohrenwend. New York: Wiley, pp. 45–72.

—————— Rahe, R. H. (1967), The social readjustment rating scale. *J. Psychosom. Res.*, 11:213–218.

Horne, R. L., & Picard, R. S. (1979), Psychosocial risk factors for lung cancer. *Psychosom. Med.*, 41:503–514.

Imboden, J. B., Canter, A., & Cluff, L. E. (1961), Convalescence from influenza: A study of the psychological and clinical determinants. *Arch. Intern. Med.*, 108:393–399.

Jacobs, M. A., Anderson, L. S., Eisman, H. B., Muller, J. J., & Friedman, S. (1967), Interaction of psychologic and biologic predisposing factors in allergic disorders. *Psychosom. Med.*, 29:572–585.

Jacobs, M. H., Spelken, A. Z., Norman, M. M., & Anderson, L. S. (1970), Life stress and respiratory illness. *Psychosom. Med.*, 32:233–242.

Jacobs, S., & Myers, J. (1976), Recent life events and acute schizophrenic psychosis: A controlled study. *J. Nerv. & Ment. Dis.*, 162:75–87.

Kalis, B. L., Harris, R. E., Sokolow, M., & Carpenter, L. G. (1957), Response to psychological stress in patients with essential hypertension. *Amer. Heart J.*, 53:572–578.

Kavanagh, T., & Shepard, R. J. (1973), The immediate antecedents of myocardial infarction in active men. *Can. Med. Assn. J.*, 109:19–22.

Kissen, D. M. (1963), Personality characteristics in males conducive to lung cancer. *Brit. J. Med. Psychol.*, 36:27–36.

Knapp, P. H. (1977), Psychotherapeutic management of bronchial asthma. In: *Psychosomatic Medicine, Its Clinical Applications*, ed. E. D. Wittkower & H. Warnes. New York: Harper & Row, pp. 210–219.

Kohn, M. L. (1973), A social class and schizophrenia: A clinical review and a reformulation. *Schiz. Bull.*, 7:60–79.

Lazarus, R. S. (1966), *Psychological Stress and the Coping Process*. New York: McGraw-Hill.

Leff, J. P., Hirsch, S. R., Gaind, R., Rohde, P. D., & Stevens, B. C. (1973), Life events and maintenance therapy in schizophrenic relapse. *Brit. J. Psychiat.*, 123:659–660.

LeShan, L. L. (1966), An emotional life-history pattern associated with neoplastic disease. *Ann. N.Y. Acad. Sci.*, 125:780–793.

—— Worthington, R. E. (1956), Personality as a factor in the pathogenesis of cancer: A review of the literature. *Brit. J. Med. Psychol.*, 29:49–56.

Levi, L., Frankenhaeuser, M., & Gardell, B. (1982), Report on work stress related to social structures and processes. In: *Stress and Human Health: Analysis and Implications of Research*, ed. G. R. Elliott & C. Eisdorfer. New York: Springer, pp. 119–146.

Levine, S., Strebel, R., Wenk, E. J., & Harman, P. J. (1962), Suppression of experimental allergic encephalomyelitis by stress. *Proc. Soc. Exp. Biol. Med.*, 109:294–298.

Liebman, R., Minuchin, S., & Baker, L. (1974), The use of structural family therapy in the treatment of intractible asthma. *Amer. J. Psychiat.*, 131:535–540.

Lown, B., DeSilva, R. A., & Lenson, R. (1978), Roles of psychologic stress and autonomic nervous system changes in provocation of ventricular premature complexes. *Amer. J. Cardiol.*, 41:979–985.

—— Verrier, R. L., & Rabinowitz, S. H. (1977), Neural and psychologic mechanisms and the problem of sudden cardiac death. *Amer. J. Cardiol.*, 39:890–902.

Luparello, T., Lyons, H. A., Bleecker, E. R., & McFadden, E. R., Jr. (1968),

Influence of suggestion on airway reactivity in asthmatic subjects. *Psychosom. Med.*, 30:819–825.

Marsh, J. T., Lavender, J. F., Chang, S., & Rasmussen, A. F., Jr. (1963), Poliomyelitis in monkeys: Decreased susceptibility after avoidance stress. *Science*, 140:1415–1416.

Mason, J. W. (1971), A reevaluation of the concept of non-specificity in stress theory. *J. Psychiat. Res.*, 8:323–333.

—— (1974), Specificity in the organization of neuroendocrine response profiles. In: *Frontiers in Neurology and Neuroscience Research*, ed. P. Seeman & G. Brown. Toronto: University of Toronto, pp. 68–80.

McCoy, J. W. (1976), Psychological Variables and Onset of Cancer. Unpublished doctoral dissertation, Oklahoma State University.

Meyer, R. J., & Haggerty, R. J. (1962), Streptococcal infections in families: Factors altering individual susceptibility. *Pediatrics*, 29:539–549.

Nathan, M. A., Tucker, L. W., Severini, W. H., & Reis, D. J. (1978), Enhancement of conditioned arterial pressure responses in cats after brainstem lesions. *Science*, 201:71–73.

Orth-Gomer, K., & Ahlbom, A. (1980), Impact of psychological stress on idiopathic heart disease when controlling for conventional risk indicators. *J. Hum. Stress*, 6:7–15.

Parkes, C. M., Benjamin, B., & Fitzgerald, R. G. (1969), Broken heart: A statistical study of increased mortality among widowers. *Brit. Med. J.*, 1:740–743.

Paykel, E. S. (1976), Life stress, depression, and attempted suicide. *J. Hum. Stress*, 2:3–10.

—— (1982), Life events and early environment. In: *Handbook of Affective Disorders*. New York: Guilford Press.

—— Myers, J. K., Dienelt, M. N., Klerman, G. L., Lindenthal, J. J., & Pepper, M. P. (1969), Life events and depression: A controlled study. *Arch. Gen. Psychiat.*, 21:753–760.

—— Tanner, J. (1976), Life events, depressive relapse and maintenance treatment. *Psychol. Med.*, 6:481–485.

Pokorny, A. D., & Kaplan, H. B. (1976), Suicide following psychiatric hospitalization. *J. Nerv. & Ment. Dis.*, 162:119–125.

Purcell, K., Brady, K., Chai, H., Muser, J., Molk, L., Gordon, N., & Means, J. (1969), The effect on asthma in children of experimental separation from the family. *Psychosom. Med.*, 31:144–164.

Rabkin, J. G. (1980), Stressful life events and schizophrenia: A review of the research literature. *Psychol. Bull.*, 87:408–425.

Rahe, R. H., & Arthur, R. H. (1978), Life change and illness studies. *J. Hum. Stress*, 4:3–15.

—— O'Neil, T. O., Hagan, A., & Arthur, R. J. (1975), Brief group therapy following myocardial infarction. Eighteen month follow-up of a controlled trial. *Internat. J. Psychiat. Med.*, 6:349–358.

—— Romo, M., Bennett, L., & Siltanen, P. (1974), Recent life changes, myocardial infarction, and abrupt coronary death. *Arch. Intern. Med.*, 133:221–228.

Reiser, M. F., Brust, A. A., Ferris, E. B., Shapiro, A. P., Baker, H. M., & Ransohoff, W. (1951a), Life situations, emotions, and the course of patients with arterial hypertension. *Psychosom. Med.*, 13:133–139.

—— Rosenbaum, M., & Ferris, E. B. (1951b), Psychologic mechanisms in malignant hypertension. *Psychosom. Med.*, 13:147–159.

Ricks, D. L., & Dohrenwend, B. S., eds. (1983), *Origins of Psychopathology: Problems in Research and Public Policy.* New York: Cambridge University Press.

Rogentine, G. N., Jr., van Kammen, D. P., Fox, B. H., Docherty, J. P., Rosenblatt, J. F., Boyd, S. C., & Bunney, W. E., Jr. (1979), Psychosocial factors in the prognosis of malignant melanoma: A prospective study. *Psychosom. Med.*, 41:647–655.

Rosenman, R. H. (1978), Role of Type A behavior pattern in the pathogenesis of ischemic heart disease and modification for prevention. *Adv. Cardiol.*, 25:35–46.

Rotter, J. I., Petersen, G., Samloff, M., McConnell, R. B., Ellis, A., Spence, M. A., & Rimoin, D. L. (1979), Genetic heterogeneity of hyperpepsinogenemic I and normopepsinogenemic I duodenal ulcer disease. *Ann. Intern. Med.*, 91:372–377.

Ruskin, A., Beard, O. W., & Shaffer, R. L. (1948), Blast hypertension: Elevated arterial pressures in the victims of the Texas City disaster. *Amer. J. Med.*, 4:228–236.

Sapira, J. D., Scheib, E. T., Moriarty, R., & Shapiro, A. P. (1971), Differences in perception between hypertensive and normotensive populations. *Psychosom. Med.*, 33:239–250.

Schleifer, S. J., Keller, S. E., Camerino, M., Thornton, J. C., & Stein, M. (1983), Suppression of lymphocyte stimulation following bereavement. *J. Amer. Med. Assn.*, 250:374–377.

Schmale, A. H., & Iker, H. (1971), Hopelessness as a predictor of cervical cancer. *Soc. Sci. Med.*, 5:95–100.

Schwartz, G. E., Shapiro, A. P., Redmond, D. P., Ferguson, D. C., Ragland, D. R., & Weiss, S. M. (1979), Behavioral medicine approaches to hypertension: An integrative analysis of theory and research. *J. Behav. Med.*, 2:311–363.

Selye, H. (1950), *The Physiology and Pathology of Exposure to Stress.* Montreal: Acta.

—— (1975), Stress and distress. *Comp. Ther.*, 1:9–13.

Serban, G. (1975), Stress in schizophrenics and normals. *Brit. J. Psychiat.*, 126:397–407.

Shapiro, A. P. (1960), Psychophysiologic mechanisms in hypertensive vascular heart disease. *Ann. Intern. Med.*, 53:64–83.

———— (1961), An experimental study of comparative responses of blood pressure to different noxious stimuli. *J. Chronic Dis.*, 13:293–311.

———— Miller, R. E., King, H. E., Gincherean, E., & Fitzgibbon, K. (1980), Behavioral consequences of mild hypertension. *Circulation 62*, Suppl. III:36.

Solomon, G. F., & Amkraut, A. A. (1981), Psychoneuroendocrinological effects on the immune response. *Ann. Rev. Microbiol.*, 35:155–184.

Sturdevant, R. A. L. (1976), Epidemiology of peptic ulcer. *Amer. J. Epidemiol.*, 104:9–14.

Syme, S. L. (1975), Social and psychological risk factors in coronary heart disease. *Mod. Concepts Cardiovasc. Dis.*, 44:17–21.

Terr, L. C. (1979), Children of Chowchilla: A study of psychic trauma. *The Psychoanalytic Study of the Child*, 34:547–623. New Haven, CT: Yale University Press.

Theorell, T., & Rahe, R. H. (1975), Life change events, ballistocardiography and coronary death. *J. Hum. Stress*, 1:18–24.

Thomas, C. B., Duszynski, K. R., & Shaffer, J. W. (1979), Family attitudes reported in youth as potential predictors of cancer. *Psychosom. Med.*, 41:287–302.

Uhlenhuth, E. H., Lipman, R. S., Balter, M. B., & Stern, M. (1974), Symptom intensity and life stress in the city. *Arch. Gen. Psychiat.*, 31:759–764.

———— Paykel, E. S. (1973), Symptom configuration and life events. *Arch. Gen. Psychiat.*, 28:744–748.

U.S. Department of Health, Education, and Welfare, (1979), *Smoking and Health*. Washington, DC: U.S. Government Printing Office, DHEW Publ. No. (PHS) 79-50066.

Vaughn, C. E., & Leff, J. P. (1976), The influence of family and social factors on the course of psychiatric illness: A comparison of schizophrenic and depressed neurotic patients. *Brit. J. Psychiat.*, 129:125–137.

Verrier, R. L., Calvert, A., & Lown, B. (1975), Effect of posterior hypothalamic stimulation on ventricular fibrillation threshold. *Amer. J. Physiol.*, 228:923–927.

Weiner, H. (1970), Psychosomatic research in essential hypertension: Retrospect and prospect. In: *Psychosomatics in Essential Hypertension*, ed. M. Koster, H. Musaph, & P. Visser. Basel: S. Karger, pp. 58–116.

———— (1977), *Psychobiology and Human Disease*. New York: Elsevier.

———— (1978), Emotional factors. In: *The Thyroid*, ed. S. C. Werner & S. H. Ingbar. New York: Harper & Row, pp. 627–632.

———— Singer, M. T., & Reiser, M. F. (1962), Cardiovascular responses and their psychological correlates: I. A study in healthy young adults and patients with peptic ulcer and hypertension. *Psychosom. Med.*, 24:477–498.

—— Thaler, M., Reiser, M. F., & Mirsky, I. A. (1957), Etiology of duodenal ulcer. I. Relation of specific psychological characteristics to rate of gastric secretion (serum pepsinogen). *Psychosom. Med.*, 19:1–10.

Weisman, A. D. (1956), A study of the psychodynamics of duodenal ulcer exacerbations with special reference to treatment and the problem of "specificity." *Psychosom. Med.*, 18:2–42.

Weissman, M., & Klerman, G. L. (1977), Sex differences and the epidemiology of depression. *Arch. Gen. Psychiat.*, 34:98–111.

—— Myers, J. K. (1978), Affective disorders in a U.S. urban community: The use of research diagnostic criteria in an epidemiological survey. *Arch. Gen. Psychiat.*, 35:1304–1311.

Wolf, S. (1969), Psychosocial forces in myocardial infarction and sudden death. *Circulation 39-40*, Suppl. IV:74–83.

—— Almy, T. P., Bachrach, W. H., Spiro, H. M., Sturdevant, R. A. L., & Weiner, H. (1979), The role of stress in peptic ulcer disease. *J. Hum. Stress*, 5:27–37.

—— Wolff, H. G. (1943), *Human Gastric Function*. New York: Oxford University Press.

3.

Disregulation Theory and Disease: Toward a General Model for Psychosomatic Medicine

GARY E. SCHWARTZ, PH.D.

INTRODUCTION AND OVERVIEW

The purpose of this chapter is to present a general theory of disease derived from general systems theory (von Bertalanffy, 1968) and to apply it to key issues in psychosomatic medicine. As will become clear, this theory—called *disregulation theory*—has broad implications not only for the role of psychosocial factors in the etiology and pathogenesis of disease, but for the role of psychosocial factors in the treatment and prevention of disease. This chapter is based on an article by the author (Schwartz, 1983), which provides a progress report on the theory's development (Schwartz, 1977, 1979).

Disregulation theory can be briefly summarized as follows. All functioning systems are, by definition, self-regulating. If the various components of a self-regulating system are disrupted, or in extreme cases disconnected, it will become disregulated. A disregulated system will show properties of disordered behavior that, in extreme cases, may be defined medically as disease. One psychological state hypothesized to produce a critical neuropsychological disconnection is disattention to essential negative feedback processes. Defense mechanisms, especially repression, involve excessive disattention, which should promote demonstrable neuropsychological disconnections leading to disregulation, disorder and disease. Hence, (1) disattention should involve (2) disconnections, creating (3) disregulations, promoting (4) disorder, which then contributes to (5) disease. Conversely, (1) self-attention (to a negative feedback process) should involve (2) re-connection, creating (3) self-regulation, promoting (4) order (e.g., homeostasis), which would thus contribute to (5) "ease" or health.

A framework that stimulates the synthesis of theory and research across such diverse areas as psychodynamic psychiatry, cognitive and personality psychology, clinical neuropsychology, psychophysiology, and pathophysiology deserves to be considered seriously and scrutinized closely. It has been proposed that significant progress in psychosomatic medicine and the emerging interdisciplinary field of behavioral medicine (Schwartz and Weiss, 1978) will require general theories that can effectively integrate biological, psychological, and social data and analysis (e.g., Engel, 1977; Leigh and Reiser, 1980). General systems theory (von Bertalanffy, 1968; Miller, 1978; deRosnay, 1979) has the potential to provide such an integrative organization (see Schwartz, 1980, 1981, 1982b, for a synthesis of systems theory applied to behavioral medicine, or Schwartz, 1982a, 1982c, for a synthesis of systems theory applied to research on emotion and cardiovascular psychophysiology).

The first half of this chapter reviews some basic tenets of general systems theory and illustrates how self-regulation and disregulation theory are derived from it; the second half applies disregulation theory to the relationship between psychological defense mechanisms and physical disease, using cardiovascular disease as a model system.

WHAT IS SYSTEMS THEORY?

Systems theory, a shorthand for general systems theory (von Bertalanffy, 1968), is concerned with general principles that are hypothesized to be applicable to all aspects of nature. These general principles were not "contrived," but rather were "derived" from a close analysis of findings independently discovered in diverse disciplines. Considered collectively, these findings led to the discovery of more general principles that, quite remarkably, apply to and therefore unite the separate findings and disciplines. Of course, it is impossible to develop the principles of systems theory here given the limited space available (see deRosnay, 1979; Miller, 1978). However, a few general points must be made in order to discuss disregulation theory in any depth.

As shown in Table 1, it is possible to organize various systems in nature in terms of their *level* of complexity. Curiously, this organization not only parallels evolutionary theory as it explains the development of physical, biological, psychological, and social systems, in that order (Boulding, 1978), but also illustrates how various scientific disciplines have evolved to study the unique properties that emerge at each level. In systems language these unique properties are called *behaviors*. All systems *behave* (they can act and react), and scientists, be they physicists, physiologists, or psychologists, ultimately study the *behavior* of systems at their appropriate emergent level.

The reader will note, of course, that the term behavior can be (and has been) used in different ways to encompass various levels of systems. (See Table 2.) Whereas at one extreme "behavior therapists" use the term "behavior" to refer to a subset of the field of psychology, at the other extreme, systems theorists use the term as applied to the concept of behavioral medicine (Schwartz, 1979). For clarity of presentation, I will capitalize BEHAVIOR from now on to refer to the general systems concept, and reserve small letters for its more common and limited use in psychology.

Table 1
Four Definitions of Behavior, Using Behavioral Medicine as an Example,
Moving Up Levels of Complexity (in Systems Terms)

1. Behavior from the perspective of systems theory. Behavior here refers to the study of behavior of systems, not just organisms. All scientific disciplines, including physics, chemistry, biology, as well as the "behavioral sciences" mentioned in Definition 3, would be reclassified here as Behavioral Sciences. Behavioral medicine here refers to the application of systems theory, and the integration of all scientific disciplines, to medicine (Schwartz, 1979).

2. Behavior from the perspective of the arts and sciences. Behavior here refers to the study of behavior of organisms, very broadly defined, and encompasses not only the discipline of psychology, but the disciplines of anthropology, sociology, political science, and so forth. Behavioral medicine here refers to the application of all behavioral sciences (psychology being only one such science) to medicine. This is the definition of behavioral science used at the Yale Conference on Behavioral Medicine (Schwartz and Weiss, 1978a).

3. Behavior from the perspective of general psychology. Behavior here refers to the study of behavior of organisms, broadly defined, and encompasses the entire discipline of psychology. Here psychology is "the" behavioral science. Behavioral medicine here refers to the application of all subareas of the discipline of psychology to medicine.

4. Behavior from the perspective of behaviorists and behavior therapists. Behavior here refers to one subarea in the discipline of psychology, emphasizing learning and the strict measurement of observable events. Behavioral medicine here refers to the application of behavior therapy per se (learning theory) to medicine.

Systems, by definition, are composed of *units* or *parts*. These parts *interact* with each other, directly or indirectly. The term *interact* rather than *act* is used to signify that the *actions* occur

Table 2
Levels of Complexity in Systems and Associated Academic Disciplines[a]

Level and Complexity of the System	Academic Field Associated with the Level of the System
Beyond earth	Astronomy
Supranational	Ecology
National	Government, political science, economics
Organizations	Organizational science
Groups	Sociology
Organism	Psychology, ethology, zoology
Organs	Organ physiology (e.g., neurology, cardiology)
Cells	Cellular biology
Biochemicals	Biochemistry
Chemicals	Chemistry, physical chemistry
Atoms	Physics
Subatomic particles	Subatomic physics
Abstract systems	Mathematics

[a]According to systems theory, in order to understand the behavior of an open system at any one level, it is essential to have training in the academic disciplines below that level, plus have training at least in the relevant discipline at the next highest level as well.

in both directions, i.e., each part or unit influences the other. I use the term *reciprocal regulation* to refer to the fact that parts in a system regulate each other. Out of the reciprocal regulation of its parts, a system takes on properties (BEHAVIORS) that can exist only when the system is *whole*. Therefore, emergent BEHAVIORS in systems arise out of the interactions of their parts. It is this property of reciprocal regulation that leads to the concept of feedback and self-regulation in systems (see below).

Note that virtually every system is composed of parts that in turn are themselves smaller systems; each part is in turn composed of its own parts. Thus virtually all systems are composed of subsystems; conversely, virtually all systems are simultaneously parts of larger systems. In other words, a given system is both composed of specific subsystems and is simultaneously part of a larger suprasystem(s). The external environment is actually, in systems terms, a part of the larger suprasystem of which the given system is a part. Therefore, every system is reciprocally regulated not only by its subsystems, but is simultaneously regulated by, and in turn actively regulates, systems in its external environment (of which it is part).

It is hypothesized that there may be two exceptions to the subsystem-system-suprasystem principle; they occur at the extreme microscopic and macroscopic levels. An assumption is made that at the extreme microscopic level, a fundamental particle (a system) does not contain any units (subsystems), and at the extreme macroscopic level, the universe (a system) does not exist alongside other systems (the universe is not part of a larger suprasystem). The reader might reflect upon the remarkable conclusion that the *unique* BEHAVIORS observed in particular systems at particular levels (which is what justifies the emergence of separate scientific disciplines and bodies of knowledge) simultaneously reflect *universal* properties derived from general, organizing principles.

WHAT IS CONTROL THEORY?

Control theory is a subset of systems theory. It is concerned with how parts in systems regulate each other to achieve order and stability. The concept of *feedback*, both *positive* and *negative*, is a general one, referring to the process whereby information about the BEHAVIOR of a system (its "output") is fed back to some "input" in the system in order that the system may regulate itself (control itself). A self-regulating system requires feedback of its BEHAVIORS.

The use of feedback in machines has a long history (Mayr, 1970), going back thousands of years. However, it was not discovered to be a general concept until the important work of Wiener (1948), who provided the mathematics of negative feedback systems and established the new field of cybernetics. It is impossible to develop the principles of control theory here given the limited space available (see Jones, 1973, for a particularly lucid account of principles of biological regulation as an introduction to feedback systems). However, a few general points must be made in order to discuss disregulation theory in any depth.

Negative feedback is not negative in a value judgment sense, but rather refers to the process of subtracting information about a system's BEHAVIOR from its input so as to counteract the BEHAVIOR and thereby return it to some *reference level*. This reference level can be changed. For example, a thermostat can be set at 65 degrees to maintain the temperature in a house within certain limits. This is an example of a negative feedback system with a given reference level. Note that not only is the thermostat connected to the furnace, but the furnace by way of the air is ultimately connected to the thermostat. The thermostat, therefore, regulates the furnace (it turns the furnace on when the temperature drops below the reference level, and turns the furnace off when the temperature rises above the reference level). However, the furnace, in turn, regulates the thermostat (it acts to raise the electricity above the reference level by increasing the temperature in the air and lower the electricity below the reference level by not increasing the temperature).

Most control theorists presume that the concept of reciprocal regulation is understood in order for the thermostat-furnace combination to become and act as a system. The parts must be appropriately *connected*, and they must appropriately *regulate each other*, if ordered self-regulation is to occur.

The reader will note that if the conditions inside and outside the house are kept relatively constant, the furnace-thermostat system will go on and off in a regular, rhythmic fashion. Out of the interaction of the thermostat and the furnace, as these components interact with the house (and its inhabitants and surroundings), the whole system will become rhythmic, producing regular, ordered BEHAVIOR. *Regularity* emerges when certain combinations of variables interact with self-regulating, negative feedback systems. *Ordered* BEHAVIOR over time, therefore, emerges out of reciprocal regulation (self-regulation).

The reader will also note that a *positive* feedback system, though it does not hover around a reference level, nonetheless reflects a self-regulating process. Positive feedback is not positive in a value judgment sense, but rather refers to the process of adding information about a system's BEHAVIOR to its input so as to augment the BEHAVIOR, and thereby move the BEHAVIOR further in the direction it is already going. In fact, it is an error to think that positive feedback leads to *disordered* BEHAVIOR. On the contrary, positive feedback BEHAVIOR is quite ordered and quite predictable. A positive feedback system is a self-regulating system because it achieves a particular goal through the controlled interaction of its parts. It follows that a positive feedback system can only BEHAVE as one if its parts are appropriately connected.

Note that both negative and positive feedback systems BEHAVE with *purpose*, that is, their parts interact in such a way as to achieve a certain goal. This BEHAVIOR is *automatic*, i.e., it emerges out of the manner in which the parts are connected and how the information is processed. The latter is critical to the final BEHAVIOR. Of course, if the information is not transmitted (the parts are disconnected), the system will be unable to BEHAVE as a self-regulating system. However, if the information is transmitted, how it is processed will determine whether the system BEHAVES as a negative or positive feedback system, and therefore *to what purpose* the system will act. Purpose arises in self-regulating systems (Wiener, 1948), which are systems that become ordered and BEHAVE in a systematic way because of feedback processes that allow reciprocal regulation.

REGULATION IS TO ORDER AS _____ IS TO
DISORDER?

Disregulation theory (Schwartz, 1977, 1979) can be thought of as the converse of control theory, or what I will hereafter refer to as regulation theory. As discussed above, regulation theory was created to help specify the conditions under which regulation leads to ordered BEHAVIORS in systems. As illustrated in Table 3, the concept of *regulation* is used to help explain the emergence and existence of *order* (according to Webster, the word regulation is derived from *regulare,* which means to make regular or ordered through rule).

A basic tenet of science is that order cannot occur unless the regulatory processes generated by the subsystems within a system (plus regulatory processes generated by systems outside the given system) are connected (or more appropriately, interconnected). Psychologically, one way to connect various psychobiological processes (within the brain as well as between brain and body) is through the process of self-attention. Doing so should lead to relatively automatic self-regulation, which should produce a certain "ease" in the system. An appropriately regulated negative feedback system will show balance, properties of homeostasis, negentropy (as in physics), and stability. It directly follows that an ordered system can (and in fact, must) become disordered if the essential regulatory processes are, for whatever reason, *disconnected.* This too, of course, is a basic tenet of science, though often it is assumed implicitly rather than stated explicitly.

Table 3

Terms That Parallel the Analogy, "Regulation Is to Order as Disregulation Is to Disorder"

Regulation Theory	Disregulation Theory
Order	Disorder
Connection	Disconnection
Attention	Disattention
Ease	Disease
Balance	Imbalance
Homeostasis	Heterostasis
Negentropy	Entropy
Stability	Instability

Table 4
Types of Disregulation in a Negative Feedback System

Type 1-Disregulation:	Attenuation of negative feedback
Type 2-Disregulation:	Distortion of negative feedback
Type 3-Disregulation:	Delay of negative feedback
Type 4-Disregulation:	Disconnection of negative feedback

Clearly, disconnection represents the extreme means of dis-rupting regulation. Regulation can be attenuated, distorted, delayed, or disconnected, and all of the above will lead to var-ious degrees of disregulation in a regulated system (Table 4). Space does not permit a detailed discussion of these different types of disregulation and their different effects in systems of differing degrees of complexity (e.g., the *specific* consequences of disregulating a system containing both positive and negative feedback processes can vary markedly depending upon whether and how these processes are disregulated). However, the *general* principles are the same in each case. Disregulation of a regu-lated, stable system *must* lead to a relative increase in disorder as measured in the system's BEHAVIOR.

Returning to Table 3, one psychological way to disconnect (to various degrees) various psychobiological processes (within the brain as well as between brain and body) is through the process of disattention to self. Doing so should lead to relatively automatic disregulation, which in turn should contribute to "dis"-ease in the system. A disregulated, negative feedback sys-tem will show imbalance, properties of heterostasis, entropy (as in physics), and instability.

To summarize, we can say that regulation is to order as disregulation is to disorder. However, until now we have lacked a term in the English language to complete this analogy. I coined the term "disregulation" (Schwartz, 1977, 1979) to fill this void. The absence, however, is not merely semantic; it is evident in most of the major texts on systems theory and regulation (control) theory. For example, mechanisms of disorder and order-disorder relationships are either ignored or mentioned minimally in most of the books referenced above, and will not be found in most of their indexes. The justification for balancing the concepts of regulation and order with concepts of disregulation and disorder is not merely to aesthetically complete the symmetry, but more importantly, to help focus our attention on the nature of disorder and the role that the disruption of key regulatory processes play in its promotion.

Of course, like the concept underlying feedback (Mayr, 1970), the concept behind disregulation is really quite old and has been previously applied to specific problems in specific disciplines. For example, leading theorists in hypertension have referred to its being a "disease of regulation" (see Page, 1960). However, my experience is that focusing on disregulation *per se* as it leads to disorder raises new questions, stimulates the development and use of new statistical techniques, and helps to organize conflicting theories and data across disciplines.

WHEN DOES REGULATION LEAD TO DISORDER?

Regulation theory presumes that an ordered system is a regulated system; and ordered systems show orderly (predictable, even rhythmic) BEHAVIOR. It follows that for an ordered system to become a disordered system, some key regulatory forces must be disrupted (see Table 4). How can this disruption occur? A basic tenet of science is that the disruption of a regulatory force requires some regulatory process! This takes effort. For example, perpetual motion machines are considered untenable because undesirable regulatory forces (e.g., friction) use energy in the system. Theoretically, the only way to create a perpetual motion machine is to completely disconnect the system from any constraining, regulatory processes that use energy. This degree of disregulation is presumed to be impossible.

It follows, therefore, that in order to disregulate an ordered system, it is essential to use a regulatory process! This, of course, is the logic of the germ theory of disease (i.e., germs and viruses cause certain diseases). Some diseases do occur because germs and viruses act to disconnect certain essential regulatory processes, thereby causing the particular biochemical and physiological processes to become disordered (to BEHAVE in a disorderly way) and be labeled as a disease, but many other stimuli (regulators) can act in such a way as to disregulate key biological regulatory processes. These regulatory processes can occur at the social and psychological levels as well and thereby modulate biological processes (recall Table 1). Furthermore, in complex systems, combinations of regulatory processes can interact, contributing to *multiple* disregulation within and between levels. For example, a person's sensitivity to becoming disregulated by a given germ may in part be determined by (i.e., regulated by) psychological stimuli that are acting as disregulators (e.g., life stresses disregulating the immune system).

The key here concerns the concept of *interactions* of various regulatory processes. Disregulation theory provides a general structure for organizing the various combinations of regulatory processes that may be disregulating key regulatory processes in an additive or even synergistic fashion to produce disorder. Parenthetically, a fundamental regulatory system in the body is DNA. Genes can disregulate systems in the same way that they regulate systems. Genes can either (1) generate certain regulatory processes that will act to disregulate others, or (2) lack certain regulatory processes to begin with (hence such a system will begin relatively disordered).

The English language requires that we use the term regulation to infer the process of producing *order* in a system. Then what does it mean in English to say that regulation can produce *disorder*? The answer, of course, is that this use of the term "regulation" is meaningless *unless* we posit that regulation can lead to disorder *only if* it acts to *disrupt* some other key regulatory process that in turn is producing order. In terms of stages, regulatory process X may control regulatory process Y in such a way that Y can no longer effectively regulate process Z. I refer to this chain of events as "disregulation." A *disregulatory process* is one that is used in such a way as to produce a *state of disregulation* somewhere in the system, which reflects the relative disconnection of a key regulatory process.

DISREGULATION AND THE SCIENTIFIC METHOD

Disregulation theory is the complement of regulation theory, and both, when combined, provide a general theory for understanding order and disorder. The theory, therefore, can potentially be applied to any system, which is why it qualifies as being a general theory. The reader will note that stated in this way, disregulation theory is ultimately a statement of the basis of the scientific method. Saying it, of course, does not mean that we typically think of the scientific method in quite this way.

Briefly, in science we first attempt to discover order in some system. That is, we *observe* that a system BEHAVES in a particular, and hence ordered, fashion. Then, we *hypothesize* that the order is caused by something (or a combination of things), i.e., that the order is produced by some regulatory process(es).

Using the previous example, we *observe* order (call it Z) and we *hypothesize* that Z is caused by Y (assuming other regulatory processes are held constant or assuming that they vary "randomly"). How do we *prove* that Y is regulating Z, and thereby is responsible for the order we observe as Z? The most convincing, and ultimate proof, is to somehow *remove* Y and show that Z *changes accordingly*. That is, to prove that Y regulates Z, we attempt to disregulate Y experimentally and show that the order in Z is changed. Now, how do we disregulate Y experimentally? We use some other regulatory force! We employ X to disregulate Y so as to produce disorder measured at Z. X is therefore the disregulating regulatory force used to prove that Y regulates Z.

We thus infer that regulation produces order in a system

by disregulating the system and showing that this leads to disorder. Of course, the extreme experimental application of the scientific method cannot often be achieved, so we resort to lesser forms of direct (regulated) disregulation (e.g., attenuation of a regulatory force, type 1-Disregulation), or we look to nature for accidents of disregulation. Disregulation is therefore as much a part of the method of science as is regulation.

WHEN IS DISREGULATION "UNHEALTHY"?

Whether disregulation of a system is deemed good or bad is a value judgment. This value judgment depends upon (1) the purpose of disregulating the system, and (2) the desire to maintain degrees of order and disorder in a given system. In the case of physical disease, we assume that (1) the purpose of disregulating the system, though it may have been good for the disregulator (e.g., the germ), is not necessarily valued by the individual who is disregulated (and/or the society), and (2) the individual's (and/or the society's) desire that his or her system should be healthy (optimally ordered) rather than unhealthy (disordered to some defined critical degree). As we will see, sometimes the individual's desire to repair a disregulated system expressed in the periphery, may inadvertently contribute to disregulation at a group or social level, since the initial causes of the peripheral disregulation were not corrected (Schwartz, 1977, 1979).

The principle that treating symptoms rather than causes is ultimately maladaptive becomes clearer when we take a systems perspective and apply disregulation theory to it (Schwartz, 1977). Simply stated, treating symptoms rather than causes is inherently disregulatory, since it removes the key regulatory processes that would motivate the organism to alter the cause (to leave the environment). In other words, the existence of disorder in a system is often accompanied by feedback that motivates an individual to change his or her behavior for the sake of his or her health, i.e., *disorder* is often experienced as *distressing*. In regulation terms this is extremely *adaptive*. To remove this feedback process is to remove a key stabilizing force that allows the brain and body to act together as a "health care system" (Schwartz, 1979). This implication of disregulation theory can now be discussed and specifically applied to recent basic and clinical findings.

THE REPRESSION/CEREBRAL DISCONNECTION/CARDIOVASCULAR DISORDER HYPOTHESIS

The experience of distress is a negative feedback process that serves as a prerequisite for engaging in appropriate health-seeking behavior. If the body were not designed to generate signals that could be processed by the brain as distress when the body was disordered, the brain could not take corrective self-regulatory actions to help restore order and health. For various reasons, people may not process these distress signals. For example, disattention to negative feedback from the body, regardless of its cause, theoretically could lead to a relative increase in disregulation in the brain-body homeostatic relationship, thereby contributing to physiological disorder and disease.

One mechanism for producing disattention is a psychological defensive coping style, broadly termed "repressive." Individuals prone to use this coping style will tend to deny experiencing distress in stressful situations and will deny experiencing negative emotions in situations where such emotions are normal and appropriate. Repressive individuals, therefore, should show a *discrepancy* or a *dissociation* between their verbal reports of stress and what they are experiencing physiologically.

In a classic paper, Galin (1974) proposed that repressed subjects achieved this dissociated state by producing a functional cerebral disconnection syndrome, in which the left (the more verbal, analytic hemisphere) became functionally disconnected, relatively speaking, from the right (the more nonverbal, emotional hemisphere). Following upon Galin's suggestion (1974), I proposed that this functional cerebral disconnection syndrome would be accompanied by disregulation between the two hemispheres at various sites, and between the brain and body. This disregulation would lead to greater physiological reactivity to stress and poorer recovery from stress (indicative of physiological disorder), which in turn could contribute to disease (Schwartz, 1977).

However, to test this broad theory required that it be possible to (1) measure repressive coping styles psychometrically, and to demonstrate the following: (2) that repressive subjects show greater physiological disorder in the face of stressful stimuli (e.g., they should appear to be physiologically and behaviorally "anxious" despite verbal claims to be "relaxed"), (3) that cerebral laterality involving emotion is accentuated in repression, (4) that the accentuated cerebral laterality in repression is associated with physiological disorder, and (5) that all of the above are related to physical illness. Recent data from our laboratory illustrate progress toward reaching each of these goals.

Concerning the measurement of repressive tendencies (Weinberger, Schwartz, and Davidson, 1979), it is possible to separate subjects who report experiencing little distress in everyday situations (as indicated by low scores on such instruments as the Taylor Manifest Anxiety Scale, TMAS, 1953) and are accurate in their perceptions (i.e., "true low anxious subjects") from subjects who report experiencing little distress in everyday situations and are inaccurate in their perceptions (i.e., are deceiving themselves, using a repressive coping style). It also turns out that the Marlowe-Crowne Social Desirability Scale (Crowne and Marlowe, 1964), which is not a good measure of social conformity, is quite a good measure of defensiveness (for simplicity, defensiveness is referred to here as "repressive"; and since other psychological defenses may be involved, the term "repressive coping style," rather than the term "repression," is preferred). Since the Marlowe-Crowne scale is correlated only minimally with scales tapping subjective distress, it is possible to split subjects reporting low distress into two subgroups on the basis of their scores: low TMAS/lowMarlowe-Crowne subjects are labeled true low anxious, whereas low TMAS/high Marlowe-Crowne subjects are labeled repressive.

These two subgroups were compared to true high anxious subjects in a psychophysiological study (Weinberger et al., 1979). All subjects performed a moderately stressful sentence-completion task involving neutral, aggressive, and sexual content, while heart rate, skin resistance, and frontalis region muscle tension were continuously recorded. In addition, their verbal responses were scored for latency and verbal content. The results indicated that for all dependent measures, true low anxious subjects showed less evidence of stress than true high anxious subjects, whereas repressive subjects showed stressful reactions equal to or greater than the true high anxious subjects. Interestingly, the repressive subjects reported experiencing significantly less distress than even the true low anxious subjects. These data suggest that it is possible to measure repressive tendencies psychometrically and to demonstrate increased physiological and behavioral reactivity in subjects who incorrectly report low levels of distress.

The next question that arises concerns the relationship between repressive coping styles and cerebral laterality in emotion. At the time of Galin's article (1974), it was generally believed that in right-handed subjects, the left hemisphere was relatively more involved with verbal and analytic processes, while the right hemisphere was relatively more involved with spatial, holistic, and emotional processes (e.g., Schwartz, Davidson, and Maer, 1975). However, recent research questions this simple dichotomy, suggesting instead that the hemispheres are differentially involved in positive versus negative emotions, especially those emotions accompanying approach versus avoidance behaviors.

As reviewed in Ahern and Schwartz (1979), various findings suggest that the left hemisphere may be more involved with positive emotions and the right hemisphere more involved with negative emotions. Furthermore, as indicated by their data, the positive-negative emotion dichotomy may be more fundamental than the verbal-spatial cognitive dichotomy (i.e., the positive-negative emotion dichotomy may be mediated subcortically). Differential lateralization for positive versus negative emotions has been reported for lateral eye movements (Ahern and Schwartz, 1979), facial expression (Schwartz, Ahern, and Brown, 1979), and EEG from the frontal regions (Davidson, Schwartz, Saron, Bennett, and Goleman, 1979). These data are important because they suggest how it might be possible neuropsychologically for a person to "verbally" think he or she is happy, yet simultaneously be otherwise. These individuals should show marked laterality for positive versus negative emotions if the hemispheres are functioning in a relatively disconnected manner (and therefore cannot equilibriate via self-regulation).

We have recently collected data consistent with the hypothesis that defensive individuals evidence greater cerebral laterality for positive versus negative emotions than do control subjects. For example, Polonsky and Schwartz[1] examined laterality in zygomatic region muscle tension (a muscle involved in the smile) and corrugator region muscle tension (a muscle involved in the frown) during various types of positive, negative, and mixed positive-negative images. The results showed relatively greater muscle tension on the right side for positive images (indicative of relative left hemispheric activation) for the zygomatic region, and relatively greater muscle tension on the left side for negative images (indicative of relative right hemispheric activation) for the corrugator region. However, these laterality findings occurred most strongly and reliably in *repressive* subjects. True low anxious subjects showed virtually no laterality differences as a function of positive versus negative affective images. It may be that the large individual differences typically observed in the laterality literature are in part due to personality differences in defensive coping styles.

[1]Polonsky, W. H., & Schwartz, G. E. Facial electromyography and the self-deceptive coping style: Individual differences in the hemispheric lateralization of affect. (Manuscript.)

More striking are findings that emerge above and beyond the specific cognitive or affective nature of the stimuli. For example, Schwartz and Schwaab[2] have observed that repressive subjects produce a preponderance of left lateral eye movements in response to reflective questions (above and beyond lateral eye movement differences elicited by the specific content of the questions), whereas true low anxious subjects produce a preponderance of right lateral eye movements in response to reflective questions. Since left lateral eye movements tend to occur more under conditions of stress (e.g., in Schwartz and Schwaab, all subjects generated relatively more left eye movements during a stressful condition of being evaluated than during a nonevaluation control condition), the data suggest that repressive subjects are relatively more stressed by the laboratory situation in general and are more right hemispherically active (indicative of more avoidant, negative emotions). Repressive subjects, therefore, appear to be more cerebrally lateralized in negative emotions and in situations that are potentially threatening.

Theoretically, the suppression of the experience of negative feelings should take effort (recall our previous discussion of effort and the use of regulatory processes to produce disorder), and should presumably be mediated cortically. Therefore even under "resting" conditions in a psychophysiology experiment, repressive subjects should show relatively low levels of alpha EEG activity, whereas true low anxious subjects should show relatively high levels of alpha EEG activity. Schwartz and Ahern[3] found that repressive subjects showed remarkably low levels of resting alpha (both anterior and posterior) whereas true low anxious subjects showed very high levels. And importantly, defensive high anxious subjects (subjects scoring high on the TMAS and high on the Marlowe-Crowne) were closer to the repressive subjects in their resting EEG alpha levels, whereas

[2]Schwartz, G. E., & Schwaab, M. Repressive coping style, cerebral lateralization and cardiovascular disregulation. (Manuscript.)
[3]Schwartz, G. E., & Ahern, G. L. EEG patterning in repressive subjects. (Manuscript.)

true high anxious subjects were closer to the true low anxious subjects. (The order of groups from repressive to defensive high anxious to true high anxious to true low anxious is consistent with the other findings reported above.)

These findings clarify why previous research has failed to uncover consistent relationships between self-reports of distress and measures of physiological reactivity, resting levels of EEG alpha activity, or indices of cerebral laterality. In most of the previous research, two different subgroups of subjects (repressive subjects and true low anxious subjects) have been treated as a single group of "low anxious" subjects. Note that although most of our research to date has examined subjective reports of anxiety, the same issue of accuracy versus inaccuracy in self-perception should apply to other emotions such as depression and anger. This is why the general term "distress" is preferred.

The above data, although they are consistent with the repression/cerebral disconnection hypothesis, do not constitute proof. More direct measures of interhemispheric communication, such as those employed in the cognitive-performance literature (e.g., T scope/hemifield presentation/reaction time studies) are needed. R. J. Davidson and colleagues[4] have collected performance data in two studies, and find a relative attenuation of information transfer from right to left hemisphere in repressive, as compared to true low anxious, subjects.

Do subjects who show repressive tendencies psychometrically as well as enhanced cerebral laterality also show greater physiological disregulation? To date we have completed one experiment that addresses this question, and the data are consistent with the general theory. In Schwartz and Schwaab,[5] subjects were administered reflective questions while heart rate and respiration were recorded. During a 15-second period in which subjects formulated their answers silently, changes in heart rate and respiration were continuously sampled by computer, and measures of mean heart rate, heart rate variability, and heart

[4]Personal communication, May 1983.
[5]Schwartz and Schwaab, op. cit.

rate–respiration covariation (a measure of respiratory homeo-static control of heart rate) were computed on-line. Repressive subjects and true low anxious subjects showed comparable *mean* increases in heart rate during that time. However, the repressive subjects showed significantly greater increases in heart rate *variability*, and significantly reduced *heart rate–respiration covariation*, during these periods than true low anxious subjects. These data suggest that beat by beat homeostatic control of heart rate during the mental task was disrupted more in repressive subjects than in true low anxious subjects. In other words, the repressive subjects' cardiovascular system appeared to be responding (BE-HAVING) in a more "disordered" (less ordered) fashion, which is suggestive of increased disregulation. Current research in our laboratory is attempting to replicate and extend these initial findings.

How do all of the above findings relate to cardiovascular disease, and possibly, to disease in general? We have completed two studies thus far that bear on this question, one on hypertensive subjects, the other on normal college students. Warrenburg, Crits-Christoph, and Schwartz[6] compared normotensive and hypertensive subjects on measures of defensiveness, cerebral laterality in facial expression, cardiovascular reactivity, and self-reports during a stressful speech task. First, using a clinical cutoff for "repression," hypertensives showed a significantly higher percentage of trait repressors (45 percent) compared to standardized samples (11 percent). These data suggest that hypertension and defensiveness covary in a significant number of patients. Interestingly, blood pressure responses during the speech task were *positively* correlated with self-reported state anxiety in normotensive subjects but *negatively* correlated in hypertensive subjects. This striking discordance between physiological response and self-report suggests the operation of a

[6]Warrenburg, S., Crits-Christoph, P., & Schwartz, G. E. (1981), Biobehavioral etiology and treatment of hypertension: A comparative outcome study of stress management and diet change approaches. Presented at the NATO Symposium on Behavioral Medicine, Greece, July.

defensive mechanism in hypertensives that is proportional to their physiological arousal to stress.

When the hypertensives were split into "true low anxious" and "repressive" subgroups, the latter displayed (1) increased corrugator region muscle tension during resting conditions (suggesting they were more distressed), (2) enhanced elevation of corrugator activity during the stress conditions, and (3) reduced recovery in the corrugator during the rest period following the stress conditions. These subjects also showed increased facial laterality, especially during stress. Finally, blood pressures were recorded from both arms. The discrepancy between readings taken from the left and right arms was greatest in those hypertensives who reported the *least* distress during the stress condition. (Although these data are generally consistent with the theory, they should be viewed as tentative until they have been replicated in a second sample of patients.)

The effects of defensiveness need not be limited to hypertension or cardiovascular disease *per se*. Individuals who disattend to negative emotional states and associated physiological sensations should be less likely to engage in various health promoting behaviors. Repressive subjects, because they are actually quite stressed, should be likely to show more stress-linked physical illnesses than subjects who are truly low anxious. In a study by Polonsky and Schwartz,[7] subjects were asked to list the various physical illnesses they had experienced over the preceding year. The repressive subjects (who, it will be recalled, showed the large facial laterality effects to positive versus negative affective images) reported having significantly more physical illnesses than the true low anxious subjects. These data are striking in view of the fact that the repressive subjects (1) reported being significantly less aware of symptoms of distress than the true low anxious subjects, and (2) scored higher on the "social desirability" scale, yet reported higher levels of physical illness (which is not necessarily a "socially desirable" response).

---

[7]Polonsky and Schwartz, op. cit.

IMPLICATIONS OF DISREGULATION THEORY
FOR TREATMENT AND PREVENTION

Clearly, the data reviewed above represent only a beginning of possible research that is needed to examine the relationship between psychological defense, neuropsychological disconnection, disregulation, physiological disorder, and disease. To the extent that the above data are consistent with disregulation theory, they provide the impetus for continuing the challenging task of integrating findings and methods from different areas using general systems theory. Although it is obviously premature at this time to accept the theory and directly apply it to treatment and prevention, we can hypothesize at this point what some of the possible applications might be.

First, the theory predicts that if (1) disattention can promote (2) a neuropsychological disconnection, resulting in (3) a disregulated state leading to (4) disorder and thereby contributing to (5) disease, then (1) self-attention should (under certain conditions) promote (2) neuropsychological connections producing (3) enhanced self-regulation leading to (4) order in the system, and thereby contributing to (5) "ease" (Schwartz, 1977, 1979). In other words, self-attention *may* have automatic, self-regulatory, homeostatic effects which increase the system's ability to engage in appropriate healing processes. I emphasize "may" because, as discussed above, the way in which the feedback is processed (interpreted) should influence whether the feedback will act as a negative or positive feedback process. The hypochondriac may perpetuate physiological hyperactivity not simply through the process of self-attention but by interpreting the signals in a worried, threatening way, which could serve to further activate the physiology.

Schwartz and Rennert[8] have found that self-attention to heart rate versus respiration in a passive, nonstressful way, has specific self-regulatory effects on heart rate versus respiration. In particular, each response becomes selectively more ordered

[8]Schwartz, G. E., & Rennert, K. Effects of attention and sensory feedback on automatic self-regulation of heart rate versus respiration. (Manuscript.)

(less variable) when subjects specifically attend to it, especially if the subjects' attention is augmented by "natural" biofeedback (e.g., feeling one's pulse, or feeling the air come out of one's nose). These data are consistent with the observation that self-attention in various meditation techniques seems to have specific, automatic, self-regulatory, stabilizing effects on physiological functioning. For example, respiration becomes deeper, slower, and more *regular* (ordered), especially in those meditation practices that involve attention to breathing (or in specific self-attention to respiration tasks, as used by Schwartz and Rennert). It is conceivable that self-attention can promote localized healing, especially if the self-attention is guided by relevant imagery that is targeted to the appropriate part(s) of the body.

Self-monitoring of all sorts (behavioral, physiological, subjective) may, under appropriate conditions, help engender self-regulation at multiple levels. Variables such as the subject's motivation, attentional style, attitude toward mind and body, and style of coping, should all interact with the above. In certain individuals, self-monitoring may actually make them more anxious and distressed. Furthermore, making these individuals become aware of their distress may be a prerequisite for successful clinical treatment and compliance.

For example, Heide and Borkovec[9] have reported a phenomenon that they call "relaxation-induced anxiety." Some subjects show psychophysiological evidence of anxiety enhancement while practicing relaxation. Is it possible that these subjects are actually repressors who actively (though not necessarily consciously) disattend to various negative subjective experiences? Is it possible that self-attention tasks may automatically increase a repressor's awareness of his or her actual distress? Schwartz and Polonsky[10] measured zygomatic and corrugator region

[9]Heide, F. J., and Borkovec, T. D. (1980), Relaxation-induced anxiety: Psychophysiological evidence of anxiety enhancement in tense subjects practicing relaxation. Presented at the Fourteenth Annual Convention of the Association for the Advancement of Behavior Therapy, New York, November 21–23.

[10]Schwartz, G. E., and Polonsky, W. H., Facial electromyography and the

muscle tension in repressive and low anxious subjects who were meditating for the first time. True low anxious subjects found the experience enjoyable and relaxing, whereas repressive subjects found it boring, if not unpleasant; most interestingly, only the repressive subjects showed increased facial muscle laterality during meditation!

Will measures of defensiveness or cerebral disconnection predict noncompliance due to repression? Will more sophisticated measures of physiological disorder (time series, rhythmicity, variability, recovery) reveal improvements with successful psychological therapies (e.g., Will successful psychotherapy for defensive subjects be accompanied by increased cerebral interconnectedness and reduced physiological disregulation?). These and many other questions are raised when the therapeutic implications of the theory are considered.

SUMMARY AND CONCLUSIONS

Ideally, a new theory should (1) organize disparate, if not discrepant, theories and findings, and (2) suggest new methods, experiments, and findings. Disregulation theory has the potential to organize a substantial body of knowledge and to utilize recent advances in psychometrics, statistics, and systems research design to uncover new findings. As mentioned above, the concept of disregulation is by no means new; it is implicit in most models of disease and is the basis of the scientific method. However, specifying more clearly the relationship between regulation and order, and disregulation and disorder, should make it possible to use these concepts more effectively.

For example, current research in the Department of Psychology at Yale is applying disregulation theory to cancer (an extreme example of disregulation at the cellular level) and to eating disorders. Current clinical work at the Yale Behavioral

---

self-deceptive coping style: Individual differences in response to meditation. (Manuscript.)

Medicine Clinic in the Department of Psychiatry has found disregulation theory useful in conceptualizing and implementing biobehavioral treatments for certain urologic disorders (where disattention contributes to an apparent functional disconnection in the self-regulation of urination), tension and migraine headaches (where instability and failure to recover effectively from stressful stimuli is observed in a substantial number of patients), and type A behavior (where individuals disregard feedback of frustration, fatigue and early warning symptoms of impending cardiovascular disease). Hopefully the reader will see applications of the general concepts outlined here to areas of his or her particular interest. If this chapter stimulates the reader's interest in modern systems theory and its possible applications to psychosomatic medicine, then it will have achieved its goal.

References

Ahern, G. L., & Schwartz, G. E. (1979), Differential lateralization for positive versus negative emotion. *Neuropsychologia*, 17:693–697.

Boulding, K. E. (1978), *Ecodynamics*. Beverly Hills, CA: Sage.

Crowne, D., & Marlowe, D. (1964), *The Approval Motive*. New York: Wiley.

Davidson, R. J., Schwartz, G. E., Saron, C., Bennett, J., & Goleman, D. J. (1979), Frontal versus parietal EEG asymmetry during positive and negative affect. *Psychophysiology*, 16:202–203.

deRosnay, J. (1979), *The Macroscope*. New York: Harper & Row.

Engel, G. L. (1977), The need for a new medical model: A challenge for biomedicine. *Science*, 196:129–136.

Galin, D. (1974), Implications of left-right cerebral lateralization for psychiatry: A neurophysiological context for unconscious processes. *Arch. Gen. Psychiat.*, 9:412–418.

Jones, R. W. (1973), *Principles of Biological Regulation*. New York: Academic Press.

Leigh, H., & Reiser, M. F. (1980), *The Patient: Biological, Psychological and Social Dimensions of Medical Practice*. New York: Plenum.

Mayr, O. (1970), *The Origins of Feedback Control*. Cambridge, MA: M.I.T. Press.

Miller, J. G. (1978), *Living Systems*. New York: McGraw-Hill.

Page, I. H. (1960), The mosaic theory of hypertension. In: *Essential Hypertension*, ed. K. D. Bock & P. T. Cottier. Berlin: Springer-Verlag.

Schwartz, G. E. (1977), Psychosomatic disorders and biofeedback: A psychobiological model of disregulation. In: *Psychopathology: Experimental Models*, ed. J. D. Maser & M. E. P. Seligman. San Francisco: Freeman, pp. 270–307.

——— (1979), Disregulation and systems theory: A biobehavioral framework for biofeedback and behavioral medicine. In: *Biofeedback and Self-Regulation*, ed. N. Birbaumer & H. D. Kimmel. Hillsdale, NJ: Erlbaum, pp. 19–48.

——— (1980), Behavioral medicine and systems theory: A new synthesis. *National Forum*, Winter:25–30.

——— (1981), A systems analysis of psychobiology and behavior therapy: Implications for behavioral medicine. *Psychother. Psychosom.*, 36:159–184.

——— (1982a), Psychophysiological patterning and emotion revisited: A systems perspective. In: *Measuring Emotions in Infants and Children*, ed. C. Izard. Cambridge, MA: Cambridge University Press, pp. 67–96.

——— (1982b), Testing the biopsychosocial model: The ultimate challenge facing behavioral medicine? *J. Consult. Clin. Psychol.*, 50:1040–1053.

——— (1982c), Cardiovascular psychophysiology: A systems perspective. In: *Perspectives in Cardiovascular Psychophysiology*, ed. J. T. Cacioppo. New York: Guilford Press, pp. 347–372.

——— (1983), Disregulation theory and disease: Applications to the repression/cerebral disconnection/cardiovascular disorder hypothesis. *Internat. Rev. Appl. Psychol.*, 32:95–118.

——— Ahern, G. L., & Brown, S. L. (1979), Lateralized facial muscle response to positive versus negative emotional stimuli. *Psychophysiol.*, 16:561–571.

——— Davidson, R. J., & Maer, F. (1975), Right hemisphere lateralization for emotion in the human brain: Interaction with cognition. *Science*, 190:286–288.

——— Weiss, S. M. (1978), Behavioral medicine revisited: An amended definition. *J. Behav. Med.*, 1:249–251.

Taylor, J. A. (1953), A personality scale of manifest anxiety. *J. Abnorm. Soc. Psychol.*, 48:285–290.

von Bertalanffy, L. (1968), *General Systems Theory*. New York: Braziller.

Weinberger, D. A., Schwartz, G. E., & Davidson, R. J. (1979), Low anxious, high anxious, and repressive coping styles: Psychometric patterns and behavioral and physiological responses to stress. *J. Abnorm. Psychol.*, 88:369–380.

Wiener, N. (1948), *Cybernetics of Control and Communication in the Animal and Machine*. Cambridge, MA: M.I.T. Press.

4.
Onset Situation in Three Psychosomatic Illnesses

HAROLD LEVITAN, M.D.

INTRODUCTION

Precipitation of a psychosomatic illness requires the concurrence of three factors: (1) the person who is about to become ill must possess a particular somatic predisposition; (2) he or she must possess a particular psychological predisposition; and (3) he or she must be placed in a particular reality situation.

Much is already understood about the nature of each of these factors. With regard to the predisposing somatic factor, we know, for example, that persons who are at risk to develop a peptic ulcer secrete unusually high levels of pepsinogen starting at birth (Menguy, 1964). Presumably an as yet undiscovered predisposing somatic factor of this sort is present in each of the other psychosomatic illnesses as well.

With regard to the predisposing psychological factor, we know that persons who are at risk to develop one or another of the psychosomatic illnesses tend to have difficulty in generating fantasy (de M'Uzan, 1974) and in experiencing their own affect (Sifneos, 1973). Both of these limitations of mental function, which apparently reflect two sides of the same phenomenon, may materially reduce the individual's ability to mod-

119

ulate the bodily component of his emotional responses. Although it has been determined that this predisposing psychological factor is more often present in psychosomatic patients
than in nonpsychosomatic patients (Sifneos, 1973), there is as
yet no evidence that it is present to a greater degree in one
rather than in another of the various diagnostic categories that
make up the realm of psychosomatic disease. With regard to
the reality situation necessarily present at the onset of illness,
we know that it is never a pleasant one. Indeed, we know from
the work of Engel (1968) that it tends to be intolerable enough
to induce in the potential patient a sense of hopelessness and
helplessness.

As just noted, Engel has acquainted us with a significant
quantitative aspect of the interaction between the psychosomatic
patient and his environment during the onset phase of illness.
The question now arises as to whether there is also a qualitative
aspect to this interaction. Does the life situation tend to be the
same in those persons who are about to develop the same illness,
and does it tend to be different in those persons who are about
to develop different illnesses? In other words, is there a specificity regarding the circumstances at onset of the various psychosomatic illnesses? In this chapter I will present some data
bearing on this issue derived from two sources: (1) retrospective
reports of the life situation at onset provided during psychotherapy by patients with either rheumatoid arthritis or ulcerative colitis; and (2) reports of dreams which culminated in
attacks, which were provided by patients with asthma. These
data have been published in several previous papers (Levitan,
1973, 1976, 1977–1978, 1981, 1983), which dealt separately
with one or another of these three illnesses. Here I shall bring
my material together for purposes of comparison.

The possible role of a specific intrapsychic factor in the
etiology of each psychosomatic illness has been extensively studied over the past five decades. The particular intrapsychic parameters that have been investigated include personality type
(Dunbar, 1943), unconscious conflict (Alexander, 1950), and
unconscious attitude (Graie and Graham, 1952).

While it is true that the patient's mental state at onset and the external circumstances at onset are closely related, it is to be expected that the fresh angle of vision obtained by focusing more directly on the external circumstances will yield new information.

ONSET SITUATION IN RHEUMATOID ARTHRITIS

In 25 female patients with well diagnosed rheumatoid arthritis (RA), it was found that each woman was confronted by a similar overwhelming situation at the onset of illness. The following very brief vignettes will serve as illustrations.

Mrs. B., age 56
This patient had developed RA at age 47 in the context of her discovery of her husband's chronic unfaithfulness. He was (and is) a very narcissistic and arrogant man who behaved in an exceedingly unfeeling manner to her. A few years prior to onset of her illness, he rejected her outright and left her for a much younger woman. She was the more disappointed because she had given up on his behalf her own prospects for a career.

Her rage at her husband, which was extreme, existed side-by-side with a continuing love for him. For example, at the same time that she contemplated the idea of having both him and his new wife murdered by contract, she welcomed him back into her home and even into her bed. Also, during this period she had many dreams in which he was once more in love with her.

Mrs. L., age 40
This patient had developed RA at age 35 in the context of her agonizing marriage. Her husband was (and is) a narcotics addict who in the two years prior to her illness experienced

several episodes during which he became totally mute for periods of a month or more. At other times he behaved in a very sadistic fashion toward her. She is constantly in a state of tremendous rage at her husband but cannot bring herself to leave him.

Mrs. D., age 38

This patient had developed RA at age 25 in the context of a forced exile from her native land following the discovery by her family of Mrs. D.'s long-standing incestuous love affair with her brother-in-law. During the period of exile she was in a continuous rage at her ex-lover and at the rest of her family. She tore up their letters and refused to answer their long-distance phone calls. However, at the same time, she was having dreams of reconciliation with them nearly every night.

As illustrated by these examples from my own patient survey, each woman was caught at the time of onset in an insoluble conflict between her feelings of dependency and of rage. Since she was unable to give up the particular person in question she was forced to bear indefinitely the torment inflicted by that person as well as her own anger at him. It is interesting that although each woman was conscious of her rage she never acted upon it. In addition, it is not at all clear why the bond between the patient and her tormentor persisted for so long. Possibly it represents a direct transfer from the bond between the child and its mother, which tends to persist regardless of circumstances. The fact that this intolerable situation of an unrelenting attachment to a rage-provoking object had gone on for months and even years before the illness began suggests that a chronic rather than acute aggravating situation was the key psychological factor contributing to the illness.

It is important to note that the marked prevalence of the configuration reported here supports earlier data (Johnson, Shapiro, and Alexander, 1947) derived from the only other longitudinal clinical studies on a substantial number of rheumatoid patients.

ONSET SITUATION IN ULCERATIVE COLITIS

My first studies of the onset situation in ulcerative colitis included 10 patients who, in addition to their ulcerative colitis, suffered from a preexisting condition of either deafness or organic brain syndrome. These cases were especially helpful because the preexisting conditions had created a clear-cut and easily recognizable psychological state that clearly played a role in the production of the illness. The following brief histories are typical:

Mrs. V., age 52 (ulcerative colitis and deafness)

Mrs. V.'s hearing difficulty dated back to her preschool days when she contracted chronic bilateral mastoiditis. She had an 80 percent hearing loss on the left side, combined with a loss of less than 50 percent on the right side. She consistently refused to wear a hearing aid.

The initial episodes of her ulcerative colitis had taken place at age 48, at a time when she was very upset by the forthcoming engagement and separation of her older son, as well as by the news that her younger son would be attending a high school known for its drug traffic. In fact, she had become so enraged on this latter point that she had given up her religion. The act of separating from God, on the part of this extremely pious woman, was an indication of her marked withdrawal from the object world.

When I came to know her she had been quite isolated for a period of years. During our sessions she volunteered nothing at all. At no time did I feel that I established any real contact with her.

Mr. S., age 35 (ulcerative colitis and organic brain syndrome)

Mr. S. had developed ulcerative colitis five years before at age 30 in the context of the following series of traumatic events. Six months earlier his mother, from whom he had never been separated for more than one night, was hospitalized for repair of a detached retina. The detachment had been caused by a blow which the patient had struck to her face. Mr. S. was extremely agitated during the two weeks of his mother's absence; he became less agitated but more withdrawn after her return home following successful surgery.

Apparently, as a result of the direct damage that she sustained at the patient's hands, the mother, who had always been very loving, changed her attitude toward her son. She began to treat him very roughly and often struck and cursed him. He became increasingly withdrawn and started spending a good part of the day in bed, with his head under the covers. He developed ulcerative colitis on the very day that his mother left home to return to her part-time job.

Psychological testing disclosed a full scale I.Q. of 51. The Bender-Gestalt indicated brain damage, which was probably sustained at birth as the consequence of a difficult delivery. He learned to walk and talk very late. It was impossible to carry on any conversation with Mr. S. He tended to repeat his interlocutor's words verbatim. He talked to himself a great deal, breaking out from time to time in bursts of uncontrolled laughter, which were associated with loss of control of his bladder. His only relationship is with his mother, and when she was at home he shadowed her closely. When she was not at home he remained under the covers. His father, who is terrified of him, lets him do as he pleases.

Scrutiny of the prodromal period in these illustrative histories reveals the following set of events: a certain traumatic event caused the patient to separate from a key object; the handicap of either deafness or brain damage caused the patient to be impervious to fresh ties, and the rage that had been provoked by the traumatic event continued to mount. Finally, in this context of objectlessness and spiraling rage, the first signs of illness appeared.

In a later project I studied two adult patients with ulcerative colitis, each of whom had been traumatically separated from his mother during infancy. The actual events of the prodromal period in both of these cases revealed a strong associative link with the infantile loss.

Mr. S., age 57

Mr. S. is an unsuccessful artist and inventor who developed ulcerative colitis at age 55 in the midst of a period of great stress. Shortly before the onset of bleeding he realized that his cherished dream of returning to live in Europe would never come true. He had based his hopes of returning on the prospect of royalties to be paid by certain manufacturers for the rights to one of his inventions. No manufacturer accepted his invention, however. Though he refused to disclose the nature of his invention to me his whole plan seemed quite unrealistic.

His initial reaction to his realization was panic; it now seemed to him that he would be trapped in North America forever. In a matter of days, however, his response changed to rage. He had been in a constant rage ever since. There was room for little else in his mind. He violently and indiscriminately hated every aspect of life in North America. He cursed it with an astonishing string of terms.

Mr. S.'s father had been killed in World War I in the last months of his mother's pregnancy. After his birth his mother tried to maintain both herself and her baby, but when the patient was six months old she was forced to hand him over to her mother in the country. He had little contact with his mother from that time until he was four years old, at which point he was returned very much against his will to live with her in the city. He recalls hating his mother and his new life. In the four-year interval he had become very attached to his grandmother. It is important to stress that within four years he had suffered a double loss. First he was wrenched from his mother at age six months and then at four years from his grandmother.

He adapted very poorly throughout childhood and adolescence. He was very rebellious at school and was often expelled. At the first opportunity in adolescence he left home never to return. Thus began a process of aimless wandering about the world. On several occasions he was jailed for flaunting the authorities. In his early twenties he married an alcoholic woman who gave him two children and then disappeared. After many adventures he arrived in Canada 15 years ago.

It is particularly important to note that since leaving home in his teens he had only the most minimal contact with his mother. Up to the present moment he had not seen her for 30 years. He considered her a worthless creature, whom he described in terms very similar to those he used to describe North America. His mother, however, lives in Europe, to which he had wished so desperately to return. It is clear that he has rejected his actual mother while, at the same time, he has continued to worship her symbol, the motherland.

The therapeutic relationship was short-lived because of his refusal to return for visits despite persistence of his illness. There was no meaningful contact with him; sessions consisted almost entirely of angry outbursts at his surroundings, which included the therapist. Usually it was literally impossible for the therapist to utter a word.

Mr. R., age 22

Mr. R. is a student, of East Indian descent, who developed ulcerative colitis at age 21, one week after his sister, with whom he was living, left town for a one-month vacation. Initially, after she left for the airport, he had a sharp sense of panic accompanied by an urge to run after her and catch her before she could board the plane. Once she was actually away, however, his mood shifted and he experienced a strong anger toward her. Shortly after her departure he experienced another disappointment when a second sister, who was to supply him with his meals during the absence of his other sister, proved to be very irregular in the performance of her tasks.

In the ensuing days he noted that he had lost complete interest in his girlfriend. He was at first unable to explain this sudden loss of interest. She herself had done nothing to provoke him; he only knew that she was the last person in the world he wanted to see. Then he realized that he was repelled by all females. Significantly, at the time the author met him, which

was six months after his sister's departure, his interest in females—including his sexual interest—had not yet returned.

When he was six months old Mr. R.'s mother had abruptly
left home to join a lover. From that point on until he was six
years old when his father remarried he was brought up by the
very sister, five years older than himself, whose departure precipitated his illness 21 years later. He had seen his mother only
rarely since infancy. He was very resentful that he had been
deprived of a mother's care, which he states is "every person's
birthright." Most of the time, however, he has acted as if she
never existed. For example, it is his custom to leave the room
when his mother is discussed by his older sisters.

Throughout childhood and adolescence he displayed a violent temper. Often he would throw food or break dishes if his
meals were not on time. Most of his wrath was directed at his
oldest sister who had assumed the mothering role. Another
interesting feature of his childhood and adolescence was his
unduly sharp rage response to being on the losing side in games.
The defeat of his team seemed to act as a trigger that stirred
the memory of his previous losses.

Mr. R. was very unpredictable about keeping appointments.
When he did come he was impossible to engage. Often during
the interviews he acted as if the therapist were not present. On
these occasions he looked out the window and hummed audibly
to himself.

It is evident that during the prodromal period both Mr. S.
and Mr. R. showed the intense rage reaction and trend to objectlessness that was displayed by the patients with deafness and
with organic brain damage described above.

The predominant role of the patients' objectlessness and
rage during the onset phase in these very transparent cases
alerted me to the role of such issues in other cases. One hears
from patient after patient with ulcerative colitis that just prior
to the onset of illness there had been a sharp increase in the
level of rage leading to a break in communication with one's
mother or mother substitute. For example:

Miss H.

Miss H. developed ulcerative colitis at age 17. Five months earlier she had reluctantly submitted to an abortion at her older sister's insistence. This older sister had assumed the role of mother since the death of their actual mother when the patient was 12. Shortly after her own abortion the patient discovered that her sister was also pregnant and, though single, did not intend to have an abortion. Although continuing to live in the same house with her sister, the patient, furious at this discovery, broke off all communications with her. Miss H.'s ulcerative colitis began a few months later, when she received a most distressing note from the father of the aborted child suggesting that they both start dating others.

Mr. F.

Mr. F. developed ulcerative colitis at age 20, some months after his family had moved to a new neighborhood from the home in which he had been born. After the move he began quarreling with his very dominating mother on issues of independence. The relationship between the patient, an only child, and his mother had been a symbiotic one, marked by the belief that they were in constant communication via their thoughts. Shortly after the quarreling began, by apparently mutual agreement, mother and son stopped talking to each other altogether. This loss of external communication entailed as well a loss of internal dialogue via their thoughts. The patient managed without overt difficulty until five months after cessation of communication. At that time he developed ulcerative colitis following a severe disappointment regarding his grades in pre-med courses.

It is important to note that prior to a rupture, the relationship of the ulcerative colitis patient with his primal object retains many features of the early symbiosis. Indeed, as stressed by Engel (1958) many years ago, it is the presence of these symbiotic features prior to the rupture which causes the withdrawal from the object to be so global afterward.

Dreams That Culminate in Asthma Attacks

Scrutiny of dream sequences in an illness like asthma, in which symptoms occur episodically, provides an excellent opportunity to observe at very close range the particular constellation of psychological events that immediately precede onset of symptoms. Of course here we are dealing with the relapse of an illness rather than with its onset.

Forty-five pre-asthmatic dreams drawn from 11 patients were available for examination. This group comprised seven who had been reported in previous literature (French and Alexander, 1941; Dunbar, 1943; Kris, 1948) and four of my own patients.

Despite the problem of overlap it was possible to divide the 45 dreams culminating in asthma attacks into four types: (1) dreams in which the dreamer is the perpetrator of a violent act (19, or 42 percent); (2) dreams in which the dreamer is the victim of a violent act (12, or 27 percent); (3) dreams in which the dreamer is involved in a sexual act (7, or 16 percent); and (4) dreams which contain disturbing memories (7, or 16 percent). It is important to note that at least 69 percent of these dreams (types 1 and 2) portrayed acts of ongoing violence.

Examples

1. Dreams in which the dreamer is the victim of a violent act:

A dream of C.H., a 59-year-old woman: "a tiny cat bites into my index finger, I cannot get it to release itself. A large cat appears and bites the little cat, which lets go. There are clear teeth marks around my finger. I wake up wheezing."

This dream occurred while Mrs. H. was in the midst of a very bitter conflict with a younger sister. She immediately associated the vicious and tenacious little cat to this sister.

2. Dreams in which the dreamer is the perpetrator of a violent act:

A dream of D.B., a 40-year-old man: "Two boxers are slugging away . . . snarling with hatred . . . they become two beasts like jackals or dogs . . . one of the beasts is me . . . the other beast lunges out at me, ready to kill, I tear its neck and realize I have to act quickly and murderously or be brutally killed myself by this primitive, lustful animal. I try to mutilate it to be sure it is dead, but stop, not wishing to have an obsession as primitive as that of the other beast. I wake up wheezing."

This dream occurred while the patient was in the midst of a tremendous struggle with his common-law wife over the issue of her possible unfaithfulness. As in the dream he was often tempted to do her real violence in waking life.

3. Dreams containing sexual scenes:

Another dream of D.B.: "The manager of a pub throws a man out onto the street . . . he looks like he has been killed by the fall but suddenly he revives . . . then he and another naked man are violently humping each other, like two beasts or behemoths . . . I wake up wheezing."

This violent sexual dream occurred during the same period as the violent dream reported above. It clearly reflects his latently homosexual orientation which was also evident in his almost delusional jealousy.

4. Dreams containing disturbing memories:

A dream of P.C., a 40-year-old woman: "I have lost my suitcase. Then I see it . . . someone has put it on the windowsill . . . I wake up wheezing."

The scene in this dream depicts the most disturbing memory in Miss C.'s life. Some 20 years ago a particular landlady who was a mother surrogate had decided to throw Miss C. out of her house and had placed Miss C.'s suitcase and all belongings on the stoop. It is important to note that her life situation at the time of the dream paralleled the situation referred to in the dream, since she was in effect barred from returning to her own family.

It is fair to surmise on the basis of proximity alone that in each instance the impact of the traumatic event triggered the hormonal and autonomic responses that led to asthma. It is evident, however, that some other factor in addition to the psychological situation, probably a state of physiological read-iness, was necessary in order to set the asthmatic attack into motion. I say this because very often I came across a nearly identical dream in the same patient, or for that matter in an-other asthmatic patient, which does not culminate in an attack. Also, it should be noted that I have not come across any in-stances in which a bland dream culminated in an attack.

With regard to the types of situations that precede asthma attacks, data from waking life tend in a broad way to support my data from dreams. Knapp and Nemetz (1960), for example, noted that 20 to 25 percent of the attacks in their series were preceded by an "angry-excited" state, and 10 to 15 percent by an "elated-erotic" state; Leigh (1953) noted that one third of the asthma attacks in his series were preceded by a sudden emotion, usually anger or sadness. Treuting and Ripley (1948), without giving precise figures, noted the frequent presence of sudden intense emotions prior to asthma attacks. However, the emotional setting immediately prior to an asthmatic attack in dreams appears to be endowed with considerably more intensity than is the comparable setting in waking life. It is possible that dreams simply reveal more clearly the forces that are also pres-ent during the day, but which are obscured by the various complexities associated with wakefulness.

DISCUSSION

The onset situations in the three illnesses under consider-ation differ from each other in several ways. Perhaps the most obvious difference is to be found in the temporal relationship of the onset circumstances to the actual onset of illness. When illness began, the patients with rheumatoid arthritis were locked into a masochistic relationship with their key object, which had been going on for years; the patients with ulcerative colitis had freshly separated from their key object; and the patients with asthma were in the very midst of struggle with their key object. Put succinctly, the stressful circumstances at onset of the three illnesses were chronic, subacute, and acute, respectively. However, while considering this issue of the differing temporal relationship of the onset circumstances to the actual onset of illness, it is important to remember that the physiology of each disease is a crucial factor in determining its rate of development. For example, it is impossible to imagine an episode of rheumatoid arthritis developing almost instantaneously in the manner of an asthmatic attack.

Another important aspect of the differing circumstances of the three illnesses at onset relates to the identity of the key figure with whom the patient is so passionately involved: In rheumatoid arthritis the key figure is regularly a spouse, or at least a sexual partner; in ulcerative colitis the key figure is regularly a parent; and in the dreams of asthma patients the key figure is more variable, and may be a spouse, a child, a parent, or very often, a sibling. Evidently, of the three groups of patients, those with ulcerative colitis who, as noted, had just broken the symbiotic bond with their original object at the time of onset of illness were closest to the circumstances of their early childhood.

Yet another important aspect of the different circumstances during the onset period relates to the nature of the interaction between the patient and the key figure: in rheumatoid arthritis the patient had been abused repeatedly by the key figure; in ulcerative colitis the patient had separated from the key figure; and during the dreams that culminated in asthma attacks the patient was engaged in an ongoing struggle with the key figure. It seems that the rheumatoid arthritis patients, who clung to their key figure regardless of circumstances, were more passive than either the ulcerative colitis patients, who withdrew cathexis from their key figure, or the asthmatic patients, who at least in their dreams engaged in struggle with their key figure. Although the interactions between the patient and the key figure were different in each diagnostic group, all three types were characterized by the presence of rage. Thus rage appears to be the common precursor to psychosomatic disease. However, it is likely that rage, rather than constituting a unitary response, differs in subtle ways, depending upon the circumstances that have provoked it. It is easy to imagine, for example, that chronic abuse, as in the case of the rheumatoid patients, may provoke a quality of rage which is different from that provoked by one or two discrete traumatic events, such as occur in the case of the ulcerative colitis patients. In one variation the rage may be directed more at the self than at figures in the outside world. In another variation the rage may contain more oral sadistic than anal sadistic components, and so on. At the present stage of our knowledge it is difficult to make these distinctions with any degree of confidence. Nonetheless, it is important that we attempt to do so because the quality of rage may turn out to be a key factor in determining the particular pattern of physiological disruption characteristic of each syndrome.

REFERENCES

Alexander, F. (1950), *Psychosomatic Medicine*. New York: Norton.
de M'Uzan, M. (1974), Psychodynamic mechanisms in psychosomatic symptom formation. *Psychother. Psychosom.*, 23:103–110.
Dunbar, F. (1943), *Psychosomatic Diagnosis*. New York: Hoeber.
Engel, G. (1958), Studies of ulcerative colitis: Psychological aspects and their implications for treatment. *Amer. J. Dig. Dis.*, 3:315–337.
——— (1968), A life setting conducive to illness: The giving-up, given-up complex. *Ann. Intern. Med.*, 69:293–300.
French, T., & Alexander, F. (1941), Psychogenic factors in bronchial asthma. *Psychosomatic Medicine*, Monogr. IV, Part II. New York: International Universities Press.

Graie, W., & Graham, D. (1952), Relationship of specific attitudes and emotions to certain bodily diseases. *Psychosom. Med.*, 14:243–251.

Johnson, A., Shapiro, L. B., & Alexander, F. (1947), Preliminary report on a psychosomatic study of rheumatoid arthritis. *Psychosom. Med.*, 9:295–300.

Knapp, P., & Nemetz, S. (1960), Acute bronchial asthma. *Psychosom. Med.*, 22:42–56.

Kris, E. B. (1948), Bronchial asthma. *Psychiat. Quart.*, 22:257–269.

Leigh, D. (1953), Some psychiatric aspects of asthma. *The Practitioner*, 170:381–385.

Levitan, H. (1973), The etiologic significance of deafness in ulcerative colitis. *Internat. J. Psychiat. Med.*, 4:379–387.

——— (1976), Psychological factors in the etiology of ulcerative colitis: Objectlessness and rage. *Internat. J. Psychiat. Med.*, 7:221–228.

——— (1977–1978), Infantile factors in two cases of ulcerative colitis. *Internat. J. Psychiat. Med.*, 8:185–190.

——— (1981), Patterns of hostility revealed in the fantasies and dreams of women with rheumatoid arthritis. *Psychother. Psychosom.*, 35:34–43.

——— (1983), Dreams which culminate in asthma attacks. In: *Psychosomatic Medicine*, ed. C. Kimball & A. Krabowski. New York: Plenum.

Menguy, R. (1964), Physiologic, psychologic and social determinants in etiology of duodenal ulcer. *Amer. J. Dig. Dis.*, 9:199–211.

Sifneos, P. E. (1973), The prevalence of alexithymic characteristics in psychosomatic patients. *Psychother. Psychosom.*, 22:255–262.

Treuting, T., & Ripley, H. (1948), Life situations, emotions and bronchial asthma. *J. Nerv. & Ment. Dis.*, 108:380–398.

5.
Failure of the Defensive Functions of the Ego in Psychosomatic Patients

HAROLD LEVITAN, M.D.

INTRODUCTION

The ego is constantly occupied on two fronts. It must contend with threats which come at it from the outside world and with dangerous drives, affects, and memories which come at it from within the mind. In its struggle against the dangers of the outside world the ego utilizes mental operations based upon its powers of cognition and judgment. It is important to note that the mental operations directed toward the outside world are largely conscious and preconscious.

As weapons in its struggle against the dangers of the inside world, on the other hand, the ego has at its disposal a different roster of mental operations. These complex operations, which are known as the defense mechanisms of the ego, are based upon various primary process functions such as repression, projection, and displacement. In contrast to the mental operations facing the outside world, those facing the inside world are largely unconscious.

In psychotic and neurotic patients, the defense mechanisms of the ego meet halfway the threatening elements that are pressing from within. As a result of this encounter a relatively enduring mental structure, the psychiatric symptom, is created. Which symptom is created depends, of course, upon which inner elements and which defense mechanisms of the ego are involved in a given instance. For example, the creation of a compulsive neurosis depends upon the transformation of the patient's sadistic drive into its opposite by the defense mechanism known as reaction formation. Likewise, the creation of a manic psychosis depends upon the transformation of the patient's depressive affect into its opposite by the defense mechanism of denial.

What is the relationship between the elements threatening from within and the defense mechanisms of the ego in the psychosomatic patient? In this chapter I will present data indicating that the situation of these opposing structures in the psychosomatic patient is not at all similar to the situation in neurotic and psychotic patients. In the psychosomatic patient no compromise product between the ego and the inner elements is created. On the contrary, the ego of the psychosomatic patient often fails to make any contact at all with the dangerous inner elements, with the result that they go on to achieve full expression.

Investigators have been slow to consider the relationship between the ego and the threatening inner elements of the psychosomatic patient. Perhaps the main reason for this delay lies in the fact that the psychosomatic patient's symptoms are physiological rather than psychological, and as such do not contain externalized fragments of the inner world which enable us to reconstruct the process leading to symptom formation in psychotic and neurotic patients. It has been natural under these circumstances to focus attention on the attempts of the psychosomatic patient to cope with the outer world. Thus, it is not surprising to find that nearly all of the physiological mechanisms proposed to explain changes leading to psychosomatic disease have had as their basis either the "flight or fight" reaction of Cannon (1929) or the "conservation-withdrawal reaction" of Engel (1968), both of which constitute responses to external danger.

As noted, the symptoms of the psychosomatic patient are physiological and do not illuminate for us the psychological processes which have led up to them. However, it is possible to obtain some concept of the relationship between the threatening inner elements and the defense mechanisms of the ego of such patients by looking at certain aspects of their behavior and at the manifest content of their dreams.

FAILURE OF THE DEFENSIVE FUNCTIONS OF THE EGO IN THE DREAMS OF PSYCHOSOMATIC PATIENTS

Most psychosomatic patients who report a reasonably large number of dreams reveal four recurrent themes (Levitan 1980a,b, 1981a,b,c). The fact that these types of dreams are remarkably similar in one psychosomatic patient after another, irrespective of diagnosis, strongly supports the concept of a commonality of mental structure in this group of patients. The four types are as follows:

1. Dreams which contain acts of extreme cruelty. This type of dream demonstrates the psychosomatic patient's intense aggressive drive as well as the failure of his ego to neutralize it.

2. Dreams in which the persona of the dreamer himself is subjected to extreme violence. This type of dream, like the previous type, demonstrates the failure of the psychosomatic patient's ego to neutralize his intense aggressive drive; it also

demonstrates the failure of his ego to deflect the aggressive drive away from the self.

3. Dreams which contain acts of frank incest. This type of dream demonstrates the psychosomatic patient's powerful illicit sexual drive as well as his failure to control it.

4. Dreams in which a character other than the dreamer experiences affects which properly belong to the dreamer himself. This type of dream demonstrates the psychosomatic patient's powerful affects as well as the failure of his ego to truly master them. While the ego in these dreams does influence the affects, it does so merely to the extent of displacing awareness of them onto another dream character.

It is evident that the dreams in the first three categories demonstrate a total failure of the defensive functions of the ego, while the dreams in the last category demonstrate a less total failure of these functions.

Why is the ego so helpless in the dreams of psychosomatic patients? One factor relates to the strength of the drives, which are certainly very powerful in their own right. Another factor involves the absence of a proper response to the drives on the part of the ego itself, which appears to be caused by an inefficient signaling system. As will be seen when the dreams are presented, the psychosomatic patient is handicapped by a general inability to experience negative affects, the crucial signals that incite the ego to set its defensive operations into motion.

Apart from my own recent studies, literature on the dreams of psychosomatic patients is scanty. Exceptions to the general neglect of this subject are an early paper by Saul and Sheppard (1956), which demonstrates high levels of hostility in the dreams of patients with essential hypertension; a paper by Schneider (1973) dealing with an episode of coronary disease that developed immediately following a dream; and a paper by Warnes and Finkelstein (1971), which demonstrates the increased number of instances of hostility and physical injury in the dreams of psychosomatic as compared to neurotic patients.

Clinical Examples of Four
Types of Dreams

A. A dream in which a character other than the dreamer himself experiences feelings properly belonging to the dreamer (Type = Projected Affect):

(I am presenting this type of dream first because the vicissitude of affect that is its central feature often appears to play an important role in the other types of dreams as well.)

Miss S. is a 60-year-old secretary with rheumatoid arthritis. Her unawareness of her own feelings is astonishing. For example, she sought an ophthalmological consultation for the complaint of "wet eyes" without any recognition of the fact that her eyes were wet because she was crying.

In the midst of our therapy her mother died. Although she was deeply attached to her mother she was aware of few signs of sadness. The following dream illustrates the process by which she was able to avoid awareness of her grief:

"We were all at mother's funeral. . . . Suddenly my brother Jack burst into tears . . . I never saw anybody cry so hard . . . I felt very sorry for him. . . ."

Although she had noted during the dream how sorry she felt for her brother whose suffering was intense, it is clear that her grief on behalf of him was easier to bear than would have been her own grief at first hand.

On awakening from this dream her pillow was wet. This dream sequence serves to emphasize how wide may be the split between the mental and physiological components of emotion: while she was an observer in the process of watching someone else cry, her own body was actively shedding tears.

It is evident that the dream ego in this type of dream possesses a paucity of defensive resources. A dream ego equipped with a more powerful range of defenses might have been able to prevent the affect of grief from appearing in the dream at all. The projection of the experiential aspect of the grief reaction onto another dream character seems to represent a last

ditch effort, which accomplishes the warding off of an awareness of the affect only after it has already undergone considerable development. The fact that the dreamer continues to cry
during the dream is a clear indication that the only aspect of
the affect complex that has been altered by his defensive operations is his awareness of it.

The affect in this type of dream is without doubt especially
intense because it is unmonitored. Also, awareness of a traumatic affect such as grief usually causes the dreamer to awaken.
However, in these instances, because the dreamer himself is not
experiencing the affect he fails to awaken from the episode,
which continues for an unduly long period of time.

Furthermore, this type of dream has significance with regard to the general theory of affects. Freud and most workers
after him have held the opinion that there are no unconscious
affects in the sense in which there are unconscious ideas; while
an idea consists of cathexes of memory traces, an affect corresponds to a process of discharge which, if it is unconscious,
exists only as a potential disposition rather than as an entity
with concrete properties. In fact, this very difficulty in conceptualizing the existence of unconscious affect has constituted one
of the major stumbling blocks in the development of our understanding of psychosomatic mechanisms. The configuration
in this type of dream demonstrates at least one way in which
affect can flourish in a fully developed form and yet remain
outside of consciousness.

B. A dream which contains an act of extreme cruelty (Type
= Dreamer as Aggressor):

Mrs. B., a married woman with ulcerative colitis, had the
following dream while she was contemplating a divorce in order
to take up a liaison with another man. The dream relates to the
circumstance that recently she had had an inkling that she might
be pregnant.

"I have three little children . . . (in fact she is childless)
. . . they are standing in the way of something important
. . . I decide to kill them . . . I tore the first one apart. . . . My

husband was horrified. . . . I decided to continue and I tear the other two children apart as well. . . ."

I want to draw attention to the fact that in this dream it is the husband, rather than the dreamer herself, who feels the horror because of her acts. The avoidance of awareness of the affect of horror by means of projection of it onto another dream character is regularly encountered in dreams of psychosomatic patients in which the dreamer commits acts of extreme cruelty. In these situations in which the dreamer is not aware of the affect of horror, his superego remains dormant and he is left free to continue on his tremendously sadistic course.

C. A dream which contains an act of frank incest (Type = Incestuous):

Mr. C., a middle-aged executive with asthma, reported the following dream shortly after noticing the onset of his daughter's pubescence:

"I am with my daughter . . . she wants to have sex . . . we walk around the block trying to find a secluded place . . . everywhere is too public . . . finally we hide in a clump of bushes . . . and have sexual intercourse there. . . ."

It is interesting to note that at least initially he attributed the sexual impulse to his daughter. Also, throughout the dream he experienced no compunction. This type of dream, like the previous type, demonstrates the fact that while the dreamer is not aware of negative affects the superego remains dormant and the dreamer is left free to pursue his illicit aims.

D. A dream in which the persona of the dreamer himself is subjected to extreme violence (Type = Dreamer as Victim):

The following dream was reported to Schneider (1973) by a patient with coronary heart disorder who had had news of a severe setback in his financial affairs on the previous day. A massive heart attack occurred a few minutes after the patient awakened from the following dream:

"I am a great violinist . . . I come out on the stage to tremendous applause . . . I bow . . . I turn to my violin case . . . I take out not a violin but a machine gun, and swiftly I put the muzzle to my mouth and rat-a-tat-tat, I blow my brains out . . . I fall to the ground."

The positive tone that exists in the first part of the dream prior to the outbreak of violence is a crucial feature. This positive tone masked awareness of the developing onslaught to such a degree that the dreamer had no opportunity to modify the onslaught, or failing that, to awaken prior to the denouement. I want to stress that in a large percentage of dreams in this category the traumatic events pass beyond the point of threat to the point of consummation.

Dreams of this type are very common in psychosomatic patients. Indeed, they may occur several times during the same night. It is interesting to note they are at variance with Freud's clinical experience. He states that "the unconscious seems to contain nothing that could give any content to our concepts of the annihilation of life" . . . as opposed, for example, to "castration," which "can be pictured on the basis of the daily experience of the faeces being separated from the body or on the basis of losing the mother's breast at weaning . . . but nothing resembling death can ever have been experienced; or if it has, as in fainting, it has left no observable traces behind" (Freud, 1926, pp. 129–130). It is likely that Freud (and the other early analysts) never encountered such traumatic dreams because the psychosomatic syndromes had not yet come under scrutiny during their working lifetimes.

Table 1 presents the percent frequency of the four types of dreams, taken from nine of the author's psychosomatic patients who reported the largest number of dreams.

It is evident that the total percentage of the four types of dreams was fairly high, ranging from 19 to 68 percent.

INTENSITY AND DIRECTION OF AGGRESSION IN DREAMS OF PSYCHOSOMATIC PATIENTS

Method: In this study (Levitan, 1982a), a total of 300 dreams reported by each of the three matched groups (three female

Table 1
Frequency of Four Types of Dreams
in Psychosomatic Patients

Patient	Diagnosis	No. Dreams Reported (N)	Dreamer as Aggressor (%)	Dreamer as Victim (%)	Dreams of Incest (%)	Dreams of Projected Grief (%)	Four Dream Types Total (%)
A	Rheumatoid arthritis	405	9	13	1	1	24.0
B	Hypertension	68	12	5	20	1.5	38.5
C	Regional ileitis	198	40	25	4	1	70.0
D	Ulcerative colitis	121	19	26	1	1	47.0
E	Asthma	160	4	11	2	2	19.0
F	Hypertension	91	21	28	4	2	55.0
G	Urticaria	108	50	15	0	3	68.0
H	Asthma	360	9	10	0.5	0.5	20.0
I	Rheumatoid arthritis	172	13	11	0	0	24.0

patients with asthma, rheumatoid arthritis, and psychoneurosis, respectively) were compared along several parameters related to the issue of management of aggression. The psychoneurotic patients were used as controls for the two groups of psychosomatic patients. Table 2 presents the results when a binomial test of proportion was applied to the data.

Comment: As demonstrated in Table 2, significant differences at the .05 level were found as follows:

1. The *asthmatic* group reported a significantly greater number of dreams containing the presence of *physical threat to the self* as against the number of such dreams reported by the psychoneurotic group.

This finding indicates that the defense mechanisms of the asthmatic patients are less successful than those of the neurotic patients with respect to the control of expression of aggression toward the self. Here we are assuming that in creating those dreams that are scored positively for the presence of physical

Table 2
Types of Agrression in Dreams
of Psychosomatic
vs. Psychoneurotic Patients

Type of Dream Event (in Order of Intensity)	Asthma	Level of Significance Psychoneurosis	Arthritis
A. Ego as Victim			
Consummated physical attack	n.s.	n.s.	n.s.
Physical threat	.05	n.s.	n.s.
Verbal threat	n.s.	n.s.	n.s.
Feeling of being threatened	n.s.	.05	n.s.
B. Ego as Aggressor			
Consummated physical attack	n.s.	n.s.	n.s.
Physical threat	n.s.	n.s.	n.s.
Verbal threat	n.s.	n.s.	n.s.

threat to the self, the dreamers are at some level choosing to represent themselves as victims.

2. The *psychoneurotic* group reported a significantly greater number of dreams containing scenes in which the dreamer is experiencing the *feeling of being threatened* as against the number of such dreams reported by the asthmatic group.

This finding appears to be a corollary of the finding reported above, which indicated that the defensive mechanisms of the asthmatic patients are less effective than the defensive mechanisms of the neurotic patients in controlling the expression of aggression against the self. Here we see that, instead of visualizing themselves face-to-face with a threat as the asthmatic patients tend to do, the neurotic patients apparently feel that they are being threatened. It is important to remember that even in a dream there is a great difference between the experience of being attacked and entertaining the idea that "someone is after me." This finding reflects the greater ability of the neurotic patients as compared to the asthmatic patients to anticipate danger.

The overall results of this controlled study support the clinical impression that the defenses against the expression of aggression in psychosomatic patients are markedly less effective than in psychoneurotic patients.

THE FAILURE OF THE DEFENSE MECHANISMS OF THE EGO IN DREAMS OF PATIENTS WITH THE ANOREXIA-BULIMIA NERVOSA SYNDROME

Although the anorexia-bulimia nervosa syndrome is not one of the classical psychosomatic syndromes, psychosomatic factors clearly play an important role in its development and maintenance.

A study (Levitan, 1981a) of the repetitive dreams of six patients with this syndrome revealed a pattern of failure of the defensive mechanisms of the ego during dreaming, which was very similar to that described for the classical psychosomatic patients. Table 3 gives the rate of occurrence of each type of dream.

Table 3
Frequency of Three Types of Dreams in Patients with Anorexia-Bulimia
Nervosa Syndrome

Patient	No. Dreams Reported (N)	Dreamer as Aggressor (%)	Dreamer as Victim (%)	Dreams of Incest (%)
A	99	27	17	8
B	91	28	23	8
C	32	10	3	7
D	89	6	18	1
E	72	8	18	2
F	3	0	66	0

It seems possible that the reliance of bulimic patients on the pleasure produced by eating represents an accessory defensive process, which is made necessary by the total failure of the usual intrapsychic defenses. This hypothesis is supported by the observation that very often the patients commenced binging immediately after awakening from an upsetting dream.

FAILURE OF THE DEFENSIVE MECHANISMS
OF THE EGO IN DREAMS THAT CULMINATE
IN PSYCHOSOMATIC SYMPTOMS

The data presented have raised the possibility that the failure of the defensive functions of the ego in dreams constitutes an essential early step leading to physiological dysfunction. It was easy to imagine the following sequence: repetitive failure of the defensive functions of the ego in the dreams permits the repetitive occurrence of traumatic events; the traumatic events in turn produce an abnormally intense physiological response; the abnormally intense physiological response in turn interferes with the regular functioning of the internal organs.

It is fair to assume, I believe, that a dream immediately preceding a symptom has contributed to the production of that symptom. In the study reported below (Levitan, 1983a), I examined the dream-symptom sequence in asthma patients in order to determine the types of dreams that appear to play this role.

DREAMS CULMINATING IN ASTHMA ATTACKS

Forty-five pre-asthmatic dreams drawn from 11 patients were available for examination. The group was comprised of seven patients recorded in the literature (Dunbar, 1938; French and Alexander, 1941; Kris, 1948), and four of my own patients.

Despite the problems of overlap it was possible to divide the 45 dreams culminating in asthma attacks into four types: (1) dreams in which the dreamer is the victim of a violent act (19, or 42 percent); (2) dreams in which the dreamer is the perpetrator of a violent act (12, or 27 percent); (3) dreams in which the dreamer is involved in a sexual act (7, or 16 percent); and (4) dreams which contain disturbing memories (7, or 16 percent).

It was evident immediately that except for the fourth category in each set the dreams preceding asthma attacks fell into the same categories as those I had found regularly in other psychosomatic patients. This overall congruence provides support for the idea that traumatic events in dreams contribute to stress leading to symptom formation in other nonepisodic psychosomatic syndromes.

Clinical Examples

A. A dream of a 40-year-old woman in which the dreamer is the victim of a violent act:

"A dog and a fox are fighting . . . the fox was too slow and was about to be killed . . . it was torn up. I wake up wheezing."

This dream occurred while the patient was in the midst of a struggle to the death with her husband. She immediately recognized herself as the fox who was getting the worst of the battle. At the time of this dream she was actually taking steps to buy a shotgun to kill her husband, her children, and herself.

B. A dream of a 41-year-old woman in which the dreamer is the perpetrator of a violent act:

"My son and I are in a struggle . . . I try to cloak the violence of the struggle by pretending that it's all in fun . . . then the floor is littered with blood . . . most revolting of all, I see the torn bloody shreds of a kitten . . . especially its head . . . I wake up wheezing."

This dream as well as her other 15 violent dreams reflected Mrs. A.'s intense ambivalence toward her young son whom she immediately recognized as the kitten. It is interesting to note that her presenting symptoms were an intense overreaction to stories involving cruelty to children and a compulsion to lock her pet cats in the furnace.

C. A dream of a 33-year-old man containing an incestuous homosexual act:

"I am taking a penis in my mouth . . . I think it is my father's. I wake up wheezing."

This homosexual dream reflects the patient's negative Oedipus complex, which was also evident in other aspects of his life. His prolific dream material was of further interest because he had numerous heterosexual dreams that were also incestuous but which did not provoke asthma attacks.

D. A dream of a 60-year-old woman which contained a disturbing memory:

". . . a body of a young soldier lying on the battlefield . . . riddled with wounds . . . I wake up wheezing."

The scene in this dream depicts her vision of her sweetheart's death on the battlefield which occurred some 40 years ago. She had five other asthma-provoking dreams which contained memories of events surrounding his death. Despite the passage of time his death still moved her to a point at which she cried each time we discussed it.

Comment: An outstanding feature of these dreams culminating in asthma attacks is the extreme situations that they contained. Thus, in the dreams of category A the dreamer's body was usually damaged rather than merely threatened. In the dreams of category B the angry acts ended in murder. In the dreams of category C the sexual acts were incestuous or at least perverse rather than legitimate, and in the dreams of category D, not just any memory but the patient's worst memories were revived. The presence of these extreme situations in the dreams reflects the failure of the defensive processes, including the process of awakening, which are usually available to the ego during dreams.

In considering the issue of the traumatic dream as a possible point of inception of psychosomatic disorders, as the patient's Achilles' heel so to speak, three points are especially relevant. First, the autonomic and hormonal systems are more labile and therefore more susceptible to stimulation during dreams than during waking life. Second, the events in dreams of this type are vastly more traumatic than any event that could possibly occur in waking life. Third, the traumatic dreams tend to be repetitive, unlike traumatic events in waking life. In some cases, for example, a psychosomatic patient may undergo the experience of being killed in several dreams during the same night.

FAILURE OF THE DEFENSIVE MECHANISMS OF THE EGO IN THE WAKING LIFE OF PSYCHOSOMATIC PATIENTS

Failure of the defensive mechanisms of the ego occurs less frequently in the waking life of psychosomatic patients than in their dreams. As a group, psychosomatic patients are extremely well adapted to the outside world. Their "supernormality," as their excellent adaptation is sometimes called, is probably the consequence of a characteristic mental style (dubbed '*la pensée opératoire*' by Marty and de M'Uzan, 1963) which leads them to focus on outside reality at the expense of fantasy and symbolic thinking. Nonetheless, the failure to control their impulses, which occurs so often in their dreams, occurs from time to time in their waking life as well. I demonstrate this point in the two studies that follow.

Explicit Incestuous Motifs in Psychosomatic Patients

Over the years I had been impressed by the large numbers of psychosomatic patients who reported incestuous dreams, fantasies, and/or behavior. In order to put my clinical impression on a firmer basis I decided to conduct a survey of the charts of my own patients with this issue in mind (Levitan, 1982).

Method: I reviewed the notes I had made on all psychosomatic patients (n = 62) seen by me in at least 40 interviews between 1975 and 1980. In order to establish a control group I also reviewed the notes I had made on all nonpsychosomatic patients (n = 48) seen by me in at least 40 interviews between 1970 and 1975. This group consisted largely of patients with neuroses and character disorders.

Results: I found that 31 percent of the psychosomatic patients as against 10.4 percent of the nonpsychosomatic patients had reported explicit incestuous motifs. This difference was significant at the .02 level. Also, the incestuous motifs reported by the psychosomatic patients were much more intense and pervasive than those reported by the nonpsychosomatic patients.

Some Typical Case Reports of
Psychosomatic Patients Who
Reported Incestuous Motifs

I. Mr. A., age 38, is a stand-up comic with regional ileitis.

He seems to be almost totally incapable of experiencing negative affect. His very funny jokes consist largely of transformations into their opposite of his own traumatic experiences. He reported many sexual dreams in which his wife was suddenly revealed as his sister. Also, after the birth of his daughter he dreamed repeatedly of having a sexual relationship with a teen-age girl who turned out to be his daughter. During waking life he wonders if he will be able to restrain himself when she becomes older. He wonders how other fathers deal with this situation.

II. Mr. B., age 35, is a successful executive with essential hypertension. He reported many dreams in which he is masturbating his young son. Furthermore, in waking life, after having taken a few drinks, he fondles his son's genitals. While carrying out this incestuous homosexual act he experiences feelings of deep affection for his son. Though he knows his behavior runs counter to accepted morality and is not in the best interests of his son, he seems unable to restrain himself when his controls are the least bit lessened.

III. Mr. C., age 40, is a college professor with essential hypertension. He experiences an immense sexual attraction to his four daughters who range in age from 9 to 21. He is constantly making passes at them. In nearly all his dreams he is depicted in a sexual relationship with one or another of them. Like the previous patient he is aware that his behavior runs counter to accepted morality and is not in the best interests of his children. He rationalizes his desires with the claim that if the act of love is carried out in a tender fashion it is not harmful to the other party, even if the other party is one's own child. It is interesting to note that as a teen-ager he had invited his mother to make love with him.

IV. Mrs. D., age 38, is a schoolteacher with rheumatoid arthritis, who was forced by her family to leave her native country when her long-standing love affair with her brother-in-law was discovered. The brother-in-law was clearly a substitute for her father who had died just before the affair began. She reported numerous dreams in which she was having intercourse with her father.

Comment: To the best of my knowledge an association between incest and the psychosomatic diseases had not been recognized as a phenomenon in its own right prior to this study. However, in a random search through the psychosomatic literature I had turned up several case histories containing explicit incestuous motifs (see Saul, 1939; French and Alexander, 1941; Schur, 1955).

SUICIDAL TRENDS IN ASTHMATIC AND HYPERTENSIVE PATIENTS

As was the case with the incestuous trends, I had been struck by the large percentage of my psychosomatic patients who reported suicidal trends. Once again I conducted a chart study (Levitan, 1983b) to test my clinical impression.

Method: Charts of patients who had been hospitalized with bronchial asthma, essential hypertension, chronic obstructive pulmonary disease (COPD), and cholelithiasis were searched for evidence that the patient had made a suicidal attempt or had entertained suicidal ideation. The patients with COPD and cholelithiasis, which are presumably not psychosomatic diseases, were intended as controls for the patients with asthma and hypertension, respectively. The results are presented in Table 4.

In a further step, the patients were sorted by the time the suicidal trend first appeared. This was an attempt to control for the possible effects of diagnosis and treatment of the illness on the production of the suicidal trend.

Table 5 indicates the number of patients in whom the sui-

Table 4
Suicidal Trends in
Asthmatic and Hypertensive Patients

Diagnosis	Total no. of pts.	No. of pts. with suicidal trend	Significance p value
Asthma	100	12	
COPD	75	1	< .01
Hypertension	200	9	
Cholelithiasis	200	3	< .02
Asthma & hypertension	300	21	< .005
COPD & cholelithiasis	275	4	< .005

Table 5
Timing of Appearance of Suicidal Trend

Diagnosis	Suicidal trend before diagnosis of illness (N)	Suicidal trend after diagnosis of illness (N)
Asthma	3	9
COPD	0	1
Hypertension	4	5
Cholelithiasis	0	3

cidal trend appeared prior to the time the particular diagnosis had been made versus after the diagnosis had been made.

The suicidal trends in the asthma patients appeared three times as often after the diagnosis had been made than before it had been made. This finding probably reflects the fact that a great many of the cases of asthma had begun in early childhood. Unfortunately, however, the charts of the nine cases in which the asthma preceded the appearance of the suicidal trend did not contain information as to the exact time of onset of the asthma. It might be argued on the basis of this finding that the occurrence of suicidal trends in these asthma patients was heavily influenced either by the presence of the disease itself or by the effects of the drugs used to treat the disease. However, the low incidence of suicidal trends in the patients with COPD, who, like the patients with asthma, were suffering from a serious lung disease, weakens to some degree the argument regarding the possible effect of the presence of the disease. As regards the possible effect of the drugs used to treat asthma, it should be noted that none of them is known to enhance depressive and/or suicidal trends.

The rate of appearance of suicidal trends in the hypertensive patients was more or less the same before and after the diagnosis had been made. It is important to note that none of the five hypertensive patients who demonstrated a suicidal trend after the diagnosis had been made had been treated with amine-depleting drugs such as reserpine, which are known to enhance depressive and/or suicidal trends.

Comment: It is important to note that the findings of this study support those of Dorpat, Anderson, and Ripley (1968). These investigators found that a startlingly high percentage of persons who successfully committed suicide as well as of those who merely attempted suicide were suffering from one or more of the classical psychosomatic diseases at the time they undertook the act. The congruence between their findings and mine is especially meaningful since they started out from a point of view precisely the opposite of my own.

Interestingly, to return to dreams for a moment, I found in a general survey of the dreams of psychosomatic patients several examples of dreams, some of them repetitive, which depicted an ongoing act of suicide that was ultimately consummated within the dream. It is probably significant that though I have studied the dreams of many suicidal patients, I have never encountered this phenomenon in suicidal patients who were not also psychosomatic patients.

DISCUSSION

It is evident from the data I have presented that the defensive mechanisms of the ego of the psychosomatic patient often fail to control the threatening elements of his internal world. During waking life this failure of defense may result in pathological forms of behavior such as incest or suicide; during the night it may result in a traumatic dream which trips off a physiological symptom such as asthma. It is likely that the failure of the defensive mechanisms of the ego plays a role in the tripping off of physiological symptoms in waking life as well. However, because of the way in which information on such matters becomes available to us during waking life, it is very difficult to demonstrate this sequence with any precision.

As noted earlier, it is likely that failure of the defensive mechanisms of the ego in psychosomatic patients is based upon an inefficient signaling system, which is in turn based upon an inability to fully perceive negative affect. The inability to fully perceive negative affect has been dubbed "alexithymia" (Sifneos, 1973). Patients who are without full awareness of their affects as they are unfolding can be compared to persons without awareness of pain who are injured, because they do not receive warning of ongoing trauma.

It is important to note that the failure of the signaling functions in psychosomatic patients causes more disruption within the system of unconscious defense mechanisms, which are charged with controlling the threatening elements of the internal world, than it does within the system of conscious adaptive mechanisms, which are charged with maintaining an adjustment to the outside world. It is probable that the intense focus on the outside world, which is a key feature of the psychosomatic patient's 'opératoire' style of mental functioning, is a means of compensating for the feebleness of the guidance systems that are based on affect.

Finally, I want to stress once more the great vulnerability of the psychosomatic patient. According to the conception of symptom formation that I have presented here, the failure of the psychosomatic patient's defensive mechanisms does not constitute an occasional factor. Rather it is, along with a particular somatic proclivity, a defining factor. Indeed, it can be stated that psychosomatic patients have physiological rather than psychological symptoms precisely because their defensive mechanisms are unable to contend with threatening internal elements.

REFERENCES

Cannon, W. (1929), *Bodily Changes in Pain, Hunger, Fear and Rage*. New York: Appleton-Century-Crofts.

Dorpat, T., Anderson, W., & Ripley, H. (1968), The relationship of physical illness to suicide. In: *Suicidal Behaviors: Diagnosis and Management*, ed. H. Resnik. Boston: Little, Brown.

Dunbar, F. (1938), Psychoanalytic notes relating to syndromes of asthma and hay fever. *Psychoanal. Quart.*, 7:25–68.

Engel, G. (1968), A lifesetting conductive to illness: The giving-up–given-up complex. *Ann. Intern. Med.*, 69:293–300.

French, T., & Alexander, F. (1941), Psychogenic factors in bronchial asthma. *Psychosomatic Medicine*, Monogr. IV, Part II, New York: International Universities Press.

Freud, S. (1926), Inhibitions, Symptoms, and Anxiety. *Standard Edition*, 20. London: Hogarth Press, 1956.

Kris, E. B. (1948), Bronchial asthma. *Psychiat. Quart.*, 22:257–269.

Levitan, H. (1980a), Dreams of psychosomatic patients. In: *The Dream in Clinical Practice*, ed. J. Natterson. New York: Aronson.

——— (1980b), Dreams in traumatic states. In: *The Dream in Clinical Practice*, ed. J. Natterson. New York: Aronson.

——— (1981a), The implications of certain dreams reported by patients with the anorexia-bulimia nervosa syndrome. *Can. J. Psychiat.*, 30:137–149.

——— (1981b), Patterns of hostility revealed in the fantasies and dreams of women with rheumatoid arthritis. *Psychother. Psychosom.*, 34–43.

——— (1981c), Failure of the defensive functions of the ego in dreams of psychosomatic patients. *Psychother. Psychosom.*, 36:1–7.

——— (1982), Explicit incestuous motifs in psychosomatic patients. *Psychother. Psychosom.*, 37:22–25.

——— (1983a), Dreams which precipitate asthma attacks. In: *Psychosomatic Medicine*, ed. C. Kimball & A. Krakowski. New York: Plenum.

—— (1983b), Suicidal trends in patients with asthma and hypertension. *Psychother. Psychosom.*, 39:165–170.

—— (1984), Vicissitudes of the suicidal impulses in dreams. *Suicide and Life-Threatening Behavior*, 14:201–206.

—— (1985), Intensity and direction of aggression in dreams of psychosomatic patients. (Manuscript.)

Marty, P., & de M'Uzan, M. (1963), *L'Investigation Psychosomatique*. Paris: Presses Universitaires de France.

Saul, L. (1939), Hostility in cases of essential hypertension. *Psychosom. Med.*, 1:153–161.

—— Sheppard, E. (1956), An attempt to quantify emotional forces using manifest dreams: A preliminary study. *J. Amer. Psychoanal. Assn.*, 4:486.

Schneider, D. (1973), Conversion of massive anxiety into heart attack. *Amer. J. Psychother.*, 360:360–378.

Schur, M. (1955), Comments on the metapsychology of somatization. *The Psychoanalytic Study of the Child*, 10:119–164. New York: International Universities Press.

Sifneos, P. E. (1973), The prevalence of alexithymic characteristics in psychosomatic patients. *Psychother. Psychosom.*, 22:255–262.

Warnes, H., & Finkelstein, A. (1971), Dreams that precede a psychosomatic illness. *Can. Psychiat. Assn. J.*, 16:317–325.

6.

Current Concepts of Character Disturbance

PIERRE MARTY, M.D., and
ROSINE DEBRAY, PH.D.

The title of this chapter reflects both the area of our major interest and the central psychological problem in somatic illness. Indeed, it appears that most somatizations occur in subjects in whom psychological disturbances in the nature or intensity of character traits are in the foreground and are often much more prominent than neurotic or psychotic problems.

This does not mean, however, that neurotic or psychotic subjects are thereby protected from all somatic ailments—this simplification is contradicted daily in clinical practice—but that the amount and frequency of somatizations are greater in subjects with few or primitive solid defense mechanisms and who show "signs" and behavior involving character traits.

It is still debatable whether this situation applies to temporary disorganizations of mental functioning or to more enduring weaknesses linked to insufficient or incomplete development of the mental apparatus. This issue is discussed by various authors elsewhere in this work (see chapters by Weiner and Fawzy, and Levitan, in this volume). The subject is a complex one and we propose to explain our position by presenting four aspects of our thinking.

ASPECT 1

The use of the word "psychosomatic" to distinguish certain patients or certain diseases is reductionist, without the conditions of the reduction being defined. It limits the goal of the science that psychosomatic medicine can become.

OUR PRESENT POSITION

1. We use the word "psychosomatic" to designate an individual presenting any bodily alteration, whether it be lesional or functional. Likewise, any bodily illness, whatever its nature, is designated by us as "somatic." We therefore abandon all classification that applies to nosological entities such as somatic or psychosomatic, as well as to individuals called "psychosomatic" in contrast to others who are not.

2. In our Hôpital de la Poterne des Peupliers[1] psychoanalysts and medical doctors with different specialties or trained in psychology conduct investigations and apply psychotherapy to almost all somatic illnesses regardless of the nature of the complaint. Exceptions are made only for acute cases where medical or surgical urgency is in the foreground, for example, accidents and acute toxic or infectious states.

It goes without saying that treatment like this, whose psychotherapeutic character is obvious from the first evaluation, rests on the thesis that supporting the mental functions must improve the general psychosomatic economy of the patient, and thus, his somatic condition. (We will defend the theoretical validity of this statement in the fourth aspect of this chapter.)

3. Our guiding frame of thought is Freudian. Although we do not use classical psychiatric, psychoanalytic, or medical no-

---

[1]The Hôpital de la Poterne des Peupliers (H.P.P.) is a day hospital. It receives adult and child patients with somatic complaints. The pediatric ward is directed by Dr. Leon Kreisler. The H.P.P. operates under the auspices of the Psychosomatic Institute (I.P.S.O.). It is located at 1 rue de la Poterne des Peupliers, 75013 Paris, France.

sological classifications as an exclusive base of our thinking about each patient, we do use them if they seem helpful and likely to clarify our diagnostic and prognostic evaluation.

4. We reserve the use of the word "psychosomatic" to designate the topographical, dynamic, and economic relationships established between the psychic and somatic phenomena observed in our subjects. It is in this sense only that a so-called psychosomatic nosology can be considered.

DISCUSSION

We find the use of the words "somatic" and "psychosomatic," as just defined, simple and not likely to limit new concepts that might appear in the future. The choice of our theoretical base, strictly Freudian, i.e., classical psychoanalytic, may be subject for discussion. A psychiatric or medical base might seem more propitious to some people. We, however, think Freudian theory offers the best known instrument to evaluate mental processes from a triple point of view—topographical, dynamic, and economic. It is also the richest and most solidly supported. Moreover, the psychoanalytic model is a methodology centered on the analytic study of man with a broad perspective that includes a multitude of factors and, more than any other, lends itself to the study of psychic and somatic phenomena as well as to their evolution in time.

ASPECT 2

A precise research orientation, isolated from clinical practice, limits the objectives of research and reduces the prospect of fundamental clinical and theoretical discoveries.

OUR PRESENT POSITION

1. Our diagnostic evaluation of the characteristics of the ill subject's psychosomatic economy is inseparable from our psy-

chotherapeutic activity; the latter aids the former, and vice versa. The psychotherapeutic commitments are generally of long duration with seriously ill somatic patients.

2. For each individual the basic goal of the first clinical evaluation is to determine the form of the initial psychotherapeutic approach. We must, therefore, evaluate the presenting state of the patient, his recent state, and his usual former state, especially if it is obviously different from his present one. The data of the anamnesis are thus compiled with this goal in mind. We also try to get a view, necessarily approximate, of the patient's heredity, major developmental milestones, and sociocultural dimensions.

DISCUSSION

It is through the transference that forms between the subject and the investigator during the first session that the characteristic elements of the subject's present psychosomatic economy progressively appear. It is these that will permit the determination of the initial form of psychotherapy. The transference and countertransference "reactions" of the patient and therapist are identified from the outset. How they evolve during the first session, as well as during the subsequent therapy, will lead to confirmation or modification of the initial evaluation. This is our basic methodological approach. It aims at using the evolution of the therapeutic treatment to validate or invalidate "a posteriori" the diagnostic and nosological evaluations of the first investigation.

Tests, up to this point, are used more to confirm theoretical advances than as a means of research in and of itself. For example, it is our experience that the idea of a "common psychological profile" for a population of 21 insulin-dependent diabetics is inadequate to account for the variety of mental organizations in question. The patients vary greatly, and their individual characteristics of mental organization determine qualities of the treatment that each diabetic will be able to assume for himself. These considerations can lead to considerable differences in the evolution of the illness, which only superficially appears identical for everyone. In this research, aside from the usual clinical evaluation, we used the Thematic Apperception Test (T.A.T.) (in English in original), the "Figure Complexe de Rey" (in French), and the Draw-a-Person test. Practitioners who know and use projective techniques will be interested to learn that the data furnished by the T.A.T. and the drawing tests turned out to be in complete agreement in evaluating each subject's economic psychosomatic characteristics. The two types of approach validated each other here (Debray, 1983).

Although we make little use of tests in our own research, we pay close attention to research that does; we look to it for verification of our ideas. Tests, however, often tend to limit research (since findings are only obtained in the specific areas explored) and slow it down if one spends a long time verifying partial and premature hypotheses. Therefore, we agree on this point with the authors of the preceding chapter. They have formulated the same kind of criticism.[2] Furthermore, formulations of fundamental hypotheses, and their testing by objective methods, represent different motivations and aptitudes in researchers.

In clinical investigations, the comparison between the presenting state (at the time the illness is triggered) and the usual state (which reflects the subject's stable character structure) leads to a dynamic and economic evaluation of areas where the illness has infiltrated. Likewise, interview data from the course of the therapy are compared with data drawn at the early stages of the evaluation. Information comes out progressively during the interviews in a more distant, vague and possibly erroneous way, about memories, family history and the subject's development. These data, offered spontaneously or in response to the therapist's questions during the investigation, are compared with data from the initial evaluation on presenting, recent, and usual states, as well as with the patient's immediate relationships

[2]See chapter on alexithymia, pp. 189–237.

(including the transference). This process extends in time the dynamic and economic perspective on patients' illness.

It is also necessary to consider sociocultural dimensions during the investigation. They appear in a relatively objective way through the subject's appearance, style and, especially, language, but also in terms of countertransference, i.e., how they evoke the investigator's interest in the patient's cathexes and countercathexes (with their respective topographical, dynamic, and economic weights). However, because of our present limited means, our own studies lack a general evaluation of finer sociocultural dimensions of psychosomatic medicine. This seems all the more regretable to us, since the evolution of Western society cannot help but influence the evolution of individual structures. Societal currents seem to explain both the striking reduction of neurotic organizations according to classical Freudian descriptions and the proportional increase of so-called character disorders with poor organization of personality structure and, in particular, a weakly functioning preconscious system. This last characteristic is especially well known for accompanying somatic illnesses.

More precise knowledge of patients during psychotherapy facilitates control of the initial evaluation. It especially helps to sharpen our grasp of the elements of psychosomatic interactions when clinical signs that went unnoticed during the evaluation are accentuated during treatment. The quality of investigations as well as the therapy that follows thus progressively improve.

Aspect 3

It is necessary to modify one's position and to make ongoing transitions from clinical observation to theory.

Our Present Position

We use clinical work to establish, with each patient, the broadest possible theoretical point of view. Although our approach is based on the Freudian model, we do feel free to modify our initial points of view (even the broadest) if observation seems to diminish their value or to contradict them. In this way, we have modified our early basic positions several times over the course of our work.

Those points of view that have undergone most modification mainly concern the vicissitudes of character development; and psychosomatic character structures (i.e., the usual adult organizations), their peculiarities, and the responses of the character to the appearance and course of illness. Indeed, we find it important to appreciate the patient's evolution from a precise reference point (the appearance of a somatic illness can be one), so as not to remain fixed in a static perspective reflecting an overly structured conception of the organization of human beings.

An evolutionary and genetic approach leads us to search the individual's past, from the most recent events to the most distant ones, and further back to his heredity, the genetic material of the individual's construction. It is upon this construction and through the intermediary of various anatomic psychosomatic interconnections that external events trigger or maintain illness.

A relationship (more or less difficult to prove) always exists among the following:

1. the quality of materials that have been used in the individual's construction (intervening here are details of the genetic code, the "first mosaic" presented by the newborn (Marty, 1980);

2. early mother/infant interactions, data from the environment, early childhood events, etc. (Braunshweig and Fain, 1975);

3. the traumatic quality of the events that triggered or are maintaining the illness. The notion of a "crisis" as a weakening factor at certain moments of the subject's life can intervene here (Debray, 1983); and

4. the quality of the illness. (Specifying why a specific illness appears at one moment or another still remains unresolved.)

The individual's development corresponds to a progressive "psychosomatic" structuring whose analysis allows us to consider its two main axes. These rest inevitably on the dualist psyche-soma conception, which is anchored in the history, vocabulary and way of thinking of Western civilization, and entails the following:

1. The development of the *somatic* structure, which unfolds according to a phylogenetic program altered by heredity, intrauterine life, birth, and the evolution of early childhood. For most individuals this changes less and less as life moves on, except for unexpected and unpredictable accidents.

2. The development of the *mental* structure, which also evolves according to a phylogenetic and sociocultural program (to which primitive fantasies contribute), and by way of a much more individual program related to the constituent and relational characteristics of the mother.[3] The determinant role that the mother's mental organization plays and the variations of her psychosomatic economy (according to the events of her own life), particularly during the first two years of the child's life, appears indisputable in the light of recent data, i.e., joint psychotherapeutic treatment of the mother/baby dyad in which infants with early psychosomatic troubles were treated at the Hôpital de la Poterne des Peupliers (Kreisler, 1981). Beyond the first years, the mental structuring is pursued according to an immediate familial program and, secondarily, a social program.

The relational events between the child, his mother, and successive social influences participate intensively in the psychosomatic structuring. The construction of the mental apparatus, and in particular the preconscious with its superimposed layers of representation and various interconnecting systems (Marty, 1980) is supported largely by somatic development and

[3]At best, the mental structure evolves until "the oedipal organization of the genital phase" (Luquet-Parat, 1967).

particularly by the sensory and motor acquisitions of the first two years of life.

3. The development of the *adult* structure, which does not really earn this name until the time (varying with the individual) when progressively acquired positions no longer show themselves to be modifiable. Little by little, during the time necessary for structure formation—which is made up of successive hierarchies of various psychosomatic functions—the mental apparatus plays a progressively more important role until it finally dominates the individual's functioning.

This is what leads us to say that in the majority of adults the characteristics of their mental apparatus, and in particular the qualities of their preconscious, are a testimony to an individual's health, whatever pathology may be present in other areas. More specifically, intervening decisively in the qualities of the preconscious are (1) its *depth*, linked to the number and richness of the successive layers of its representations; (2) its *internal circulation*, linked to the dynamic mobility between the different layers of representations; and (3) the *permanence of its activity* in creating a defense against excitation (or, if you will, a filter), constantly absorbing the excessive excitations or, on the other hand, protecting against insufficient stimuli from the internal or external world of the subject.

Alterations in these three dimensions will lead to faulty functioning of the preconscious system in several ways, such as appears in character neuroses, which leave the somatic organization to respond to the hazards of life.

DISCUSSION

The evolutionist and genetic approach from which we work has stood up to the tests that we have put it to. We therefore remain faithful to it in spite of the numerous unknowns that remain. One of the major unknowns is the answer to the apparently simple question—why does a particular illness, and not another illness, appear at the particular moment? On the other hand, we can predict with relative certainty in a significant number of cases the more or less imminent arrival of a somatic disorganization. (We will return to this in our last section.)

We do not hesitate to question, just as we do with our patients, our own personal concerns that might affect our thinking about the process of structure development and pathology. The risk that the theory is disturbed by our own personal problems is diminished by constant interaction with immediate colleagues who themselves present varied personality structures.

Modifying fundamental theoretical positions seems more difficult to implement than partial perspectives. However, the relative narcissistic security that one may find in some systematic and circumscribed work and which requires little or no modification of one's personal system of thought can be recovered even in changing fundamental points of view. This arises from feelings of freedom brought on by the possibility of reforming one's own thought. Moreover, once there has been some modification in the fundamental theoretical stance, it is that much easier to reclassify secondary problems.

It is in this manner that we have modified our understanding of allergic conditions in the light of our current concepts. In an early paper (Marty, 1958), major elements that characterize the object relations of allergic patients were described, leading to the formulation of a sort of profile type. It included several "signs" such as

—a marked indistinction between oneself and others constituting the base of an astonishing power of empathy.

—a great facility for establishing relationships in general.

—an astonishing aptitude at replacing the investment of one object by that of another object (an object being someone immediately invested as good), which goes hand-in-hand with a marked absence of aggressive expression.

—a striking familiarity with primary processes, which pierce the subject's speech without his being at all affected. In this way, one can note the frequency of slips, confusions of the pronouns he/she, condensations, etc.

Such a description, resting on clear clinical evidence, led us to conclude that there existed an essential allergic psychological structure at work in subjects who present these peculiarities in their object relations. However, our research shows that only about a third of allergics actually have an essential allergic structure, and that the majority of them belong, in fact, to a group of character neuroses. They do not present the entire picture that we described initially and, moreover, distinguish themselves by other "signs," which suggest more of an "evolutionary lateral chain of the allergic order" rather than a "typical central chain of allergic order" (Marty, 1980).

It is probably worthwhile to point out that the presence or absence of recognized somatic allergic manifestations, severe or mild, does not at all constitute a criterion for this nosological distinction.

These changes in our fundamental theoretical positions are similar to those that have occurred in the works of Alexander (1950) and Dunbar (1955), which also focus on the notion of the "personality profile." In our perspective, if this notion is to survive—which remains a very debatable question—it cannot, in all cases, rest on symptomatic classification of illnesses. We find that artificially regrouping subjects according to somatic symptoms is insufficient and inadequate to address the variety of their mental organizations. The major reference must become the characteristics of their psychosomatic economy of the moment, with sustained attention to influences on their mental state.

We regularly confront this issue and the results that ensue from it in our direct experience with somatic patients of differing mental structures as well as illnesses by using several devices to test our thinking. The H.P.P. and the Center for Education and Psychosomatic Research with which it is associated favor constant exchanges with immediate colleagues and with students of various disciplines and levels of psychosomatic knowledge. Young colleagues treating patients as controls in their training present supplemental and enriching psychotherapeutic material. Another way of testing our hypotheses is by our statistics system. We keep statistics for each semester at the H.P.P., the results are utilized both for research and administrative purposes. Although these results have only relative value because they reflect a limited number of cases, they do raise a certain number of points which could have otherwise passed unnoticed. For example, since the opening of the hospital in April 1978, the statistics have shown a regular tendency toward increasing presentation of an organic lesion-caused attack (77 percent) as opposed to a functional attack (23 percent).

We have also developed a new rubric, entitled "Indefinite Psychotherapeutic Surveillance" (I.P.S.), on the hospital chart that accompanies the sick person throughout his stay at the hospital. It requires the consulting physician to note, at the conclusion of the first evaluation, a tentative assessment of the patient's physical health with reference to characteristics of his psychosomatic economy, rather than to use nosographic classifications of classical medicine.

The above-mentioned "Indefinite Psychotherapeutic Surveillance" is defined:

1. by the fundamental structure of the subject, including
   (a) behavioral neuroses
   (b) character neuroses with poor mental representations
2. by the style and associated structures of his mental organization
   (a) latent depression
   (b) infantile depression
   (c) delayed infantile depression
   (d) unreachable grandiose self ("*moi-idéal irreductible*")
3. by the fragility of the foregoing ensemble at the moment of psychosomatic investigation, including
   (a) essential depression
   (b) progressive disorganization
   (c) repeated disorganizations
   (d) postoperative states
   (e) aging

After our conclusions, we will present in the first appendix several extracts of adult statistics of the H.P.P. from January 1 to June 30, 1982. They are followed by a sample of the type of new patient chart sheet, which goes into practice during the second semester of 1983.

ASPECT 4

THE PSYCHOANALYTIC MODEL IS THE MAJOR POINT OF DEPARTURE FOR OUR PRESENT POSITION

Our long study, which began in 1948, owes a debt to several sources—our close Parisian collaboration with Mustapha Ziwar, the writings of American authors, past and present, who preceded or still accompany us, and the patients whom we have studied psychoanalytically.

From the outset our position rested on important differences, in quality and kind, in the distribution of somatic illnesses between patients with symptom neuroses and psychoses on the one hand and character neuroses (neuroses of unstable and irregular mental functioning) on the other. The symptom neuroses included obsessional neuroses (reflecting sustained mental activity vis-à-vis original but displaced conflicts) and phobic neuroses (reflecting permanent vigilance vis-à-vis objects designated for repression and displacement). The psychoses reflect the permanent functioning of a massively organized psychological system. These neuroses and most psychoses are infrequently associated with somatic illness. The stability of the mental organization, even though pathological, protects the body. Therefore, we might add, parenthetically, our belief that current psychopharmacological agents, which aim to "socialize" the mentally ill, raise the risk of the emergence of somatic illnesses in personalities that previously appeared protected from them.

The neuroses of unstable mental functioning (character

neuroses without permanent classical symptomatology) constitute, on the other hand, the terrain of the most diverse somatic
illnesses.

Therefore, we analyzed the entire group of neuroses of
unstable mental functioning and regrouped them around two
poles: the behavioral neuroses and the character neuroses. The
behavioral neuroses generally apply to subjects whose psychological functioning (according to the two Freudian topogra-
phies) was never solidly established; that is to say, these subjects
live out their drives almost directly without their actions first
being submitted to mental elaboration. In contrast, character
neuroses apply to subjects whose psychological functioning is
unstable in time (hence, the absence of symptomatic permanence) and who consequently are fragile in the face of emotional
trauma.

Two points deserve clarification. First of all, this distinction
does not imply any moral or social value judgments—these categories are not linked to one or another social class. Depending
upon circumstances, each of us may ultimately live happily with
the psychological equipment at his or her disposal. In the second
place, most individuals usually considered "normal," including
the majority of psychosomaticians like ourselves, belong in the
group of character neuroses. The habitual availability of the
mental apparatus (e.g., identification, release of identifications,
awareness of self and of others, reflection, utilization of multiple
mechanisms of defense while maintaining a rational whole)
seems to go hand-in-hand with fragility of this apparatus during
emotional strain, and consequently, with a permeability which
leaves the body susceptible to illnesses.

Having thus noted the protective role in somatic health that
is played by the symptom neuroses and by the psychoses, our
attention turns to the genesis of symptomatic neuroses, to the
organization of the conscious and unconscious, and finally to
the construction of the preconscious, which Freudian theory
defines as the repository of early object representation.

We will consider as a point of departure some of the principal processes of somatization:

1. the failure of somatic responses to adapt to stimulation from the unconscious through the intermediary of inhibition or of prolonged suppression of representations or inhibition of affects;

2. the fundamental inadequacy of preconscious functioning in behavioral neuroses;

3. the posttraumatic weaknesses of the ego and of the preconscious in character neuroses; and

4. psychosomatic regressions.

The effects of these processes are different: With regard to (1), the failure of somatic responses to adapt to stimulation from impulses by inhibition or prolonged suppression of their representations is frequently found even in the mental neuroses (which, in fact, only irregularly show classical symptoms). The representations are consciously put aside, the affect preserved, by processes that occur at psychological levels other than that of repression. Nevertheless, they are similar to repression and may coexist with it. Such putting aside leads, in any case, to a direct release of instinctual energy into the somatic sphere, as is often seen in the unweaned infant and in the small child; the problem, however, is more complex in the adult. Many acute, short-lived illnesses arise from this process. For example, motor disorders of smooth and striate muscles, such as cramps and muscle tension problems, and elevations in blood pressure in times of life crises.

The headaches can be considered as a passageway between frustration and suppression. The representations of fantasies that underlie the headaches are often precise and touch on the oedipal conflict, as a screen. These representations and fantasies appear "on the surface of consciousness," more frustrated than repressed. The mental inhibition during these headaches (which correspond to a lack of freedom of movement of thought) as well as the pain (undoubtedly through vascular intermediaries) can be considered neither an offshoot of the subconscious toward the conscious, nor a classical symptom compromise; nor does the repression in question result in a simple release of energy into somatic expression (moreover, we don't find headaches in children younger than five).

As to the hysterical conversions (transfer of a frustrated psychological conflict into somatic symptoms, principally of a sensorimotor order), they will progressively cause the disappearance of the gap between psychic and somatic innervation. It seems that apart from the primary somatic libidinal expression (the type of somatic expression of the unweaned infant, or of the little child in whom the idea of conversion is already evoked), secondary somatic expression, also libidinal, may appear in subjects who are particularly hysterical. These secondary expressions thus take charge, also secondarily, of the sense of the repressed representations and take on a symbolic sensorimotor form, which rests both in the primary expression as well as in secondary identifications.

With regard to (2), the fundamental inadequacies of the preconscious in behavioral neuroses are much more frequent in Western populations than classical psychoanalysts not directly concerned with the somatically ill imagine. They use Freud's discoveries concerning the psychological apparatus of the symptom neuroses, denying the psychological deficiencies of these patients and attributing to them assets—at least latent—that they may not have. Many inhibitions and suppressions, like some repressions, can be attributed to a functional weakness of the preconscious.

The deficiency of the preconscious (by the lack of an appropriate sensorimotor maturation, lack of sensorimotor relationships, lack of connections between the diverse categories of representations, lack of possibilities for introjection) and the inadequacy of the ego that results give rise to a reduced mental apparatus, unable to use repression adaptively. The subconscious also finds itself lacking the capacity for psychological elaboration of instincts mobilized by affects. The subjects thus are particularly at the mercy of the objects, or, more precisely, of the partners which constitute their relationships. Since the introjects are faulty the loss of relationships cannot be mourned and is experienced as a narcissistic loss. Without the possibility of a mental elaboration and without direct expression of the instincts in question through more or less immediate behaviors (which most of the time require partners), the unconscious finds itself alone. Without hierarchical mental organization, the most varied somatic dysfunctions rapidly come into play.

Two points of vocabulary are in question here:

1. We use the term "unconscious" to refer to the first Freudian topography. We could, from another perspective, use the term "id."

2. The term "impulse" implies, among other things, the notion of "object." It is difficult to specify before at least eight months of age, as it is impossible to specify in somatic matters, what can be an "object." Thus we prefer to use the term "instinct."

We must point out that the fundamental inadequacies of preconscious organization that one finds in behavioral neuroses are at times accompanied by serious somatic illnesses that begin in childhood (e.g., severe allergic manifestations, insulin-dependent diabetes), as if corresponding to the fragile mental organization there were a somatic organization of equal fragility.

With regard to (3), the posttraumatic weaknesses of the ego and of the preconscious in character neuroses give rise, finally, to somatic disorganizations. These disorganization processes begin by attacking the mental apparatus. They generally work in the opposite way to that of the progressive organization which marks development. They are counterevolutionary and run in the opposite direction to the steps of maturation.

The disorganizations of the mental apparatus in character neuroses last longer in general than those that attack the mental apparatus of behavioral neuroses. They meet a relatively consistent and appropriately hierarchical system capable of levels of regression that at least slow the movement of disorganization. The regressions consist of character attitudes or symptomatologies too unstable to arrest the disorganization. They merely slow down the process. It is again at the level of the preconscious that one can best recognize at its beginning, with disruption of more and more fundamental functions, a disorganization that threatens to progress to the somatic domain.

These processes of disorganization manifest themselves in an original way in each individual. Certain factors of their originality can be related to the individual, hereditary, developmental, psychosomatic fixations of the subjects, to the vicissitudes of their libidinal investments, and to their level of vitality (which decreases with age). These factors include the rate of disorganization, the timing of its abatements, the duration and order of the disorganization, the nature, quality, and concomitants of the specific illness. Because of all these, most illnesses which arise in the course of disorganization appear atypical in form as well as in course, when compared to the same illnesses arising when there is a regressive arrest capable of bringing solid psychosomatic defenses into play.

The form of illness that develops is, of course, also affected by the host of other somatic symptoms that may have become a part of the individual patient's mental organization and by other somatic systems arising from his heredity that are also stirred up by the progressive disorganization. These individual variables account for yet further individual differences in the manifestation of a particular illness in a psychosomatically vulnerable patient as compared with a less psychosomatically vulnerable patient who presents with the same somatic diagnosis.

With regard to (4), the psychosomatic regressions are thus those that, relying on consistent systems of fixations, have the capacity to arrest primitive movements of disorganization emerging from emotional traumata.

The arrest of disorganizations by regressions can be produced at psychological as well as somatic levels. The regressions are distinguished by affects with theoretically classical form and evolution, and large systems of fixations generally are the same from one individual to the next. From the point of the regressive arrest, such patients are able to reconstitute to the level that existed prior to the disorganization.

The essential and determining factor is the fixation point. The capacity of the patient to arrest the potential disorganization by regression to firmly established fixation points is what stabilizes the pathological process and allows a point of departure for reorganization. It may appear that a patient's ability to preserve certain personal assets or strengths or external supports is what interrupted the disorganization; but that is only an illusion. The fixation points are what arrest the process and become the stable base from which reorganization proceeds.

We find two types of regression which in theory depend on the role of fixations in the development of the individual, his individual psychosomatic evolution: (1) global regressions, in which the whole psychosomatic evolution of the individual comes into play and is recapitulated on former bases, whatever somatic aspects (e.g., sensory, motor, allergic) are part of the person's history; and (2) partial regressions, in which a system developed during the psychosomatic evolution, mental (e.g., an emotional organization) or somatic (e.g., an allergic organization), is specially subject to regression, without the whole developmental evolution being the subject of the regression. The partial regressions (all regressions are more or less partial in the end) are usually recognized as "cleavages," for descriptive purposes. Our group is currently interested in the varieties of individual evolutionary movements that create what we later find to be "cleavages," that is, passages from one economic system to another.

Between the poles of "global regressions" and "partial regressions" are intermediary regressions. These are currently the subject of analysis and study, especially for topographical, dynamic, and economic psychosomatic research.

To finish the presentation of our current point of view on the principal processes of somatization, we must add that it is never wise to trust in the long-term stabilizing capacity of these processes. This caution particularly applies to the hysterical conversions emerging from repression, suppressions of representation, and psychosomatic regressions of all kinds. A number of factors are likely to intervene to cause a patient to pass from one process (that was believed basic) to another. The researcher, the psychotherapist, and the therapist-physician must be regularly on the alert to such shifts.

Discussion

We prefer the psychoanalytic model over any other because it rests on functionally less static bases. On the other hand, this choice requires the use of an exact vocabulary—for effective communication.

We will proceed with the following comments:

1. It is appropriate to insist on the major fact that the mental apparatus is not "standard," that is, uniform for all. It follows that the noteworthy modifications at the level of the first Freudian topography (Ucs, Pcs, Cs) and at the second level of topography (id, ego, superego) will vary according to the individual and to the moments in each person's life.

2. "Failure of the ego" is a term used more specifically and precisely to mean poor functioning of the preconscious which make the ego (in the sense of the second topography) precarious.

The superego can often appear impoverished in its contents, reduced to an ideal of an all-powerful self, heir of primary narcissism, and not at all moderated by the play of identifications and counteridentifications. It is this play that marks the complete structuring of the individual, permitting the progressive appropriation by the superego of various forms of the ego-ideal which promote mediation among the imperatives of superego, ego, impulses, and those of reality.

3. The need for precision extends to specifying the exact nature and quality of emotional distress arising in a patient because it can be a question of diffuse distress caused by primary problems of individuation and not of distress caused by a particular relationship to a particular object. Similarly, phobias can

be phobias of "environment" (agoraphobias, claustrophobias —even cancerophobias, for example) and not phobias concerning a determined object.

4. Stimulation and its traumatic impact, eventually traumatic on the subject, deserve to be studied. It is fitting to define the nature of these excitations in terms of the functional organization (in its present references) which receives them. It is also fitting to define the nature of weak para-excitation systems. Is it a matter, for example, of excessive sensory stimulation or of a lack of relational stimulation? The specificity is important. How would one use analytically a formulation like that of Harold Levitan (see his chapter in this volume) which evokes without specifying the "menacing elements"?

It does not seem useful to employ a term of defense without indicating which defense, against what. The defensive operations can refer to various mechanisms of completely heterogeneous functional value, much more of a quantitative than qualitative point of view.

5. Fantasies emerge from liaisons and elaborations arising from very different levels of representation, which refer back to, in our view, these diverse states of the preconscious system that we have already addressed. It is a question then of an important area of future research.

Dreams constitute an aspect of mental activity which we particularly endorse. One cannot treat in the same way dreams made from elementary representations at the limit of the subconscious and from the preconscious, without actual work of elaboration, and dreams of an entirely different nature in which condensations, displacements, and repetitions, for example, translate into evidence of the richness of the work of the dream. A dream cannot be analyzed according to its simple manifest content, and it seems useful to recall that the dreamer's associations remain equally indispensable as elements of an interpretation. These considerable differences of quality in representations, fantasies, and dreams constitute some of the most pertinent indices from which technique emerges, different for each individual, which we adopt during the course of the evaluation and then in the psychotherapy (Marty and Parat, 1974).

6. Variations in the quality of representations, fantasies, and dreams deserve to be observed in the same individual. This indeed reveals a significant characteristic that character neuroses electively present—the irregularity of their mental functioning. Now, as we have said, it is very often at the occasion of weaknesses in the functioning of the preconscious system that a movement toward disorganization will become clear, which can result in a more or less serious somatization. When this happens and constitutes a central element in the general psychosomatic economy of the subject, the therapist will be particularly attentive to the variations of the quality of the representations, fantasies, and dreams. These can present as so many "signs" and allow the anticipation of a reorganization favoring an eventual remission of the somatic pathology or, to the contrary, a possible aggravation. We return here to what we said at the start of our chapter: we seek to determine what supports the mental function—what facilitates the quality of exchanges between this complex system that constitutes the preconscious at its core—and serves to support the general psychosomatic economy of the subject and thus his somatic state. We see that from this perspective a somatic symptom is often no more than a temporary sign, depending entirely on the place it holds in the general psychosomatic economy of the subject at the moment it appears.

7. As to behavioral and character neuroses, the precise definition of their nosological limits remains an open discussion. In our opinion, it is a question of many and varied mental organizations, which extend the length of a continuum from frank neurotic organizations to what we have called apparent unorganizations, characterized by extreme precariousness and operative since the origins of the patient's mental functioning.

All of these subjects risk having to appear at one moment or another, notably during what we've termed functional weaknesses of the preconscious system, a state of "essential depression." This depression is called essential because it consists of a veritable "lowering of instinctual and libidinal pressure," without having psychotic, neurotic or emotional symptomatology appear, which will at least promise a recovery, a clutch on the instincts or on the libido of previously living systems. The subject, often, will thus not complain of anything. He is barely conscious of his mechanical countenance, truly without life, which envelops his customary activities. It is therefore his family and friends rather than the subject himself who worry about his peculiar state. It is a profoundly significant state for the psychosomatician since it is the main menace of eventual somatic disorganizations. It is in the course of these states of essential depression, temporary or more enduring, that the *"vie opératoire"* can appear. We prefer to say *vie opératoire* rather than *pensée opératoire*, the latter term having assumed a meaning over time which no longer corresponds to the course of our thought.

Since we first introduced this term *pensée opératoire* with Michel de M'Uzan (Marty and de M'Uzan, 1963), we have indiscriminately mixed subjects presenting disorganized behavioral neuroses and disorganized character neuroses. This is to say that the *vie opératoire*, like the essential depression which precedes and accompanies it, can appear in subjects presenting extremely disparate mental organizations, and therefore would not constitute a sign having a unitary nosological value.

The *vie opératoire* usually constitutes a stage of more or less lasting chronicity in the course of a progressive disorganization. One does not find, in the *vie opératoire*, the qualities of regression which make the subjects hope for a spontaneous reorganization. It represents a period of automatic life at all the functional psychosomatic levels. Thought is reduced to a type of secondary cognition, moreover sometimes very operational, but not from its roots. It is a question of a block or a solid inhibition producing a veritable freezing that affects the systems of liaison between the diverse representations of the preconscious, which concerns only the factual and the current. The verb is reduced to its utilitarian aspect. The subconscious and the id find themselves isolated, stopped. The libido does not manifest itself. The instincts barely penetrate the repetitive behaviors that show, and the impulses are not elaborated at all on the psychological level. The risk of grave somatizations is permanent and increases when the *vie opératoire* continues for a long time. The improvement of a state of *vie opératoire* requires the intervention of psychotherapy, even in the absence of a somatic symptomatology. The *vie opératoire* appears superficially identical to the life of behavioral neuroses, as the disorganizations approach the unorganizations. In the meantime the behavioral neuroses are living characters in whom the instincts sustain one's conduct, and sometimes, one's sublimations. The patients with *vie opératoire* evoke the image of the living dead.

To make a global concept like the *vie opératoire* into an entity, such as the concept of alexithymia seems to have become (the inventors of which have always pointed out that it emerged from *pensée opératoire*), where the emphasis is placed on the impossibility of expressing feelings with words, appears to us unsatisfactory for descriptive and phenomenologic reasons. It is altogether too fixed to recognize the richness and complexity of inter-individual and intra-individual differences throughout the unfolding of a life.

Today we willingly defend the idea that outside of cases clearly marked by permanent psychotic or neurotic mental functioning, no one, no matter how well provided with mental mechanisms of defense belonging to the neurotic and/or the psychotic lineage, is truly protected from an eventual course of disorganization—starting with the appearance of an essential depression, whether temporary or more lasting, and eventuating in the arrival of the *vie opératoire* and of a possible somatic disorganization. The conditions for the occurrence of such an outburst can be linked to multiple variables: economic overloading affecting either the internal impulse world or the external world life stress. It is at this level that we stress the importance of the notion of a "crisis" with the character fragility that is stirred in the person who is living it.

It is therefore on the accumulation of negative factors, intervening more at the internal level than at the relational external level and in a well-defined temporal sequence, that the nature of the subject's response will depend. Life goes on in this way and when a sequence of events and their negative impacts bring about a state of essential depression or the *vie opératoire*, death is often the result.

CONCLUSION

We chose four questions for exploring certain of our current positions. They gave the opportunity to discuss issues which we think are likely to shed some light on major hypotheses that form the science of psychosomatic medicine of the future. Our position in this text is designated as theoretical. Perhaps we have shown ourselves to be too much of the theoretician. Therefore, we do not hesitate to expose, in the appendix which follows under schematic forms, some aspects of the application at the H.P.P. of our positions. These could not have been established and could not be usefully modified without our daily clinical and psychotherapeutic activity.

REFERENCES

Alexander, F. (1950), *Psychosomatic Medicine.* New York: Norton.
Braunschweig, D., & Fain, M. (1975), La nuit le jour. In: *Essai Psychoanalytique sur le Fonctionnement Mental.* Paris: Presses Universitaires de France.
Debray, R. (1983), L'Équilibre psychosomatique. In: *L'Organisation Mentale des Diabétiques.* Paris: Dunod.
Dunbar, H. F. (1955), *Emotions and Bodily Charges: A Survey of Literature on Psychosomatic Interrelationships.* New York: Ayer.
Kreisler, L. (1981), *L'Enfant du Désordre Psychosomatique.* Paris: Pivot.
Luquet-Parat, C. (1967), L'Organisation oedipienne de stade génital. *Rev. Psychanalyse,* 21.
Marty, P. (1958), La relation d'objet allergique. *Rev. Psychanalyse,* 22:30–35.
——— (1969), Notes cliniques et hypothèses à propos de l'économie de l'allergie. *Rev. Psychanalyse,* 33:243–254.

184 PIERRE MARTY—ROSINE DEBRAY

184 PIERRE MARTY—ROSINE DEBRAY

—— (1976), *Les Mouvements Individuels de Vie et de Mort, Essai d'Économie Psychosomatique*. Paris: Payot.

—— (1980), *L'Ordre Psychosomatique—Désorganisations et Régressions. Les Mouvements Individuels de Vie et de Mort*, Tome II. Paris: Payot.

—— de M'Uzan, M. (1963), La pensée opératoire. *Rev. Psychanalyse*, 27:345–356.

—— —— David, C. (1963), *L'Investigation Psychosomatique*. Paris: Presses Universitaires de France.

—— Parat, C. (1974), De l'utilisation des rêves et du matériel onirique dans certains types de psychothérapie d'adultes. *Rev. Psychanalyse*, 38:1069–1076.

APPENDIX

HÔPITAL DE LA POTERNE DES PEUPLIERS

A semiannual statistics abstract about adult patients admitted and leaving the hospital from January 1, 1980, to June 30, 1984

	No. of admissions	Patients leaving the hospital	Total
October 30, 1980			187
From October 30, 1980, to December 31, 1980	12	6	
December 31, 1980			193
From January 1, 1981, to June 30, 1981	50	19	
June 30, 1981			224
From July 1, 1981, to December 31, 1981	30	30	
December 31, 1981			224
From January 1, 1982, to June 30, 1982	55	67	
June 30, 1982			212
From July 1, 1982, to December 31, 1982	35	37	
December 31, 1982			210
From January 1, 1983, to June 30, 1983	36	34	
June 30, 1983			212
From July 1, 1983, to December 31, 1983	58	16	
December 31, 1983			254
From January 1, 1984, to June 30, 1984	51	27	
June 30, 1984			278

	Number	Sex (%)		Average Age (Year)	
		M	F	M	F
December 31, 1980	193	38	62	40	41
June 30, 1981	224	39	61	40	41
December 31, 1981	224	34	66	43	40
June 30, 1982	212	33	67	42	40
December 31, 1982	210	31	69	42	40
June 30, 1983	212	31	69	43	41
December 31, 1983	254	31	69	43	42
June 30, 1984	278	32	68	43	42

Main diseases treated on June 30, 1984	Percent
1. Cancer	11.51
2. Bronchial asthma	9.71
3. Hypertonice	8.27
4. Colopathy	7.91
5. Cephalea	7.56
6. Arterial hypertension	6.47
7. Obesity	6.12
8. Hemorrhagic rectocolitis, Crohn's disease	5.75
9. Algia (cansalgia)	5.40
10. Eczema	4.68
11. Migraine	4.68
12. Ulcus (peptic ulcer)	3.96
13. Various infections	3.96
14. Psoriasis	3.96

Frequency of psychotherapy

	Patients 6/30/84	Percent
2 sessions a week	10	4
1 session a week	243	87
3 sessions a month	0	0
2 sessions a month	14	5
1 session a month	1	0
4 sessions a year	0	0
2 sessions a year	0	0
Irregularly (at the patient's request)	10	4
TOTAL	278	100

Duration of treatment for patients
discharged over the past 6 months

	Number	Percent
More than 3 years	11	41
More than 2 years	1	4
About 2 years	5	19
About 1 year	6	22
About 6 months	2	7
Less than 6 months	2	7
TOTAL	27	100

REASONS FOR TERMINATION OF PSYCHOTHERAPY

Psychosomatic functioning

	Good	Much better	Some-what better	No results	Total	Percent
A. Good psychosomatic functioning						
B. Treatments abandoned early:						
(a) By the patient		2	4	3	9	33.33
(b) By the doctor		2			2	7.42
(c) By both		12	1		13	48.15
(d) Other reasons						
C. Treatments done in another place		1			1	3.70
D. Treatments temporarily stopped upon agreement of both patient and doctor			1		1	3.70
E. Other cases						
F. Death					1	3.70
Total		17	6	3	27	
Percent		62.96	22.22	11.11		100

Mr
Mrs
Miss   **M**   wife name   first name   Colette

Address: 52, rue Serpente 75006 Paris   Socio-professional status   Tel.
Profession: Secretary   Chief doctor from
Data written by Dr. MARTY Pierre   Consulting doctor   Origin
from notes Dr: DURAND Henri   Therapist   Correspondent's Name and
   and: Mme BRAUN Renée   Treatment end   Address:
Record number: 83-12   28/04/85

FIRST CONSULTATION: 03/07/83	Answer to the correspondent oral
	Date: 04/07/83 written x

PSYCHOSOMATIC CLASSIFICATION

Basic structure: Character neuroses with
unstable mental functioning
Main usual particularities: agoraphobias
   diffuse anxiety
Main actual characteristics: essential
   depression
Psychotherapic indefinite survey:
   (YES) [NO]

Observations:

CLASSIC MEDICAL REFERENCES

Diseases leading to psychosomatic consultation: Hemorrhagic rectocolitis

Past diseases revealed: Enterocolitis during the first year of life.

Organic (○)   Functional □   Nonorganic □
lesion   trouble   trouble

TREATMENT STARTED ON: 02/09/83

**PSYCHOSOMATIC CLASSIFICATION
REVISED:**
Basic structure: character neuroses with
good mental functioning
Main usual particularities:
Canceled:
Revealed: good mental functioning

Observations:
Frequent states of essential depression;
artistic activities of painting stopped during these states.

Past diseases revealed (during the treatment):

MEDICAL REFERENCES
New somatic events: 2 acute crises of hem-
orrhagic rectocolitis: November 1983 and
July 1984

EXIT — Last session: 02/20/85

Treatment duration: 1 year and 6 months
(without interruptions) Psychosomatic functioning
End of treatment   good + +   +   0

Normal (good functioning)
Before time by: patient's decision
doctor's decision
both decision   X
other cases
Treatment done in another place
Temporary end decision
Other cases
Death

CLASSED the:

Observation and chief doctor's signing
[R]

SESSIONS, RHYTHMS, BREAKS Dates of the decision	rhythm expected	sessions programmed	absences expected	sessions expected	absences unexpected	real sessions
03/07/83	1.W					

Observations   %   %

Good psychosomatic functioning
Regular painting activity
No hemorrhagic rectocolitis for 6 months

Statistics
□ enter and leave the hospital in the same half
   year

7.
Alexithymia

FERNANDO LOLAS, M.D., and
MICHAEL VON RAD, M.D.

DEFINITION

The term *alexithymia* designates a cluster of behavioral manifestations observed mostly in the interview situation. It was coined by Sifneos (1972, 1973), alluding to the inability of some patients to describe their feelings in words, a characteristic not infrequently associated with thought processes described as "concrete," "pragmatic" or "instrumental," and marked by a preoccupation with minute details of external environmental events and a striking absence of fantasies expressing inner drives and affects. Although objections have been raised about the appropriateness of the term (Philippopoulos, 1977), it has gained acceptance and is now being used in a wide variety of contexts. Its significance in the present context derives from the fact that it was originally used for describing behavioral characteristics in bearers of so-called "psychosomatic conditions." This chapter will be devoted to a selective rather than exhaustive review of the voluminous literature concerning alexithymia, emphasizing empirical data and directions for further research.

THE CLINICAL PICTURE

Alexithymia encompasses several different behavioral characteristics. Although they are frequently observed together, the

189

precise nature of their relationship is still a matter of debate. At a descriptive level, the current usage of the term "alexithymia" connotes several disturbances. Krystal (1979) divides them into cognitive, affective, and object-relations disturbances.

On the cognitive side, alexithymic individuals are said to present a particular way of approaching events and persons in their lives. They tend to lack fantasy and to concentrate on lengthy descriptions of the minutiae of their environments and daily life in a sort of "stimulus-bound rather than drive-directed" (Nemiah and Sifneos, 1970b) mentation. They seem to be oriented toward "pragmatic" thought content and to prefer action rather than reflection and fantasy. "The word repeats what the hand does" (Marty and de M'Uzan, 1963). These features, psychodynamically interpreted, constitute the core description of the so-called *pensée opératoire* proposed by French psychoanalysts in the 1960s within the framework of a characterization of a "psychosomatic structure," which they contrasted with the neurotic and the psychotic (Marty and de M'Uzan, 1963; Marty, de M'Uzan, and David, 1963).

Affectively, observers have emphasized that subjects labeled alexithymic are characterized by the inability to express feelings verbally, employing a language devoid of affective resonance, meager in the use of emotionally laden metaphors. Although these individuals may use words that refer to affects (they may describe themselves as being "nervous," "angry," or "happy"), they are unable to describe their inner experience if they are pressed by the interviewer to do so. This lack of affective connotation or relatedness to inner experience is not of the same quality as the verbalization deficits attributed to low intelligence or educational level, although this point also has been hotly disputed. Verbal deficit often occurs with an inability to localize feelings in the body and an unawareness of the common somatic reactions that usually accompany the experience of a variety of affects. A lack of differentiation between different feeling states has also been described, as if the individual lacked the capacity for distinguishing among them. Despite the fact that alexithymic individuals give little external evidence of experiencing affect (this has led to the question of whether they experience it at all or are merely unable to put it into words), they sometimes manifest brief but violent outbursts of affective behavior, which the individual cannot explain and which remain incomprehensible to the observer.

The psychoanalytic bias of many students of alexithymia finds expression in the description of their disturbances in object relations. The French authors have drawn attention to the peculiar ways of relating to significant others that seemed to appear along with the *pensée opératoire* phenomenon. The psychotherapeutic relationship was described as dull and boring—"*relation blanche.*" A phenomenon of "projective reduplication" was also described as the inability of these individuals to perceive the other as another person, in his or her individuality. They tended to view the therapist, for instance, as another version of themselves or as not separated from themselves. Related formulations have been put forward by other authors, although in some cases—as we shall see below—no distinction is made between alexithymic individuals and so-called psychosomatic patients. Shands (1958) has noted the unsuitability of many of these patients for psychotherapy and has spoken of a disorder of individuation to allude to a psychodynamic constellation in which the patient, unable to compensate for losses in essential human relatedness, sees the lost human other as "malignant" (in the pattern of the phantom limb) (Shands, 1981).

Before clarifying the relationship between alexithymia and somatic disease, it does not seem advisable to further expand the concept to cover all aspects of psychic functioning described in relation to somatic illness. This consideration also applies to other qualities observed in conjunction with alexithymic features in some patients and thought to constitute part of their behavioral syndrom^ ^nportant among these is the so-called "pseudonormality" ernormality." It is meant to imply that these persons often ₁t exhibit behavioral aberrations of the type that usually qu.......y as pathological. They seem to lead ordered lives, work hard, and be professionally as successful as other people. It is under certain circumstances, and particularly in the course of psychodynamically oriented psychotherapy, that deficits may appear (Brede, 1971, 1972; McDougall, 1974, 1980). As negative phenomena, these deficits are not always clearly recognized. It must also be added that this labeling may be just a reflection of the psychoanalyst's frustration with a patient who does not behave in the way he expects (Ahrens, Gyldenfeldt, and Runde, 1979) and that societal constraints must be considered in any discussion of normality. We shall refer to some of these points when discussing the causation models proposed to account for alexithymic behavior.

HISTORICAL ASPECTS: RELATED BEHAVIOR PATTERNS

The studies of the Boston group (Sifneos, Nemiah, and coworkers), which finally led to the proposal and refinement of the construct of alexithymia, were conducted within the framework of psychosomatic theories. Inspired by the observations of Ruesch (1948) and Marty and de M'Uzan (1963), they became interested in determining the nature of the psychosomatic patient's thought content and expression of affect. Reexamining earlier material Nemiah had collected from patients afflicted by psychosomatic illnesses, they found that the majority of the interview protocols were characterized by an impoverishment of fantasy life and a constriction in emotional functioning. These features appeared in sharp contrast to the richness and vividness of the interviews from psychoneurotic patients. Since their work, the comparison between psychoneurotic and psychosomatic patients has been a key issue in discussions about alexithymia and a basic research strategy. It has also been a source of confusion and criticism from psychodynamically oriented writers, in explaining the causation of this behavior pattern and its relation to somatic disease. Pointing toward two different psychic organizations this work revived earlier distinctions that can be traced back to the one proposed by Freud (1895) between conversion neuroses and actual neuroses. This contrast has been repeatedly pointed out by a number of authors and can also be found in Alexander's (1950) distinction between hysterical conversion and vegetative neurosis (considered a psychosomatic condition), which was based upon the notion that while the former was a symbolic attempt to relieve emotional tension, the latter was just the physiological concomitant of emotions, nonsymbolic in nature. It is well known that early psychosomaticists expanded the conversion model beyond the limits of its explanatory power. Psychoanalysts in particular, while acknowledging the differences between the two conditions, insisted upon what Stephanos and Berger (1979) (quoting Sami-Ali) have called a "homogeneous" model, meaning to imply that in both cases the participation of ego defense mechanisms was decisive in accounting for the somatic symptom formation. The position espoused by Alexander (1950), for instance, emphasized the dual nature of affect and invoked intrapsychic defenses to explain the apparent absence of fantasy and affect in psychosomatic patients.

Alexithymia-like characteristics had also been observed by Ferenczi (1924) in describing patients who produce no fantasy invested with affect and who speak of the most emotional experiences and recollections without becoming agitated. He attributed this behavior to the repression of psychic material and to the supression of affect, thus adhering to a defense model. Zilboorg (1933) incorporated the Freudian notion of "affect equivalents" to describe anxiety attacks very much like the emotional outbursts appearing in alexithymic individuals. Aside from invoking the defenses of denial and repression to explain this behavior, he added that the absence of the ideational aspect of affect was due to a regression to a primitive developmental state characterized by an undifferentiated fusion between soma and psyche.

Ruesch (1948) proposed the concept of the "infantile personality" for designating certain personality traits common to all patients suffering from psychosomatic illnesses, irrespective of the clinical picture. Aside from departing from specificity theories then current for explaining somatic symptom formation, Ruesch emphasized the notion that infantile personalities (the "core problem of psychosomatic medicine") were the result of a developmental arrest. Psychoneuroses, instead, should be viewed as the result of pathological development. Infantile personalities would be individuals whose psychic development became arrested at some point. For them the problem was not one of defense mechanisms but of immaturity—their developmental arrest would produce a "sham maturity." Persons affected by it would be incapable of discharging tension through verbal or creative symbolism; instead they would express themselves through somatic expression or action. The absence of symbolic ability and language skills would impair their ability to cope with tension and deal in an elaborated manner with frustration.

The value of Ruesch's contribution may be seen in his having identified common denominators in symptomatology, personality structure, and social techniques of patients suffering from different conditions (posttraumatic syndromes, chronic disease in general, duodenal ulcer and thyroid conditions). His emphasis on a primitive level of organization was subsequently taken up by other authors. In his etiopathogenic discussion, Ruesch's work stressed the possibility that a failure in the functions of communication, symbolization, and self-expression might be associated more often than not with somatic illness (Ruesch, 1948, 1972).

A related behavioral pattern was described by Shands in his studies on suitability for psychotherapy. As early as 1958, he had described the main components of a complex syndrome found in so-called "difficult patients": a conspicuous inability to describe feelings; a peculiar type of relatedness to others, especially the physician, who is implicitly regarded as important but not valued as an individual; an undeveloped ability to use the pronoun "I" in an emotionally meaningful context; a tendency to mention a number of bizarre, diffuse bodily sensations that cannot be localized, and a great deal of circumstantiality in conversations with others. Referring to Ludwig's notion of the "psychosomatic core," he observed that many psychosomatic patients—as opposed to psychoneurotics—seem to belong to the category of difficult patients. He stressed the "primitive" level of mental functioning that seemed to characterize many of them. At the same time, he cautioned against overgeneralizations: ". . . there is a group of characteristics which can be defined by content analysis of recorded interviews . . . these characteristics will be significantly positively correlated on the one hand to the sort of culture from which the person emerges and on the other hand to the sort of disease from which he suffers" (Shands, 1958, p. 518). He thus anticipated one of the key issues in later discussions about the causation of alexithymia and its societal or cultural determination. In this and subsequent papers, Shands (1958, 1975, 1977, 1981) has repeatedly addressed the relationships between these behavioral characteristics and psychodynamic formulations about physical illness and has contributed insights into the psychotherapeutic approach to "difficult" (alexithymic) patients.

Pursuing studies of affective disturbances in alcoholism and drug dependence, a pattern was found that consisted of affect dedifferentiation, deverbalization, and resomatization (Krystal and Raskin, 1970; Krystal, 1974, 1975, 1978). Emotions came in vague, undifferentiated, somatic form, i.e., like sensations rather than feelings. These subjects were not able to put their emotions into words, and therefore could not use them as signals to themselves (Krystal, 1974). A similar coincidence of impairment of symbolization and affect disturbance in drug addicts has been reported by Wurmser (1974). An affective-cognitive disturbance (which might be described as an inability to "cognitize" the emotion) was also observed in severely traumatized survivors of concentration camps, who also "showed an extremely high rate of psychosomatic diseases." Krystal's elaboration of the genetic development of affect permits him "to understand psychosomatic conditions as a regression in regard to affect—in that affects are resomatized and dedifferentiated, with a concomitant impairment in verbalization and symbolization" (1978, p. 211). While this view has been put forward many times in relation to psychosomatic disease, attention has not always been drawn to the communication pattern or behavioral syndrome that concerns us here. Krystal (1974) has remarked that his observations coincide precisely with those of Sifneos, Nemiah, Marty, de M'Uzan, and others who have studied psychosomatic patients, and that he has adopted the term "alexithymia" for referring to them (Krystal 1974, 1975, 1977, 1979).

We have already referred to the pivotal work of the French psychoanalysts, which laid some of the foundation for later theory (Fain, 1966; Marty et al., 1963; Marty and de M'Uzan, 1963; de M'Uzan, 1974; McDougall, 1974). From a phenomenological psychodynamic point of view they described three components of the syndrome: operational thinking (la pensée opératoire), a cognitive style which adheres closely to materially present facts and the usefulness of thoughts; the basic representative inhibition (la inhibition fantasmatique ou l'inhibition represéntative de base) by which dreaming and fantasy are either totally absent or reduced to situations perceived in the external environment; and projective reduplication, a type of narcissistic perception whereby others are seen as stereotyped images of oneself. (We shall be concerned with their psychodynamic interpretation of these phenomena in the next section.)

From the vantage point of neuroanatomy and neurophysiology, MacLean remarked in 1949 that "a notable deficiency attendant on psychosomatic theory . . . is the inability to point to a mechanism of emotion that would account for the variety of ways the affective qualities of experience may act on autonomic centers" (p. 338). Quoting the then available evidence, MacLean drew attention to the fact that psychosomatic patients "often advance to superior attainments in the intellectual sphere, and at the same time . . . show evidence that their emotional life has been arrested at or near the oral level" (p. 340). He emphasized the paradox that the patient with psychosomatic illness (where lesions are present) showed an apparent intellectual inability to verbalize his emotional feelings.

(His formulations regarding mechanisms will be discussed in the next section.)

It is clear from this brief presentation that some of the features embodied in the concept of alexithymia have been independently described by many observers and related to a wealth of clinical conditions. We have selected only those descriptions that explicitly refer to alexithymia-like phenomena observed in similar settings and within frameworks comparable to those employed by the Boston group. At present there seems to be a consensus regarding the existence of characteristics such as those summarized by the term *alexithymia*. Rooted in a large body of consistent clinical and phenomenological observation, it is an empirical question to determine whether alexithymia is indeed a novel phenomenon or simply represents classical psychopathological features in a new guise. We will refer to this when discussing its assessment. Alexithymic characteristics could be conceived of as a syndrome, a communication pattern, or a psychic structure, depending upon the level of observation and the theoretical bias of the observer. However, despite agreement at the phenomenological level, disparate views are often presented regarding the etiology of the behavioral characteristics, their interpretation, their relation to illnesses and to other behavioral patterns, and their therapeutic modifiability. A related problem in the present state of research is that of assessment and measurement.

ETIOLOGIC AND PATHOGENIC MODELS

As a current review points out, "despite the fact that alexithymia is a relatively recent term, there has been no dearth of attempts to explain its etiology from neurophysiological, psychoanalytic, social learning, developmental, and genetic points of view" (Lesser, 1981, p. 531). The author rightly emphasizes the fact that in many theoretical considerations the issues seem to be confounded. For example, some writers have taken for granted that alexithymic characteristics could be equated with certain forms of somatic illness. In this way, when they propose a model for somatic symptom formation they believe they are accounting for alexithymia, and vice versa. Another problem is determining exactly what is to be accounted for in a theoretical model. It may seem somewhat surprising that despite the important body of psychodynamic theory related to the inability to express feelings verbally, only sketchy presentations are made about the "normal" state of affairs. On the other hand, while some models adequately explain part of the syndrome, this does not imply that alexithymia, with all its aspects, is a unitary phenomenon that can be singled out and understood in causal terms by means of straightforward explanatory concepts. These and other problems justify that we refer only cursorily to the vast amount of literature that has accumulated during the last years.

Nemiah (1977) considers two main groups of theories: psychologic and neuroanatomic. Of all the models he reviews, only three—a psychological model, a deficit model, and a neuroanatomical model—provide a satisfactory explanation for the presence of alexithymic characteristics. The psychological model is based on the defense mechanism of denial, with its implication of a massive, global inhibition of affects and its power for explaining the disappearance of alexithymic characteristics and somatic symptoms in cases of chronic or catastrophic physical illness (secondary alexithymia). The deficit model, which refers not to an inhibition of function but to an absence of functions related to the experience of affect and fantasy, accounts for the seeming irreversibility of alexithymic characteristics in some patients. And the neuroanatomical model has the advantage of "making possible the translation of intangible, unmeasurable psychoanalytic constructs into the concepts of neurochemical processes taking place in neuronal pathways and centers" (p. 205).

Similarly, Kleiger (1979) divides the etiologic theories of alexithymia into deficit models (absence of function), defense models (inhibition of function), and sociocultural models (social variables modify function). In point of fact, however, many of the hypothetical explanations presented would not qualify as "models" in the sense of providing adequate accounts of the mechanisms that make possible the appearance of alexithymic characteristics. In some instances we find only anecdotal reports about remarkable coincidences between alexithymia-like behavior and other types of behavior, or repetitive observational data unsupported by careful testing. In the following discussion we shall therefore refer to three major contexts in which the phenomenon of alexithymia has been placed and shall try to indicate where testable formulations are being offered.

Psychodynamic Theories

Psychodynamically oriented writers have discussed alexithymia from two main vantage points—as a defense mechanism or as a deficit in psychic organization. We have already observed that the explanation Ferenczi (1924) offered for alexithymia-like features included "repression of psychical material and suppression of affect" (p. 8). In classical psychoanalysis, defensive processes presuppose a psychic organization capable of investing energy to reelaborate experiences at the service of other functions. Some writers have discussed the defensive process of regression in relation to alexithymic characteristics, according to which psychic functioning goes back to a more primitive stage along a developmental line. Schur (1955), for instance, hypothesized that resomatization of responses is tied up with a prevalence of primary process thinking and the use of unneutralized energy; in the presence of conflict which cannot be dealt with appropriately by psychic means, the ego regresses to an earlier organization, a pre-verbal, pre-ego state of development where reaction to stimuli is in the closest sense psychosomatic. A similar stance has been taken by Krystal, who, in addition, has provided a reformulation of the psychoanalytical theory of affect, stating that "the developmental lines of affect are verbalization, desomatization, and differentiation out of the common precursor patterns into refined forms of specific emotions" (1978, p. 240). Moreover, in terms of defense mechanisms the concept of conservation-withdrawal (Engel and Schmale, 1972) may be brought to bear on behavior patterns characterized by a lack of affective expression and supposedly subserving a homeostatic or restorative function in the presence of conflict or trauma.

Nemiah, Freyberger, and Sifneos (1976) have remarked that one of the essential features of Alexander's work was the use of psychoanalytical concepts of psychic conflict, attempting to define for each of the illnesses studied the nature of the psychological stress involved, the character of the drives and affects aroused by the stressful situation, and the type of ego defenses employed to control the drives and affects. They recall that "in particular, the concept of denial became prevalent as the significant defence against drives and affects in patients suffering from these illnesses—denial in this context being used to refer to a defence against internal psychic elements as opposed to its more proper and restricted designation of a psychological mechanism aimed at denying external reality" (p. 435). This psychodynamic model, they point out, does not provide an adequate explanation for the difference in the clinical manifestations of conversion hysteria and psychosomatic disorders. "Given the initial repression of affect and fantasy in both types of disorder, the model does not enable one to state why symbolization enters into the formation of symptoms of the one and not of the other" (p. 435)—unless, we might add, the conversion model is expanded to cover all forms of somatization, assuming that all possess symbolic meaning.

However, the nonsymbolic nature of psychosomatic disorders has been stressed by many theorists (James, 1979). In a series of theoretical papers, Nemiah (1973, 1975, 1977) has commented on the conceptual difficulties inherent in the notion of denial on the basis of two main arguments: the restricted efficacy of insight therapy in such patients, and phenomenological descriptions suggesting that the inner experience of feelings and fantasies is of a different order from that of other individuals. These arguments have led him to propose a more physiological model (to be discussed below). Freyberger (1977), on the other hand, assuming a more eclectic position, draws a distinction between "primary" and "secondary" alexithymia. The former would be truly psychosomatic in nature, while the latter suggests a somato-psychic process that involves a protection against the emotional significance of serious and catastrophic illnesses, thereby interpretable in terms of defensive constriction of emotional expression.

A psychodynamic-developmental model based primarily on a deficit concept, which in many ways resembles Ruesch's (1948) lack of progression, has been espoused by the French psychosomatic group and by other authors. Its basic tenet is an impairment of function based on a deficiency in psychic structure because of disturbances in the earliest mother-child relationship. In the discussion of these issues, few authors have followed the prospective strategy adopted by Spitz (1963) and Bowlby (1969); rather, they have dwelled upon the reconstruction which takes place in the psychotherapeutic situation. This retrospective strategy—which probably lies at the core of the psychoanalytical point of view—has generated a wealth of hypotheses and observations, all related in one way or another to the mother-infant relationship and its etiopathogenetic relevance (Müller-Braunschweig, 1980).

McDougall (1974) has brilliantly summarized some of the basic concepts of the French psychoanalysts. Based on her own work with adult analysands and on the observations by Fain (1971), she concludes: ". . . there are two predominant trends in disturbed baby-mother relationships which are apt to create a predisposition to somatic pathology. The first is an unusually severe prohibition of every attempt on the baby's part to create autoerotic substitutes for the maternal relationship, thus initiating the nodal point for the creation of inner object representations and the nascent elements of fantasy life. The second trend is the antithesis of this, namely, a continual offering of herself on the mother's part as the only object of satisfaction and psychic viability" (p. 447). Having observed children who could not go off to sleep, Fain (1971) theorized that instead of a *mère satisfaisante* some had a *mère calmante*, i.e., a mother who because of her own problems cannot permit her baby to create a primary identification that will enable him to sleep without continual contact with her. The other end of the spectrum is represented by the child who engages in a type of autoeroticism that seems to eliminate the mother as an object. In these cases, "instinctual aims and autoerotic activity . . . run the risk of becoming literally autonomous, detached from any mental representation of an object" (McDougall, 1974, p. 447). The interpretation given to these observations is that they imply an absence of good object representations on a symbolic level, which has to be substituted for by concrete supplies. This would be the paradigm for the symbolization deficit embodied in the phenomenon of operational thinking and in the particular type of relatedness to others, modeled on the experience with the mother. The result, in developmental terms, is an inability to experience feelings or to achieve the capacity for fantasy as a means of gratifying instinctual drives. A super-adaptation to external reality ensues, the price for not being able to deal with instinctual drives by psychic elaboration because of deficient representation and diminished affective response. Thus, while hysterical symptom formation would be the result of repressed fantasy elaborations, these subjects would be characterized by the lack of such psychic activity. Other features of the psychodynamic-developmental model based on the deficit model can be found in Stephanos (1979a,b) and von Rad (1983).

Based on studies of drug addicts and severely traumatized persons, Krystal (1978) does not share the conclusion that alexithymic traits (which he sees related to the incapacity for self-care) are the result of a "deficiency-resulting-from-a-failure-in-internalization." He contends that there is a psychic block, an inhibition in their functions of self-soothing and self-caring, as well as others. He insists that under placebo-like conditions—in many ways related to transitional objects—these capacities may be regained. The transitional object has been associated with the origin of the capacity to symbolize and represents the first reality-based division between the self and object representations, serving as a means of alleviating anxiety arising from the threat of separation and abandonment (Winnicott, 1958). It is believed that prohibition or failure of attachment to a transitional object due to disturbed baby-mother "dialogue," may result in alexithymia-like characteristics (Gaddini, 1970).

Other theorists, while agreeing on an early fault, believe that the more primitive defense mechanism of splitting might be operative (Benedetti, 1980; Müller-Braunschweig, 1980). Further discussion of psychodynamic hypotheses has been presented elsewhere (von Rad and Lolas, 1978). Zepf (1977) has presented a comprehensive theory of "psychosomatogenesis" based on Lorenzer's (1971) studies on language, symbol formation, and interaction. Some authors (Benedetti, 1980) have invoked psychodynamic processes similar to those found in narcissistic disturbances to account for the coexistence of alexithymic-like characteristics and somatic symptom formation. An overview of this thesis is offered by von Rad (1982).

A major difficulty with psychodynamic theory is the relatively untestable nature of its constructs. They cannot be easily translated into measurable variables or formulated in terms of high consensual validity. Unless this is attempted by means beyond mere analogies, there is truly no way to decide whether a defense or a deficit model accounts better for alexithymia and leads to clearer prognostic and therapeutic predictions. While recognizing the intuitive appeal that most of this theory possesses and the many insights it has contributed, psychoanalytic writers do not usually separate the conceptual discussion of alexithymia from that of symptom formation. Despite increased efforts in this direction, it must be recognized that the underlying "ideal state" or normal person's expression of emotions has only been very vaguely described. Implicit in the psychoanalytic perspective is the assumption that the verbal expression of emotions is healthy and mature. This is a value judgment, which may not conform to norms in other, non-Western cultural settings, as has been pointed out by Lesser (1981). Although it does not seem reasonable to label someone abnormal because he or she does not conform to such standards, this has often been considered as a diagnostic criterion. The discussion of the problems posed by alexithymia from a psychoanalytical point of view certainly requires a more precise reconstruction of early events from retrospective as well as prospective points of view. Above all, more attention should be devoted to providing appropriate mechanisms linking the various components in the causal chain of events.

PHYSIOLOGICAL MODELS

Several authors have tried to account for alexithymia from a biological or physiological point of view. A possible genetic contribution was reported by Heiberg and Heiberg (1977, 1978) based on two twin studies (15 monozygous and 18 dyzygous pairs rated on the Beth Israel Alexithymia Questionnaire). Their conclusion of a strong hereditary component in alexithymia should be interpreted with caution because there were no data on sociocultural variables and rearing practices. Aside from the usual critique of such studies (the sharing of similar environments by twins), to consider alexithymia a clear-cut unitary phenomenon on the basis of a questionnaire is premature. These data, nonetheless, are valuable for their contribution to the study of alexithymia in nonpatient populations.

Neurophysiological explanations of alexithymic behavior have also been advanced. Building upon both the Papez theory of emotions (1937) and the work of several clinical researchers (especially Ruesch, Lindemann, and Ludwig), MacLean (1949) postulated that there may be an inadequate exchange between the phylogenetically more primitive rhinencephalon (visceral brain) and the neocortex (word brain) in psychosomatic patients (many of whom are alexithymic). In this way "emotional feelings built up in the hippocampal formation, instead of being relayed to the intellect for evaluation, found immediate expression through autonomic centers. In other words, emotional feelings, instead of finding expression and discharge in the symbolic use of words and appropriate behavior might be conceived as being translated into a kind of 'organ language'" (p. 350). He then compared psychoneurosis and psychosomatic illness on the basis of these postulated mechanisms. In a later reformulation of his theoretical views, MacLean (1977) has spoken of three "brains" (reptilian, paleomammalian, and neomammalian), each with its own special history, intelligence, subjective sense, memory, and sense of time and space. What is most interesting, he speculates, is the lack of a commonly shared neural code for intersignaling in verbal terms. Misunderstanding generated by this situation "might result in intrapersonal and interpersonal conflict." MacLean further proposes two types of "cerebration" subserving "emotion" and "cognition" and puts forward interesting analogies to psychodynamic formulations. Recognizing that "in the light of Freudian psychology the visceral brain would have many of the attributes of the unconscious id," he argues that this would not be the case; it rather "eludes the grasp of the intellect because its animalistic and primitive structure makes it impossible to communicate in verbal terms" (p. 209).

Starting from the above clinical observations and drawing upon both the work of MacLean and more recent neurophysiological data, Nemiah (1975, 1977) has proposed a tentative neurophysiological model. "Neurophysiology, like psychodynamic psychology is grounded on those intervening variables in the causal chain between input and output, stress and somatic symptom, whose elucidation is necessary to the understanding of psychosomatic mechanisms" (1975, p. 143). Either because of genetic factors or developmental arrest in infancy, there would exist a lack of adequate neuronal connections between those areas of the brain subserving drives and affects (limbic system) and those in the neocortex underlying the conscious representation of feeling and fantasy. The resulting failure in the "elaboration" of drives and the pathogenic short-circuiting of energy (a conception not too far from the psychodynamic theories of the French group) would result in a dissociation between physiological arousal and expression of feeling through symbolic means. The "gnostic" and "pathic" aspects of information-processing would be inappropriately integrated, and the individual would not experience conscious awareness of feelings but would undergo autonomic emotional changes from the hypothalamus, "changes which we must perhaps further postulate to be intensified and prolonged because of the short-circuiting of neocortical pathways with their potential modulating effect on the somatic processes" (1975, p. 145).

Nemiah particularly postulates the paleostriatal dopamine tract as a locus related to alexithymic phenomena and psychosomatic processes. The paleostriatum modulates the transmission of impulses from the amygdala and other limbic structures via the substantia innominata to neocortex. Following the lead of Stevens (1973), who suggests that schizophrenia might be the result of insufficient modulation by the limbic striatum of impulses reaching the cortex, alexithymia could then be viewed as the obverse of schizophrenia. Although data are scarce, Nemiah proposes several consequences of his thesis, such as the particular sensitivity to the complication of parkinsonism with phenothiazines that alexithymics should exhibit and the beneficial effects of levodopa in the alexithymic capacity to experience feeling. However, Schneider (1977) has commented that if a brain disturbance such as the one postulated by Nemiah were present, then one should expect more profound and intense behavioral manifestations.

Although no direct proof is available, physiological data might be interpreted as supporting some of Nemiah's contentions. In the study of slow event-related potentials of the brain in arousing situations (fixed foreperiod reaction-time tasks) Dongier and associates (Dongier and Koninckx, 1970; Dongier, Dubrovsky, and Engelsmann, 1976) have found that vertex negativity was more pronounced in psychosomatic than in neurotic patients, a result they interpreted within the framework of the *pensée opératoire* hypothesis. They theorized that the pragmatic orientation of these subjects (probably alexithymics) might lead to their higher involvement in the task and to the resulting higher arousal indicators (vertex negativity). Similarly, other workers (Lolas, de la Parra, and Gramegna, 1978), using the same experimental situation and the same physiological indicators, have come to the conclusion that while highly neurotic subjects *reduce* their cerebral indicators of arousal in the presence of demanding tasks, hyperthyroid subjects do not show this "inverted U" relationship. Framed within the alexithymia hypothesis, the suggestion was developed that psychosomatic (alexithymic) subjects differ from high-neuroticism ones in measures of anticipatory arousal because they are not easily distracted by the "worry" component (Sarason, 1975) or the attendant covert verbalizations commonly associated with anxiety (Lolas, 1978).

Further scrutiny of these studies must take into consideration the difficulties in the operationalism of alexithymia and the report by Anderson (1981), who has shown that although various physiological measures, such as electrodermal response, digital temperature and forearm muscle tension, showed significant increases during a stressor, a tendency was observed "for correlations between physiological level and subjective ratings of stressfulness to be negative" (p. 143). This tendency, the author writes, "did not . . . appear to be differentially expressed across the five subject groups studied. Most importantly, normal subjects did *not* show a reduced tendency toward this relationship as compared to psychosomatic subjects" (p. 149). However, Nemiah, Sifneos, and Apfel-Savitz (1977) compared the oxygen consumption of normal and alexithymic subjects in response to affect-provoking thoughts and found that the latter showed less somatic responsiveness, even though no subjective report on stressfulness was available. The authors interpreted their findings as lending support to the notion that alexithymic subjects do not process affect-provoking stimuli in the same manner as normals. However, no evidence was found of a more intense somatic response in alexithymia, as one could have predicted on the basis of Nemiah's (1975) earlier description.

Hoppe (1975, 1977a), in studying possible neural mechanisms underlying alexithymic behavior, has called attention to the "horizontal" rather than "vertical" organization of the brain.

He relates the concept of alexithymia to the cognitive and affective characteristics of patients who have undergone therapeutic cerebral commisurotomies. Dwelling upon an extensive literature documenting hemispheric asymmetry in relation to task, cognitive mode, and affective expression (Galin, 1974; Wexler, 1980), he suggests that the alexithymic characteristics of "split brain" patients might be due to an interruption of the exchange of information between the two hemispheres, which causes a separation of word representations from thing representations. Hoppe's conclusions, however, have departed from the physiological point of view and have been phrased in psychoanalytical terms, alluding to a theory of biphasic defense processes in psychosomatic patients (Hoppe, 1975, 1977a; Kleiger, 1979). An experimental approach to the relationship between hemispheric asymmetry and alexithymia was made by Kaplan and Wogan (1976–1977), who found that left hemisphere activation was associated with a reported increase in pain, while right hemisphere activation was associated with a reported decrease in pain and with apparent mobilization of fantasies. Buchanan, Waterhouse, and West (1980) theorize that the use of affect-laden speech is influenced by impaired function of the right hemisphere or a disconnection between the two hemispheres. They believe that alexithymia may be a symptom in individuals with subtle organic dysfunction, which becomes manifest in a specific social-developmental environment that inhibits emotional expression. They present a case of agenesis of the corpus callosum in which severe alexithymia was demonstrated by means of the Beth Israel Alexithymia Questionnaire.

Sociocultural Theories

Under the rubric sociocultural models we should first consider those attempts at explaining alexithymia as an artifact due to the artificial conditions under which interviews have been conducted. A number of authors have indicated that the setting employed by the French theorists—in which the patient is confronted by a group of interviewers—blocks the expression of fantasy and affect. They also point out that social class may be an important factor in any discussion of this problem in light of research that suggests a positive correlation between lower social class and psychosomatic disease (Hollingshead and Redlich, 1958). Both Cremerius and Borens conclude that the so-called "psychosomatic structure" is not disease-specific but related to social class and probably intellectual differences between middle-class and lower-class patients (Borens, Grosse-Schulte, Jaensch, and Kortemme, 1977; Cremerius, 1977; Cremerius, Hoffmann, Hoffmeïster, and Trimborn 1979). These authors, along with others (Pierloot and Vinck, 1977; Lesser, Ford, and Friedman, 1979), suggest that alexithymia is a phenomenon related to social origin and degree of sophistication of the patient. In this regard, it is interesting to recall the recommendation by Bräutigam (1974) to consider the extent to which therapist and patient may use different "languages" or "codes," particularly if they belong to different social classes. Bernstein's (1972) distinction between an "elaborated" and a "restricted" code is relevant in this context, although no empirical work has been done to explicitly test its application to alexithymia or its predictive power.

Aside from the social influence on speech, a major difficulty seems to be the types of measures employed. Schöfer, Koch, and Balck (1979) and Rost (1981) have presented data showing that lower-class subjects tend to have *higher* scores in Gottschalk-Gleser affective content categories of speech and other indices, so that the importance of differences in social class, education, psychological-mindedness or intellectual sophistication cannot be construed as the sole interpretation of alexithymia. On the other hand, it may be correct to stress the fact that the phenomenon of alexithymia has been described mainly, though not exclusively, from an analytical point of view. Certain persons seem particularly suitable for this type of therapy with its heavy emphasis on verbalization, whereas others are not. Ahrens, Gyldenfeldt, and Runde (1979) suggest that labeling someone as alexithymic might simply reflect the frustration of the psychoanalyst at not being able to obtain a response in accordance with his expectations. These authors view alexithymia as a consequence of secondary socialization processes as they manifest themselves in industrialized societies. Thus, alexithymia should not be viewed as a psychopathological phenomenon but as the end-product of sociostructural determinants of action and conscious experience.

Others (Brede, 1971, 1972, 1977; Wolff, 1977a; Zepf, 1976, 1981) have also contributed to the alexithymia framework from a sociological perspective. Although their theories are somewhat different, Zepf (1976, 1981) and Wolff (1977a) both believe that alexithymic individuals grew up in an atmosphere in which they received little encouragement to develop their communicative skills and abilities for symbolization. Such individuals might thus develop "a false self," who relates in an emotionless manner with relevant others. The social learning model implicit in these considerations would lead one to expect that parents, and even families, may display alexithymic traits. Waring (1977) has theorized that alexithymia might be a trait in psychosomatic families characterized by a kind of cohesion that limits the expression of strong feelings.

The different contexts of discussion presented here cannot be said to be mutually exclusive because they involve different levels of conceptualization, different starting points, and more or less speculative links for their respective arguments. All share the basic assumption that certain verbal expressions of affect could be defined as "normal," and each defines alexithymia as a pathological deviation from it. Since the construct was born and has continued to be studied within the framework of comparisons between neurotic and psychosomatic patients, the problems presented by sample bias should be carefully considered. As Anderson (1981) points out, the possibility should also be entertained that the neurotic samples consist of individuals with exaggerated verbalization of affect, who might also constitute the best candidates for psychodynamic insight therapies. On the other hand, a neurophysiological explanation certainly does not invalidate attempts at understanding, in psychodynamic terms, the clinical features of the alexithymic syndrome. A neurophysiological model is not necessarily the expression of therapeutic nihilism, and it does not imply that organism-environment interactions are of less importance than inherited factors. Neuroscientific research has repeatedly shown how interdependent structure and function are in the nervous system and how early experience definitely modifies the pattern of structural relations in those neural networks mediating behavior and affect (Walsh, 1980). On the basis of the empirical support offered it seems premature to focus too heavily on etiological considerations, particularly if the basic phenomenon to be explained has not been adequately operationalized nor its relevance for somatic pathology precisely determined. We shall deal briefly with these issues in the following discussion.

ASSESSMENT

Whether considered a behavioral syndrome, a communication pattern or a psychic structure, alexithymia needs to be assessed, measured, and evaluated if its potential value for psychosomatic theory is to be fully developed. One would expect that this process would benefit from the theories outlined earlier, but in reality development of psychometric instruments or diagnostic indicators has proceeded at a slower pace than the rapid generalizations about etiology and pathogenesis. The problem is essentially one of identifying appropriate observable clues that may serve as guides for inference regarding the hypothetical construct. This process should also provide a basis for comparison among different studies and serve as a starting point for prognostic and therapeutic considerations.

Some authors have espoused the view that alexithymia is an "all or none" phenomenon, that is, any given individual is or is not alexithymic (Flannery, 1977). Others support the view that it is more useful to approach its assessment from a dimensional point of view, stressing quantification along a continuum

(Bräutigam and von Rad, 1977; Lolas, 1981c). Since, as we shall see, there is not a one-to-one relationship between the diagnostic indicators used thus far and the presence of alexithymia, the solution probably lies somewhere in between; any measurable characteristic should be studied both on the basis of its theoretical relevance and its degree of generalizability. Another preliminary consideration is the population studied, since the problem of sample bias is extensive in psychosomatic research (Singer, 1977). As a complex construct intuitively derived from clinical impression, alexithymia must be evaluated with regard to the observed phenomenon, the observer, and the setting of the observation (Schneider, 1977), recognizing the biases wrought by this interaction of factors. Even assuming that alexithymia is a bona fide phenomenon, it is clear that social and cultural factors must influence its depiction to some degree. It should also be pointed out that the components of the behavioral syndrome described thus far may be more prominent in some groups of subjects than in others, or be interrelated in complex ways.

From a simple descriptive point of view, we may distinguish between three types of approaches to the assessment of alexithymia. The *direct* approach is characterized by employing clinical rules or psychometric instruments with face validity developed on the basis of observational criteria. The *indirect* approach tries to assess some expected consequence of outcome of alexithymia using indicators related to the clinical observations and theoretically relevant. To this we add the *comparative* approach which tries to answer, usually by analogy, the question of the relationship between alexithymia and other psychopathological dimensions or theoretical constructs. The latter would help answer the question whether alexithymia represents a new phenomenon or is simply an already known psychopathological dimension in a new guise.

As we stated earlier, the definition of alexithymia incorporates both a cluster of traits and an observational setting represented by the interview situation. A secondary, though no less relevant, criterion is the comparative strategy which separates alexithymic subjects from so-called psychoneurotic ones, even if the issue here is somewhat confounded by the assumed association between the alexithymic pattern and certain somatic illnesses. When all these criteria are put together, the interview situation offers the best observational setting, provided it is so standardized as to yield significant descriptors that take into account the clinical judgment of the observer.

This is precisely what the Beth Israel Alexithymia Questionnaire (BIAQ) developed by Sifneos (1973) tries to accomplish. The 23-item instrument is filled out by the interviewer after the completion of a diagnostic interview. Seventeen items refer to patient behavior and six to the observer's reactions to the patient, utilizing "yes"/"no" assessments of such aspects as use of action to avoid conflicting situations, tendency to describe circumstances rather than feelings, difficulty in communicating with the interviewer, and the like. If these questions are answered "yes," they suggest alexithymia. Eight items are considered "positive" with respect to the presence of alexithymia, so that scores may vary from 0 to 8. Although in earlier studies a score of 6 or more was considered indicative of alexithymia, subsequently it was felt that almost all 17 items were related to the phenomenon in some way (Apfel and Sifneos, 1979).

Many studies have employed this questionnaire, both in comparing patient populations and in validating scores obtained by means of other instruments (e.g., Pierloot and Vinck, 1977; Heiberg and Heiberg, 1977, 1978; Kleiger and Jones, 1980). According to Apfel and Sifneos (1979), psychiatrically experienced interviewers need no more than 30 minutes to become acquainted with its basic assumptions and to achieve a high interrater reliability. High reliability was also reported by Kleiger and Kinsman (1980). When taken at face value, however, connotations associated with the formulation of the different items lead to differences between experienced and inexperienced interviewers (experience referring here both to interviewing skills and knowledge about the hypothesis). It was suggested that the dichotomous nature of the items led to forced decisions regarding otherwise subtle gradations in the behaviors depicted by each item. Under the assumption of a continuous dimension it has been proposed that polarity profiles and analogue scales be used for each of the eight "alexithymia" items (Lolas, de la Parra, and Gramegna, 1978; Lolas, 1981c). Scores on the latter alexithymia questionnaire and on the classic BIAQ showed a high correlation when utilized by trained interviewers. Despite the fact that the BIAQ has been widely employed, large populations of normals have rarely been studied with this instrument (Heiberg, 1980). Nonetheless, it represents the most comprehensive attempt to operationalize the construct within the framework of the patient-doctor relationship.

What we call the "indirect" approach usually starts from an expected outcome or consequence of alexithymia either upon an interpersonal relationship or upon a pattern of dispositional behaviors that can be measured through self-administered questionnaires. For instance, many studies have relied upon language usage in different groups of subjects by means of formal indices, such as on-off patterns of speech interaction, or by means of content analysis depicting affective content of utterances. It has not always been clearly recognized that alexithymia is an umbrella term encompassing different elements. The exact description of the components of the syndrome and of their interrelationships is still an incompletely performed task.

There are also problems with the instruments themselves, which have produced varying results. Apfel and Sifneos (1979), in describing the two self-administered questionnaires they have used for measuring alexithymia, observed that one of them was so lengthy that almost none of the patients completed it. The other psychometric instrument, the Schalling-Sifneos Personality Profile (SSPP), consists of 20 items rated on a 1 to 4 scale. Scores can range from 20 to 80, a score of 50 or below indicating alexithymia (as reported by Blanchard, Arena, and Pallmeyer, 1981, based on Sifneos' indications). However, these scores do not seem to correlate with those derived from the Beth Israel Alexithymia Questionnaire (Kleiger and Jones, 1980).

An Italian version of the SSPP discriminated between hypertensives and controls with cardiovascular disorders other than hypertension (Fava, Baldaro, and Osti, 1980). In studies conducted on a sample of 230 undergraduates, it was found that scores were approximately normally distributed for each sex, with 8.2 percent of males and 1.8 percent of females in the alexithymia range (Blanchard et al., 1981). The same authors reported that a factor analysis of the Schalling-Sifneos Personality Profile revealed three factors, accounting for 58.4 percent of the common variance. These factors were labeled "difficulty in expression of feelings," "importance of feelings about people" and "daydreaming or introspection."

Kleiger and Kinsman (1980) have presented a 22-item MMPI alexithymia scale, validated against BIAQ scores and highly stable over time. This scale yields an 82 percent success rate when predicting alexithymia scores. A construct validation study by Doody and Taylor (1983) suggests that this scale largely measures personality features involving social overconformity. High MMPI alexithymia scorers tended also to score high on measures related to social appropriateness and defensiveness and low on the tendency to admit either to psychopathology or to psychological distress. An inverse correlation with the schizophrenia scale was also reported. The scale did not correlate with verbal expression of feelings or the capacity for fantasizing, thus suggesting that it measures only partial aspects of the alexithymia syndrome.

These results highlight the fact that it is probably too early for the fruitful development of a single instrument to measure alexithymia and that further study of the relationships between alexithymia and other psychometric indices should be pursued before attempting it. Kleiger and Jones (1980) found, for instance, lower MMPI Psychasthenia (Pt) and higher MMPI Lie (L) scores in alexithymics (rated with the BIAQ). Blanchard et al. (1981) found that the Schalling-Sifneos scale is orthogonal to other psychological tests including commonly accepted measures of depression, anxiety, and assertiveness, but correlates with a Psychosomatic Symptoms Checklist. Fava et al. (1980) reported negative correlations between the

Schalling-Sifneos scores and Neuroticism and Extraversion of the Maudsley Personality Inventory. It is interesting to note that only the negative correlation with extraversion reached statistical significance, a finding also reported for BIAQ scores (Lolas, 1981c). The last study, on the other hand, also agreed with other observations in that no significant correlations with Beck and Zung depressiveness scores were found. Thus, the question of whether alexithymia constitutes a new psychopathological dimension or not needs further study.

An interesting possibility opened by studies of this kind should nonetheless be mentioned. As Kleiger and Dirks (1980) show, subjects who scored high both on the MMPI alexithymia scale and on a 15-item MMPI Panic-Fear Scale were judged by their physicians to be more severely ill than other patients, independent of the objective severity of the patient's illness (asthma in this particular case). This observation might lead to the definition of subtypes within populations of alexithymic subjects on the basis of combined scores on different psychometric tests. It may also contribute to a better definition of the construct itself. Instruments trying to tackle its depiction in a definitive manner should separate alexithymia as a psychological dimension from alexithymia as a feature of psychosomatic or other patients.

This separation is all the more important when considering the results provided by those studies that rely upon more indirect measures. A certain circularity of argument is present in many of them, since a great majority involve a research strategy that consists of comparisons between physically ill patients and neurotic ones. Any difference between these groups, if not contradicting the basic tenets of the alexithymia hypothesis, might be taken erroneously to indicate that a useful definition and measurement of the construct has been achieved, while in point of fact just another set of observational criteria has been added.

These studies, nonetheless, may help introduce further refinements at the conceptual level and improve the design and development of more valid and reliable diagnostic instruments. This is the case, for instance, in those studies that operationalize alexithymic phenomena by equating them with the expression of fantasy in projective tests. Starting from a psychoanalytical framework and defining a "fantasy syndrome" by five categories from Rorschach protocols, Vogt, Bürckstümmer, Ernst, Meyer, and von Rad (1979) have presented comparative data which could be interpreted in terms of alexithymia. The same holds true for observations derived from T.A.T protocols, completion of stories, and personality assessment of self-image versus ideal self-image (Overbeck, 1977; von Rad and Lolas, 1978; Vogt et al., 1979; von Rad, 1979, 1982). If alexithymia is not defined in terms of the indicators used, the analogy between these observations and the clinical picture raises a question about the fit between them (as pathognomonic or paradigmatic aspects of the construct) and alexithymia itself. There is also the problem of incorporating poorly validated or unreliable measures to the data set. Although they may substantiate a distinction between psychosomatic and psychoneurotic patients or between subgroups of psychosomatic patients, these measures may be related to alexithymia in an as yet undefined form.

A number of studies have concentrated upon speech and communication patterns in bipersonal interactions, employing automatic analysis of speech patterns and complex forms of content analyses (Overbeck and Brähler, 1974; Overbeck, 1977; von Rad, Lalucat, and Lolas, 1977; von Rad, Drücke, Knauss, and Lolas, 1979; Berger, Brähler, Kunkel, and Stephanos, 1981; Lolas and von Rad, 1982a,b), as well as more experimentally oriented studies of connotative meaning (Zepf, 1976). With the Gottschalk-Gleser (Gottschalk and Gleser, 1969) method of content analysis of speech, patients suffering from organ-destructive psychosomatic illnesses generally express less anxiety and hostility during an initial interview than patients with predominantly psychic complaints. The situational dependency of this difference has also been pointed out (Lolas, von Rad, and Scheibler, 1981) with the possibility that alexithymia might appear only in interactive bipersonal situations and not in monological ones, thus constituting an attribute of the dyad rather than of its individual members (Lolas and von Rad, 1982a; von Rad, 1983).

This brief presentation of some approaches to the assessment of alexithymia and attempts to operationalize it discloses that the most widely employed psychometric instruments have not yet been extensively validated, that they possess little more than face validity and that alexithymia, as measured by them, does not seem to represent a unitary phenomenon that can be unambiguously isolated from other behavioral patterns, at least in the present state of research. The alexithymia concept has brought to light many important dimensions of analysis applicable not only to the understanding of psychosomatic illness, but which lead to a reformulation of many critical problems in medicine in general. One of its important dimensions is probably the communication of emotional meaning in patient-doctor interactions (Lolas and von Rad, 1982b), which, properly evaluated, may constitute a true biopsychosocial approach to every form of illness.

ALEXITHYMIA AND ILLNESS

It should be pointed out that there is not a one-to-one correlation between alexithymic characteristics and psychosomatic illness, since patients with the latter are found without the former, and a number of alexithymic individuals are seen without evidence of psychosomatic problems. There are clinical indications that there may be a significant relationship between alexithymia and problems of addiction as well as with patients who resort under stress to acting out . . . but, in general, the question of the distribution of alexithymic characteristics and their relationship to clinical disorders remains to be determined by further study [Nemiah, Freyberger, and Sifneos, 1976].

Since Nemiah and associates made this statement, several authors have presented material in which alexithymic characteristics have been explored in different groups of subjects. No justice can be done to the explosive growth of this descriptive literature, and only a few examples can be cited. Alexithymic traits have been reported in digestive diseases, including ulcerative colitis, peptic ulcer, and chronic pancreatitis (Overbeck, 1977; Jackson, 1977; Fava and Pavan, 1976–1977; Nakagawa, Sugita, Nakai, and Ikemi, 1979; Nakai, Sugita, Nakagawa, Araki, and Ikemi, 1979; Taylor, Doody, and Newman, 1981). They have also been described in chronic respiratory illnesses, particularly asthma (Zepf, 1976; Kleiger and Jones, 1980; Künsebeck and Zepf, 1981), skin diseases (Marty, 1958, 1969; Lefebvre, 1980), heart diseases (Dongier, 1974; Defourny, Hubin, and Luminet, 1976–1977), obesity (Waysfeld, Le Barzic, Aimez, and Guy-Grand, 1977), myofacial pain dysfunction (Heiberg, Helöe, and Krogstad, 1978), somatic complaints in general (Flannery, 1978; Heiberg, 1980), and other comparative studies (Tress, 1979; Tempfer, 1981).

Some unresolved issues still pervade the discussion of the relationship of alexithymia and illness. Sifneos (1973) reported that 25 "psychosomatic" patients outnumbered 25 control patients by more than two to one for possession of alexithymic characteristics. According to his data, alexithymic traits occurred at a base rate of 44 percent in his psychosomatic sample, the same percentage found by Kleiger and Jones (1980) in a sample of asthmatics. Overbeck (1977) reported that about 15 percent of his ulcer patients might be described as alexithymic, whereas about 50 percent of patients having peptic ulcer showed alexithymic features in a study by Nakagawa et al. (1979). These results call attention to problems of sample bias as well as to the possible influence of other factors. We have already referred to intelligence, social class, and educational level as contaminating factors (Borens et al., 1977; Cremerius, 1977; Pierloot and Vinck, 1977; Schneider, 1977).

Still other studies, most notably those by Heiberg (1980) and Kleiger and Jones (1980), have called attention to the possible influence of age. Heiberg (1980) found a significant correlation between high scores on the BIAQ and many reported somatic diseases in women 40 years of age or older, and Kleiger and Jones (1980) reported that age may account for about one-fourth of the variance in the judgment of alexithymia. However, this relationship has not been consistently reported by others (Pierloot and Vinck, 1977). Kleiger (1979) elaborates further on the need for a more careful examination of the role of aging in certain adaptational patterns that may resemble alexithymia.

Another complicating factor in these studies is the nature of the assessment procedures employed, which, as we have already seen, are not entirely devoid of problems of validity and generalizability. Many authors have suggested wider applications oriented to the development of assessment instruments (Singer, 1977; Wolff, 1977b; Lolas, de la Parra, Aronsohn, and Collin, 1980; Taylor et al., 1981). Standardization and clarification of the main dimensions of behavior that should be evaluated must be taken into consideration when using any given assessment procedure.

While it is clear that alexithymic characteristics do in fact appear in a wide variety of clinical pictures—irrespective of the contaminating factors mentioned—the relationship between these characteristics and the processes of symptom formation and their maintenance are still rather speculative. In this regard, two main directions can be discerned. One is related to the etiologic significance of alexithymia in the development of somatic symptomatology. The other, represented by what Kleiger (1979) and Kleiger and Dirks (1980) call "psycho-maintenance aspects," focuses both on how alexithymic characteristics, regardless of etiology, maintain the intractability of an illness, and how certain environmental factors help to support and perpetuate alexithymic traits in physically ill patients. A good example of the former is the description provided by Sifneos, Apfel-Savitz, and Frankel (1977):

An alexithymic individual who is faced with a potentially dangerous situation, particularly in the interpersonal sphere, which requires the awareness of feelings, and who is deficient in this area by virtue of his inability to have appropriate fantasies and language to cope with it, may find himself in a progressively frustrating situation. At first totally helpless to describe any inner feelings which do not exist, he tries to deal with the problem by going into the endless details of the "pensée opératoire." This totally inadequate reaction gives rise to further tension and he soon finds himself in a progressively helpless situation. On the verge of giving up he is forced either to withdraw in order to conserve himself or to take impulsive action in a final effort to correct a seemingly hopeless state of being. While all these changes take place in the psychological sphere, physiological reactions to this stress mobilize the autonomic and endocrine systems.

This integrative view suggests that the pathogenic signifi-cance of alexithymia resides in its reflecting a lack of appro-priate coping mechanisms for stressors, which would lead to physical symptoms if a specific (inborn or acquired) peripheral organ vulnerability does exist. As previously pointed out, this view assumes that it is healthy and mature, in our culture at least, to deal symbolically with emotion-producing stimuli.

Maintenance theories, avoiding questions concerning pri-mary etiology, are interesting insofar as they draw attention to the many factors that may lead to the intractability of illness in general, and to which attention should be devoted in any com-prehensive treatment program. Among these factors, the atti-tude of the physicians involved and of the whole network of health-related institutions deserves further scrutiny. They are particularly relevant to a consideration of therapeutic ap-proaches to alexithymic individuals.

THERAPEUTIC CONSIDERATIONS

It seems to be relatively agreed upon that physically ill per-sons are difficult to treat from a psychotherapeutic or psychi-atric point of view. We have already referred to Shands (1977) who identified the basic dimension of "unsuitability for psy-chotherapy," relating this concept to alexithymic-like charac-teristics. Other authors have found that psychotherapy with these patients is often difficult and unsatisfying, for they show low motivation and high dropout rates in forms of psychother-apeutic treatment characterized by provoking anxiety in order to achieve insight (Kellner, 1975; Karasu, 1979; Salminen, Lehtinen, Jokinen, Jokinen, and Talvitie, 1980; Sifneos, 1975; Pierloot and Vinck, 1977). Flannery (1977), like many others, believes that the presence of alexithymic traits is responsible for an exclusive orientation in some patients toward seeing organic causes as the only valid ones.

A therapeutic approach to alexithymia from the standpoint of structural nervous system damage would certainly include treatment modalities that bypass the deficit and act directly on the underlying defect. Until now, no therapies of this kind have been studied and reported. On the other hand, insofar as one of the historically important facts in the development of the alexithymia construct was the inability of alexithymic patients to profit from psychodynamic psychotherapy, the main issue for discussion will be the appropriateness of psychotherapy for these patients, and, if indicated, what modifications seem necessary.

It is interesting to note in this connection that those authors who have made observations during analytical psychotherapy of psychosomatic or physically ill patients have a tendency to consider alexithymia as developmentally determined (and hence psychodynamically understandable) and to suggest that patients with these characteristics can be brought in touch with their feelings and fantasies. To accomplish this, the investigator should make vigorous efforts to stimulate associative material concerning the patient's relationships, life experiences, and illness. Wolff (1975, 1977b) has stressed that the aim of any such therapy must be to achieve what Winnicott (1966) has called "psychosomatic integration." Patients should be helped to move out of the area of preoccupation with their body into the area of psychic experience. In dealing with the body-mind split, the therapist has at times to function as a holding mother who is able to respond adequately to the patient's bodily and emotional needs in order to make up for what his original mother was unable to provide. "When confronted with alexithymic patients the therapist is dealing with a different though related split. Here the split is between thinking and action on the one hand

and feeling and fantasy on the other" (p. 59). After devoting some comments to the problem of countertransference when dealing with these patients, Wolff (1977a) adds:

In essence, faced with an alexithymic patient the interviewer's and therapist's task is first and foremost to avoid being cast into the role of a frustrated, angry and rejecting parent figure. Instead, he has to provide a corrective experience by being a better parent than the patient's original one. . . . Interpretations alone are rarely enough to bring this about because they are so often of a cognitive rather than of an affective nature. The therapist, therefore, has to be prepared to act as a model for his patient by communicating more openly than is the rule in classical analysis how he feels, and by using the sessions for creative play in terms of shared fantasies and exploration of feelings, desires and bodily sensations [p. 62].

A similar stance had been taken by Ruesch in his pivotal 1948 article. After defining psychotherapy as "a corrective experience which enables the patient to develop his growth potentialities," Ruesch went on to state that the first phase of therapy is concerned with "making the patient aware of himself as a psychologic and biologic entity distinct from the therapist." "The therapist," he writes, "must be explicit and even primitive. . . . He must express his own emotions so that the patient can learn; he must be a concrete figure—approachable, visible, understandable, and comprehensible. The therapeutic procedure is more one of learning than of repetition of single traumatic events. . . ." (p. 138). Ruesch also pointed out that the therapist has to be aware that nonverbal expression is the only means of communication that the patient understands, thus anticipating the now widespread belief that nonverbal therapeutic approaches should have a place in dealing with alexithymic patients (Becker, 1977). Kinston and Wolff (1975), as well as Lowen (1975), have called attention to the fact that the modification of posture or breathing pattern may help release feelings which the patient has been unaware of or suppressed for many years. Wolff (1977a) remarks that it is essential to combine these other methods with proper psychodynamic understanding and ongoing analytical work.

Shands (1958), after indicating that the therapist "must insinuate himself into the patient's 'social orbit' as a real participant," observes that the process of attempting to change basic frames of reference in the patient is one which must of necessity be extremely prolonged, slow, and incomplete. Ruesch (1948) and Krystal (1979) are of the same opinion. The latter stresses the fact that alexithymic characteristics, aside from being widespread among patients, seriously diminish the success of psychotherapeutic efforts and methods. He describes roughly three phases of treatment. In the first, the patient should be helped to observe the nature of his alexithymic disturbances. The second task is helping the patients to develop what he calls affect tolerance (Krystal, 1975); in this phase the patients should reacquaint themselves with their emotions as "useful signals to themselves" rather than as "dangerous demonic forces which possess them." The next task is to gradually verbalize emotions. In these efforts, Krystal (1979) notices that there will be an underutilization (because of unavailability) of dreams and transference, and that the process may be a slow and tedious one. There is the need to demonstrate to the patients the primitive forerunners of affective experiences, and to this end the therapist must make observations, comments, elucidations, and confrontations regarding the patients' "outside" experiences. Gradually, it may become possible to shift emphasis and begin to make direct transference interpretations. An important notion in Krystal's scheme is the reconstruction of the cognitive elements of the emotion, namely, the meaning of the emotion or the "story behind it." Krystal concludes that while alexithymia represents a serious and widespread hindrance to the psychotherapeutic process, it should not be considered an insuperable barrier to it. He suggests that by studying the problems posed by alexithymic individuals, the theory and technique of psychoanalytic psychotherapy might be enriched.

Group psychotherapy of patients with somatic illnesses and alexithymia has been advocated by several clinicians for theoretical and practical reasons. A collection of papers describing various experiences of this kind has been presented in Bräutigam and von Rad (1977). Combined inpatient and outpatient group psychotherapy as well as combinations of group and individual therapy have been discussed within this framework (von Rad and Rüppell, 1975; Sellschopp and Vollrath, 1979; von Rad, 1983). These endeavors assume that the group atmosphere and the interaction with other people may lead to a facilitation of expression of feelings. Stephanos (1979a) has discussed a psychoanalytically based therapeutic milieu that in his opinion seems particularly suited to overcoming the main difficulties found in patients with *pensée opératoire*. Von Rad (1983) discussed further some therapeutic strategies for dealing with alexithymic characteristics from a psychodynamic point of view. In general, there seems to be some degree of consensus as to the usefulness of a therapeutic approach, recapitulating some of the notions involved in the concept of "anaclitic therapy" advanced by Margolin (1954), that is, those procedures that repeat stages in the relationship between the infant and the mother.

However, as we have already observed, there is a basic disagreement between psychodynamically oriented authors as to the causes underlying alexithymic behavior and to the mediating links between this behavior and illness. This fact seriously hampers any attempt to compare therapeutic strategies on the basis of theoretically sound predictions. Because of the basic framework of reference within which alexithymia is usually described, alternative nonpsychodynamic therapeutic modalities have not been extensively explored. However, some efforts in this direction have been made, such as the use of hypnosis (Schraa and Dicks, 1981), biofeedback (Rickles, 1981), and movement therapy (Becker, 1977). Although further study of such treatment modalities is necessary, many workers are presently experimenting with modifications of classical psychodynamic psychotherapy for the "reconstruction of emotionality," one of the basic endeavors in dealing with alexithymia. Whether alexithymia is a modifiable transitory phase in any psychodynamic process (Benedetti, 1980) or a permanent structural deficit—a still unresolved issue—should not deter investigators and clinicians from seeking ways to deal more effectively with this phenomenon and its possible etiopathic influence. It is hoped that a deeper probing into its etiology and assessment may help to develop more reliable and effective treatment techniques.

THE VALUE OF THE ALEXITHYMIA CONCEPT

Summarizing the Heidelberg Conference of 1976, Wolff said, "The value of such words as alexithymia and 'pensée opératoire' is that they help us more easily to communicate with each other to convey with a single word instead of lengthy descriptions what phenomena we are talking about" (Wolff, 1977b, p. 379). He also points out that the danger in using such short-cut expressions is that they might become reified, be thought of as a thing or concrete object. Much ill-directed criticism has been due to hasty generalizations and simplicity in argumentation. In view of the still confusing picture, one may conclude that the wrong question to ask is whether alexithymia exists or not. Believers and nonbelievers alike fight an endless war here.

It should not be forgotten that the value of any scientific construct resides in its fertility, in the new vistas it provides, and in the problems it opens. The first value of the alexithymia concept has been to cast doubt on any simple generalization about etiological factors in disease. Pointing toward certain behavioral regularities, it has generated a revision of current theories of affect, psychodynamic or physiological, calling attention to the already known connections between coping strategy, style of life, and illness from a perspective still incompletely explored. However poorly systematized the observations still are, the alexithymia construct has brought the communicative style of people to the foreground. To what extent communicative structures reflect psychic structures (Freedman and Grand, 1977) and under which theoretical framework their relationship should be studied will still be a matter of disagreement for years to come. Pointing toward a specific human function —language —the alexithymia construct may give further impetus to the search for organizing principles in clinical science rooted in communication and cognition (Knapp, 1980). As one psychoanalyst has put it, the ego may, in fact, be regarded as a vocal/auditory organization—a language-determined and language-determining structure which functions as a characteristic human organ of adaptation (Edelheit, 1969). A reformulation of basic theory concerning emotions, cognition, expression, symbolization, and meaning is certainly equivalent to adding a new dimension of analysis, shared by clinicians and researchers alike and incorporating biological, psychological, and social languages (Lolas and von Rad, 1982a; Lolas, 1981b).

In the treatment sphere, the alexithymia concept has brought into sharper focus certain frequently encountered difficulties in psychotherapy and will certainly stimulate new research and fresh insights into treatment modalities and alternative therapies.

There are still many unresolved issues in this area of research. The cause of alexithymic behavior is as enigmatic as the ultimate cause of any behavior pattern and will have to be further elucidated from interpretative as well as from quantitative and physiological points of view. The relationship between this communication pattern and illness is still an open question. The problems posed by the observational setting and the biases of the observers will have to be more clearly formulated and examined by empirical means. The practical implications of the concept for therapeutic measures are in need of further exploration. Despite all this, for the time being, this construct may serve a bridging function and stimulate further research.

REFERENCES

Ahrens, S., Gyldenfeldt, H. V., & Runde, P. (1979), Alexithymie, psychosomatische Krankheit und instrumentelle Orientierung. *Psychother. Med. Psychol.*, 29:173–177.

Alexander, F. (1950), *Psychosomatic Medicine*. New York: Norton.

Anderson, C. D. (1981), Expression of affect and physiological response in psychosomatic patients. *J. Psychosom. Res.*, 25:143–149.

Apfel, R. J., & Sifneos, P. E. (1979), Alexithymia: Concept and measurement. *Psychother. Psychosom.*, 32:180–190.

Axelrod, S., Noonan, M., & Atanacio, B. (1980), On the laterality of psychogenic somatic symptoms. *J. Nerv. & Ment. Dis.*, 168:517–525.

Beck, A. T., Ward, C. H., Mendelson, M., Mock, J., & Erbaugh, J. (1961), An inventory for measuring depression. *Arch. Gen. Psychiat.*, 4:561–570.

Becker, H. (1977), A non-verbal therapeutic approach to psychosomatic disorders. *Psychother. Psychosom.*, 28:330–336.

Benedetti, G. (1980), Beitrag zum Problem der Alexithymie. *Nervenarzt*, 51:534–541.

Berger, F., Brähler, E., Kunkel, R., & Stephanos, S. (1981), Untersuchungen zum Sprechverhalten und Kommunikationserleben von psychosomatischen Patienten im Zusammenhang mit dem Konzept der "pensée opératoire." *Zschr. für Psychosomatische Medizin und Psychoanalyse*, 27:45–59.

Bernstein, B. (1972), *Sozialisation und Sprachverhalten*. Düsseldorf: Schwann.

Blanchard, E. B., Arena, J. G., & Pallmeyer, T. P. (1981), Psychometric properties of a scale to measure alexithymia. *Psychother. Psychosom.*, 35:64–71.

Borens, R., Grosse-Schulte, E., Jaensch, W., & Kortemme, K. H. (1977), Is "alexithymia" but a social phenomenon? *Psychother. Psychosom.*, 28:193–198.

Bowlby, J. (1969), *Attachment and Loss*. London: Hogarth.

Bräutigam, W. (1974), Pathogenetische Theorien und Wege der Behandlung in der Psychosomatik. *Nervenartz*, 45:354–363.

—— von Rad, M. (1977), *Toward a Theory of Psychosomatic Disorders: Alexithymia, Pensée Opératoire, Psychosomatisches Phänomen*. Basel: Karger.

Brede, K. (1971), Die Pseudo-Logik psychosomatischer Störungen. In: *Psychoanalyse als Sozialwissenschaft*. Frankfurt: Suhrkamp.

—— (1972), *Sozialanalyse psychosomatischer Störungen*. Frankfurt: Athenäum.

—— (1977), Ein sozialpsychologischer Zugang zur Spezifität psychosomatischer Störungen. *Psyche*, 31:355–360.

Buchanan, D. C., Waterhouse, G. J., & West, S. C. (1980), A proposed neurophysiological basis of alexithymia. *Psychother. Psychosom.*, 34:248–255.

Cremerius, J. (1977), Some reflections about the conception of "psychosomatic patients" in the French School. *Psychother. Psychosom.*, 28:236–242.

—— Hoffmann, S. O., Hoffmeister, W., & Trimborn, W. (1979), Die manipulierten Objekte. Ein kritischer Beitrag zur Untersuchungsmethode der französischen Schule der Psychosomatik. *Psyche*, 33:801–828.

Defourny, M., Hubin, P., & Luminet, D. (1976/1977), Alexithymia, "pensée opératoire" and predisposition to coronopathy. *Psychother. Psychosom.*, 27:106–114.

de M'Uzan, M. (1974), Psychodynamic mechanisms in psychosomatic symptom formation. *Psychother. Psychosom.*, 23:103–110.

—— (1978), Zur Psychologie der psychosomatisch Kranken. In: *Hrsg. Seelischer Konflikt—Körperliches Leiden*, ed. G. Overbeck. Hamburg: Rowohlt & Reinbek (S. 170–184). (Vortrag im Sigmund-Freud-Institut, 19.11.1976: "A propos du fonctionnement mental des malades psychosomatique".)

—— Bonfils, S., & Lambling, A. (1958), Etude psychosomatique de 18 cas de rectocolise hemorragique. *Sem. Hop. Paris*, 34:922–928.

Dongier, M. (1974), Psychosomatic aspects in myocardial infarction in comparison with angina pectoris. *Psychother. Psychosom.*, 23:123–131.

—— Dubrovsky, B., & Engelsmann, F. (1976), Event related slow potentials: Recent data on clinical significance of CNV and PINV. *Res. Comm. Psychol. Psychiat. Behav.*, 1:91–104.

—— Koninckx, N. (1970), Present-day neurophysiological models of mindbody interaction. *Psychother. Psychosom.*, 18:123–129.

Doody, K., & Taylor, G. (1983), Construct validation of the MMPI alexithymia scale. In: *Psychosomatic Medicine*, ed. A. J. Krakowski & C. D. Kimball. New York: Plenum.

Edelheit, H. (1969), Speech and psychic structure. *J. Amer. Psychoanal. Assn.*, 17:342–381.

Engel, G. L., & Schmale, A. H. (1972), Conservation—withdrawal: A primary regulatory process for organismic homeostasis. In: *Physiology, Emotion and Psychosomatic Illness*. Ciba Foundation Symposium 8. Amsterdam: Elsevier, pp. 57–86.

Fain, M. (1966), Regression et psychosomatique. *Rev. Franc. Psychoanal.*, 30:452–456.

—— (1971), Prélude à la vie fantasmatique. *Rev. Franc. Psychoanal.*, 35:291–364.

Fava, G. A., Baldaro, B., & Osti, R. M. A. (1980), Towards a self-rating scale for alexithymia. A report on 150 medical patients. *Psychother. Psychosom.*, 34:34–39.

—— Pavan, L. (1976/1977), Large bowel disorders II: Psychopathology and alexithymia. *Psychother. Psychosom.*, 27:100–105.

Ferenczi, S. (1924), Über forcierte Phantasien. *Zschr. für Psychoanalyse*, 10:6–16.

Flannery, J. G. (1977), Alexithymia I. The communication of physical symptoms. *Psychother. Psychosom.*, 28:133–140.

—— (1978), Alexithymia II. The association with unexplained physical distress. *Psychother. Psychosom.*, 30:193–197.

Freedman, N., & Grand, S. (1977), *Communicative Structures and Psychic Structures*. New York: Plenum.

Freud, S. (1895), Über die Berechtigung von der Neurastenie einen bestimmten Symptomenkomplex als "Angstneurose" abzutrennen. *Gesammelte Werke I*, p. 341.

Freyberger, H. (1977), Supportive therapeutic techniques in primary and secondary alexithymia. *Psychother. Psychosom.*, 28:337–342.

Gaddini, R. (1970), Transitional objects and the process of individuation. *J. Amer. Acad. Child Psychiat.*, 9:347–365.

Galin, D. (1974), Implications for psychiatry of left and right cerebral specialization. *Arch. Gen. Psychiat.*, 31:572–583.

Gottschalk, L. A., & Gleser, G. C. (1969), *The Measurement of Psychological States Through the Content Analysis of Verbal Behavior*. Berkeley: University of California Press.

Heiberg, A. N. (1980), Alexithymic characteristics and somatic illness. *Psychother. Psychosom.*, 34:261–266.

—— Heiberg, S. (1977), Alexithymia—an inherited trait? A study of twins. *Psychother. Psychosom.*, 28:221–225.

—— —— (1978), A possible genetic contribution to the alexithymia trait. *Psychother. Psychosom.*, 30:205–210.

—— Helöe, B., & Krogstad, B. S. (1978), The myofascial pain dysfunction: Dental symptoms and psychological and muscular function. An overview. A preliminary study by team approach. *Psychother. Psychosom.*, 30:81–97.

Hollingshead, A., & Redlich, F. (1958), *Social Class and Mental Illness*. New York: Wiley.

Hoppe, K. (1975), Die Trennung der Gehirnhälften. *Psyche*, 29:919–940.

—— (1977a), Split brains and psychoanalysis. *Psychoanal. Quart.*, 46:220–244.

—— (1977b), Destruction-reconstruction of language and forms of interaction: Clinical aspects of Lorenzer's concepts. *Contemp. Psychoanal.*, 13(1):52–63.

Jackson, M. (1977), Psychopathology and "pseudo-normality" in ulcerative colitis. *Psychother. Psychosom.*, 28:179–186.

James, M. (1979), The non-symbolic nature of psychosomatic disorder: A test case of both Klein and classical theory. *Internat. Rev. Psycho-Anal.*, 6:413–422.

Kaplan, C. D., & Wogan, M. (1976–1977), Management of pain through cerebral activation: An experimental analogue of alexithymia. *Psychother. Psychosom.*, 27:144–153.

Karasu, T. B. (1979), Psychotherapy of the medically ill. *Amer. J. Psychiat.*, 136:1–11.

Kellner, R. (1975), Psychotherapy in psychosomatic disorders. A survey of controlled studies. *Arch. Gen. Psychiat.*, 32:1021–1028.

Kinston, M., & Wolff, H. H. (1975), Bodily communication and psychotherapy. A psychosomatic approach. *Internat. J. Psychiat. Med.*, 6:195–201.

Kleiger, J. H. (1979), Alexithymia: Theoretical foundations, clinical issues, and new directions in research. Psy. D. Thesis. Graduate School of Arts and Sciences, University of Denver.

—— Dirks, J. F. (1980), Psychomaintenance aspects of alexithymia: Relationships to medical outcome variables in a chronic respiratory illness population. *Psychother. Psychosom.*, 34:25–33.

—— Jones, N. F. (1980), Characteristics of alexithymic patients in a chronic respiratory illness population. *J. Nerv. & Ment. Dis.*, 168:465–470.

—— Kinsman, K. A. (1980), The development of an MMPI alexithymia scale. *Psychother. Psychosom.*, 34:17–24.

Knapp, P. H. (1980), Free association as a biopsychosocial probe. *Psychosom. Med.*, 42:197–219.

Krystal, H. (1974), The genetic development of affects and affect regression. *Ann. Psychoanal.*, 2:98–126.

—— (1975), Affect tolerance. *Ann. Psychoanal.*, 3:179–219.

—— (1977), Aspects of affect theory. *Bull. Menn. Clin.*, 41:1–26.

—— (1978), Self representation and the capacity for self care. *Ann. Psychoanal.*, 6:209–246.

—— (1979), Alexithymia and psychotherapy. *Amer. J. Psychother.*, 33:17–31.

—— (1981), Alexithymia and the effectiveness of psychoanalytic treatment. Presented at the 6th World Congress of the International College of Psychosomatic Medicine (ICPM), Montreal.

—— Raskin, H. A. (1970), *Drug Dependence: Aspects of Ego Function*. Detroit: Wayne State University Press.

Künsebeck, H. W., & Zepf, S. (1981), Zur Verhaltensnormalität bei Patienten mit Asthma bronchiale. *Therapiewoche*, 31:1015–1020.

Lang, P. J. (1979), A bio-informational theory of emotional imagery. *Psychophysiol.*, 16:495–512.

Lefebvre, P. (1980), The narcissistic impasse as a determinant of psychosomatic disorder. *Psychiat. J. Univ. Ottawa*, 5:5–11.

Lesser, I. M. (1981), A review of the alexithymia concept. *Psychosom. Med.*, 43:531–543.

—— Ford, C. V., & Friedman, C. T. (1979), Alexithymia in somatizing patients. *Gen. Hosp. Psychiat.*, 1:256–261.

Levitan, H. L. (1977–1978), Infantile factors in two cases of ulcerative colitis. *Internat. J. Psychiat. Med.*, 8:185–190.

Lipowski, Z. J. (1977), Psychosomatic medicine in the seventies: An overview. *Amer. J. Psychiat.*, 134:233–242.

Lolas, F. (1978), Event-related slow brain potentials, cognitive processes, and alexithymia. *Psychother. Psychosom.*, 30:116–129.

—— (1981a), The categorization of behavior and the expression of emotions. In: *Proceedings, 13th European Conference on Psychosomatic Research*, ed. G. Koptagel-Ilal & O. Tuncer. Istanbul: Turkish Psychosomatic Society.

———— (1981b), Psicofisiología y medicina conductual: Hacia una reformulación de la aproximación psicosomática. *Acta psiquiat. psicol. Amer. Lat.*, 27:97–106.

———— (1981c), The quantitation of alexithymia: Observations and perspectives. In: *Proceedings, 13th European Conference on Psychosomatic Research*, ed. G. Koptagel-Ilal & O. Tuncer. Istanbul: Turkish Psychosomatic Society.

———— (1982), Basic concepts in psychophysiological personality research. In: *Life Stress*, ed. S. B. Day. New York: Van Nostrand Reinhold, pp. 39–94.

———— de la Parra, G., & Aronsohn, S. (1979), Cuantificación del síndrome alexitímico: Un estudio preliminar. *Rev. Chil. Neuropsiquiat.*, 17:24–30.

———— ———— ———— Collin, C. (1980), On the measurement of alexithymic behavior. *Psychother. Psychosom.*, 33:139–146.

———— ———— Gramegna, G. (1978), Event-related slow potential correlates of thyroid grand function level. *Psychosom. Med.*, 40:226–235.

———— von Rad, M. (1982a), Communication of emotional meaning: A biopsychosocial dimension in psychosomatics. In: *Life Stress*, ed. S. B. Day. New York: Van Nostrand Reinhold, pp. 138–144.

———— ———— (1982b), Psychosomatic disease and neurosis: A study of dyadic verbal behavior. *Compr. Psychiat.*, 23:19–24.

———— ———— Scheibler, D. (1981), Situational influences on verbal affective expression of psychosomatic and psychoneurotic patients. *J. Nerv. & Ment. Dis.*, 169:619–623.

Lorenzer, A. (1971), *Sprachzerstörung und Rekonstruktion*. Frankfurt: Suhrkamp.

Lowen, A. (1975), *Bioenergetics*. New York: Coward, McCann & Geoghegan.

MacLean, P. D. (1949), Psychosomatic disease and the "visceral brain." *Psychosom. Med.*, 11:338–353.

———— (1977), The triune brain in conflict. *Psychother. Psychosom.*, 28:207–220.

Margolin, S. C. (1954), Psychotherapeutic principles in psychosomatic practice. In: *Recent Developments in Psychosomatic Medicine*, ed. E. D. Wittkower & R. A. Cleghorn. London: Pitman.

Marty, P. (1958), La Relation objectale allergique. *Rev. Franc. Psychoanal.*, 22:5–33.

———— (1969), Notes cliniques et hypotheses à propos de l'économie de l'allergie. *Rev. Franc. Psychanal.*, 33:243–253.

———— de M'Uzan, M. (1963), La pensée opératoire. *Rev. Franc. Psychanal.*, 27:34–356.

———— ———— David, C. A. (1963), *L'Investigation Psychosomatique*. Paris: Presses Universitaires de France.

McDougall, J. (1974), The psychosoma and the psychoanalytic process. *Internat. Rev. Psycho-Anal.*, 1:437–459.

———— (1980), A child is being beaten. *Contemp. Psychoanal.*, 16:417–459.

Mitscherlich, M. (1976), Ein Beitrag zur Frage der Alexithymie. *Therapiewoche*, 26:909–915.

Müller-Braunschweig, H. (1980), Gedanken zum Einfluß der frühen Mutter-Kind-Beziehung auf die Disposition zur psychosomatischen Erkrankung. *Psychother. Med. Psychol.*, 30:48–59.

Nakagawa, T., Sugita, M., Nakai, Y., & Ikemi, Y. (1979), Alexithymic feature in digestive diseases. *Psychother. Psychosom.*, 32:191–203.

Nakai, Y., Sugita, M., Nakagawa, T., Araki, T., & Ikemi, Y. (1979), Alexithymic features of patients with chronic pancreatitis. *Psychother. Psychosom.*, 31:205–217.

Nemiah, J. C. (1973), Psychology and psychosomatic illness: Reflections on theory and research methodology. *Psychother. Psychosom.*, 22:106–111.

——— (1975), Denial revisited: Reflections on psychosomatic theory. *Psychother. Psychosom.*, 26:140–147.

——— (1977), Alexithymia: Theoretical considerations. *Psychother. Psychosom.*, 28:199–206.

——— Freyberger, H., & Sifneos, P. E. (1976), Alexithymia: A view of the psychosomatic process. In: *Modern Trends in Psychosomatic Medicine*, Vol. 3, ed. O. Hill. London: Butterworths, pp. 430–439.

——— Sifneos, P. E. (1970a) Psychosomatic illness: A problem in communication. *Psychother. Psychosom.*, 18:154–160.

——— ——— (1970b), Affect and fantasy in patients with psychosomatic disorders. In: *Modern Trends in Psychosomatic Medicine*, Vol. 1, ed. O. Hill. London: Butterworths.

——— ——— Apfel-Savitz, R. (1977), A comparison of the oxygen consumption of normal and alexithymic subjects in response to affect-provoking thoughts. *Psychother. Psychosom.*, 28:167–171.

O'Connor, K. P. (1981), The intentional paradigm and cognitive psychophysiology. *Psychophysiol.*, 18:121–128.

Overbeck, G. (1977), How to operationalize alexithymic phenomena—some findings from speech analysis and the Giessen Test. *Psychother. Psychosom.*, 28:106–117.

——— Brähler, E. (1974), Eine Beobachtung zum Sprechverhalten von Patienten mit psychosomatischen Störungen. *Dyn. Psychiat.*, 7:100–108.

Papez, J. W. (1937), A proposed mechanism of emotion. *Arch. Neurol. Psychiat.*, 38:725–743.

Philippopoulos, G. S. (1977), Some remarks on the etymological and grammatic aspects of the term "alexithymia." *Psychother. Psychosom.*, 28:68–70.

Pierloot, R., & Vinck, J. (1977), A pragmatic approach to the concept of alexithymia. *Psychother. Psychosom.*, 28:156–166.

Plaum, F. G., & Stephanos, S. (1979), Die klassischen psychoanalytischen Konzepte der "pensée opératoire." In: *Lehrbuch der Psychosomatischen Medizin*, ed. T. Uexküll. München: Urban & Schwarzenberg, pp. 203–216.

Rickles, W. H. (1981), Biofeedback therapy and transitional phenomena. *Psychiat. Ann.*, 11:23–41.

Rigatelli, M. (1981), A global psychosomatic study of 16 consecutive patients with ulcerative colitis. *Psychother. Psychosom.*, 35:22–33.

Rost, W. D. (1981), Objektpsychologische Modellvorstellungen zur Theorie, Erforschung und Behandlung psychosomatischer ("alexithymer") Störungen. Fallstudie einer analytischen Gruppe. Thesis Psychology, Frankfurt/M.

Ruesch, J. (1948), The infantile personality. *Psychosom. Med.*, 10:134–144.

——— (1972), *Semiotic Approaches to Human Relations*. The Hague: Mouton.

Salminen, J. K., Lehtinen, V., Jokinen, K., Jokinen, M., & Talvitie, A. (1980), Psychosomatic disorder: A treatment problem more difficult than neurosis? *Acta Psychiat. Scand.*, 62:1–12.

Sandler, J. (1972), The role of affects in psychoanalytic theory. In: *Physiology, Emotion and Psychosomatic Illness*. Ciba Foundation Symposium 8 (new series). Amsterdam: Elsevier-Excerpta-North Holland, pp. 31–56.

Sarason, I. G. (1975), Anxiety and self-preoccupation. In: *Stress and Anxiety*, Vol. 2, ed. I. G. Sarason & C. G. Spielberger. London: Wiley.

Schneider, P. B. (1977), The observer, the psychosomatic phenomenon and the setting of the observation. *Psychother. Psychosom.*, 28:36–46.

Schöfer, G., Koch, U., & Balck, F. (1979), The Gottschalk-Gleser content analysis of speech: A normative study. In: *The Content Analysis of Verbal Behavior: Further Studies*, ed. L. A. Gottschalk. New York: Spectrum, pp. 97–118.

Schraa, J. C., & Dicks, J. F. (1981), Hypnotic treatment of the alexithymic patient: A case report. *Amer. J. Clin. Hypnosis*, 23:207–210.

Schur, M. (1955), Comments on the metapsychology of somatization. *The Psychoanalytic Study of the Child*, 10:119–164. New York: International Universities Press.

Sellschopp, A., & Vollrath, P. (1979), Psychoanalytisch-klinische therapie. In: *Psychologie des XX. Jahrhunderts*, Vol. 9, ed. P. Hahn. Zürich: Kindler, pp. 961–977.

Shands, H. C. (1958), An approach to the measurement of suitability for psychotherapy. *Psychiat. Quart.*, 32:500–521.

——— (1975), How are "psychosomatic" patients different from "psychoneurotic" patients? *Psychother. Psychosom.*, 26:270–285.

——— (1977), Suitability for psychotherapy. II. Unsuitability and psychosomatic disease. *Psychother. Psychosom.*, 28:28–35.

——— (1981), Psychosomatic disease: A disorder of individuation? In: *Proceedings, 13th Conference of Psychosomatic Research*, ed. G. Koptagel-Ilal & O. Tuncer. Istanbul: Turkish Psychosomatic Society, pp. 89–96.

Sifneos, P. E. (1972), *Short-term Psychotherapy and Emotional Crisis*. Cambridge, MA: Harvard University Press.

—— (1973), The prevalence of "alexithymic" characteristics in psychosomatic patients. *Psychother. Psychosom.*, 22:255–262.

—— (1975), Problems of psychotherapy of patients with alexithymic characteristics and physical disease. *Psychother. Psychosom.*, 26:65–70.

—— Apfel-Savitz, R., & Frankel, F. H. (1977), The phenomenon of "alexithymia." *Psychother. Psychosom.*, 28:47–57.

Singer, M. T. (1977), Psychological dimensions in psychosomatic patients. *Psychother. Psychosom.*, 28:13–27.

Spitz, R. A. (1963), Ontogenesis: The proleptic function of emotions. In: *Expression of Emotion in Man*, ed. P. E. Knapp. New York: International Universities Press.

Stephanos, S. (1975), Über die Objektbeziehungen des psychosomatischen Patienten. *Z. Psychosomat. Med. Psychoanal.*, 21:1–15.

—— (1979a), Die analytisch-psychosomatische Theorie und ihre therapeutischen Modelle. *Praxis Psychother. Psychosom.*, 24:113–131.

—— (1979b), Libidinal cathexis and emotional growth in the analytical treatment of psychosomatic patients. *Psychother. Psychosom.*, 32:101–111.

—— (with F. Berger) (1979), Das Konzept der "pensée opératoire" und "das psychosomatische Phänomen." In: *Lehrbuch der Psychosomatischen Medizin*, ed. T. von Uexküll. München: Urban & Schwarzenberg, pp. 217–242.

—— Auhagen, V. (1978), Pathologische primäre identifikationen und ihre auswirkungen auf die "psychosomatische" ökonomie des individuums. *Psychotherapie, Medizinische Psychologie*, 28:37–49.

Stevens, J. R. (1973), An anatomy of schizophrenia. *Arch. Gen. Psychiat.*, 29:177–189.

Taylor, G., & Doody, K. (1982), Psychopathology and verbal expression in psychosomatic and psychoneurotic patients. *Psychother. Psychosom.*, 38:121–127.

—— —— Newman, A. (1981), Alexithymic characteristics in patients with inflammatory bowel disease. *Can. J. Psychiat.*, 26:470–474.

Tempfer, H. (1981), Different modes of expression of psychosomatic and neurotic patients in gynecology and obstetrics. In: *Proceedings, 13th European Conference on Psychosomatic Research*, ed. G. Koptagel-Ilal & O. Tuncer. Istanbul: Turkish Psychosomatic Society.

Timsit, M., Urbain, E., Sabatier, J., & Timsit-Berthier, M. (1975), Statische Untersuchung der psychosomatischen Kopfschmerzen. *Münch. Med. Wochenschr.*, 117:1515–1520.

Tress, W. (1979), Die diagnostische Bedeutung der Alexithymie. *Medizinische Psychologie*, 5:95–106.

Vogt, R., Bürckstümmer, G., Ernst, L., Meyer, K., & von Rad, M. (1979), Experimentelle Rorschach-Untersuchung zur "pensée opératoire." *Psyche*, 33:829–873.

von Rad, M. (1979), Comments on theory and therapy of psychosomatic patients with a follow-up study. *Psychother. Psychosom.*, 32:118–127.

―――― (1980), Psychoanalytische Konzepte psychosomatischer Symptombildungen. Der gegenwärtige Stand. *Nervenarzt*, 51:512–518.

―――― ed. (1983), *Alexithymie*. New York: Springer.

―――― (1983), Überlegungen zur psychoanalytischen Psychotherapie alexithymer Patienten. In: *Alexithymie*, ed. M. von Rad. New York: Springer, pp. 160–168.

―――― Drücke, M., Knauss, W., & Lolas, F. (1979), Alexithymia: A comparative study of verbal behavior in psychosomatic and psychoneurotic patients. In: *The Content Analysis of Verbal Behavior: Further Studies*, ed. L. A. Gottschalk. New York: Spectrum, pp. 641–674.

―――― Lalucat, L., & Lolas, F. (1977), Differences of verbal behavior in psychosomatic and psychoneurotic patients. *Psychother. Psychosom.*, 28:83–97.

―――― Lolas, F. (1978), Psychosomatische und psychoneurotische patienten im vergleich. Unterschiede des sprechverhaltens. *Psyche*, 32:956–973.

―――― ―――― (1982), Empirical evidence for alexithymia. *Psychother. Psychosom.*, 38:91–102.

―――― ―――― (1983), Begriff, symptomatik und gegenwärtiger forschungsstand in der alexithymie-diskussion. In: *Alexithymie*, ed. M. von Rad. New York: Springer.

―――― Rüppell, A. (1975), Combined inpatient and outpatient group psychotherapy: A therapeutic model for psychosomatics. *Psychother. Psychosom.*, 26:237–243.

Walsh, R. N. (1980), Effects of environmental complexity and deprivation on brain chemistry and physiology: A review. *Internat. J. Neurosci.*, 11:77–89.

Waring, E. (1977), The role of the family in symptom selection and perpetuation in psychosomatic illness. *Psychother. Psychosom.*, 28:253–259.

Warme, G. E. (1980), Emotion as personal creation: A psychoanalytic and psychological perspective. *Amer. J. Psychiat.*, 137:456–459.

Waysfeld, B., Le Barzic, M., Aimez, P., & Guy-Grand, B. (1977), "Pensée opératoire" in obesity. *Psychother. Psychosom.*, 28:127–132.

Wexler, B. E. (1980), Cerebral laterality and psychiatry: A review of the literature. *Amer. J. Psychiat.*, 137:279–291.

Winnicott, D. W. (1958), *Through Pediatrics to Psychoanalysis*. London: Tavistock.

―――― (1966), Psycho-somatic illness in its positive and negative aspects. *Internat. J. Psycho-Anal.*, 47:510–516.

Wolff, H. H. (1975), Psychotherapy. Its place in psychosomatic management. *Psychother. Psychosom.*, 22:233–249.

―――― (1977a), The contribution of the interview situation to the restriction of phantasy life and emotional experience in psychosomatic patients. *Psychother. Psychosom.*, 28:58–67.

———— (1977b), The concept of alexithymia and the future of psychosomatic research. *Psychother. Psychosom.*, 28:376–388.

Wurmser, L. (1974), Psychoanalytic considerations of the etiology of compulsive drug use. *J. Amer. Psychoanal. Assn.*, 22:820–943.

Zepf, S. (1976), *Die Sozialisation des Psychosomatische Kranken.* Frankfurt: Campus-Verlag.

———— (1977), Primary socialization and alexithymic defects in symbol and concept formation. *Psychother. Psychosom.*, 28:278–284.

———— (1981), *Psychosomatische Medizin auf dem Wege zur Wissenschaft.* Frankfurt: Campus-Verlag.

Zilboorg, G. (1933), Anxiety without affect. *Psychoanal. Quart.*, 2:48–67.

Zung, W. W. K. (1965), A self rating depression scale. *Arch. Gen. Psychiat.*, 12:63–70.

Section 2.
RECENT ADVANCES IN PSYCHOPHYSIOLOGY

8.
Physiology of Stress Reviewed

ERWIN K. KORANYI, M.D.

GENERAL REMARKS

In *The Act of Creation* Arthur Koestler remarked that yesterday's discoveries are today's commonplaces. Introductory remarks frequently contain such commonplaces and truisms, if not platitudes, and thus fall victim of the reader's inattention. I was tempted to avoid this risk, but in dealing with the subject of stress it was not possible to omit a brief review of some general principles.

Stress is an elusive concept, a linguistic monster to some, the scrutiny of which poses a considerable methodological challenge to the researcher. There are those who express their scientific reservations by putting a derogatory quotation mark around the word. This is so, because stress is neither measurable nor definable. What keeps the research alive is that the other half of the equation—stress-response—is indeed eminently measurable.

On a continuum, stress is poorly delineated from its immediate left and right neighbors of stimulus and trauma. This alone explains the terminological confusion that has reigned since the early days of investigation. What most contemporary researchers, practitioners, and lay public call stress—the external force evoking a response—was named "stressor" in the early work of Hans Selye, who reserved the word *stress* to depict

241

the ensuing reaction itself. Today this would generally be referred to as the "stress-response."

With variations in meaning and emphasis, the concept of stress has been known since ancient times but its current significance has come into focus over the last 45 years, particularly through the life work of Hans Selye. The foundation was laid by Claude Bernard's recognition of the tissue need for stability and for a steady *milieu intérieur*, a concept which preceded Walter Cannon's principle of homeostasis and his study of fight/flight responses. As stress research increasingly became the concern of cellular biologists, immunologists, endocrinologists, and neurophysiologists, it also fired the imagination of psychologists and even sociologists and eventually grew to be confluent with psychophysiological research. The stress concept also became the overpopularized target of the media and the public, and nowadays it is fashionable to point an accusing finger at "stress" as a proverbial culprit behind the widest range of medical problems that happen to be difficult to explain otherwise. This popularity led directly to the modern-day alchemist formula, used by friends and practitioners alike, to "take it easy"—a prescription cheap to dispense and near-impossible to follow. In this simplistic sense "stress" has little to do with the carefully charted cellular and psychophysiological responses to external and to internal stimuli, which concerns the scientific inquirer of this question.

Stress—the word probably derives from the Latin *stringere*: to draw tight—is not easily defined. An earlier portrayal stated that stress is "the sum total of all nonspecific biological phenomena elicited by adverse external influences, including damage and defense" (Selye, 1956). However, stress is not only biological but can be psychological; is not necessarily adverse but can be challenging and instructive; is not only external but can be internal.

The original observation of the then teen-ager Hans Selye (1936)—that a collection of commonly shared symptoms regularly occur in many patients suffering from the most varied diseases ("the syndrome of being sick")—led him to conclude that a *nonspecifically induced specific syndrome* is elicited by diverse causes. As opposed to a Local Adaptation Syndrome (LAS) induced by topical tissue pathology, he regarded the assembly of shared systemic symptoms as a stress-induced General Adaptation Syndrome (GAS) consisting of three sequential steps: (1) an alarm reaction with the two subphases of shock and countershock responses; (2) a stage of resistance; and finally (3) a stage of exhaustion. He highlighted that the body's defensive reaction to adverse influences—"stressors"—can in itself cause "diseases of adaptation" as a sort of wild biological overshoot. He pointed out that stress is not a "nervous tension," nor just an emergency discharge of the suprarenal medullary, cortical, and pituitary hormones, or simply a homeostatic disbalance. He regarded the GAS as a specific entity, stating that its release, however, occurs as a result of nonspecific causes. Despite the dozen pages filled with his clarifications (Selye, 1956, 1982), the concept of stress retained some of its original ambiguity.

As it is understood by Selye, and contrary to the popularized contemporary meaning, stress is a "common feature of all biological activity" (Selye, 1956), a wear-and-tear of life itself, the consequences of which can range from harmful and destructive to invigorating and beneficial. Thus, a presumed "stress-induced" myocardial infarction is remedied by eventually prescribed physical exercises, that is, by a "stress" in its own right. Others have seen stress as "demands which tax or exceed the adjustive resources" (Lazarus, 1976) or as "the anticipation of inability to respond adequately" (McGrath, 1970). At a later date, Selye drew a somewhat nebulous and overlapping distinction between innocuous stress (also called eustress) and deleterious distress (Selye, 1974). Doing so, he consented to the growing observations of others, particularly those of Lazarus that often it is the perception and subjective mental elaboration of the individual and endowments of the personality which act as a "first mediator" (Mason 1970, 1975) in allocating a human experience to the category of stress or to distress (Lazarus, 1966; Lazarus, Cohen, Folkman, Kanner, and Shaefer, 1980). Thus, starting from cellular biology, Selye too arrived at the field of interpersonal psychology. The main thrust of stress research for the last two decades has shifted from the purely biological toward the psychophysiological direction (Lazarus, 1966; Mason, 1975). This trend was well reviewed recently by Mikhail (1981).

For some time Selye maintained that the specificity of the GAS is relative. The issue of the *specificity* of the GAS was seriously questioned by Lacey (1967) who found discrepancies —"directional fractionations"—and deviances in responses from the expected hormonal and autonomic patterns dependent upon the quality of the external stressors. Therefore, he disagreed with the uniformity of the GAS. Mason (1971) was the first to challenge its specificity by an experiment, but his research design was not quite convincing (Koranyi, 1977). Other studies (Bourne, 1969; Rose, 1969) support the idea that the quality of the environmental stress determines some of the psychoendocrine responses in conjunction with experiential factors and ego defenses.

Because stress research has so grown in size and has progressed to a complex interdisciplinary matter, its valid discussion demands some sort of partitioning. As long as the essentials are covered and the reader's attention can be upheld, it is secondary which way one goes about this task.

In pursuit of a comprehensive representation, cautiously and with some reluctance an inductive type of philosophy will be followed, highlighting first those principles that appear to be valid for the entire mammalian class. Mason (1970) cites Claude Bernard in stating that mere accumulation of data, as important for progress as it may be, would fail to provide a broader, integrated design of biology. But bold syntheses without total experimental support, at times, are known to further scientific progress. Thus, we must begin by reiterating some of the undisputed biological postulates.

Darwin's work made it abundantly clear that the physical environment over many generations gradually shapes and molds the morphology of the succeeding organisms; this is the evolutionary principle. Life is an ongoing transaction with the environment. Descent by continuous differentiation is coerced by the harshness of the external milieu, eventually evolving to multicellular systems. Such organisms not only give rise to cellular specialization and to the evolvement of the diverse viscera but simultaneously offer shelter for them against the gross changes of the environment by maintaining a nearly constant internal milieu. However, within modest limits the balance of this internal milieu, or homeostasis, is modifiable and acts like a gyroscope. This cushioned mobility represents the precondition of adaptation, and the force that challenges it is stress.

Repeated stress of the same type, essentially conditioned learning, can bring about adaptive and/or maladaptive responses. The quality of responses will depend largely on the brain-reward system. Lasting experimental functional alterations, such as hypertension, were brought about by using "reward" (Miller, 1969). Such findings confirm the assumption that even some "hard-wired" brain functions are modifiable by learning.

Confluent with a multitude of other responses, stress mobilizes both the suprarenal medulla and the suprarenal cortex, probably in that order. Recognizing that these functions are nearly simultaneous and inseparable, the primary activation of the sympathico-adrenal system in face of danger will be a good point of departure for this discussion, if for no other reason than that it would follow the historical sequence of stress research.

THE SYMPATHICO-ADRENAL
MEDULLARY ALARM REACTION

The enzymatically determined breakdown sequences of L-tyrosine to dopamine, to norepinephrine, and to epinephrine are clustered under the name of catecholamines in a close relationship, although the physiological effects of these substances

are vastly different. Cannon (1914) presumed that both norepinephrine and epinephrine are produced in the adrenal medulla and recognized their close connection both with physiological
(pain, hunger) and psychological (anxiety, anger) states. He
concluded that norepinephrine is the "everyday" hormone and
epinephrine the "emergency" hormone (Cannon, 1929). His
observation that adrenalectomized dogs failed to show functional deficit unless they were placed under stress (Cannon,
1931) supported his assumption that epinephrine is indeed secreted under emergency conditions. Directed by hypothalamic
stimuli, the outpouring of epinephrine raises blood pressure,
heart and respiratory rates, enhances neuromuscular transmission, elevates blood sugar by glycogenolysis, mobilizes fat,
redirects hemodynamic patterns to suit muscular activity, and
while increasing blood oxygenation also increases oxygen consumption. Other consequences of raised levels of epinephrine
are alertness, pupillary dilation, piloerection, and sweating,
some of which are explained in sociobiological terms relating
to readiness, enhanced visual fields, threatening body shape,
and intensified spreading of pheromones (Barash, 1977).

It is indeed impressive that upon the effusion of epinephrine
such a rapid and energetic collection of widely dispersed physiological responses occur, bringing about a state eminently
suited to face the impending task of fight or flight. It is also
apparent that this alarm reaction subserves phylogenic and on-
togenic purposes; there is something common between fight
and flight. Both share the same limbic sight in the (crudely
described area) of basolateral amygdala in relation to which an
aggression-anxiety axis (Goldstein, 1974; Lorenz, 1966) was
postulated. Empowered by the catecholamines, both fight and
flight require an immediate powerful motoric outlet. There is
a circularity between anxiety and epinephrine release—each
can initiate the other. In fact anxiety, a normal, necessary, and
required emotional modality enhancing adaptive learning, can
be viewed as the side effect of the catecholamines. Bilateral
removal of the basolateral amygdala not only causes tameness
with loss of territorial interest but also leads to lack of anxiety.

As long as the mainstay of human existence primarily required an "immediate powerful motoric outlet" for survival, our physiology remained in harmony with our life style. Civilization, however, rapidly evolved to be essentially "antimotoric" in nature, and in an artificial, particularly urban setting, some of our physiological responses became outdated. Supporting this assertion is Charvat, Dell, Folkow, and Folkow's (1964) finding that the load on the heart function is greater in the absence of motoric outlet. The clockwork of our purposeful response to danger and epinephrine release still occurs with regularity in our contemporary cultural scene, but the character of the danger has fundamentally changed, a powerful motoric outlet is rarely needed, and the chemical alterations, instead of being adaptive, serve only to undermine our composure. The now futile responses—tachycardia, rise of blood pressure, respiration rate, and blood sugar levels, and other homeostatic alterations—become a physiological burden, a source of wear-and-tear and the fons origo of conflict between neocortical and subcortical functions. Importantly, not only veritable but also anticipated danger releases these hormones. Koestler (1964) aptly called some experiences "adrenotoxic."

The physiological differences between epinephrine and norepinephrine were known for a long time (Cannon, 1931; von Euler, 1967; Frankenhaeuser, 1975), and considerable effort was spent on trying to relate mood and personality factors to the selective alteration of these substances under varied social conditions. Elmadjian, Hope, and Lamson (1957) analyzed the norepinephrine to epinephrine ratio in active hockey players during the game compared to passive spectators. In the active players, large increases of norepinephrine and small increments of epinephrine were noted, the exact opposite of findings in passive spectators. Contrary to that, Kety (1967) proposed that epinephrine is secreted whenever a motoric outlet happens to be the behavioral choice, and norepinephrine output occurs when the outcome of events is inevitable and muscular activity is futile. The findings of Bloom, von Euler, and Frankenhaeuser (1963) on experienced and novice parachute jumpers proved that under the conditions of really dangerous stress, epinephrine secretion outweighed the effect of training and habituation. Funkenstein's (1956) experiments made him conclude that people who habitually keep "anger-in" are epinephrine secretors as opposed to those who externalize "anger-out" and tend to produce higher levels of norepinephrine. Folkow and von Euler (1954) described that epinephrine and norepinephrine are released in isolation when different hypothalamic sites are stimulated, and Kety (1967) found that epinephrine passes through the blood brain barrier at certain hypothalamic regions. The latter finding is fundamental from the point of view of central regulation.

Much of the work on selective excretion of epinephrine and norepinephrine was done by Frankenhaeuser and associates (Frankenhaeuser and Jarpe, 1962; Frankenhaeuser and Patkai, 1965; Frankenhaeuser, 1974, 1978). They also showed that sex differences, with higher epinephrine output occurred in the male versus female engineering students under achievement-stress (Collins and Frankenhaeuser, 1978), which was confirmed later by Lundberg, de Chateau, Weinberg, and Frankenhaeuser (1981). Selective output of these substances in relation to social situations was also described in this study. Not only distressful but also pleasurable stimuli cause epinephrine and norepinephrine release. In an earlier study Johansson and Frankenhaeuser (1973) related ego-strength to hormone secretion and found that a rapid normalization of epinephrine level signified good adjustment. Lazarus and Alfert (1964) showed "scary" film strips to an audience while measuring their physiological parameters and found that those who tended to deny fear or threat showed more significant departure from baseline levels.

A wide variety of interhormonal patterns was described in dominant, aggressive, submissive, and defensive behaviors, commonly referred to as "agonistic behavior," without providing any distinct or predictive clues that are uniformly acceptable. Many of these investigations were carried out by using less reliable, old laboratory techniques and were performed on collected urine samples of the subjects. More accurate, radioen-zymatic assays on plasma have been available for less than 14 years (Engelman, Portnoy, and Lovenberg, 1968). This fact may account for some of the controversial results. Although Ahlquist (1948) had already described α- and β-adrenergic receptors, not until the arrival of modern techniques (Iversen, 1975) were the effects of epinephrine and norepinephrine on receptor sites understood. Both of these substances act on both kinds of re-ceptors but the receptors mediate different effects. The α-ad-renergic receptor activation will cause constriction of the blood vessels, the sphincters of the stomach, urinary bladder trigone, and uterine smooth muscles and will inhibit insulin effects. Its activation probably occurs via cyclic-guanidine-monophosphate (Goldberg, O'Dea, and Haddox, 1975). The β-receptor function will result in increased heart rate, contractibility and conduction velocity, and shorter A/V refractory period, dilatation of the blood vessels, and relaxation of the smooth muscles of the bron-chi, stomach, urinary bladder, and uterus. The β receptors are activated via cyclic-adenosine-monophosphate, as second mes-senger (Lefkowitz, 1976). More recently, dopamine-β-hydrox-ylase release (Mathew, Beng, and Taylor, 1982), the level of the enzyme responsible for converting dopa to norepinephrine, was used as a measurement of anxiety.

Epinephrine is produced mainly in the adrenal medulla, a sort of sympathetic postganglion without axons, and is trans-ported to its receptor sights via the blood circulation; therefore epinephrine is a hormone, par excellence. While the adrenal medulla also contains some norepinephrine, this substance is mainly a neurotransmitter which is released from the axon ter-minals of the sympathetic postganglionic neurons and acts as a hormone only under exceptional circumstances, such as in hypoglycemia (Cryer, 1980). A most interesting investigation was performed by Cryer who gave graded doses of norepi-nephrine and epinephrine in infusion to subjects and found that only about ten times the base levels of norepinephrine could cause hemodynamic and metabolic changes. Graded in-fusion of epinephrine, on the other hand, produced different responses at different levels of plasma concentration: increased heart rate at 50 to 100 pg/ml; lipolysis and systolic pressor effect at 75 to 125 pg/ml; hyperglycemia, ketogenesis and glycolysis at 150 to 200 pg/ml and suppression of insulin secretion at 400 pg/ml. All of these levels are commonly reached both in health and sickness and prove that epinephrine is an important regulatory hormone both in states of stress and without it. Cryer also found that both epinephrine and norepinephrine are rapidly cleared from the system and that they appeared to facilitate their own metabolic clearances. The clearance is modulated only by the β receptors. An α-adrenergic blockade by administration of phentolamine had no effect on the rate of metabolic degradation of the catecholamines. However, a β-adrenergic blockade by propranolol reduced catecholamine levels to more than 50 percent below the basal rate (Cryer, 1980).

The clinical significance of the altered sympathico-adrenal activity will be discussed later. As a way of emphasizing the significance of this issue, I wish to recall the experiment of von Holst (1972) who found that shrews, confronted simply with aggressive cage mates, died of uremia in less than 20 days. The autopsy showed extensive glomerular damage due to ischemia.

THE HYPOTHALAMIC-ADRENOCORTICAL SYSTEM

Under conditions of stress, more enduring than the effect of the catecholamines is the function of the steroid hormones of the suprarenal gland. This hormonal response represents the cornerstone of Selye's research. Built from acetate in the liver, cholesterol is the master substance of all steroids. Three subvarieties of such hormones are produced in the cortical part of the suprarenal gland: sex steroids, mineral steroids, and glucosteroids. The biosynthesis is determined by the locally available unique assortment of tissue-bound enzymes.

The release of the steroids into the circulation is under the hierarchical control of the anterior pituitary gland and of the central nervous system. The anterior pituitary adrenocortico-tropin hormone (ACTH), a polypeptide, is secreted in the chromophobe b-3 cells. ACTH is a rate-limiting step in hydro-lyzing cholesterol esters to cholesterol and initiating steroido-genesis (Rees, 1977). In turn, ACTH secretion is regulated by the corticotropin-releasing factor (CRF), a peptide, the first of the nine hypothalamic neurohormones described by Saffran and Schally (1955), which is still not isolated. Edwards (1977) believes that vasopressin acts as CRF. The CRF is produced in the palisadic zone of the hypothalamic median eminence (Kor-don, Enjalbert, Hery, Joseph-Bravo, Rotsztejn, and Rutberg, 1981). In this area neocortical and limbic connections coexist with neurofibers sensitive to corticosteroids, thus closing the cybernetic feedback loop. Fibers responsive to rhythmic changes and those responsive to internal and external stress have also neuronal input in this anatomic area. Such stimuli can initiate direct release of CRF, indirectly leading to ACTH output and rise in corticosteroid levels. Elevated corticosteroids then can shut down CRF production. The function of an intermediate lobe C-peptide is unknown. Some details of steroidogenesis is shown in Figure 1.

ACTH, like many other vital neurosubstances, derives from the large polypeptide, β-lipotropin, and in fact represents spe-cific fragments of it. The β-lipotropin contains 91 amino acids in unique sequences. The 61st to the 91st portion of it is known as C-peptide, or endorphin. A still smaller part of the C-peptide, from the 61st to 65th, is enkephalin. ACTH is the 1st to 39th amino acid sequence of the β-lipotropin.

Corticotropin release is not the only action of the ACTH. DeWied (1973) found that smaller fragments of the ACTH, namely from the 4th to the 10th amino acid sequences, have a positive effect upon learning and memory, along with other neurosubstances, such as vasopressin. This was well reviewed by Ungar (1980).

Unlike proteins, the steroid hormone production is not un-der direct genetic control, but the biological activity of the local

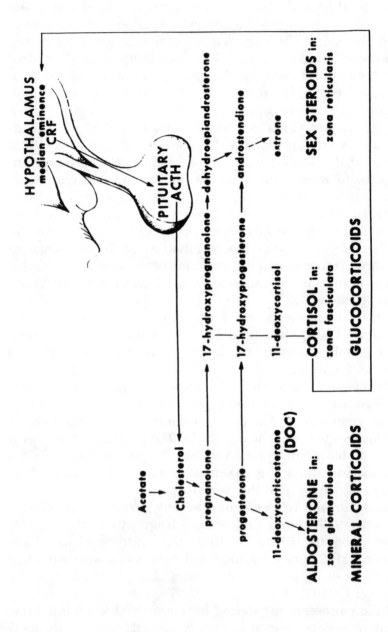

Figure 1. Suprarenal steroidogenesis and its central control.

enzymes involved in their biosynthesis, ACTH as well as CRF, is determined by the genetic code, its transcription, translation and regulation.

Cortisol represents 70 to 80 percent of the total 17-hydroxycorticoids in the circulation. Only about half of this is in a biologically active state, protected by corticosteroid-binding globulins (transcortin) and by albumin. The other half is bound to glucuronic acid in an inactivated state. Blood cortisol levels are subject to diurnal variation, the highest levels being reached around 6 A.M., the lowest around midnight.

The response to threat and to danger is a confluent, multihormonal and autonomic nervous system dislocation from the resting baseline, which does not easily permit a separate analysis of the effect of a particular single component. Nevertheless, especially in the countershock phase, the biological profile of the cortisol secretion clearly emerges. The partial antagonism between mineral corticoids (DOC, aldosterone) and glucocorticoids (cortisol) was emphasized by Selye (1956) since his early observations and in fact led him to the formulation of the Local and the General Adaptation Syndromes. He viewed aldosterone as a "pro-inflammatory" agent responsible for the Local Adaptation Syndrome and cortisol as the "anti-inflammatory" agent relating to the General Adaptation Syndrome. Biological stress originally was induced with foreign-protein injections to rats by Selye, who in the shock phase observed lowering of the blood pressure, temperature, glucose, sodium and alkali reserve along with hyperkalemia, lymphocytosis, and hemoconcentration. In the subsequent countershock phase, a rebound of defenses, intensive ACTH activation and cortisol outpour, elevation of glucose levels, cardiac output, blood pressure and total white blood count, with decrease of lymphocytes, eosinophils, and basophils, constriction of the renal vessels, gastric hyperemia, sometimes with ulcers, will occur. The thymolymphatic suppression and eventually the atrophy of the thymus, spleen, and lysis of the lymphatic nodes have a major impact upon the immune responses. No countershock response can be elicited in hypophysectomized animals.

Chronic stress sometimes will cause circumscribed, not encapsulated, proliferative nodules surrounded by atrophic tissue in the suprarenal cortex. With endogenous elevation of cortisol, as in the "side effects" of exogenous cortisone administration, water retention, rarification of the bones with disordered calcium metabolism, muscular atrophy, altered metabolism of fat (buffalo hump), diabetes, reduced resistance to infections, hypertension, and worsening or even perforation of duodenal or gastric ulcers can be seen. Enhancement of seizure tendency due to central GABA suppression occurs in the epileptic patient. All of these consequences are usually less pronounced in stress-related elevation of cortisol compared to what occurs with administration of pharmacological doses.

Sustained overproduction of cortisol is the hallmark of the stage of resistance with a LAS–GAS imbalance (Fernandez, 1981).

Corticosteroids are not produced in the central nervous system and they pass freely the blood-brain barrier. Catecholamines are synthesized within the centrums, however, and are strictly separated by the blood-brain barrier from their peripherally produced counterparts. Cortisol increases the re-uptake of norepinephrine in the brain tissue by accelerating the degradation of the norepinephrine through the enzyme monoamineoxidase and eventually leads to its depletion (Maas, 1972). Prolonged administration of cortisone will not only impoverish the brain of norepinephrine but also of serotonin. Cortisol also facilitates the enzyme phenylethanolamine-N-methyltransferase, which is required for norepinephrine-epinephrine conversion. These interactions explain the frequent depression with cortisone therapy and in Cushing's syndrome.

Psychosocial stress response is rarely as extreme and overpowering as the one observed in physical pathophysiology, such as toxic or septic illness, but its significance is remarkable.

The differences in mean cortisol levels in the absence of physical illness are quite varied in the population and are subject to body weight, nutritional status, external temperature, mood, genetic makeup, and a wide assortment of factors. Mason,

Buescher, Belfer, Mougey, Taylor, Wherry, Ricketts, Young, Wade, Early, and Kenion (1967) attempted to separate out features of personality type, psychological defenses utilized and even historical and developmental variables by the baseline levels and by endocrine responses of the 17-hydroxycorticosteroids (17-OHCS). Poe, Rose, and Mason (1970), in analyzing 17-OHCS, found that those young men whose parents died in their childhood had high- or low-range but still normal mean baseline levels of 17-OHCS. Those with maternal death had a high range of 17-OHCS and those with paternal death showed low to normal values. It was also observed that under conditions of group living, such as in Army camps, after some time the cortisol levels tended toward a common median (Marchbanks, 1958).

Brady's (1958) classical experiment with monkeys tied to a restraining chair and getting pre-signaled unpleasant electric shock has shown that the available behavioral repertoire is a crucial factor in the outcome of stress. Those monkeys who had no choice but to endure the displeasure faired better. The ones who upon a signal heralding the shock could prevent the shock by pressing a lever, the so-called "executive monkeys," developed ulcers.

Bourne, Rose, and Mason (1968) studied the 17-OHCS urinary output in two groups of soldiers. The first group consisted of untrained soldiers undergoing strenuous basic training in New Jersey. They showed a uniform elevation of 17-OHCS. The second group was a platoon of extremely well-trained Green Beret soldiers in an actual precombat situation in Viet Nam. Of this group, all of the enlisted men showed a lowering of the 17-OHCS values, the lowest levels being measured on the day of the attack. The two officers and the radio man in this group, facing a different quality of stress with less mobility and being challenged by the more experienced enlisted men, revealed an elevation of the 17-OHCS levels. All had lowered testosterone levels, except one, whose behavior pattern was such that he avoided commitments to his work.

In the absence of physical pathology, a moderate elevation of cortisol levels may indicate the presence of nonspecific psychosocial stress. This may be observed in a variety of psychiatric illnesses. Cortisol levels ordinarily may be suppressed by the administration of a synthetic steroid, dexamethasone, which is a standard test used in diagnosing steroid-producing tumors. More recently Carroll, Feinberg, Greden, Tarika, Albala, Huskett, James, Kronfal, Lohr, Steiner, de Vigne, and Young (1981), who gave smaller doses of dexamethasone to patients, described a relative nonsuppressibility or an "early escape" from depression (particularly in reference to the 4 P.M. sample) and were able to differentiate depressions from other psychiatric disorders in 50 percent of the cases. Some major stressors, such as surgical stress can override powerful dexamethasone (5 mg/hour) or cortisol (50 mg/hour) administration (Rees, 1977).

OTHER ENDOCRINE RESPONSES TO STRESS

Even one single chemical alteration will change the values of a string of others in vivo, sending ripples through the endocrine-metabolic pool. Selective sets of agonistic and antagonistic chemical-neural responses, corresponding to a real or to an anticipated task ahead, will be funneled into predetermined patterns. The activation of the hypothalamo-pituitary-adrenal axis resulting in elevation of catecholamines and steroids occurring upon stress was already outlined, along with a multitude of secondary and compensatory biochemical changes. Additionally, there are other neuro-peptides and hormones that will respond to stress in their own right. Of these, the pituitary growth hormone, the prolactin, and their hypothalamic regulatory substances occupy a prominent position.

Among other biological roles, the growth hormone is one of the important links in the regulation of glucose levels. Hypoglycemia, which is a powerful biological stress, is a trigger of growth hormone release, so much so that insulin-induced hypoglycemia is a standard clinical method to test the function of the pituitary with respect to the release of the growth hormone. Conversely, high blood sugar levels will shut off growth hormone production.

The rate of growth hormone secretion occurs in small pulsatory patterns during daytime, but a sharp rise takes place upon falling asleep and throughout the slow wave sleep stages. A nocturnal rise of growth hormone with an irregular secretion pattern was found in depression (Schildkraut, Chaudra, Osswald, Ruther, Baarfusser, and Matussek, 1975). The degree of this hormonal alteration was proportionate with the severity of the depression. Administration of arginine, estrogen and L-dopa will elevate growth hormone levels, as will physical exercise and fasting. An excessive release of growth hormone can also be achieved following apomorphine injection, a procedure that is now used to predict the effectiveness of lithium therapy in some psychiatric conditions (Hirschowitz, 1982).

Growth hormone values readily rise upon internal or external stress (Brown and Reichlich, 1972), although not nearly as consistently as is the case with the elevation of cortisol levels. Such capricious growth hormone levels during stress were found by Suematsu, Kurokawa, Tamai, and Ikemi (1974) and Mason (1975) who blamed it on individual response patterns and elusive psychological variables, and by Rose, Hurst, and Herd (1979) who thought that growth hormone elevation may occur only in acute and major stress, such as parachute jumping. Their study of approximately 400 air traffic controllers over a period of three years could not reveal any positive relationship between stress, cortisol, growth hormone levels, or cardiovascular or psychiatric illnesses but established categories of habitual high-, middle- and low-hormone responders.

The growth hormone production is under the dual control of two opposing factors in the hypothalamus. The growth hormone releasing factor which stimulates the growth hormone secretion is not yet identified but there is little doubt as to its existence. On the other hand, the growth hormone inhibiting factor, somatostatin, is well known. Somatostatin is ubiquitous in the brain with highest concentration in the preoptic area and the median eminence. However, somatostatin is also produced in other parts of the body, and its physiological role in all of these locations is similar, that is, inhibition of glandular productivity. Somatostatin halts growth hormone secretion in the pituitary, insulin, and glucagon secretion in the pancreas and the excretion of secretin and acidity in the stomach. Somatostatin causes nitrogen retention and elevation of both intracellular and blood levels of amino acids. It also bears a close relationship to dopamine.

In view of the inconsistencies of the measured growth hormone levels under stress, a recent finding of Engelhardt and Schwille (1981) is most interesting. These experimenters administered graded series of stress to mice and found elevated levels of circulating somatostatin. If these results also refer to hypothalamic somatostatin excretion, and if the experiment can be duplicated as well as applied to human responses, a lowered, rather than raised growth hormone level under stress could be expected.

Despite a striking elevation of prolactin levels to stress (Noel, Suh, and Stone, 1972), its behavioral correlates are subtle, and due to difficulties with its exact measurement until recently, it is still not explored sufficiently. Prolactin secretion is also under dual hypothalamic control. Prompted by the prolactin-releasing factor, its secretion is suppressed by the prolactin-inhibiting factor (PIF). The latter is triggered by the tuberoinfundibular dopaminergic tract; therefore, dopamine-suppressing drugs, such as phenothiazines and butyrophenones, will raise prolactin levels, as will the administration of arginine. Decrease of prolactin production occurs with the use of L-dopa, MAOI, and such ergot alkaloids as bromocriptine.

Of the many physiological effects (Frantz, 1978) of prolactin the best known is its effect on lactation, with a delicate circularity between the suckling style of the infant and maternal levels of prolactin. In many species prolactin also has a positive impact upon the behavioral modality of mothering, and both in animals and humans it has a distinct "antisexual" action with undue elevation causing an anorgastic state and impotence (Koranyi,

1982). In human pathologies such as galactorrhea-amenorrhea (Kleinberg, Noel, and Frantz, 1977) and pituitary microtumors (Wilson and Dempsey, 1978), the sexual dysfunction can be reversed by administration of bromocriptine. Prolactin levels are low to normal in anorexia nervosa. Prolactin is secreted in the anterior pituitary in a fast changing pulsatile manner, the levels being higher at night, with the notable exception of the REM periods when it falls to the lowest levels (Thorner, 1977). Nocturnal elevation of prolactin was thought to be mediated by serotonin. Prolactin responses strikingly support Mason's (1975) conclusion that a high degree of endocrine selectivity exists corresponding to psychological variables. An experiment by Kolodny, Jacobs, and Daughaday (1972) found that self-stimulation of the nipples of women caused some rise in the prolactin levels but the elevation was much more pronounced when the nipples were stimulated by their husbands. Males had no rise of prolactin levels with self-stimulation of the nipples but did show some augmentation when stimulated by their wives.

Prolactin levels rise with the stress of surgery. In small doses prolactin elevates and in higher doses it lowers the blood pressure (Horrobin, 1974). It also causes retention of sodium, potassium, and water. Importantly, prolactin restores the sensitivity of the human adrenals to ACTH.

Since the thyroid-releasing hormone (TRH) promptly elevates prolactin levels, a process prevented by the administration of L-dopa, it was thought that this substance is identical with the prolactin-releasing factor. It was found, however, that prolactin can be released without TRH.

Thyroid response to stress remained a vague area, despite the ancient custom in Tyrol to measure the bride's neck before and after the wedding night as an estimation of the "endured stress." Unlike most other hormones, large quantities of active and inactive hormones are stored in the thyroid gland in the form of T_3 and T_4. They are discharged into the circulation upon the anterior pituitary thyroid-stimulating hormone (TSH), a glycoprotein, which works on the gland via the cyclic AMP. In turn, the TSH is activated by the TRH.

The TRH, a tripeptide, is present in all parts of the brain with the exception of the cerebellum, reaching high concentration in the septal regions with the highest values in the preoptic area (Schally and Arimura, 1977). The TRH not only raises thyroid hormone levels via the TSH but has a nonendocrine direct effect on the brain. This was first suggested by Prange, Wilson, and Rabon (1969), who found a therapeutic potentiation of imipramine when given together with TRH. Although Ehrensing and Kostin (1977) report that 25 to 50 percent of the depressed patients have reduced TSH response to TRH provocation, the hormonal studies have not contributed markedly to the understanding of the depressive syndrome (Anisman and Lapierre, 1982).

The most outstanding stress response of the thyroid hormone consists of a pronounced elevation upon exposure to cold (Yuwiler, 1976). In fasting and in anorexia nervosa the circulating thyroid levels are low but the TSH shows no elevation, probably an expression of an energy-conserving mechanism. In surgical stress, the TSH levels are thought to be low although the measurement of TSH by radioimmune assay is notoriously unreliable at levels of "low" values. Glucocorticoids tend to suppress thyroid hormone levels, while catecholamines and serotonin facilitate its release.

The stress-related aspects of the prostaglandins are that ACTH activation of the adrenals will regularly elevate certain forms of this substance and lower other ones.

ASPECTS OF PSYCHOIMMUNOLOGY

One of Selye's (1956) earliest observations was an atrophy of the spleen and of the thymolymphatic system under the stress of injected foreign protein. This procedure resulted in a cortisol-mediated immunodeficiency, expressed by lymphopenia, the degree of which was found to be dose-related according to the quantum of the injected material. A stress-induced elevation of the "anti-inflammatory" steroid, cortisol, as Selye postulated, permits foreign proteins, microbes included, to coexist with the host.

Selye's description proceded by many years the spectacular evolution of modern immunology, let alone psychoimmunology, which in those days rested on no more evidence than the anecdotal connections between psychic traumatization and enhanced susceptibility to illness. Kabat, Wolf, and Bezer's (1947) discovery that injected whole brain tissue with Freund's adjuvant caused an experimental allergic encephalomyelitis is commonly held to be the cornerstone of neuroimmunology (Oldstone, 1975), but it was not until the development of the surface antigen markers in the early seventies (Kunkel, 1975) that the bone marrow-derived B lymphocyte could be differentiated from the thymus-derived T lymphocytes and their respective roles in the immune responses be mapped out. An attempt to cover only the most important principles of immunology as they relate to psychiatry is a task far beyond the scope of this chapter. The reader is referred to Rogers' chapter in this volume and to reviews by Kies (1975), Alvord, Shaw, Hruby, Petersen, and Harvey (1975), and McFarlin (1975). Nevertheless, a few selected facts, so necessary for the grasp of stress research in immunology and for the understanding of the reviewed material, will be briefly outlined.

The B lymphocytes produce the antibodies, the five classes of immunoglobulins—IgG, IgM, IgA, IgD, IgE—and their subvarieties, each within rigidly quantified physiological limits, of which the IgG is the largest component. When the receptors, mainly IgD and IgM, on the surface of the B lymphocyte are stimulated the cell becomes a plasma cell. Antigens—unique and specific chains of amino acids—are made up from a light and a heavy protein chain containing "variable" and "hypervariable" zones. Their enormous capacity to produce diverse antigen combinations is not entirely determined genetically, although fragments of information are carried in gene segments. From some 300 genetic segments 18 billion antigens can ensue (Lader, 1982). B lymphocytes can be distinguished and numerically counted in different ways, one of which utilizes the propensity of the antibody—and complement-coated erythrocytes to form characteristic rosettes (EAC-rosetting) around the B cells, which bear membrane surface immunoglobulins.

The T lymphocytes and their subvarieties, coming in contact with antigens to which the lymphocyte happens to be sensitized, release lymphokines, such as the migration-inhibiting factor, and cause a delayed, cell-mediated immune reaction. Such cellular immunity has many clinical consequences, one of which is the demyelinating diseases in the central nervous system (McFarlin, 1975). The T lymphocyte also has surface antigens or receptors, and when it is activated the T lymphocyte becomes a blast cell or blastogenic response. Under such conditions the T lymphocytes emit mediator substances which in turn aid the function of the B lymphocytes (Friedman, 1975). The T lymphocytes produce a remarkably different kind of rosetting with sheep erythrocytes (E-rosetting), a propensity which permits counting of their numbers.

Not only are there techniques available to establish the number of the lymphocytes, but there are ways to measure the degree of their functional competence as well. T cell functions can be explored by stimulating the cell with mitogenic substances, such as phytohemagglutinin, concanavalin A, or by agents such as purified protein derivate of tuberculin (PPD). Subvarieties of T cells are of several kinds, such as suppressor and helper cells, regulating the immune response. The suppressor cells are found to be higher in the young and lower in older age, a fact which contributes to the understanding of the increased autoantibody formation in presenescence (Folch and Waksman, 1974).

Both the T cell mediated cellular immunity and the B cell mediated humoral immunity represent a highly specific antigen-antibody reaction, and are so precisely regulated and have such a predictable outcome that they determine whether there will be an immune response to an antigen at all, and if so, of what magnitude, what classes of antibodies will be formed, and which subsets of the antigen-specific T cells will be induced (McDevitt, 1980).

It is the characteristic of the injured tissue that a sensitivity to its own components may ensue, giving rise to titreable antibodies to cellular fragments. This hypersensitivity may then lead to numerous varieties of autoimmune diseases (Allison, 1976), some of which have a major significance in neuropsychiatry.

The study of the immunological responses surged with the advent of the era of organ transplantation and was prompted by the concern with the problems of foreign tissue rejection. The responsible agents for this, the transplantation antigens, were first identified in the peripheral lymphocytes and named human leukocyte antigens, HLA or HLA system (McDevitt, 1980). Soon many subvarieties of HLA antigens were recognized and their origin in the sixth chromosome was determined. The significance of the HLA system in a wide variety of physical illnesses now is evident, and the ongoing research with these substances is beginning to have a major impact on psychiatry. The relatedness of the HLA markers to mental depression (Smeraldi, Negri, Melica, and Scorza-Smeraldi, 1978; Weitkamp, Stancer, Persad, Flood, and Guttormsen, 1981) was recently explored. Interestingly, these authors found that genes deriving from a nondepressed parent might in fact be the determinant of the tendency for depression in the offspring. The autoimmune model of schizophrenia was furthered and reviewed by Pandey, Gupta, and Chaturvedi (1981), and its possible association with malabsorption syndrome was reported (McGuffin, Gardiner, and Swineburne, 1981). In addition, experimental evidence for stress-induced suppression of T cells in the etiology of the arteriosclerosis was described (Lattime and Strausser, 1977).

Many of Selye's original observations of stress-induced immunosuppression were confirmed. Monjan and Collector (1974) assayed the splenic lymphocytes obtained from a standardized male mice population following immunization with a T cell dependent antigen. After this the colony was exposed to daily auditory stressors. The in vitro measurement of the lymphocyte functions by blastogenic activity of concanavalin A and by other means revealed that short exposure to the sound stressor caused immunosuppression, and longer exposure resulted in enhancement of the immunity. One is tempted to parallel these results with Selye's countershock phase and the stage of resistance in the GAS. Keller, Weiss, Schleifer, Miller, and Stein (1981) subjected rats to a graded series of stressors consisting of measured electric shocks. They reported a proportionate suppression of the immune responses as measured by the mitogen-induced blastogenic transformation of the lymphocytes.

Social stress consisting of change from an individual to group housing, or of social isolation in mice, was found to favor tumor growth following tumor cell transplantation (Sklar and Anisman, 1979). Prolonged competition for basic life needs under difficult conditions or in face of predictable failure was found to heighten the risk for arteriosclerosis, kidney failure, hypertension, or cerebrovascular accidents in animals (Gottschalk, 1982).

Demonstration of stress-induced immunosuppression in human stress conditions is naturally more interesting for the clinician. Bartrop, Luckhurst, Lazarus, Kiloh, and Penny (1977) explored the T and B cell numbers and measured their functional changes occurring in the bereavement of 26 people after two, and again in six weeks subsequent to the loss of their respective spouses, as compared to a control group. No change in the number of T cells, as measured by E-rosetting had occurred, and the EAC-rosetting showed no numerical alterations in the B cells. The B cell functions with regard to IgG, IgA, and IgM during the bereavement were also normal. However, striking immunosuppression was demonstrated in the T cell functions in response to mitogenic stimulation with phytohemagglutinin and with concanavalin A in the bereaved group of individuals. Serial measurement of mean levels of cortisol, growth hormone, prolactin, and thyroid hormones yielded no significant differences in the two groups. The authors interpreted these results by assuming that T cell immune alterations are independent processes, not directly resulting from the influences of the measured hormones. They cited the only other prospective study reporting a lymphocyte suppression and rosette formation, which occurred in astronauts on the day of the splashdown by the NASA Center.

It was already implied that sport and physical exertion is a stress in its own right. Immunoresponses to short, brisk exercise were measured by Steel, Evans, and Smith (1974) and by Yu, Clements, and Pearson (1977). A transient increase of B cells and a decreased response of the isolated lymphocytes to mitogens and to PPD was observed. Hedfors, Holm, and Ohnell (1976) demonstrated decreased immunocompetence of the peripheral lymphocytes to stimulation with concanavalin A, phytohemagglutinin, and PPD after 15 minutes of bicycling. Eskola, Ruuskanan, Soppi, Viljanen, Jaruinen, Toivonen, and Kouvalainen (1978) showed graded responses with moderate (35 minutes of running) and heavy (2 to 5 hours marathon running) exercises in terms of immunological parameters. While both kinds of exertion resulted in lymphocytosis and in elevated cortisol levels, only the marathon running caused a transient, 24-hour lymphocytic hyporesponsivity, measured by mitogenic substances and PPD.

Immune system responses represent a meeting point between genetic determinants and environmental influences, contributing to the overall adaptation of the organism. Defining its role in this fashion, it becomes strikingly evident that the hitherto untapped resources of the immune system, the endocrine system and the central nervous system all share similar roles, a fact only recently recognized. All of these three major organizations thoroughly interact with one another. The far-reaching impact of the immune system upon the widest varieties of pathological conditions, including carcinogenesis and psychiatric illnesses, is now beginning to unfold. Stein, Schiavi, and Camerino (1976) emphasized the complexity of the psychoimmunological responses. They reviewed the results of the neurophysiological and neuroanatomical research, particularly that of the hypothalamic area, as it relates to cell-mediated immune responses.

It is certainly not far-fetched to conclude that immunological technology and expertise will contribute a great deal more to psychiatry and to the stress concept in the near future.

ON THE ISSUE OF BEREAVEMENT

Bereavement, an inescapable human experience, as it is known for the clinician and indeed for all of us, has no controllable animal model. The grief experienced is subjective and so variable that it lends itself poorly to comparison on an individual basis. Ever since Lindemann's (1944) original observations on the Coconut Grove nightclub fire and his impressions of "normal," "morbid," and "partial" grief reactions, many classical studies established the expected responses of a mournful event in various individuals and its effect upon their physical and mental health. Suggestions were made that bereavement should be classified as a disease because of the significant adverse effect such an experience exerts on the mourner's somatic functions and on his life expectancy (Rees and Lutkins, 1967). The loss of a beloved one was compared to the loss of a limb, and the enhanced mortality rate—broken heart syndrome—was confirmed in widows during the first year of mourning (Parkes, Benjamin, and Fitzgerald, 1969; Parkes, 1970). Arbitrary cutoff points of relative recovery of some three months were proposed by Clayton (1974) as the physiological limit of mourning.

Altered physiological measurements occurring during the bereavement were scanty. I refer back to the work of Bartrop et al. (1977) who found graded immunological impairment in two and in six weeks after the loss of spouses. These authors did not find any abnormal elevation of cortisol or other hormone levels—these may have been already normalized. However, all of their research subjects were expecting the death of their spouses and may have shown a different pattern of phys-

iological alterations than those who lose their beloved ones unexpectedly. The findings of these authors were recently
confirmed by Shuchter (1982). The physiological parameters
of the bereavement remain a poorly explored area. This may
be for compassionate reasons but also because experimenters
reach out more readily for data that play a "causative" rather
than a consequential part in pathological conditions. Sleep research, REM latency, REM duration, dexamethasone suppression test, measurement of hormone levels, and immunological
parameters are admittedly cumbersome to get immediately
after the loss of a spouse or a child, and I doubt that the ones
consenting to such procedures during their shock or bereavement would relfect the physiological values in those who may
be too distraught to undergo such testing.

Gorka, Ossowska, and Stach (1979) produced "behavioral
despair" in rats, a condition which is responsive to imipramine
administration unless, as the authors demonstrated, a unilateral
lesion is induced in the basolateral part of the amygdala. The
relevance of this experiment to human conditions is obviously
limited but reveals the inadequacies of animal experiments in
some areas of psychiatry.

Raphael (1977) studied the usefulness of preventive interviews in a randomly selected, recently widowed group of women
compared to a control group. Predictably, she found a significant lowering of morbidity with less instances of hospital ad-
missions and health problems in the professionally cared for
group.

An additional problem in research on bereavement is a diagnostic one. True grief is sometimes difficult to separate from
unipolar depression (Andreasen and Winikur, 1979) on the one
hand, and from attention-seeking feigned bereavement (Snowdon, Solomons, and Druce, 1978) on the other.

Bereavement of a different nature is the one with malignant
depression and secondary personality change with nightmares
and with a regressive life style, which can develop in severely
traumatized persons, such as survivors of concentration camps
(Eitinger, 1962; Chodoff, 1966; Koranyi, 1969), Hong Kong

prisoners of war (Kral, Pazder, and Wigdor, 1967) or in survivors of Hiroshima (Lifton, 1963). Another form of stress, loss,
bereavement, and readaptation is ubiquitous in new immigrants
(Eitinger, 1981), particularly among the elderly with enhanced
somatic pathologies and mortality rate (Koranyi, 1981).

CONCLUSION

The overall profile of this chapter compared to the portion
which deals with bereavement is glaringly different. It was not
done with intention and the contrast merely reflects the gap
between biological and psychosocial approaches to psychiatry.
It also demonstrates the already emphasized fact that while
stress-response is accurately measurable, stress as an external
event cannot be gauged objectively at the present. Only a few
words can be added on some of the reasons. A detailed account
on the research implications of stress was given recently by
Elliott and Eisdorfer (1982) and is addressed by Elliott in his
chapter of this volume.

The genetic factor or what is referred to as "genetic predisposition," which determines individual responses to "stress
resistance," is a hazy concept which, as such, may not even exist
on gene levels. We know that amino acid products, thus a wide
variety of chemicals, hormones, and enzymes, their level, and
probably their resiliency, are determined by many genes. These
substances regulate many others in an indirect fashion. Friedman and Iwa (1976) found some evidence of a genetic disposition with regard to hypertension, induced by psychic stress in
a special strain of rats. This to me, however, still does not constitute absolute proof of the existence of a genetic disposition.
Such concepts in biology sooner or later turn out to be nothing
else but word constructs. In general terms the notion of genetic
disposition remains an enigma. This, of course, does not mean
that physiological responses are not genetically controlled.
Quite the contrary, but there are a multitude of responses con-

trolled polygenetically, the abstract and nonbiological collection of which is referred to as "genetic disposition." The variants of intertwin differences between identical and fraternal twins, introduced by Sir Francis Galton in 1875 to provide a guideline separating the proportionate contribution of the environmental and genetic factors of a trait, or more sophisticated genetic studies in stress research, could not be located in the literature. See the chapter by Kidd and Morton in this volume.

Furthermore, what sometimes appears to be genetic in nature in fact turns out to be environmental after all. Roth and Herrenkohl (1979) subjected pregnant rats to heat, restraint, and bright light stress during the latter two-thirds of their gestation. She found that female offspring of such mothers in their subsequent gender functions proved to be less fertile and had more spontaneous abortions. The offsprings of the stressed mother rats weighed less, had higher mortality rates than the normal ones, and the male offsprings were feminized. The considerable impact of psychosocial influences upon the emerging morphology should not be underestimated. Money, Annecillo, and Werlwas (1976) reported on 40 children with psychosocial dwarfism and impaired pituitary growth hormone production which, according to the authors, proved to be reversible by removing them from their habitual environment. In the opinion of others, however, the same condition is a nutritional deficiency.

The emotional and cognitive elaboration of an event decides what will constitute stress. From Stevens' (1966) original scale, Holmes and Rahe's (1967) Social Readjustment Scale was introduced in the psychosomatic and stress research, consisting of an account of life events converted to Life Change Units. More recently, Rahe, Ryman, and Ward (1980) issued a Simplified Scaling for Life Change Events. If the number of patients in a research project is sufficiently large, these and similar tools yield useful statistical tendencies. However, they defy a direct translation of the measurement of stress in any particular individual. How many units of life stress should one give to the patient admitted with a depression that developed after his boss shouted at him, compared, let us say, to a person who was kidnapped by murderers, chained to a bed, facing death for some six weeks, and when rescued only wanted a hamburger, a "Coke," a crew-cut, and to get back to his work? Psychosocial estimates of recently endured stress and biological measurements of stress-responses during the last decade have certainly narrowed, but they have failed to close the gap between emotional events and pathophysiological consequences. The circularity between the two mechanisms is now evident. At this stage of research there are still too many unconfirmed data that blur the clarity of an objective overview. Thus, there is a distinct need to clear up the controversies still existing in our literature. Until then one is reminded of the remark of André Maurois: "In literature, as in love, we are astonished at what is chosen by others."

REFERENCES

Ahlquist, R. P. (1948), A study of the adrenotropic receptors. *Amer. J. Physiol.*, 153:586–600.
Allison, A. C. (1976), Self-tolerance and autoimmunity in the thyroid. *New Engl. J. Med.*, 295:821–827.
Alvord, E. C., Shaw, C. M., Jr., Hruby, S., Petersen, R., & Harvey, F. H. (1975), Correlation of delayed skin hypersensitivity and experimental allergic encephalomyelitis induced by synthetic peptides. In: *The Nervous System*, Vol. 1: *The Basic Neurosciences*, ed. D. B. Towers. New York: Raven Press, pp. 647–654.
Andreasen, N. C., & Winikur, G. (1979), Secondary depression: Familial, clinical and research perspectives. *Amer. J. Psychiat.*, 136:62–66.
Anisman, H., & Lapierre, Y. (1982), Neurochemical aspects of stress and depression: Formulation and caveats. In: *Psychological Stress and Psychopathology*, ed. R. W. J. Neufeld. New York: McGraw-Hill, pp. 179–217.
Barash, D. P. (1977), *Sociobiology and Behavior*. New York: Elsevier.
Bartrop, R. W., Luckhurst, E., Lazarus, L., Kiloh, L. G., & Penny, R. (1977), Depressed lymphocyte function after bereavement. *Lancet*, 1:834–836.
Bloom, G., von Euler, U. S., & Frankenhaeuser, M. (1963), Catecholamine excretion and personality traits in paratroop trainees. *Acta Physiol. Scand.*, 58:77–89.

Bourne, P. G., Rose, R. R., & Mason, J. W. (1968), 17-OHCS levels in combat, special forces "A" team under threat of attack. *Arch. Gen. Psychiat.*, 19:135–140.

—— (1969), Urinary 17-OHCS levels in two combat situations. In: *The Psychology and Physiology of Stress*, ed. P. G. Bourne. New York: Academic Press, pp. 95–116.

Brady, J. V. (1958), Ulcers in "executive monkeys." *Sci. Amer.*, 199:95–100.

Brown, G. M., & Reichlich, S. (1972), Psychologic and neural regulation of growth hormone secretion. *Psychosom. Med.*, 34:45–61.

Cannon, W. B. (1914), The emergency function of the adrenal medulla in pain and the major emotions. *Amer. J. Physiol.*, 33:356–372.

—— (1929), *Bodily Changes in Pain, Hunger, Fear, and Rage*. Boston: Branford.

—— (1931), Studies on the conditions of activity in endocrine organs XXVII. Evidence that medulla adrenal secretion is not continuous. *Amer. J. Physiol.*, 98:447–453.

Carroll, B. J., Feinberg, J., Greden, J. F., Tarika, J., Albala, A. A., Huskett, R. F., James, N. M., Kronfall, Z., Lohr, V., Steiner, M., de Vigne, J. P., & Young, E. (1981), A specific laboratory test for the diagnosis of melancholia. *Arch. Gen. Psychiat.*, 38:15–22.

Charvat, J., Dell, P. P., Folkow, P., & Folkow, B. (1964), Mental factors in cardiovascular disease. *Cardiol.*, 44:124–141.

Chodoff, P. (1966), Effects of extreme coercive and oppressive forces: Brainwashing and concentration camp. In: *American Handbook of Psychiatry*, Vol. 3, ed. S. Arieti. New York: Basic, pp. 384–405.

Clayton, P. J. (1974), Mortality and morbidity in the first year of widowhood. *Arch. Gen. Psychiat.*, 30:747–750.

Collins, A., & Frankenhaueser, M. (1978), Stress responses in male and female engineering students. *J. Hum. Stress*, 4:43–48.

Cryer, E. P. (1980), Physiology and pathophysiology of the human sympathoadrenal neuroendocrine system. *New Eng. J. Med.*, 303:436–444.

DeWied, D. (1973), Peptides and behavior. In: *Memory and Transfer of Information*, ed. H. P. Lippel. New York: Plenum, pp. 378–389.

Edwards, C. R. W. (1977), Vasopressin. In: *Clinical Neuroendocrinology*, ed. L. Martini & G. M. Besser. New York: Academic Press, pp. 527–567.

Ehrensing, R. H., & Kostin, A. J. (1977), Clinical investigations for nonendocrine actions in man. In: *Clinical Neuroendocrinology*, ed. L. Martini & G. M. Besser. New York: Academic Press, pp. 133–143.

Eitinger, L. (1962), Concentration camp survivors in the post war world. *Amer. J. Psychother.*, 26:367–375.

—— (1981), Foreigners in our time: Historical survey on psychiatry's approach to migration and refugee status. In: *Strangers in the World*, ed. L. Eitinger & D. Schwarz. Bern: Hans Huber, pp. 16–26.

Elliott, G. R., & Eisdorfer, C. (1982), *Stress and Human Health*. New York: Springer.

Elmadjian, F. J., Hope, J., & Lamson, E. T. (1957), Excretion of epinephrine and norepinephrine in various emotional states. *J. Clin. Endocrinol.*, 17:608–620.

Engelhardt, W., & Schwille, P. O. (1981), Development of sensitive somatostatin radioimmune assay and its application to plasma of stressed and non-stressed rats. *Horm. Metab. Res.*, 13:318–323.

Engelman, K., Portnoy, B., & Lovenberg, W. (1968), A sensitive and specific double isotope derivative method for the determination of catecholamines in biological specimens. *Amer. J. Med. Sci.*, 255:259–268.

Eskola, J., Ruuskanen, O., Soppi, E., Viljanen, M. D., Jarvinen, M., Toivonen, H., & Kouvalainen, K. (1978), Effect of sport stress on lymphocyte transformation and antibody formation. *Clin. Exp. Immunol.*, 32:339–345.

Fernandez, D. (1981), Stress ulcer and the stress syndrome. *Stress*, 2:16–22.

Folch, H., & Waksman, B. H. (1974), The splenic suppressor cell, T. activity of thymus-dependent adherent cells: Changes with age and stress. *J. Immunol.*, 113:127–139.

Folkow, B., & von Euler, U. S. (1954), Selective activation of noradrenaline and adrenaline producing cells in the suprarenal gland of the cat by hypothalamic stimulation. *Circ. Res.*, 2:191–195.

Frankenhaeuser, M. (1974), Sympathetic-adrenomedullary activity, behavior and the psychosocial environment. In: *Research in Psychophysiology*, ed. P. H. Venables & M. J. Christie. New York: Wiley, pp. 71–94.

——— (1975), Experimental approaches to the study of catecholamines and emotion. In: *Emotions—Their Parameters and Measurements*, ed. L. Levi. New York: Raven Press, pp. 209–234.

——— (1978), Psychoendocrine sex difference in adaptation to the psychosocial environment. In: *Clinical Psychoneuroendocrinology in Reproduction*, ed. L. Carenza, D. Pancheri, & L. Zichella. New York: Academic Press, pp. 215–223.

——— Jarpe, G. (1962), Psychophysiological reactions to infusion of a mixture of adrenaline and noradrenaline. *Scand. J. Psychol.*, 3:21–29.

——— Patkai, P. (1965), Interindividual differences in catecholamine excretion during stress. *Scand. J. Psychol.*, 6:117–123.

Frantz, A. G. (1978), Prolactin. *New Eng. J. Med.*, 298:201–207.

Friedman, H. (1975), Stimulation of B immunocytes by a T-cell factor produced in mixed leukocyte culture. In: *Thymus Factors in Immunity*, ed. H. Friedman. New York: Ann. N.Y. Acad. Sci., pp. 261–277.

Friedman, R., & Iwa, J. (1976), Genetic predisposition and stress-induced hypertension. *Science*, 193:161–162.

Funkenstein, D. H. (1956), Norepinephrine-like and epinephrine-like substances in relation to human behavior. *J. Ment. Dis.*, 124:58–68.

Goldberg, N., O'Dea, R. F., & Haddox, M. K. (1975), Cyclic GMP. In: *Advances in Cyclic Nucleotide Research*, Vol. 3, ed. G. I. Drummond, P. Greengard, & G. A. Robinson. New York: Raven Press, pp. 155–224.

Goldstein, M. (1974), Brain research and violence: Neurochemical, endocrine, pharmacological and genetic studies. *Arch. Neurol.*, 30:8–23.

Gorka, Z., Ossowska, K., & Stach, J. (1979), Effect of unilateral amygdala lesion in imipramine action in behavioral despair in rats. *J. Pharm. Pharmacol.*, 31:647–648.

Gottschalk, L. A. (1982), Vulnerability and immune response. Presented at the 135th annual meeting of the American Psychiatric Association, Toronto, May 18.

Hedfors, E., Holm, G., & Öhnell, B. (1976), Variations of blood lymphocytes during work, studied by cell surface markers, DNA synthesis and cytotoxicity. *Clin. Exp. Immunol.*, 24:328–335.

Hirschowitz, T. (1982), Growth hormone, lithium and psychoses: A replication study. Presented at the 135th annual meeting of the American Psychiatric Association, Toronto, May 20.

Holmes, T. H., & Rahe, R. H. (1967), The Social Readjustment Rating Scale. *J. Psychosom. Res.*, 11:213–218.

Horrobin, D. F. (1974), *Prolactin 1974*. Lancaster, UK: Medical & Technical, pp. 89–94.

Iversen, L. L. (1975), Dopamine receptors in the brain. *Science*, 188:1084–1089.

Johansson, G., & Frankenhaeuser, M. (1973), Temporal factors in sympatroadrenal medullary activity following acute behavioral activation. *J. Biol. Psychol.*, 1:67–77.

Kabat, E. A., Wolf, A., & Bezer, A. E. (1947), The rapid production of acute disseminated encephalomyelitis in rhesus monkeys by injection of heterologous and homologous brain tissue with adjuvants. *J. Exper. Med.*, 85:116–130.

Keller, S. E., Weiss, J. M., Schleifer, J. S., Miller, N. E., & Stein, M. (1981), Suppression of immunity by stress: Effect of a graded series of stressors on lymphocyte stimulation in the rat. *Science*, 213:1397–1400.

Kety, S. S. (1967), Psychoendocrine systems and emotions: Biological aspects. In: *Neurophysiology and Emotions*, ed. D. C. Glass. New York: Rockefeller University Press & Russell Sage Foundation, pp. 103–107.

Kies, M. W. (1975), Immunology of myelin basic proteins. In: *The Nervous System*, Vol. 1: *The Basic Neurosciences*, ed. D. B. Tower. New York: Raven Press, pp. 637–646.

Kleinberg, D. L., Noel, G. L., & Frantz, A. C. (1977), Galactorrhea: A study of 235 cases, including 48 with pituitary tumors. *New Eng. J. Med.*, 296:589–600.

Koestler, A. (1964), *The Act of Creation*. London: Hutchinson.

Kolodny, R. C., Jacobs, L. S., & Daughaday, W. L. (1972), Mammary stimulation causes prolactin secretion in nonlactating woman. *Nature*, 238:283–286.

Koranyi, E. K. (1969), Psychodynamic theories of the survivor syndrome. *Can. Psychiat. Assn. J.*, 14:165–173.

——— (1977), Psychobiological correlates of battlefield psychiatry. *Psychiat. J. Univ. Ottawa*, 2:1–19.

——— (1981), Decline and stress: Immigrant's adaptation in the aged population. In: *Strangers in the World*, ed. L. Eitinger & D. Schwarz. Bern: Hans Huber, pp. 220–233.

——— (1982), Medical drugs and sexuality. In: *Physical Illness in the Psychiatric Patient*, ed. E. K. Koranyi. Springfield, IL: Thomas, pp. 78–90.

Kordon, C., Enjalbert, A., Hery, M., Joseph-Bravo, P. I., Rotsztejn, W., & Rutberg, M. (1980), Role of neurotransmitters in the control of adeno-hypopryseal secretion. In: *Handbook of Hypothalamus*, Vol. 2. *Physiology of the Hypothalamus*, ed. P. J. Morane & J. Panksepp. New York: Dekker, pp. 253–306.

Kral, V. A., Pazder, L. H., & Wigdor, B. T. (1967), Long term effects of a prolonged stress experience. *Can. Psychiat. Assn. J.*, 12:175–181.

Kunkel, H. G. (1975), Immune disease—Introduction. In: *Textbook of Medicine*, ed. P. B. Beeson & W. McDermott. Philadelphia: Saunders, pp. 96–103.

Lacey, J. I. (1967), Somatic response patterning and stress: Some revisions of activation theory. In: *Psychological Stress: Issues in Research*, ed. M. H. Appley & R. Trumbell. New York: Appleton-Century-Crofts, pp. 14–42.

Lader, P. (1982), The genetics of antibody diversity. *Sci. Amer.*, 246:102–115.

Lattime, E. C., & Strausser, H. R. (1977), Arteriosclerosis: Is stress-induced immune suppression a risk factor? *Science*, 198:302–303.

Lazarus, R. S. (1966), *Psychological Stress and the Coping Process*. New York: McGraw-Hill.

——— (1976), *Patterns of Adjustment*. New York: McGraw-Hill.

——— Alfert, E. (1964), The short-circuiting of threat. *J. Abnorm. Soc. Psychol.*, 69:195–205.

——— Cohen, J. B., Folkman, S., Kanner, A., & Shaefer, C. (1980), Psychological stress and adaptation: Some unresolved issues. In: *Guide to Stress Research*, ed. H. Selye. New York: Reinhold, pp. 90–117.

Lefkowitz, R. J. (1976), p-Adrenergic receptors: Recognition and regulation. *New Eng. J. Med.*, 295:323–328.

Lifton, R. J. (1963), *Psychological Effects of the Atomic Bomb in Hiroshima*. Cambridge, MA: Daedalus.

Lindemann, E. (1944), Symptomatology and management of acute grief. *Arch. Gen. Psychiat.*, 101:141–148.

Lorenz, K. (1966), *On Aggression*. London: Methuen.

Lundberg, U., de Chateau, P., Weinberg, J., & Frankenhaeuser, M. (1981),

Catecholamine and cortisol excretion patterns in three-year-old children and their parents. *J. Hum. Stress*, 7:3–11.

Maas, J. W. (1972), Adrenocortical steroid hormones, electrolytes and the disposition of catecholamines with particular reference to depressive states. *J. Psychiat. Res.*, 9:227–241.

Marchbanks, V. H. (1958), Effect of flying stress on urinary 17-OHCS levels. *J. Aviat. Med.*, 29:667–682.

Mason, J. W. (1970), Strategy of psychosomatic research. *Psychosom. Med.*, 32:427–439.

——— (1971), A re-evaluation of the concept of 'non-specificity' in stress theory. *J. Psychiat. Res.*, 8:323–333.

——— (1975), Emotion as reflected in patterns of endocrine integration. In: *Emotions—Their Parameters and Measurements*, ed. L. Levi. New York: Raven Press, pp. 143–207.

——— Buescher, E. D., Belfer, M. L., Mougey, E. H., Taylor, E. D., Wherry, F. E., Ricketts, P. T., Young, P. S., Wade, J., Early, D. C., & Kenion, C. C. (1967), Pre-illness hormonal changes in army recruits with acute respiratory infections. *Psychosom. Med.*, 29:545.

Mathew, R. J., Beng, T. H., & Taylor, D. (1982), Dopamine-β-hydroxylase response to epinephrine injection in anxious patients and normals. *Biol. Psychiat.*, 17:393–397.

McDevitt, H. O. (1980), Current concepts in immunology. Regulation of the immune response by the major histocompatibility system. *New Engl. J. Med.*, 303:1514–1517.

McFarlin, D. E. (1975), The development of immunology and its application to neuroscience. In: *The Nervous System*, Vol. 1, *The Basic Neurosciences*, ed. D. B. Towers. New York: Raven Press, pp. 655–661.

McGrath, J. E. (1970), Major substantive issues: Time, setting, and coping processes. In: *Social and Psychological Factors in Stress*, ed. J. E. McGrath. New York: Holt, Rinehart & Winston, pp. 22–44.

McGuffin, P., Gardiner, P., & Swineburne, L. M. (1981), Schizophrenia, celiac disease and antibodies to food. *Biol. Psychiat.*, 16:281–285.

Mikhail, A. (1981), Stress—A psychophysiological conception. *J. Hum. Stress*, 7:9–15.

Miller, N. (1969), Learning of visceral and glandular responses. *Science*, 163:434–448.

Money, J., Annecillo, C. H., & Werlwas, J. (1976), Hormonal and behavioral reversals in hyposomatotropic dwarfism. In: *Hormones, Behavior and Psychopathology*, ed. E. J. Sachar. New York: Raven Press, pp. 243–252.

Monjan, A. A., & Collector, M. I. (1977), Stress-induced modulation of the immune response. *Science*, 197:307–308.

Noel, G. L., Suh, H. K., & Stone, J. G. (1972), Human prolactin and growth hormone release during surgery and conditions of stress. *J. Clin. Endocrinol.*, 35:840–851.

Oldstone, M. B. A. (1975), Using immunology to understand neurobiology. In: *The Nervous System*, Vol. 1, *The Basic Neurosciences*, ed. D. B. Tower. New York: Raven Press, pp. 631–636.

Pandey, R. S., Gupta, A. K., & Chaturverdi (1981), Autoimmune model of schizophrenia with special reference to antibrain antibodies. *Biol. Psychiat.*, 16:1123–1136.

Parkes, C. M. (1970), The first year of bereavement: A longitudinal study of the reaction of London widows to the deaths of their husbands. *Psychiatry*, 33:444–467.

—— Benjamin, B., & Fitzgerald, R. G. (1969), Broken heart: A statistical study of increased mortality among widowers. *Brit. Med. J.*, 1:740–743.

Poe, R. O., Rose, R. M., & Mason, J. W. (1970), Multiple determinants of 17-hydroxycorticosteroid excretion in recruits during basic training. *Psychosom. Med.*, 32:369–378.

Prange, A. J., Wilson, I. C., & Rabson, A. M. (1969), Enhancement of imipramine and antidepressant activity by thyroid hormone. *Amer. J. Psychiat.*, 136:457–469.

Rahe, R. H., Ryman, D. H., Ward, H. W. (1980), Simplified scaling for life change events. *J. Hum. Stress*, 6:22–27.

Raphael, B. (1977), Preventive intervention with recently bereaved. *Arch. Gen. Psychiat.*, 34:1450–1454.

Rees, L. H. (1977), Human adrenocorticotropin and lipotropin (MSH) in health and disease. In: *Clinical Neuroendocrinology*, ed. L. Martini & G. M. Besser. New York: Academic Press, pp. 412–441.

Rees, W. D., & Lutkins, S. G. (1967), Mortality of bereavement. *Brit. Med. J.*, 4:13–16.

Rose, R. M. (1969), Androgen excretion in stress. In: *The Psychology and Physiology of Stress*, ed. P. G. Bourne. New York: Academic Press, pp. 117–148.

—— Hurst, M. W., & Herd, A. (1979), Cardiovascular and endocrine responses to work and the risk for psychiatric symptomatology among air traffic controllers. In: *Stress and Mental Disorder*, ed. J. E. Barrett. New York: Raven Press, pp. 237–250.

Roth, L., & Herrenkohl, L. (1979), Prenatal stress reduces fertility and fecundity in female offsprings. *Science*, 206:1097–1099.

Saffran, M., & Schally, A. V. (1955), The release of corticotropin by anterior pituitary tissue in vitro. *Can. J. Biochem. Physiol.*, 33:308–315.

Schally, A. V., & Arimura, A. (1977), Physiology and nature of hypothalamic regulatory hormones. In: *Clinical Neuroendocrinology*, ed. L. Martini & G. M. Besser. New York: Academic Press, pp. 2–32.

Schildkraut, R., Chaudra, O., Osswald, M., Ruther, E., Baarfusser, B., &

Matussek, N. (1975), Growth hormone release during sleep and with thermal stimulation in depressed patients. *Neuropsychology*, 1:70–79.

Selye, H. (1936), A syndrome produced by diverse nocuous agents. *Nature*, 138:32.

———— (1956), *The Stress of Life*. New York: McGraw-Hill.

———— (1974), *Stress without Distress*. Toronto: McLelland & Stewart.

———— (1976), *The Stress of Life*. New York: McGraw-Hill.

———— (1982), Holistic health and somatopsychic medicine as related to stress. In: *Physical Illness in the Psychiatric Patient*, ed. E. K. Koranyi. Springfield, IL: Thomas, pp. 42–58.

Shuchter, S. R. (1982), The depression of widowhood reconsidered. Presented at the 135th annual meeting of the American Psychiatric Association, Toronto, May 19.

Sklar, L. S., & Anisman, H. (1979), Stress and coping factors influence tumor growth. *Science*, 205:513–515.

Smeraldi, E., Negri, P., Melica, A. M., & Scorza-Smeraldi, K. (1978), MLA system and affective disorders: A sibship genetic study. *Tissue Antigens*, 12:270–274.

Snowdon, J., Solomons, R., & Druce, H. (1978), Feigned bereavement: Twelve cases. *Brit. J. Psychiat.*, 133:15–19.

Steel, C. M., Evans, J., & Smith, M. A. (1974), Physiological variation in circulating B cell: T cell ratio in man. *Nature*, 247:387–389.

Stein, M., Schiavi, R. C., & Camerino, M. (1976), Influence of brain and behavior on the immune system. *Science*, 191:435–440.

Stevens, S. S. (1966), A metric for the social consensus. *Science*, 151:530–541.

Suematsu, H., Kurokawa, N., Tamai, H., & Ikemi, Y. (1974), Changes of serum growth hormone in psychosomatic disorders. *Psychother. Psychosom.*, 24:161–164.

Thorner, M. O. (1977), Therapeutic implications of dopaminergic drugs in acromegaly, endocrinology. In: *Clinical Neuroendocrinology*, ed. L. Martini & G. M. Besser. New York: Academic Press, pp. 295–308.

Ungar, G. (1980), Molecular neurobiology and memory. In: *Biochemistry of Brain*, ed. S. Kumar. New York: Pergamon Press, pp. 383–406.

von Euler, U. S. (1967), Adrenal medullary secretion and its neural control. In: *Neuroendocrinology*, Vol. 2, ed. L. Martini & W. F. Ganong. New York: Academic Press, pp. 283–333.

von Holst, D. (1972), Renal failure as a cause of death in tupia belangeri exposed to persistent social stress. *J. Comp. Physiol.*, 78:236–273.

Weitkamp, L. R., Stancer, H. C., Persad, E. M. B., Flood, C. H., & Guttormsen, S. (1981), Depressive disorders and HLA: A gene on chromosome 6 that can affect behavior. *New Engl. J. Med.*, 305:1301–1306.

Wilson, C. B., & Dempsey, L. C. (1978), Transsphenoidal microsurgical removal of 250 pituitary adenomas. *J. Neurosurg.*, 48:13–22.

278   ERWIN K. KORANYI

Yu, D. T. Y., Clements, P. J., & Pearson, C. M. (1977), Effect of corticosteroids on exercise-induced lymphocytosis. *Clin. Exp. Immunol.*, 28:326–331.

Yuwiler, A. (1976), Stress, anxiety, and endocrine function. In: *Biological Functions of Psychiatry*, Vol. 2, ed. R. G. Grenell & S. Gabay. New York: Raven Press, pp. 889–985.

9.

The Interaction Between Brain Behavior and Immunity

MALCOLM P. ROGERS, M.D.

INTRODUCTION

Psychophysiologic investigations involving the immune system are currently at the forefront of psychosomatic investigation. Indeed the discoveries in this area within the past few years have injected new energy and excitement into psychosomatic research. Several factors have provided the impetus for this line of investigation. For one thing, immunology itself has been one of the most rapidly advancing areas in medical research over the last decade. Many diseases of unknown etiology, such as cancer, most rheumatic diseases, and more recently even diseases such as juvenile diabetes mellitus and Alzheimer's disease, are increasingly thought to have an underlying immunologic disturbance. Thus, an increasing number of laboratories have turned their attention to fundamental immunologic research. Important advances in genetic engineering and cell biology have spurred these developments further. The overall result has been a remarkable advance in our understanding of the complexity and interregulation of the immune system.

Historically, psychosomatic medicine has often followed advances on the somatic side of the mind-body axis. In the past, developments in endocrinology and cardiovascular and renal physiology have stimulated surges of research on the relationship between these specific areas and altered emotional states. Emerging new techniques and approaches tend to become the instruments of investigators who are trying to narrow the gap in the mind-body process referred to by Weiner (1972) as "the transduction of experience."

Another major factor is the fact that the immune system has such a fundamental role in the maintenance of body homeostasis and health (Austen, 1978). Even minor fluctuations in this system have direct implications for the development of disease. In preceding years there have been many advances in our understanding of the effect of mental states on the endocrine and autonomic nervous systems. However, the implications of many of these changes were less obvious. Were they simply adaptive changes, or did they somehow increase the organism's vulnerability to disease? Clearly the immune system provides us with a further critical link in the psychosomatic process relating to the ultimate consequences for morbidity and mortality.

A central premise of much of the work in this area is that stress and perhaps other emotional states associated with failures in coping mechanisms might lead to an increase in vulnerability to certain diseases by exerting an immunosuppressive effect, especially in those diseases intimately associated with immunologic mechanisms, such as infection, malignancy, and autoimmune disease. Recent reviews have summarized much of the recent research in this area (Amkraut and Solomon, 1974; Stein, Schiavi, and Camerino, 1976; Rogers, Dubey, and Reich, 1979; Stein, Schleifer, and Keller, 1980). The most comprehensive treatment of this field is contained in a recent volume edited by Robert Ader (Ader, 1981).

IMMUNOLOGY: A BRIEF REVIEW
INCLUDING RECENT ADVANCES

The field of immunology is expanding at an extraordinarily rapid pace. Accordingly, our knowledge of the normal regulation of immunity and the measurable immune functions that might provide the most sensitive index of immunocompetence are also changing. While we speak of the immune system in one phrase, we are of course referring to a number of different types of cells, each of which has numerous measurable dimensions of function and activity. Before focusing on more recent advances, a brief overview of the entire immune system may be helpful. For additional reading, I recommend either Gilliland's "Introduction to Clinical Immunology," in *Harrison's Principles of Internal Medicine* (Gilliland, 1980), or Roitt's (1980) *Essential Immunology.*

The principal cells of the immune system are lymphocytes, plasma cells, and macrophages, concentrated and developed in lymphoid tissues such as the thymus, lymph nodes, and spleen, and originating from the bone marrow. The immune system is generally divided into two large components: humoral and cellular immunity. The first, humoral immunity, involves antibody mediated reactions. These antigen-specific reactions are carried out by various classes of immunoglobulin molecules such as IgA, IgG, IgM, or IgE. When stimulated by specific antigens, B lymphocytes are transformed into plasma cells, actively producing specific antibodies. These antigen/antibody interactions are closely associated with amplification systems involved in the inflammatory process such as the classical or alternate complement pathways, and other mediators such as prostaglandins. Such reactions include defenses against toxic and bacterial antigens, transfusion reactions, and various forms of autoimmune reactions such as hemolytic anemia.

The second major component is cell-mediated immunity, the primary process involved in delayed hypersensitivity (such as in the tuberculin skin test) and the rejection of transplanted tissue. In this system, T cells are activated by specific antigens interacting with surface receptors to release nonantibody substances called lymphokines. Examples of lymphokines include migration inhibitory factor (MIF), macrophage chemotactic factor, interferon, cytotoxic factors, chemotactic factors for neutrophils, eosinophils, and basophils, and several other factors. These, in turn, act upon other cells to mediate and amplify cell-mediated immune responses. Neither circulating antibodies nor the complement system is involved in cell-mediated immunity. In addition to delayed hypersensitivity and transplant reactions, T cells also mediate cytotoxic responses. Approximately 2 to 10 percent of circulating lymphocytes in the blood are referred to as null cells. They lack the usual surface antigen markers for B and T cells, and may either represent immature B or T cells or natural killer cells. Another immune cell, the macrophage, facilitates the induction of the immune response, binds immune complexes, and can kill bacteria, fungi, and tumor cells.

An individual's immune system has the capacity to differentiate between self (to which there is *tolerance*) and foreign macromolecules (to which an immune response is directed). When an antigen is first introduced, it triggers a *primary* humoral or antibody response. After a brief period of time, the level of antibody declines, but following reexposure to the antigen (for example, a booster shot) an enhanced *secondary* response is elicited. In general, an antigen is taken up by a macrophage in the spleen if administered intravenously, or in the lymph node if administered subcutaneously. The macrophage in turn presents the antigen to the lymphocyte for recognition. Lymphocytes are thought to be genetically preconditioned to interact with a particular antigen. When so stimulated the B cells are transformed into plasma cells which produce immunogolulins. The B cells represent about 20 percent of peripheral blood lymphocytes and about 50 percent of spleen lymphocytes.

IgG comprises 70 to 80 percent of the serum antibodies in the human and is almost exclusively responsible for the antibodies to viruses, toxins, and gram-positive pyrogenic bacteria.

IgM makes up between 5 and 10 percent of the total serum antibody, typically elicited by antigens of gram-negative bacteria. IgA comprises about 10 to 20 percent of the total serum antibody and functions predominantly in body secretions, for example in the parotid saliva and nasal and gastrointestinal secretions. By activating mast cells in the presence of specific antigens, IgE plays an important role in immediate hypersensitivity (allergic) reactions, such as in anaphylaxis. The level of humoral immunity can be assessed by measurements of serum immunoglobulin levels, by specific antibody titers raised in response to specific antigens, or by measuring the activity of the plasma cells in the spleen after antigenic stimulation (the so-called plaque-forming assay). It is also possible in vitro to stimulate B cells differentially (with pokeweed mitogen) and to measure their capacity to proliferate in response to such stimulation.

One of the most important advances in recent years has been the differentiation of B from T cells, largely on the basis of the presence of immunoglobulins on the membrane of B cells but not on T cells. The thymus gland has a critical role in the differentiation of T cells from precursor cells and has other important regulatory functions, especially in cellular immunity. T cells, named for their derivation from the thymus, make up about 80 percent of peripheral blood lymphocytes which, as mentioned above, are involved in cell-mediated immunity. The differentiation of T and B cells has led to a proliferation of tests that provide indices of specific cellular immunocompetence. In addition to the older in vivo methods, i.e., skin testing (delayed hypersensitivity antigens such as mumps to which virtually everyone has been exposed) and the pattern of rejection of tissue transplants (which provide only crudely quantifiable measures of T cell function), a variety of new in vitro techniques have been developed. These include lymphoblast transformation—the lymphocyte response to mitogens which are substances like phytohemagglutinin (PHA) or concanavalin A (con A) that stimulate mitosis in these cells, T lymphocyte cytotoxicity (the capacity of T cells to kill culture cells to which they have been sensitized), or the even more recent natural killer cell activity first identified in 1974. The latter has emerged as an especially important index of general immunocompetence because it measures a natural function of the cells without requirement of prior sensitization and is thought to provide an important host defense against the development of malignancy and viral infections (Haller, Hansson, Kiessling, and Wigzell, 1977). For some time the immune system has been thought to perform a surveillance function in recognizing cells undergoing malignant transformation and eliminating them before tumor growth occurs.

Important interactions between T cells and B cells also occur. It turns out that another function of T cells is in regulating the humoral response of B cells, either in augmenting (helper T cells) or in suppressing (suppressor T cells) such reactions. Natural killer cells have been described as another subset of lymphocytes. Improved techniques utilizing monoclonal antibodies and fluorescence-activated cell sorter analysis based on surface antigens have helped to identify further subsets and stages in the development of T cells as well as specific abnormalities associated with clinical disorders (Reinherz, Rubinstein, Geha, Strelkauskas, Rosen, and Schlossman, 1979).

All of these lymphoid cells function in an intricate interregulatory network maintaining physiological homeostasis (Siegal, 1978). It should be obvious that the immune system is a very complex network and that there is no single measure of immunity, but many different ones. This makes a concept like immunosuppression more complicated in that the suppression of suppressor T cells, for example, may in fact augment other components of the immune system. It is known that some regulatory substances like corticosteroids have differential effects on suppressor as opposed to helper T cell subsets. In truth, relatively little is known of the normal regulation and baseline of the immune system over time in humans or laboratory animals. There is also remarkable variability in many of these laboratory measures from laboratory to laboratory and from day to day within the same laboratory. The lack of such a baseline suggests the need for some caution in interpreting the immunologic changes described later in this chapter.

A great variety of immunodeficiency syndromes, either congenital such as an isolated deficiency in IgA or acquired such as the much publicized AIDS, have been described. Beyond these gross deficiencies with obvious clinical manifestations, however, the question arises as to how much variability exists within individuals over time or between racial groups, sexes or other dimensions, and whether some of these fluctuations in both cellular and humoral immune responses have biological significance. One wonders how much variation occurs within any given individual within the course of a day, week, or month, or a lifetime. The answers are sketchy but some information does exist.

Age is certainly an important variable. It has been known for a long time that in humans humoral immunity is not fully developed at birth and becomes so only approximately at one to two years of age. Even though at that point IgM and IgG will be at adult levels, IgA levels continue to increase throughout life (Buckley and Dorsey, 1970). There is relatively little information about cellular immunity in newborns except that it is grossly intact as judged by the presence of delayed hypersensitivity reactions. At the time of puberty the thymus gland undergoes partial involution, yet no significant alteration in immunologic competence appears to occur at this time.

However, later stages of aging are known to be associated with important immunologic changes. The numerous changes in the immune system associated with aging have been well described recently (Makinodan and Yunis, 1977). In brief, these include suggestive evidence of a diminution in both cellular and humoral immunity and an increase in substances like amyloid (now identified as a fragment of immunoglobulin molecules) and autoantibodies, both of which reflect a failure in the regulation of immunity. There is some evidence to suggest that these changes associated with aging may have some biological significance. Increasing numbers of autoantibodies coincide with a rising risk of developing autoimmune disorders in an older population, although some autoimmune disorders, such as juvenile arthritis, occur in a younger population. Furthermore, the prevalence of many malignancies increases with age. One bit of direct evidence comes from a prospective study of 52 persons over the age of 80. This study showed significant correlations between diminished delayed hypersensitivity reactions and greater mortality (Roberts-Thomson, Whittingham, Youngchaiyud, and Mackay, 1974).

The immunologic theory of aging (Walford, 1974) attempts to explain the underlying pathophysiology of aging on the basis of immune dysfunction. However, contradictory evidence exists and the theory is controversial (Kent, 1977). Numerous studies in nonprimate, higher animals have established that immune potential declines with advancing age in all mammalian species tested and that autoimmunity and immunodeficiency states become more frequent in aged individuals. An interesting line of investigation involving certain strains of mice and rats has demonstrated that life span and immune competence can be augmented by dietary manipulation, specifically by caloric restriction (Walford, Liu, Mathies, Gerbase-Delima, and Smith, 1974).

There is considerable evidence that some altered developmental states associated with important endocrinologic changes such as pregnancy are also related to important changes in immunity. An impairment in cell-mediated immunity has been described both in women (Purtilo, Hallgren, and Yunis, 1972) and in animals (Fabris, 1973), presumably in protection of the fetus. In fact, complement inactivated plasma obtained from pregnant patients or at delivery has a suppressive effect on in vitro mixed lymphocyte reactivity of unrelated individuals (Jones, Curzen, and Gaugas, 1973), a measure analogous to mitogen-stimulated proliferation. Recent evidence has pointed toward a more selective rather than generalized immunosuppressive effect, specifically the induction of suppressor cells in the fetus capable of effectively shutting off maternal rejection of the fetal allograft (Goldberg and Frikke, 1980), perhaps through elaboration of a soluble factor. In summarizing recent advances in this area, Froelich, Goodwin, Bankhurst, and Williams (1980) have postulated that the hypertrophied suppressor system of the fetus acts as a temporary graft of suppressor activity in the maternal host. The immunologic changes in pregnancy are of special interest in light of the clinical associations between it and alterations in certain autoimmune disorders, to be discussed in greater detail below.

However, between the extremes of early development and old age and pregnancy, we have considerably less information about the variabilities in the normal baseline. The studies that do exist report that human immunoglobulin levels vary relatively widely between individuals, but probably by no more than about 20 percent within individuals during the course of a year (Allansmith, McClellan, and Butterworth, 1967). Differences in sex (females have 20 percent more IgM) and race (blacks have more IgG than whites) have also been reported (Grundbacher, 1974). Although no normal quantitative baselines have been established, we do know that there are significant circadian rhythms in immune functioning both in humoral and cellular functions in man and laboratory animals. Much of this work has been summarized in a recent volume (Smolenski and Reinberg, 1977), which includes papers describing circadian variations in secretory IgA, plasma cell activity, immunoglobulin titer response to antigenic stimulation, and quantitative levels of circulating lymphocytes and their response to mitogenic stimulation. A marked diurnal variation in natural killer cell activity linked with diurnal glucocorticoid levels has recently been described (Williams, Kraus, and Dukey, 1979). Cove-Smith, Kabler, Pownall, and Knapp (1978) have also focused attention on the circadian variation of the immune response in man. In all likelihood these circadian rhythms are orchestrated centrally by the brain, specifically by the hypothalamus.

These data make us cognizant of the limited knowledge of baseline patterns of immunologic variations against which attempts have been made to measure the effects of psychological stress and other emotional states. The factor of time also reminds us of the need to take into consideration the stage of the life cycle of the individual, and further, the time of day during which measurements are taken. It may turn out that changes in immunologic rhythms are as significant, or more so, than demonstrated changes in isolated levels, especially given the finely tuned regulatory balance of the immune system.

LINKS BETWEEN THE NEUROENDOCRINE AND IMMUNE SYSTEMS

Exploration of the external factors that might modify the immune system leads us to a consideration of the role of the neuroendocrine system. By now there are well-documented interactions between immune processes and neuroendocrine functions, which are described in several recent reviews (Ahlqvist, 1976; Besedovsky and Sorkin, 1977). In all likelihood the diurnal rhythmicities in the immune system described above are intimately related to well-established rhythmicities in the neuroendocrine system (Moore, 1978).

The widespread influence of cognitive and emotional experience on the endocrine system is also well established (Mason, 1968; Sachar, 1975) and, based on the known interactions between endocrine and immune systems discussed below, would by inference also have some potential to modify immune processes.

THE ENDOCRINE SYSTEM AND NORMAL IMMUNE DEVELOPMENT AND FUNCTION

The neuroendocrine system appears to be essential for the normal development of the immune system, and vice versa. In mice neonatal thymectomy leads to endocrine disturbances such as altered sexual maturation, adrenal hypertrophy, and other disturbances in addition to impairing cellular immunity (Maestroni and Pierpaoli, 1981). The thymus, so central to T cell function's overall immune balance, has been assumed for a long time to be an endocrine organ in that it produces at least four identifiable thymic hormones, known as thymopoietin, thymosin fraction V, thymic humoral factor, and serum thymic factor (Wara, 1981). These hormones, whose functions are still being further elucidated, act locally and peripherally in the maturation of lymphocytes. In turn, the thymus is dependent on a normal neuroendocrine environment, especially adrenal glucocorticoids. Many years ago Selye (1955) described accelerated thymic involution as one of the cardinal manifestations of the stress-response syndrome in conjunction with elevated corticoid steroid levels and adrenal hypertrophy, a finding that lapsed into obscurity because the importance of the thymus in immunity was not then known. Changes in both function and morphology within the thymus have been shown to occur during the light/dark cycle, suggesting a further regulation of the thymus by the neuroendocrine system (Kittell and Blume, 1977).

High doses of exogenous steroids are known to be immunosuppressive both in humoral and cellular immunity and are used for this purpose in a wide range of clinical situations. What is less well known is that physiologic levels of corticoid steroids have been found to be required for several normal functions of immunity (Ambrose, 1970). The direction of their effects on immune function is thus dose-related. In addition to the corticoid steroids, thyroid hormone, growth hormone, insulin, and sex hormones at physiologic levels have all been shown to be required for the normal development and functioning of the immune system (Fabris, 1977).

Thyroid hormone is generally thought to be a stimulator of immune actions. The decline in immune function associated with aging has been thought by some investigators to result from decreased tissue responsiveness to thyroid hormone. The effect of sex hormone modulation of immune function is probably best demonstrated in the B/W mice model for the autoimmune disorder, systemic lupus erythematosus (SLE). In this model, sex hormones modulate the expression of autoimmunity, the extent of immune complex glomerular nephritis, and mortality. Androgens suppress the disease and estrogens accelerate it, a fact which has been linked with the heavy preponderance of SLE among females (Talal, 1979).

Other studies have emphasized the importance of the neuroendocrine system during the induction of an immune response. In one study Besedovsky, Sorkin, Felix, and Haas (1977) immunized rats with two different antigens and then discovered a striking increase in serum hydrocortisone and a moderate decrease in thyroxin coinciding with the time of elaboration of antibody-forming cells. That finding, associated with the simultaneous increase in electrical activity in individual neurons in the ventral medial hypothalamus of the rat, led them to postulate an efferent pathway between the peripheral initiation of an immune response and the hypothalamus. A recent report (Pierpaoli and Maestroni, 1978) has suggested that pharmacologic interruption of that neuroendocrine response following immunization suppresses transplantation immune reactions. The authors made the empiric discovery that a combination of drugs including 5-hydroxytryptophan (5-HTP) (a serotonin precursor), dopamine, haloperidol, and phentolamine (an α-adrenergic blocking agent), when administered a few days before and after immunization led to specific and long-lasting unresponsiveness to the specific antigens administered.

RECEPTOR SITES ON LYMPHOCYTES

The existence of numerous receptors on the surface of lymphocytes at certain stages of their development and activity is noteworthy in considering the interrelatedness of the immune and endocrine systems (Helderman and Strom, 1978; Cantor and Gershow, 1979). In addition to various neurotransmitters such as histamine (Roszkowski, Plaut, and Lichtenstein, 1977), acetylcholine (Richman and Arnason, 1979), and β-adrenergic catecholamines (Singh and Owen, 1976), a variety of CNS-controlled hormones such as insulin (Krug, Krug, and Cuatrecasas, 1974), corticoid steroids (Litwack, 1975), growth hormone

(Arrenbrecht, 1974), and testosterone (Gillette and Gillette, 1979) all seem to have specific receptor sites through which they effect the functional activity of lymphocytes. Estrogens appear to have a specific thymic receptor site in the rat, located on reticuloendothelial cells (Grossman, Sholiton, Blaha, and Nathan, 1979). They all appear to exert their effect through the second messenger system, intracellular cyclic AMP and cyclic GMP (Bourne, Lichtenstein, Melmon, Henney, Weinstein, and Shearer, 1974). Some of these receptor sites, such as those for insulin and more recently transferrin and lymphocyte growth factors, appear to develop only after antigen activation of T cells. The fact that cholinergic, histaminergic, and β-adrenergic receptor sites exist on certain lymphocytes is especially relevant to our consideration of links between the central nervous system and the immune system. The capacity of these transmitter substances to inhibit or augment lymphocyte function also varies according to the activation stage of the lymphocyte and may represent secondary modulators of subimmune interactions.

β-adrenergic agonists have been shown to inhibit lymphocyte-mediated cytotoxicity, whereas acetylcholine augments that effect (Strom, Carpenter, Garovoy, Austen, Merrill, and Kaliner, 1973). The precise effects vary according to the subset of lymphocytes studied and probably also according to their level of maturation.

THE AUTONOMIC NERVOUS SYSTEM AND THE IMMUNE SYSTEM

Several anatomical studies have shown the presence in the mouse and rat of autonomic nerve endings in lymphoid tissues such as the thymus, spleen, and regional lymph nodes (Bullock and Moore, 1981; Williams, Peterson, Shea, Schmedtje, Bauer, and Felten, 1981). Bullock's study shows these thymus neurons projecting into the spinal cord and medulla. Using the electron microscope Williams and colleagues have shown what may be synaptic connections between some of these sympathetic nerve endings and adjacent mast cells. In any event, both this work and that of others (Kosohara, Tanaka, and Ito, 1977) have shown that chemical sympathectomy in mice (produced by 6-hydroxy dopamine) can enhance a primary immune response both in the antibody titers and in a number of plaque-forming cells.

STRESS AND MEDICAL ILLNESS: CLINICAL DATA

Having thus briefly considered the normal regulation of the immune system and some of the neuroendocrine influences that modulate it, let us turn to the evidence, both indirect and direct, that psychologic processes can effect immunologic function. The clinical literature and indeed clinical experience have repeatedly emphasized the importance of psychologic factors in both the onset and course of a variety of illnesses such as cancer, infectious disease, autoimmune disorders, and allergy, which are known to be influenced at least in part by a disturbance in immunity.

CANCER

Alterations in both humoral and cell-mediated immune response have long been implicated in the etiology and course of cancer (Stutman, 1975). Several retrospective studies have suggested an important role for psychologic factors in cancer (LeShan, 1959; Bahnson, 1969). More recent prospective data have heightened interest in this association. Thomas, Duszynski, and Shaffer (1979) have been conducting a long-term study of health outcome in medical students who were first evaluated psychologically in 1949. Those developing cancer were similar to those developing mental illness but different from coronary artery disease and hypertension in that they had experienced a lack of closeness with parents in childhood. Psychosocial risk factors have also been predictive of lung cancer in a semipro-spective study (Horne and Picard, 1979) and one-year survival in patients with malignant melanoma (Rogentine, Van Kam-men, Fox, Docherty, Rosenblatt, Boyd, and Bunney, 1979). Greer, Morris, and Pettingale (1979) in London found that psychologic responses observed three months after mastectomy correlated significantly with outcome at five years. Recurrence-free survival was significantly greater in patients who had ini-tially reacted to cancer by denial or who had a fighting spirit than among patients who had responded with stoic acceptance or feelings of helplessness and hopelessness. The same group of investigators (Pettingale, Greer, and Tee, 1977) also de-scribed elevations in serum IgA level associated with the ex-treme suppression of anger. Another recent study (Shekelle, Raynor, Ostfeld, Garron, Bieliauskas, Liu, Maliza, and Paul, 1981) has shown a correlation between depression and the much later development of cancer. MMPIs were performed on over 2000 middle-aged men. Those with depression were found to have a twofold increase in death from cancer over a 17-year follow-up study, an association which persisted despite adjust-ment for age, smoking, alcohol, family history of cancer, and occupational status. No particular type of cancer was associated.

INFECTIOUS DISEASE

Evidence that emotional stress can be related to the onset of infectious disease comes from a finding by Meyer and Hag-gerty (1962) that high stress in longitudinally studied families was correlated with the acquisition of streptococcal infections and to antistreptolysin antibody responses. Acute necrotizing gingivitis has long been observed by dentists to be frequently preceded by acute stresses (Dworkin, 1969). In a careful four-year prospective study of infectious mononucleosis in cadets at the West Point Military Academy the combination of high mo-tivation and poor academic performance interacted in predict-ing clinical disease (Kasl, Evan, and Niederman, 1979). Furthermore, the convalescent rate from various infectious illnesses has been correlated with psychologic factors, "ego strength" associated with more rapid recovery from infectious mononucleosis (Greenfield, Roessler, and Crosley, 1959) and, conversely, depressed mood associated with prolonged recovery from brucellosis (Imboden, Canter, Cluff, and Trever, 1959) and influenza (Imboden, Canter, and Cluff, 1961). Considerable recent attention has focused on recurrent herpes labialis infections in which a virus living in the ganglia emerges periodically, perhaps as a result of brief immunosuppressive triggers. Emotional stress has been one of the triggers frequently cited. Luborsky, Mintz, Brightman, and Katcher (1976) did demonstrate that unhappiness (as measured by the Clyde Mood Scale) predicted the frequency of recurrent episodes during a one-year follow-up. However, daily mood fluctuations were totally unrelated to these same episodes.

AUTOIMMUNE DISORDERS

This category of illness includes at least 20 mysterious disorders such as rheumatoid arthritis, systemic lupus erythematosus, ulcerative colitis, multiple sclerosis, uveitis, chronic active hepatitis, myasthenia gravis, thyroiditis, juvenile onset diabetes mellitus, and many more. Clustering of several autoimmune disorders often occurs. Their essential feature involves either an antibody or cell-mediated immune response directed toward the self. Common treatments involve immunosuppressive medications such as cytotoxic agents and steroids, Cyclosporin A, and more recent efforts with anti-T cell monoclonal antibodies. One commonly held theory is that there is an imbalance in immunoregulation and, in particular, a relative diminution in suppressor T cells which may allow the autoimmunization to occur (Horowitz, Borcherding, Moorthy, Chesney, Schulte-Wissermann, and Hong, 1977; Reinherz, Weiner, Hauser, Cohen, Distaso, and Schlossman, 1980). Recently a curious association between left-handedness and autoimmune disorders has been discovered (Geschwind and Behan, 1982). These researchers speculate that very early fetal alterations in testosterone or other endocrine influences may have simultaneously affected brain development, handedness and immunologic development, thus creating this interesting association.

Psychologic factors have been reported to have an important role in both the etiology and course of several of these disorders. Solomon and Moos (1965) compared the psychologic health of physically healthy relatives of patients with rheumatoid arthritis. Those who were positive for rheumatoid factor showed particularly high ego strength, leading the authors to hypothesize that active disease might have recurred if they had had low ego strength. Thus the combination of low ego strength and genetic predisposition might result in the onset of the disease. There are other studies pointing to an important role for psychologic factors both in the onset of this disease (Meyerowitz, Jacox, and Hess, 1968), and in its course (Feigenbaum, Masi, and Kaplan, 1979). In a study of juvenile arthritic patients, Heisel (1972) found a significantly higher incidence of life change, taken as an index of stress, in the year preceding onset compared to appropriately matched controls. Interestingly, hospitalization for minor surgery for a nonrelated disorder was the single most commonly cited life change event in the JRA population. Stress has also been associated with both the onset of systemic lupus erythematosus (SLE) (McLary, Meyer, and Weitzman, 1955; Blumenfield, 1978), and the flare-ups so characteristic of its course (Otto and Mackay, 1967). Similar observations have been made in ulcerative colitis (Engel, 1958), thyroiditis (Morillo and Gardner, 1979), uveitis (Kumar, Nema, and Thakur, 1981), and psoriasis (Seville, 1978).

OTHER DISORDERS INVOLVING THE
IMMUNE SYSTEM

Both in allergic or hypersensitivity disorders such as bronchial asthma and atopic dermatitis, and in delayed hypersensitivity reactions as in organ transplantation rejections, important psychologic factors have also been shown to operate. In reviewing the evidence in asthma, Weiner (1980) concluded that actual or anticipated separation and loss do appear to play an important role in initiating the process in about 50 percent of all asthmatic patients. Psychologic factors have been shown to be associated with allergic rhinitis (Czubalski and Zawisza, 1976) and contact dermatitis (Brown and Young, 1965). In kidney transplant patients, stressful life events and depression and anxiety have been related to the timing of rejection episodes and mortality (Eisendrath, 1969; Viederman, 1975).

EPIDEMIOLOGIC EVIDENCE

On the epidemiologic side, the measurement of the magnitude of recent life change, developed initially by Holmes and Rahe in 1967 as a quantifiable measure of stress, has provided further suggestive evidence for the contribution of stress to the development of a variety of illnesses in several different populations (Gunderson and Rahe, 1974). In addition other studies have found an increased incidence of disease in populations experiencing the same major life change, such as bereavement (Parkes and Brown, 1972) or loss of work (Cobb, 1974). These epidemiologic studies would lead us to conceptualize stress, as defined by recent life change, as a risk factor increasing the likelihood of certain diseases to a degree that is statistically significant but by no means uniformly associated with disease. In this regard it is important to avoid simplistic notions of stress and psychologic experience as the "cause" of disease, but rather, to view stress as having a complex interaction with the personality and biology of the host and hence with the expression of disease. The overt manifestations of the diseases mentioned above involve complex relationships between genetic susceptibility, developmental experience, and in some cases acute psychologic processes which may exert a subtle effect on the immune system, perhaps upsetting a delicately poised regulatory system.

Cobb (1976) and others have shown further that if social support is included in the overall equation, the relationship between stress and disease becomes more sharply defined.

Other studies have continued to demonstrate that social disconnectedness is a major risk factor for morbidity and increased mortality, and that conversely, social bonding increases host resistance (Miller and Ingham, 1976; Berkman and Syme, 1979). When social support is high, it tends to protect against the effects of stress; when it is low, it tends to magnify them. With some success other researchers have included different measures designed to evaluate subjects' capacity to cope with stress as a further modifier of this relationship (Hamburg, Adams, and Brodie, 1976).

STRESS AND EXPERIMENTAL ILLNESS: ANIMAL STUDIES

Animal experiments have also demonstrated definite but often complex effects of stress on disease susceptibility. In this discussion we are again focusing on diseases that are closely linked with failures in immune regulation.

MODELS OF TUMOR GROWTH

The incidence and rate of growth of experimental animal tumors have been altered by stress but sometimes in a conflicting and contradictory fashion. Newberry (1981) has recently reviewed the effects of what he calls "presumably stressful stimulation" on animal tumors. For example, one study found that brief daily handling but not mild electric shock, if administered early in life, retarded the rate of Walker 256 sarcoma development in rats (Ader and Friedman, 1965). Both the nature and the exact time of the stress accounted for significant variability in the response. Other investigators have also found experimental stresses to retard the growth of transplanted tumor (Gershbein, Benuck, and Shurrager, 1974; Newberry, Gildow, Wogan, and Reese, 1976).

On the other hand, however, an even more common finding

has been that stress may enhance tumor growth, presumably by suppressing the capacity of the host's immune system to delay it. In a study by Levine and Cohen (1959), stimulation by handling during the first three weeks of life has been shown to shorten the survival time of mice after transplantation of lymphoid leukemia as compared to unstimulated mice. A strain of mice carrying the Bitner oncogenic virus usually develops mammary tumors within 8 to 18 months after birth. Riley (1975) demonstrated that the usual stresses of routine housing of their laboratory animals were related to a 92 percent incidence of tumor at 400 days, while only 7 percent developed tumors in a specially designed, nonstressful environment. Elevated cortisol levels, involution of the thymus, and leukocytopenia were also found in the stressed animals. Sklar and Anisman (1979) showed that inescapable but not escapable electric shock in a mastocytoma tumor model in mice resulted in earlier tumor appearance, exaggerated tumor size, and decreased survival time, suggesting that psychologic response and coping were important intermediate variables. In fact, earlier exposure to the inescapable shock prior to the acute exposure abrogated its tumor-enhancing effect presumably by allowing for adaptation and a different neuroendocrine response (Sklar, Bruto, and Anisman, 1981). Visintainer, Volpicelli, and Seligman (1982), using a Walker 256 tumor preparation in rats, confirmed the finding that inescapable as opposed to escapable shock retarded tumor rejection. They interpreted their findings as implying that psychologic variables associated with lack of control over stressors reduced tumor rejection and decreased survival.

MODELS OF INFECTION

With regard to infection, experimental stress, typically created either by physical restraint or avoidance conditioning using electrical shocks, has been associated with increased susceptibility to numerous viral illnesses including poliomyelitis virus, coxsackie B virus (Johnsson, Lavender, Hultin, and Rasmussen, 1963) and herpes simplex (Rasmussen, Marsh, and Brill, 1957).

Other stressful manipulations such as exposure to high-intensity sound (Jensen and Rasmussen, 1963), overcrowding (Brayton and Brain, 1975), or exposure to a predator (Hamilton, 1974) have also increased susceptibility to certain infections. In the latter study, Hamilton showed that exposure to a predator—a cat—increased twofold the rate of reinfection of mice previously exposed to tapeworm, and was also correlated with adrenal hypertrophy and splenic atrophy, including an atrophy of splenic corpuscular germinal centers containing high concentrations of lymphocytes.

As with the paradoxical responses noted in some studies involving tumor models, however, it has also been observed in at least two studies that stress may have a protective effect against infection (Marsh, Lavender, Chang, and Rasmussen, 1963; Friedman, Ader, and Grota, 1973). The exact nature and timing of the stress in relation to a particular organism as well as the genetics of the host are all important factors in determining the effect that stress has on susceptibility to infection. Furthermore, the time of exposure to an infectious agent needs to be considered both in terms of the stage of the life cycle and of the diurnal rhythmicity of the host. As has been shown earlier, a variety of functions of the immune system possess a circadian rhythm.

MODELS OF AUTOIMMUNE DISEASE

Animal models of autoimmune arthritis have also been influenced by experimental stresses. Adjuvant-induced arthritis in rats has been used as an animal model for rheumatoid arthritis. Amkraut, Solomon, and Kraemer (1971) have reported that group housing stress significantly increases the intensity of this disease in male rats and that it also accelerates the time of maximal disease and rate of recovery. More recently, predator stress was shown to have profound effects on collagen-induced arthritis in rats, a model intended to be more closely analogous to the human disease. Exposure to a cat, as well as handling and transporting manipulations, profoundly diminished the development of joint inflammation without apparent effect on the expected development of cellular and humoral autoimmunity to collagen (Rogers, Trentham, McCune, Ginsberg, Rennke, Reich, and David, 1980). In a sequel to this study, Rogers, Trentham, Dynesius-Trentham, Daffner, and Reich (1983) showed that noise stress had an opposite effect, exacerbating the disease both in terms of the prevalence and severity.

Fluctuations in corticosterone have been shown to profoundly affect the course of experimental allergic encephalomyelitis (EAE), an autoimmune neurological disorder serving as a model for multiple sclerosis (Levine, Sowinski, and Steinetz, 1980). With the induction of disease following immunization with neural tissue, a rising corticosterone response associated with lysis of the thymus and a loss of T cells lead to complete clinical remission. When the corticosterone level decreases, the thymus regenerates, and clinical relapse occurs.

OTHER ANIMAL MODELS

Another interesting animal model—for arteriosclerosis—has been associated with stress-induced immunosuppression (Lattime and Strausser, 1977). Repeatedly bred female Sprague-Dawley rats developed a spontaneous arteriosclerotic condition accompanied by immune complex deposition in the arterial lesion and depressed immune responsiveness to T cell mitogens.

EXPERIMENTAL STRESS AND THE IMMUNE RESPONSE

An increasing number of animal studies have demonstrated that experimental stresses can produce alterations in both cellular and humoral immunity.

HUMORAL IMMUNITY

In one of the first such demonstrations, Solomon (1969) found that overcrowding stress in rats could reduce antibody responses to flagellin, a potent bacterial antigen, both on primary and secondary immunizations. Similar findings have been published with regard to the stress of overcrowding in mice (Vessey, 1960; Petrovskii, 1961; Edwards and Dean, 1977). If the stress is applied prior to or immediately subsequent to immunization, it is immunosuppressive but only if small doses of antigen are used. However, if stress is applied several days after inoculation, it is ineffective (Solomon, Amkraut, and Kasper, 1974). Other intriguing observations have been made, such as the variability in antibody titers in young male chickens in relationship to their social interactions (Siegel and Latimer, 1975).

The effect of stress in early life experience has also been associated with altered immunological responses later in life, but in the opposite direction. Adult rats that had been handled in infancy showed higher antibody titers in response to both primary and secondary immunization with flagellin than a control group (Solomon, Levine, and Kraft, 1968). In contrast, handling one week prior to immunization has been found to depress antibody responses to immunization. Once again, the data support the concept that the timing of stress is crucial and may lead to paradoxical results.

CELLULAR IMMUNITY

There have been several animal studies in which stress has also been associated with diminished lymphocyte response to mitogens (Gisler, 1974; Monjan and Collector, 1977), lymphocyte cytotoxicity (Monjan and Collector, 1977), lymphocyte recirculation (Spry, 1972), and lymphocyte response to antigenic stimulation (Joasoo and McKenzie, 1976). In related animal studies, suppression of cellular immunity secondary to stress has been reflected in diminished skin homograft rejection in mice (Wistar and Hildemann, 1960), diminished graft versus

host response (Amkraut, Solomon, and Kasper, 1972), and diminished delayed hypersensitivity reaction (Pitkin, 1966). An
acute immobilization stress in mice has been shown to produce
an impairment in macrophage tumoricidal function (Pavlidis
and Chirigos, 1980). The latter study demonstrated that corticoid steroids given in vivo could similarly impair function.

While most studies have thus concurred with the finding of
immunosuppressive effects of stress on cellular immunity, a few
have shown conflicting results, in which stress appears to have
augmented cellular immune functions (Mettrop and Visser,
1969; Folch and Waksman, 1974; Monjan and Collector, 1977).
One of these studies, for example, Mettrop and Visser (1969),
showed that stress increased delayed hypersensitivity. While the
discrepancy may be explained in part on the basis of differences
in the experimental animals and in the type of stress used, the
duration of stress and the length of the time interval between
the stress and of the immunologic measurements are of central
importance. For example, Monjan and Collector (1977) subjected mice to the stress of a loud noise on a chronic basis and
found a biphasic response. For the first two weeks or so of
stress, they found a 50 percent decrease in response to mitogens
and lymphocyte cytotoxicity. After three weeks, however, there
was a striking increase in these same functions. These investigators attributed the initial decrease to the increased steroid
levels occurring over the same period. They attributed the
longer-term increase to one or more circulating factors, such
as somatotrophic hormone (STH). Similarly, Folch and Waksman (1974) demonstrated that either a noise stress, a water
deprivation stress, or an injection of hydrocortisone may all
result in loss of rat suppressor T cells' adhesiveness to glass
wool (a measure of suppressor T cell activity) in the short run,
i.e., around five days. However after two to three weeks there
is a return to normal levels followed by a marked increase in
suppressor cell activity. Like Monjan and Collector, they attributed the short-term effect to elevated steroids, but wondered
whether the subsequent increase was due to altered levels of

thymic hormone(s) or a redistribution of lymphocytes (Folch and Waksman, 1974).

More recently, Keller, Weiss, Schleifer, Miller, and Stein (1981) have shown that the degree of lymphocyte suppression in the rat varies according to the severity of the stress. Four increasing levels of stress—home cage controls, apparatus controls, low shock, and high shock—were associated with sequentially increasing suppression of lymphocyte stimulation as measured by mitogen stimulation with PHA. In preliminary work, the same group of investigators (Keller, Ackerman, Schleifer, Shindledecker, Camerino, Hofer, Weiner, and Stein, 1983) has noted that early separation in rats may also diminish cellular immune function. Other investigators (Laudenslager, Reite, and Harbeck, 1982) had previously observed that early separation of monkey infants from their mothers produced some suppression in cellular immune function. Thus, there is an impressive body of evidence from animal studies demonstrating that experimental stresses can significantly alter, generally by diminishing, both humoral and cellular immune functions.

CONDITIONING AND THE IMMUNE SYSTEM

Another link connecting the brain and the immune system has been the demonstration of behaviorally conditioned immunosuppression. This phenomenon was first described by Ader and Cohen (1975) using a taste diversion paradigm in rats. Saccharin (the conditioned stimulus), a drug that can produce both gastrointestinal distress as well as immunosuppression, was paired with cyclophosphamide (the unconditioned stimulus). In a carefully controlled study, subsequent exposure to saccharin was found to exert an immunosuppressive effect, as measured in lower antibody titers raised to immunization with sheep red blood cell antigen. This basic phenomenon has been replicated by two other laboratories (Rogers, Reich, Strom, and Carpenter, 1976; Wayner, Flannery, and Singer, 1978). The mechanism accounting for this effect remains a mystery and does not seem to be due to nonspecific stress effects. When lithium chloride is substituted for cyclophosphamide, no immunosuppressive effect is seen. Furthermore, in the same paradigm, adrenocorticoid levels are equally raised by exposure to saccharin regardless of whether lithium chloride or a cyclophosphamide is used as the unconditioned stimulus (Ader, 1976), suggesting that glucocorticoids do not account for this effect. Nor does there appear to exist any synergistic relation between an elevated glucocorticoid level and the residual immunosuppressive effects of cyclophosphamide (Ader, Cohen, and Grota, 1979).

Further work by Ader and associates has shown that the effects of conditioning can be generalized to a T cell independent system in the mouse with immunization using hapten trinitrophenyl (TNP) coupled to the thymus-independent carrier, lipopolysaccharide (Cohen, Ader, Green, and Borbjerg, 1979). The conditioning paradigm has also retarded the onset of disease in the NZB mouse model of SLE (Ader and Cohen, 1982).

Brain Stimulation and the Immune Response

Several researchers have produced alterations in the immune response by directly stimulating the brain. In their studies of the dorsal hypothalamus Russian investigators have shown that destructive lesions suppress both humoral and cellular immunity (Korneva and Khai, 1963), and that stimulation can enhance antibody responses (Korneva and Khai, 1967). Fessel and Forsyth (1963) demonstrated a doubling of gamma globulin levels by electrical stimulation of the lateral hypothalamus in rats. More recently, Cross, Markesbery, and Brooks (1980) confirmed that anterior hypothalamic lesions could effect immune responses; and their associates have reported qualitative lymphocyte abnormalities in patients with primary brain tumors (Roszman and Brooks, 1980).

Bilateral hypothalamic lesions in guinea pigs have been observed to protect against lethal anaphylaxis (Freedman and Fenichel, 1958; Szentivanyi and Filipp, 1958). In subsequent studies it was found that anterior, but not posterior lesions could protect against anaphylaxis (Luparello, Stein, and Park, 1964). In addition to demonstrating the protective effect of anterior hypothalamic lesions against anaphylaxis, Macris, Schiavi, Camerino, and Stein (1970) found that the lesions lowered antibody titers and decreased cutaneous delayed hypersensitivity. The mechanism of the protective effect against anaphylaxis does not appear to be mediated by altered antibody titers, however, but by nonspecific aspects of the humoral immune response (Stein et al., 1976). For example, it appears that the vagus nerve plays an important role and that hypothalamic lesions may also mediate their immune effects via changes in thyroid-stimulating hormone or adrenocorticotrophic hormones (Stein et al., 1980). Nevertheless, the fact that hypothalamic lesions protect against lethal anaphylaxis only when placed prior to sensitization, but not postsensitization, suggests that the mechanism does involve some immune components of the anaphylactic reaction (Keller, Shapiro, Schleifer, and Stein, 1982).

Another exciting link between the hypothalamus and the immune system is revealed in studies by Besedovsky et al. (1977). A fourfold increase in the firing rate of neurons in the ventromedial nuclei of rats has been found after immunization with two different antigens. These neurons fire in concert with peak antibody formation. Further evidence of this afferent loop between the immunologic response occurring during acute immunization and the hypothalamus has been provided by the work of Shek and Sabiston (1983). Coinciding with the peak spleen plaque-forming cell response to immunization, a transient increase in circulating corticosterone was noted, along with a change in its circadian rhythmicity. This response could be blocked by the administration of diazepam. The authors speculated that lymphokines released from rapidly proliferating T cells might affect ACTH release from the hypothalamus and in turn perhaps provide a method for limiting clonal expansion of the antibody producing cells.

ALTERATIONS IN HUMAN IMMUNITY

Relative to animal studies, there is less direct evidence of altered immunity in humans as a function of altered states of emotion or behavior, but some preliminary data have begun to emerge.

STRESS

Diminished T cell response to mitogens has been noted in astronauts in the skylab program for the first three days of the post-flight period, although it is of course impossible to know whether this was more a function of physical than psychologic stress (Kimzey, Ritzmann, Mengel, and Fischer, 1975). Neuroendocrine measures taken during the same time period, however, confirmed that the day of splashdown was apparently especially stressful for the astronauts (Leach, Rambaut, and Johnson, 1974).

Greene and associates from Rochester demonstrated a statistically significant correlation between increased stress, as defined by life change units combined with alterations on a mood scale, and a decrease in lymphocyte cytotoxicity, a measure of T cells capacity to kill tumor cells to which they have been specifically sensitized (Greene, Betts, Ochitill, Iker, and Douglas 1978). In a similar study, Locke, Hurst, Heisel, and Williams (1978) found a statistically significant correlation between high stress combined with poor coping and diminished natural killer cell activity, but no significant correlations between stress and various parameters of humoral immunity. Natural killer activity provides a particularly interesting index of immunocompetence for several reasons. First, although its precise function is unknown, it is thought to provide a general host defense in combating host cells undergoing malignant transformation and also against viruses (Behelak, Banerjee, and Richter, 1976). Second, what is measured is a natural property of the cell rather than an artificially induced measure such as response to mitogens. For these reasons it appears to have particularly important clinical implications. Its disadvantage is that it is not yet as well standardized as mitogen stimulation techniques.

One other study of the effects of a naturally occurring stress on immune function investigated lymphoblast transformation in response to mitogens before and after examinations (Dorian, Keystone, Garfinkel, and Brown, 1981). Psychiatric residents were studied twice 10 to 14 days before and after important qualifying examinations in Canada. A matched control group of physicians not undergoing the examination was also studied. Lymphoblast transformation was significantly lower in those about to be examined than in controls, but returned to higher levels in the postexamination period. Interestingly, this is somewhat reminiscent of the biphasic response noted by Monjan and Collector (1977) after prolonged noise stimulation in mice.

BEREAVEMENT AND DEPRESSION

In the last few years, attention has increasingly turned toward bereavement as an important naturally occurring stress. In part this is a result of epidemiologic work suggesting increased morbidity and mortality especially in widowers following death of a spouse (Clayton, 1979) and in part from other lines of evidence showing profound and specific physiologic disruption following maternal separation (Hofer, 1975). In a landmark study (Bartrop, Lazarus, Luckhurst, Kiloh, and Penny, 1977), bereavement in humans was found to be associated with depressed lymphocyte function, specifically in T cell response to mitogens at five weeks but not at two weeks after a bereavement. There was a tenfold difference in this T cell function at five weeks between the 26 bereaved spouses, both men and women, and the controls. No difference was found in the number of T and B cells, antibody titers, presence of autoantibodies, or in the hormonal studies included. Unfortunately, the report lacks any description of the degree of severity of the grief reactions as well as sufficient detail about the presence of medications or the medical illnesses which might have altered their lymphocyte function.

In their ongoing longitudinal survey of men whose wives have died from breast cancer, Schleifer, Keller, Camerino, Thornton, and Stein (1983) at Mt. Sinai Hospital in New York have provided confirmatory evidence of immunosuppression. In the 12 subjects in whom cellular immune function was measured both before and after bereavement, there was a suppression in B cell response to mitogen (pokeweed) at one month after bereavement and in T cell function as measured by mitogen (PHA) stimulation after two months. Nine subjects later returned to normal pre-bereavement levels of cellular immune function. The three who failed to do so tended to be much younger. No change in absolute number of circulating lymphocytes was found. There was some suggestive evidence that the magnitude of the immunologic suppression, which was quite variable among subjects, was correlated with the magnitude of the psychologic disruption caused by the loss of the spouse.

Two reports at the 1982 annual meeting of the American Psychosomatic Society provided evidence of altered immune functioning in clinical depression. The first, by Linn, Linn, and Jensen (1982) looked at the degree of depression in 60 men during the first six-month period following bereavement. Those with higher levels of depression, as measured by the Hopkins symptom checklist, had significantly reduced lymphocyte response to mitogen (PHA) compared to controls as well as significantly reduced IgG and IgM antibody levels, although the latter were nevertheless in the normal range. Looking at clinical depression, Kronfol, Silva, Greden, Dembinski, and

Carroll (1982) investigated lymphocyte function in patients with melancholia and another nondepressed group of psychiatric patients compared to normal controls. They reported significant reduction in lymphocyte response to mitogens when compared to both control groups.

OTHER MENTAL ILLNESS

A number of investigators have described immunologic abnormalities in other psychiatric populations, particularly schizophrenic patients. Many of these investigations tested the hypothesis that the cause of schizophrenia might be an immune disturbance, perhaps an autoimmune disorder in which brain tissue was directly attacked. The evidence, however, has been inconsistent. Some studies have reported increases in auto-antibodies such as rheumatoid factor in schizophrenia (Oreskes, Rosenblatt, Spiera, and Meadow, 1968) and anti-DNA and anti-thyroid antibodies (Fessel, 1962); but other investigators selecting schizophrenic patients not receiving drug treatment found no increase in anti-nuclear antibodies compared to age- and sex-matched controls (Whittingham, Mackay, Jones, and Davies, 1968). Subsequent studies have linked the use of long-term chlorpromazine to the development of autoantibodies and elevations in IgM levels (Canoso and Sise, 1982). These effects appear to be mediated at the cellular level of immune responses rather than through any centrally mediated effect, in that clear in vitro alterations in immunity with chlorpromazine have also been noted (Ferguson, Schmidtke, and Simmons, 1975). Drug effects may also account for the reports of abnormal cellular immunity in both schizophrenic adults (Vanderkamp and Daly, 1968) and children (Fowle, 1968). However there are a number of studies reporting alterations in immunoglobulin levels, both in schizophrenics and other psychiatric patients (Solomon, Allansmith, McClellan, and Amkraut, 1969), in which differences did not depend on exposure to phenothiazine drugs; and in some cases, differences in clinical course were correlated with altered immunoglobulin levels (Amkraut, Solomon, and Allansmith, 1973). In summary, there is some suggestive evidence that alterations in humoral immunity exist in schizophrenia and perhaps other psychotic illnesses, but the evidence is sometimes conflicting and compounded by the effects of antipsychotic medications. Perhaps some of these immunologic changes were related to nonspecific stress associated with acute psychosis or with depression.

HYPNOSIS AND THE IMMUNE SYSTEM

Hypnosis has been found to alter the clinical manifestations of delayed hypersensitivity. Black, Humphrey, and Niven (1963) were able to inhibit the Mantaux reaction (tuberculin skin test) by direct suggestion under hypnosis in subjects known to be positive reactors. Although the typical swelling and erythema were absent, skin biopsies did reveal the expected degree of cellular infiltration. In other studies, direct suggestion under hypnosis has been shown to inhibit immediate hypersensitivity reactions in allergic dermatitis, in allergic responses to food (Ikemi and Nakagawa, 1963), and in urticarial eruptions (Kaneko and Taksishi, 1963). It would appear that hypnosis can alter the efferent but not the afferent limb of the immune system. There have as yet been no adequate replications of these interesting observations.

OTHER BEHAVIORALLY MEDIATED EFFECTS

One might speculate as to whether effects of stress and bereavement on immunologic function operate directly through brain-mediated psychophysiologic mechanisms or perhaps indirectly through associated alterations in behavior. For this reason, some of the observed effects of sleep deprivation, exercise, nutrition, alcohol, and smoking merit special consideration. Palmblad and associates at the Karolinska Institute in Sweden showed that the stress of a 77-hour sleepless continuous attention vigil in men, in which exposure to loud noise also occurred, was associated with an increase in interferon production, a product of T cells, as well as a biphasic change in phagocytic activity (Palmblad, Cantell, Strander, Fröberg, Karlsson, Levi, Granstrom, and Unger, 1976). Interferon was increased both during and shortly after the vigil. Phagocytosis, which was decreased during the vigil, rose to above baseline levels afterwards. In a further study, Palmblad, Petrini, Wasserman, and Akerstedt (1979) measured lymphoblast transformation in lymphocytes in response to mitogens in two parameters of granulocyte function in humans before, during and after 48 hours of sleep deprivation. Although no changes were observed in either measure of granulocyte function, lymphocyte response to PHA stimulation was significantly depressed at the end of the 48-hour period, returning to baseline levels within five days.

Exercise has been shown to produce alterations in both humoral and cellular immunity (Eskola, Ruuskanen, Soppi, Viljanen, Järvinen, Toivonen, and Kouvalainen, 1978), and alterations in immunity may also be produced by both under- and over-nutrition (Chandra, 1977). Dutz, Kohout, Rossipal, and Vessal (1976) have documented the residual immunologic effects resulting from malnutrition in early childhood. In addition to an increase in early infections, alterations persisted long after proper nutrition was resumed in numerous parameters of immunologic function, including phagocytosis, complement levels, cylic AMP, accelerated thymic atrophy, and an accelerated decline in cell-mediated immunity. However, whether subtle nutritional alterations in adult life as might occur in crisis situations such as bereavement influence immune function is unknown.

It is also of interest that both smoking (Kosmider and Wysocki, 1977) and alcohol (Lundy, Raaf, Deakins, Wanebo, Jacobs, Lee, Jacobowitz, Spear, and Oettgen, 1975) have been associated with diminished immune function. With regard to alcohol, other interesting effects have been observed. For example, in utero exposure to alcohol in rats produced marked suppression of lymphocyte activity in adulthood (Monjan and Mandell, 1980). In addition, surgery, anesthesia, acute viral illnesses, and a host of medications are capable of producing significant suppression of both humoral and cellular immunity.

A DISCUSSION OF MECHANISMS

The evidence presented thus far leaves little doubt that psychologic states associated with stress, grief, and depression and with direct stimulation of the central nervous system can alter different measures of the immune system. The evidence is probably somewhat stronger in animal studies, which also indicates that the degree of immunologic alteration created has significant biological consequences, i.e., relates to susceptibility to infection, autoimmune disease, or tumor growth. The human data suggest that in some naturally occurring stress situations, particularly bereavement, statistically significant diminution in cellular immune function can occur. Whether the degree of diminution noted has biological consequences for disease susceptibility in humans, however, is unknown at this point. Hopefully future investigations will help to answer the issue of biological significance by closely examining subsequent morbidity and mortality.

Another central question that arises on the basis of the above observations concerns the mechanisms for alterations in immunity. In this regard, it needs to be kept in mind that there may be several mechanisms involved, which might be induced differentially by different experimental or naturally occurring stressors. The animal data are replete with examples of paradoxical or bimodal responses. That is, sometimes the experimental stress situation can augment as well as diminish an immune response. As we have seen, timing is a crucial explanatory variable. Many of the studies have shown direct changes in the afferent limb of the immune system, i.e., alterations in antibody titers or cellular immunity as in delayed hypersensitivity cytotoxicity responses, or responses to mitogen stimulation. Other studies, however, have suggested that the efferent limb of the immune system alone is affected, producing changes in the inflammatory response, for example, in the hypnosis-altered tuberculin skin test or in the inhibition of collagen-induced arthritis.

Clearly a wide variety of stimuli and situations have been lumped together under the term "stress." Some of the stressors have included direct noxious stimuli such as loud noise or electrical shocks, whereas others have tried to capture more of a psychologic dimension such as the inescapability of a situation or exposure to a predator. It stands to reason that the physiological consequences of such divergent stimuli may be equally divergent.

Keeping these complexities in mind then, let us turn to the issue of mechanisms. A predominant hypothesis is that stress and/or bereavement, for example, can lead to immunologic change through the mechanism of hypothalamic-pituitary hormonal stimulation. Adrenocorticoid hormones have received the most attention and in fact are generally assumed to account for many of the observed immunosuppressive effects. In part this is because an elevation in adrenocorticoids has been so well substantiated as a response to stress in the work of Selye and others, and because the adrenocorticoids, at least in large doses, can suppress the immune response. Elevated corticosteroid levels have also been associated with the involution of the thymus and leukopenia. Not surprisingly, a number of the studies cited above have included measurements of corticosterone. In some of these studies, simultaneous elevations in corticosterone have been correlated with the immunologic depression observed (Gisler, 1974; Riley, 1975) and in others, exogenous administration of steroids has simulated the observed stress-induced immunosuppression (Folch and Waksman, 1974).

On the other hand, in some studies where adrenocorticoid levels have been measured, particularly in bereavement (Bartrop et al., 1977; Schleifer et al., 1983), elevations in cortisol levels have not been observed in association with immunosuppression. Furthermore, elevations in adrenocorticoid hormones alone would not seem sufficient to account for the biphasic immune response seen in prolonged noise stress in mice (Monjan and Collector, 1977). In the latter study, elevation in corticosteroid levels was correlated with initial immunosuppression but not with the later observed heightening of cellular immunity. In addition, elevated adrenocorticoid levels do not appear to account for the observed immunosuppression in the taste aversion conditioning studies. As a result of a carefully designed study to test this question, Ader et al. (1979) concluded that elevation in corticoid levels did not even have any synergistic effect to account for the conditioned immunosuppression. Finally, in at least one study in which stress has produced a depression in cellular immunity, prior adrenalectomy followed by maintenance corticosteroid treatment failed to abrogate the observed immunosuppressive effects of stress (Keller, Ackerman, Schleifer, Shindledecher, Camerino, Hofer, Weiner, and Stein, 1983). Thus, elevations in adrenocorticoid levels may account for some but not all of the observed immunosuppressive effects of stress; that mechanism does not appear to apply to conditioned immunosuppression or to studies of human bereavement. Other hormones such as growth hormone, prolactin, the endorphins, and catecholamines, either from the adrenal medulla or from the peripheral sympathetic nervous system are known to be extremely responsive to the effects of stress. Furthermore, the presence on the surface of lymphocytes of a variety of specific receptor sites for a range of hormones including insulin and sex hormones would suggest that premature closure be avoided in focusing exclusively on corticosteroids as the sole hormonal mediator of immunosuppressive effects.

Whatever the role of the pituitary, it would appear that the hypothalamus also has an important regulatory role in the immune system. The evidence for this is perhaps best exemplified by the work of Stein, Schiavi, and Camerino (1976), in which anterior hypothalamic lesions are associated with alterations in humoral immune responses, delayed hypersensitivity, as well as protection against anaphylaxis in guinea pigs. Others have described similar effects. Whether these lesions express themselves through alterations in hormones such as thyroxin and corticosteroid hormones is unclear.

Other studies also point to the role of the hypothalamus in helping to regulate and modulate the immune response. In the last several years some very exciting work has suggested that there may be an afferent loop in the connection from the immune response back to the hypothalamus, in addition to the efferent effects already discussed. The work of Besedovsky and associates, for example, has shown an increased rate of neuronal firing in the hypothalamus of mice immediately following antigen-antibody interaction and prior to any change in thyroid or corticosteroid hormones (Besedovsky et al., 1977). A peak in neuronal firing is observed approximately two days after antigenic stimulation. How could such information get back to the hypothalamus from the spleen or lymph nodes where lymphocytes would be undergoing activation following an antigenic stimulus? While the answer to this is certainly unknown at the present time, activated lymphocytes secrete a variety of products known as lymphokines, which would then be circulating in the blood and perhaps capable of triggering altered activity in the hypothalamus.

Other evidence for the presence of such a mechanism comes from the recent work of two Canadian investigators (Shek and Sabiston, 1983) that shows changes in circulating corticosterone levels following the primary antibody induction in mice. The elevation in corticosterone levels occurs at approximately two to four days after immunization. In addition to the absolute increase in levels of corticosterone, there is also an alteration in its diurnal rhythmicity. These alterations in corticosterone responses are seen only in association with a primary immune response. That is, saline injections or injections of antigen in another strain of mice known to be low responders to this particular antigen are not associated with similar hormonal changes. Furthermore, these investigators were able to block the elevations in corticosterone levels without affecting the antibody response by administering diazepam. They hypothesized that this feedback loop from the immune response to the hypothalamus with the subsequent secretion of transient increases in corticosteroid hormones were designed to down regulate the immune response, limiting further clonal enlistment. Such a feedback loop may also account for the observed pharmacologic interruption of a transplantation rejection reaction (Pierpaoli and Maestroni, 1978). These authors discovered that a combination of centrally acting psychotropic agents, when administered a few days before and after immunization, led to specific and long-lasting unresponsiveness to specific antigens administered.

Another important mechanism may involve the autonomic nervous system. The lateral specificity of the interruption of an immediate hypersensitivity reaction by suggestion (Ikemi and Nakagawa, 1963) points to a neural mechanism. Perhaps the observed effect of hypnosis on the tuberculin skin test involves similar neural mechanisms in the interruption of the secondary, efferent response of the immune system. Clearly the autonomic nervous system is exquisitely sensitive to emotional states. Adrenergic nerve endings can be found in the spleen and in the thymus and be traced to the spinal cord and brain stem. They may have a direct relationship to immunologic reactivity. Recent studies by several Japanese investigators (Kosohara et al., 1977) and by Williams et al. (1981) have demonstrated that chemical sympathectomy can alter a primary immune response. The latter study included histofluorescent mapping techniques of sympathetic fibers in spleen and thymus which suggest that nerve endings may be traced into the parenchymal tissue of the thymus and spleen in close proximity to active immune cells. Electron micrographs appeared to show adrenergic fibers adjacent to both a mast cell and lymphocytes. In fact, some of the views suggest that there might be a synaptic connection between adrenergic fibers and an adjacent mast cell, and as mentioned earlier, specific receptors for β-adrenergic substances exist on the surface of lymphocytes. These studies suggest that the autonomic nervous system, in perhaps a more targeted and localized fashion, may alter an immune response.

ISSUES FOR THE FUTURE

Future investigations in the area of so-called "psychoneu-roimmunology" will need to focus on two important questions. The first concerns the biological relevance for the observed cellular immune changes secondary to bereavement and other psychological states. Do these changes actually increase suscep-tibility of humans to certain immunologically mediated diseases, as they do in animal models of disease? Long-term follow-up studies will be required to answer this question. Inevitably the possibility of intervention to reduce the risk of such immuno-logic alteration and potential onset of disease will rise. Such an approach has the potential of not only elucidating underlying immunologic mediators, but also, if it can be shown to be ef-ficacious in carefully controlled investigations, can have pro-found effects on medical practice.

The other major focus of research for the future will be on the precise mechanisms by which psychologic states exert an influence on the immune system and their selective effects on its different components. For example, do certain kinds of stim-uli differentially affect suppressor from helper T cells? Is it the resulting imbalance in the equilibrium of the immune system that may predispose toward disease? Or perhaps a subtle effect disturbing the diurnal rhythmicity of the immune system may also predispose toward disease. Investigators will need to deal with the immune system as the complex network that it is and interpret the results of variable laboratory measures of im-munity with some caution. Certain psychologic stresses might be either immunosuppressive or enhancing of some aspects of the immune response in humans as they are in animals. That may raise the possibility that certain kinds of psychologic ex-perience or stress may protect an individual against the devel-opment of a disease to which he or she is susceptible.

The exact nature of the "stress" will need to be carefully defined. In all likelihood, this term will continue to be used to describe diverse phenomena. Because of the diversity of such stimuli and circumstances subsumed under this term, investigators will need to define precisely what is meant in any given situation by "stress." In the human situation, the obvious ethical difficulties with the use of experimental stress will continue to require that naturally occurring stressful situations be used, such as bereavement depression and perhaps a variety of test performance situations. The exact time and timing of such events and the details of the individual's capacity to cope with them psychologically and socially will need to be included as important dimensions of the overall process.

Stress may alter immunologic function by producing internal physiologic change or perhaps by altering external behavior such that an organism is exposed to different stimuli. This at least raises the question of whether a variety of behaviors can influence the functioning of the immune system. As we have seen, sleep deprivation can, and there are preliminary data suggesting that dietary changes, smoking, alcohol consumption, and exercise may alter the status of the immune system. Beyond that, of course, many experiences like pregnancy, surgery, and anesthesia, and a wide variety of drugs, can temporarily alter cellular immunity. From a methodological point of view, the influence of these other factors, aside from the psychologically experienced events and coping styles, will need to be controlled and in some cases investigated in their own right.

Finally, it would appear that not only can central nervous system initiated responses alter an immune response, but an immune response via an afferent feedback loop also appears to be capable of modifying the central nervous system, particularly the hypothalamus. The stimulation of the hypothalamus appears to be associated with transient increases in certain hormonal responses. What effect do these responses have? It has been suggested that these responses may play an important role in regulation, perhaps by turning off an immune response. Other evidence suggests that these responses may play an important role in the normal development of an organism's endocrine system.

The prospect of being able to answer some of these questions is indeed an exciting one. It is important to keep in mind that we are, nevertheless, only in the infancy of research in this area, and careful replication of the observed alterations in immune responses in humans will be needed.

References

Ader, R. (1976), Conditioned adrenocortical steroid elevations in the rat. *J. Comp. Physiol. Psychol.*, 90:1156–1163.

——, ed. (1981), *Psychoneuroimmunology*. New York: Academic Press.

—— Cohen, N. (1975), Behaviorally conditioned immunosuppression. *Psychosom. Med.*, 37:333–340.

—— —— (1982), Behaviorally conditioned immunosuppression and murine systemic lupus erythematosis. *Science*, 215:1534.

—— —— Grota, L. J. (1979), Adrenal involvement in conditioned immunosuppressions. *Internat. J. Immunopharmacol.*, 1:141–145.

—— Friedman, S. B. (1965), Differential early experiences and susceptibility to transplanted tumors in the rat. *J. Comp. Physiol. Psychol.*, 59:361–364.

Ahlqvist, J. (1976), Stability of human immunoglobulin levels. *Acta Endocrinol. Suppl.*, 206:5–136.

Allansmith, M., McClellan, B., & Butterworth, M. (1967), Stability of human immunoglobulin levels. *Proc. Soc. Exp. Biol. Med.*, 125:404–407.

Ambrose, C. T. (1970), The essential role of corticosteroids in the induction of the immune response in vitro. In: *Hormones and Immune Response*, Ciba Study Group, No. 36, ed. G. E. W. Wolstenholme & J. Knight. London: Churchill.

Amkraut, A. A., & Solomon, G. F. (1974), From the symbolic stimulus to the pathophysiologic response: Immune mechanisms. *Internat. J. Psychiat. Med.*, 5:541–563.

—— —— Allansmith, M. (1973), Immunoglobulins and improvement in acute schizophrenic reactions. *Arch. Gen. Psychiat.*, 28:673–677.

—— —— Kasper, P. (1972), Stress and hormonal intervention in the graft-versus host response. *Adv. Exp. Med. Biol.*, 29:667–674.

—— —— Kraemer, H. C. (1971), Stress, early experience, and adjuvant-induced arthritis in the rat. *Psychosom. Med.*, 33:203–214.

Arrenbrecht, S. (1974), Specific binding of growth hormone to thymphocytes. *Nature*, 252:255–257.

Austen, K. F. (1978), Homeostasis of effector systems which can also be recruited for immunologic reactions. Presidential Address, American Association of Immunologists, Atlanta, Georgia, June 6.

Bartrop R. W., Lazarus, L., Luckhurst, E., Kiloh, L. G., & Penny, R. (1977), Depressed lymphocyte function after bereavements. *Lancet*, 1:834–836.

Bahnson, C. B., ed. (1969), Second conference on psychophysiological aspects of cancer. *Ann. N.Y. Acad. Sci.*, 164:307–634.

Behelak, Y., Banerjee, D., & Richter, M. (1976), Immunocompetent cells in patients with malignant disease: The lack of naturally occurring killer cell activity in the infractionated circulating lymphocytes from patients with chronic lymphatic leukemia (CLL). *Cancer*, 38:2274.

Berkman, L. F., & Syme, S. L. (1979), Social networks, host resistance, and mortality: A nine year follow-up study of Alameda County residents. *Amer. J. Epidemiol.*, 109:186–204.

Besedovsky, H., & Sorkin, E. (1977), Network of immunoendocrine interactions. *Clin. Exp. Immunol.*, 27:1–12.

——— ——— Felix, D., & Haas, H. (1977), Hypothalamic changes during the immune response. *Eur. J. Immunol.*, 7:323–325.

Black, S., Humphrey, J. H., & Niven, J. S. (1963), Inhibition of mantous reaction by direct suggestion under hypnosis. *Brit. Med. J.*, 6:1649–1652.

Blumenfield, M. (1978), Psychological aspects of systemic lupus erythematosus. *Primary Care*, 5:159–171.

Bourne, H. R., Lichtenstein, L. M., Melmon, K. L., Henney, C. S., Weinstein, Y., & Shearer, G. M. (1974), Modulation of inflammation and immunity by cyclic AMP. *Science*, 84:19–28.

Brayton, A. R., & Brain, P. F. (1975), Proceedings: Effects of differential housing and glucocorticoid administration on immune responses to sheep red blood cells in albino to strain mice. *J. Endocrinol.*, 64:4P–5P.

Brown, D. G., & Young, A. J. (1965), The effects of extraversion on susceptibility to disease. *J. Psychosom. Res.*, 8:421–429.

Buckley, C. E., & Dorsey, F. C. (1970), The effect of aging on human serum immunoglobulin concentrations. *J. Immunol.*, 105:964–972.

Bullock, K., & Moore, R. Y. (1982), Innervation of the thymus gland by brain stem and spinal cord in mouse and rat. *Amer. J. Anat.*, 162:157–166.

Canoso, R. T., & Sise, H. S. (1982), Chlorpromazine-induced lupus anticoagulant and associated immunologic abnormalities. *Amer. J. Hematol.*, 13:121–129.

Cantor, H., & Gershow, R. K. (1979), Immunological circuits: Cellular composition. *Fed. Proc.*, 38:2058–2059.

Chandra, R. F. (1977), *Nutrition, Immunity, and Infection: Mechanisms of Interactions.* New York: Plenum.

Clayton, P. J. (1979), The sequelae and nonsequelae of conjugal bereavement. *Amer. J. Psychiat.*, 136:1530–1534.

Cobb, S. (1974), Physiological changes in men whose jobs were abolished. *J. Psychosom. Res.*, 18:245–258.

—— (1976), Social support as a moderator of life stress. *Psychosom. Med.*, 38:300–314.

Cohen, N., Ader, R., Green, N., & Borbjerg, D. (1979), Conditioned immunosuppression of a thymus-independent antibody response. *Psychosom. Med.*, 41:487–491.

Cove-Smith, J. R., Kabler, P., Pownall, R., & Knapp, M. S. (1978), Circadian variation in an immune response in man. *Brit. Med. J.*, 2:253–254.

Cross, R. J., Markesbery, W. R., Brooks, W. H., & Roszman, T. L. (1980), Hypothalamic immune interactions. I. The acute effect of anterior hypothalamic lesions on the immune response. *Brain Res.*, 196:79–87.

Czubalski, K., & Zawisza, E. (1976), The role of psychic factors in patients with allergic rhinitis. *Acta Otolaryngol.*, 81:484–488.

Dorian, B. J., Keystone, E., Garfinkel, P. E., & Brown, G. M. (1981), *Psychosom. Med.*, 43:84.

Dutz, W., Kohout, E., Rossipal, E., & Vessal, K. (1976), Infantile stress, immune modulations, and disease patterns. *Pathol. Ann.*, 11:415–454.

Dworkin, S. F. (1969), Psychosomatic concepts and dentistry: Some perspectives. *J. Periodontol.*, 40:647–654.

Edwards, E. A., & Dean, L. M. (1977), Effects of crowding of mice and humoral antibody formation and protection to lethal antigenic challenge. *Psychosom. Med.*, 39:19–24.

Eisendrath, R. M. (1969), The role of grief and fear in the death of kidney transplant patients. *Amer. J. Psychiat.*, 126:381–387.

Engel, G. L. (1958), Studies of ulcerative colitis. Psychological aspects and their implications for treatment. *Amer. J. Dig. Dis.*, 3:315–337.

Eskola, J., Ruuskanen, O., Soppi, E., Viljanen, M. K., Järvinen, M., Toivonen, H., & Kouvalainen, K. (1978), Effect of sport stress on lymphocyte transformation and antibody formation. *Clin. Exp. Immunol.*, 32:339–345.

Fabris, N. (1973), Immunological reactivity during pregnancy in the mouse. *Experientia*, 29:610–612.

—— (1977), Hormones and aging. In: *Comprehensive Immunology*, ed. T. Makinodan & E. Yunis. New York: Plenum, pp. 73–89.

Feigenbaum, S. L., Masi, A. T., & Kaplan, S. B. (1979), Prognosis in rheumatoid arthritis: A longitudinal study of newly diagnosed younger adult patients. *Amer. J. Med.*, 66:377–384.

Ferguson, R. M., Schmidtke, J. R., & Simmons, R. L. (1975), Concurrent inhibition by chlorpromazine of concavalin A-induced lymphocyte aggregation and mitogenesis. *Nature*, 256:744–745.

Fessel, W. J. (1962), Blood proteins in functional psychoses. *Arch. Gen. Psychiat.*, 6:132–148.

—— Forsyth, R. P. (1963), Hypothalamic role in control of gamma globulin levels. *Arthritis Rheum.*, 6:771–772.

Folch, H., & Waksman, B. H. (1974), Activity of thymus dependent adherent cells: Changes with age and stress. *J. Immunol.*, 113:127–139.

Fowle, A. M. (1968), Atypical leukocyte pattern of schizophrenic children. *Arch. Gen. Psychiat.*, 18:666–680.

Freedman, D. X., & Fenichel, G. (1958), Effect of mid-brain lesion in experimental allergy. *Arch. Neurol. Psychiat.*, 79:164–169.

Friedman, S. B., Ader, R., & Grota, L. J. (1973), Protective effect of noxious stimulation in mice infected with rodent malaria. *Psychosom. Med.*, 35:535–537.

Froelich, C. J., Goodwin, J. S., Bankhurst, A. D., & Williams, R. C. (1980), Pregnancy, a temporary fetal graft of suppressor cells in autoimmune disease. *Amer. J. Med.*, 69:329–331.

Gershbein, L. L., Benuck, I., & Shurrager, P. S. (1974), Influence of stress on lesion growth and on survival of animals bearing parenteral and intracerebral leukemia L1210 and Walker tumors. *Oncology*, 30:429–435.

Geschwind, N., & Behan, P. (1982), Left-handedness: Association with immune disease, migraine and developmental learning disorder. *Proc. Natl. Acad. Sci.*, 79:5097–5100.

Gillette, S., & Gillette, R. W. (1979), Changes in thymic estrogen receptor expression following orchidectomy. *Cell. Immunol.*, 42:194–196.

Gilliland, B. C. (1980), Introduction to clinical immunology. In: *Harrison's Principles of Internal Medicine*, 9th ed., ed. K. J. Isselbacher, R. D. Adams, E. Braunwald, & J. D. Wilson. New York: McGraw-Hill, pp. 315–325.

Gisler, R. H. (1974), Stress and hormonal regulations of the immune response in mice. *Psychother. Psychosom.*, 23:197–208.

Goldberg, E. H., & Frikke, M. J. (1981), The role of suppressor cells in the fetal escape of maternal immunologic rejection. In: *Suppressor Cells in Human Disease States*, ed. J. S. Goodwin. New York: Marcel Dekker, pp. 247–266.

Greene, W. A., Betts, R. F., Ochitill, H. N., Iker, H. P., & Douglas, R. G. (1978), Psychosocial factors and immunity: Preliminary report. *Psychosom. Med.*, 40:87.

Greenfield, N. S., Roessler, R., & Crosley, A. P., Jr. (1959), Ego strength and length of recovery from infectious mononucleosis. *J. Nerv. & Ment. Dis.*, 128:125–128.

Greer, S., Morris, T., & Pettingale, K. W. (1979), Psychological response to breast cancer: Effect on outcome. *Lancet*, 2:785–787.

Grossman, C. J., Sholiton, L. J., Blaha, G. C., & Nathan, P. (1979), Rat thymic estrogen receptor. Physiological properties. *J. Steroid Biochem.*, 11:1241–1246.

Grundbacher, F. J. (1974), Heritability estimates and genetic and environmental correlations for the human immunoglobulins G, M, a, A. *Amer. J. Hum. Genet.*, 26:1–12.

Gunderson, E. K., & Rahe, R. H., eds. (1974), *Life Stress and Illness*. Springfield, IL: Thomas.

Haller, O., Hansson, M., Kiessling, R., & Wigzell, H. (1977), Role of non-conventional natural killer cells in resistance against syngereic tumour cells in vivo. *Nature*, 270:609–611.

Hamburg, D. A., Adams, J. E., & Brodie, H. K. H. (1976), Coping behavior in stressful circumstances: Some implications for social psychiatry. In: *Further Explorations in Social Psychiatry*, ed. B. H. Kaplan, R. N. Wilson, & A. H. Leighton. New York: Basic Books, pp. 158–175.

Hamilton, D. R. (1974), Immunosuppressive effects of predator induced stress in mice with acquired immunity to hymenolepsisnana. *J. Psychosom. Res.*, 181:143–150.

Heisel, J. S. (1972), Life changes as etiologic factors in juvenile rheumatoid arthritis. *J. Psychosom. Res.*, 16:411–420.

Helderman, J. H., & Strom, T. B. (1978), Specific insulin binding site on T and B lymphocytes as a marker of cell activation. *Nature*, 274:62–63.

Hofer, M. A. (1975), Studies on how early maternal separation produces behavioral changes in young rats. *Psychosom. Med.*, 37:245–264.

Horne, R. L., & Picard, R. S. (1979), Psychosocial risk factors for lung cancer. *Psychosom. Med.*, 41:503–514.

Horowitz, S., Borcherding, W., Moorthy, A. V., Chesney, R., Schulte-Wissermann, H., & Hong, R. (1977), Induction of suppressor T cells in systemic lupus erythematosus by thymosin and cultured thymic epithelium. *Science*, 197:999–1001.

Ikemi, Y., & Nakagawa, S. (1963), Psychosomatic study of so-called allergic disorders. *Jap. J. Med. Prog.*, 50:451–474.

Imboden, J. B., Canter, A., & Cluff, L. E. (1961), Convalescence from influenza: A study of the psychological and clinical determinants. *Arch. Int. Med.*, 108:393–399.

———————— Trever, R. W. (1959), *Arch. Int. Med.*, 103:406–414.

Jensen, M. M., & Rasmussen, A. F., Jr. (1963), Stress and susceptibility to viral infections. II. Sound stress and susceptibility to vesicular stomatitis virus. *J. Immunol.*, 90:21–23.

Joasoo, A., & McKenzie, J. M. (1976), Stress and immune response in rats. *Internat. Arch. Allergy Appl. Immunol.*, 50:659–663.

Johnsson, T., Lavender, J. F., Hultin, E., & Rasmussen, A. F., Jr. (1963), The influence of avoidance-learning stress on resistance to coxsackie B virus in mice. *J. Immunol.*, 91:569–574.

Jones, E., Curzen, P., & Gaugas, J. M. (1973), Suppressive activity of pregnancy plasma on the mixed lymphocyte reaction. *J. Obstet. Gynecol. Brit. Common.*, 80:603–607.

Kaneko, Z., & Taksishi, N. (1963), Psychometric studies on chronic urticaria. *Folia Psychiat. Neurol. Jap.*, 17:16–24.

Kasl, S. V., Evan, A. S., & Niederman, J. C. (1979), Psychosocial factors in infectious mononucleosis. *Psychosom. Med.*, 41:445–466.

Keller, S. E., Ackerman, S. H., Schleifer, S. J., Shindledecker, R. D., Camerino, M. S., Hofer, M. A., Weiner, H., & Stein, M. (1983), Effect of premature weaning on lymphocyte stimulation in the rat. *Psychosom. Med.*, 45:75. (Abstract.)

—— Shapiro, R., Schleifer, S. J., & Stein, M. (1982), Hypothalamic influences on anaphylaxis. *Psychosom. Med.*, 44:302. (Abstract.)

—— Weiss, J., Schleifer, S. J., Miller, N. E., & Stein, M. (1981), Effect of a graded series of stressors on lymphocyte function in the rat. *Science*, 213:1397–1400.

Kent, S. (1977), Can normal aging be explained by immunologic theory? *Geriatrics*, 32:111–120.

Kimzey, S. L., Ritzmann, S. E., Mengel, C. E., & Fischer, C. L. (1975), Skylab experiment results: Hematology studies. *Acta Astronautica*, 2:141–154.

Kittell, R., & Blume, R. (1977), Untersuchungen uber das postnatale masserwachstum des thymus der albinomaus unter den einfluss verschiendener eichtfedingungen. *Verch. Anat. Ges.*, 71:275–280.

Korneva, E. A., & Khai, L. M. (1963), Effect of destruction of hypothalamic areas on immunogenesis. *Fiziol. Zh. SSSR Sechenov.*, 49:42–48.

—— —— (1967), Effect of stimulating different mesencephalic structures on protective immune response patterns. *Fiziol. Zh. SSSR Sechenov.*, 53:42–47.

Kosmider, S., & Wysocki, J. (1977), Wplyw palenia papierosow na zachowanie sie immunoglobulin w surowicy krwc. *Pol. Tyg. Lek.*, 32:1877–1879.

Kosohara, K., Tanaka, S., & Ito, T. (1977), *Chem. Pathol. Pharmacol.*, 16:687–694.

Kronfol, Z., Silva, J., Greden, J., Dembinski, S., & Carroll, B. J. (1982), Cell-mediated immunity in melancholia. *Psychosom. Med.*, 44:304. (Abstract.)

Krug, V., Krug, F., & Cuatrecasas, P. (1974), Emergence of insulin receptors on human lymphocytes during in vitro transformation. *Proc. Nat. Acad. Sci. USA*, 71:1330–1333.

Kumar, A., Nema, H. V., & Thakur, V. (1981), Stress and arthritis. *Ann. Ophthalmol.*, 13:1077–1080.

Lattime, E. C., & Strausser, H. R. (1977), Arteriosclerosis: Is stress induced immune suppression a risk factor? *Science*, 198:302–303.

Laudenslager, M., Reite, M., & Harbeck, R. (1982), Immune status during mother-infant separation. *Psychosom. Med.*, 44:303. (Abstract.)

Leach, C. S., Rambaut, P. C., & Johnson, P. C. (1974), Adrenocortical responses of the Apollo 17 crew members. *Aerosp. Med.*, 45:529–534.

LeShan, L. L. (1959), An emotional life-history pattern associated with neoplastic disease. *J. Natl. Cancer Inst.*, 22:1.

Levine, S., & Cohen, C. (1959), Differential survival to leukemia as a function of infantile stimulation in DBA/Z mice. *Proc. Soc. Exp. Biol. Med.*, 102:53–54.

——— Sowinski, R., & Steinetz, B. (1980), Effects of experimental allergic encephalomyelitis on thymus and adrenol: Relation to remission and relapse. *Proc. Soc. Exp. Biol. Med.*, 165:218–224.

Linn, B. S., Linn, M. W., & Jensen, J. (1982), Degree of depression and immune responsiveness. *Psychosom. Med.*, 44:128. (Abstract.)

Litwack, G., ed. (1975), *Biochemical Actions of Hormones*, Vol. 9. New York: Academic Press.

Locke, S. E., Hurst, M. W., Heisel, J. S., & Williams, M. (1978), The influence of stress on the immune response. Annual meeting of the American Psychosomatic Society, Washington, DC, April 1.

Luborsky, L., Mintz, J., Brightman, V. J., & Katcher, A. H. (1976), Herpes simplex virus and moods: A longitudinal study. *J. Psychosom. Res.*, 20:543–548.

Lundy, J., Raaf, J. H., Deakins, S., Wanebo, H. J., Jacobs, D. A., Lee, T., Jacobowitz, D., Spear, C., & Oettgen, H. F. (1975), The acute and chronic effects of alcohol on the immune system. *Surg. Gynec. Obstet.*, 141:212–218.

Luparello, T. J., Stein, M., & Park, D. C. (1964), Effect of hypothalamic lesions on rat anaphylaxis. *Amer. J. Physiol.*, 207:911–914.

Macris, N. T., Schiava, R. C., Camerino, M. S., & Stein, M. (1970), Effect of hypothalamic lesions on immune processes in the guinea pig. *Amer. J. Physiol.*, 219:1205–1209.

Maestroni, G. J., & Pierpaoli, W. (1981), Pharmacologic control of the hormonally mediated immune response. In: *Psychoneuroimmunology*, ed. R. Ader. New York: Academic Press.

Makinodan, T., & Yunis, E., eds. (1977), Immunology and aging. In: *Comprehensive Immunology*. New York: Plenum, pp. 1–205.

Marsh, J. T., Lavender, J. F., Chang, S. S., & Rasmussen, A. F. (1963), Poliomyelitis in monkeys: Decreased susceptibility after avoidance stress. *Science*, 140:1414–1415.

Mason, J. W. (1968), Organization of psychoendocrine mechanisms. *Psychosom. Med.*, 30:567–607.

McLary, A. R., Meyer, E., & Weitzman, E. L. (1955), Observations on role of mechanism of depression in some patients with disseminated lupus erythematosus. *Psychosom. Med.*, 17:311–321.

Mettrop, P. J., & Visser, P. (1969), Exteroceptive stimulation as a contingent factor in the induction and elicitation of delayed-type hypersensitivity reactions to 1-chloro-, 2-4, dimitrobenzene in guinea pigs. *Psychophysiol.*, 5:385–388.

Meyer, R. J., & Haggerty, R. J. (1962), Streptococcal infections in families. *J. Pediat.*, 29:539–549.

Meyerowitz, S., Jacox, R. R., & Hess, D. W. (1968), Monozygotic twins discordant for rheumatoid arthritis: A genetic, clinical, and psychological study of 8 sets. *Arthritis Rheum.*, 11:1–21.

Miller, P. M., & Ingham, J. G. (1976), Friends, confidants, and symptoms. *Soc. Psychiat.*, 11:51–63.

Monjan, A. A., & Collector, M. I. (1977), Stress-induced modulation of the immune response. *Science*, 196:307–308.

—— Mandell, W. (1980), Fetal alcohol and immunity: Depression of mitogen-induced lymphocyte blastogenesis. *Neurobehavior. Toxicol.*, 2:213–215.

Moore, R. Y. (1978), Central neural control of circadian rhythms. In: *Frontiers of Neuroendocrinology*, Vol. 5, ed. W. Janong & L. Martini. New York: Raven Press, pp. 185–206.

Morillo, E., & Gardner, L. I. (1979), Bereavement as an antecedent factor in thyrotoxicosis of childhood: Four case studies with survey of possible metabolic pathways. *Psychosom. Med.*, 41:545–555.

Newberry, B. H. (1981), Effects of presumably stressful stimulation (PSS) on the development of animal tumors: Some issues. In: *Perspectives in Behavioral Medicine*, ed. S. M. Weiss, J. A. Herd, & B. H. Fox. New York: Academic Press, pp. 329–349.

—— Gildow, J., Wogan, J., & Reese, R. L. (1976), Inhibition of Huggins tumors by forced restraint. *Psychosom. Med.*, 38:155–162.

Oreskes, I., Rosenblatt, S., Spiera, H., & Meadow, H. (1968), Rheumatoid factors in an acute psychiatric population. *Ann. Rheum. Dis.*, 27:60–63.

Otto, R., & Mackay, I. R. (1967), Psychosocial and emotional disturbance in systemic lupus erythematosus. *Med. J. Aust.*, 2:488–493.

Palmblad, J., Cantell, K., Strander, H., Fröberg, J., Karlsson, C., Levi, L., Granstrom, M., & Unger, P. (1976), Stressor exposure and immunologic response in man: Interferon producing capacity and phagocytosis. *J. Psychosom. Res.*, 20:193–199.

—— Petrini, B., Wasserman, J., & Akerstedt, T. (1979), Lymphocyte and granulocyte reactions during sleep deprivation. *Psychosom. Med.*, 41:273–286.

Parkes, C. M., & Brown, R. J. (1972), Health after bereavement—a controlled study of young Boston widows and widowers. *Psychosom. Med.*, 34:449–460.

Pavlidis, N., & Chirigos, M. (1980), Stress-induced impairment of macrophage tumoricidal function. *Psychosom. Med.*, 42:47–54.

Petrovskii, I. N. (1961), Problems of nervous control in immunity reactions. I. The influence of experimental neuroses on immunity reactions. *Zh. Microbiol.*, 32:1451.

Pettingale, K. W., Greer, S., & Tee, D. E. (1977), Serum IgA and emotional expression in breast cancer patients. *J. Psychosom. Res.*, 21:395–399.

Pierpaoli, W., & Maestroni, G. J. (1978), Pharmacologic control of the hormonally modulated immune response. *J. Immunol.*, 120:1600–1603.

Pitkin, D. H. (1966), Effect of physiological stress on the delayed hypersensitivity reaction. *Proc. Soc. Exp. Biol. Med.*, 120:350–351.

Purtilo, D. T., Hallgren, H. M., & Yunis, E. J. (1972), Depressed maternal lymphocyte response to phytohaemagglutinin in human pregnancy. *Lancet*, 1:769–771.

Rasmussen, A. F. Jr., Marsh, J. T., & Brill, N. Q. (1957), Increased susceptibility to herpes simplex in mice subjected to avoidance-learning stress or restraint. *Proc. Soc. Exp. Biol. Med.*, 96:183–189.

Reinherz, E. L., Rubinstein, A., Geha, R. S., Strelkauskas, A. J., Rosen, F. S., & Schlossman, S. F. (1979), Abnormalities of immunoregulatory T cells in disorders of immune function. *New Eng. J. Med.*, 301:1018–1082.

———— Weiner, H. L., Hauser, S. L., Cohen, J. A., Distaso, J. A., & Schlossman, S. F. (1980), Loss of suppressor T cells in active multiple sclerosis: Analysis with monoclonal antibodies. *New Eng. J. Med.*, 303:125–129.

Richman, D. P., & Arnason, B. G. (1979), Nicotinic acetylcholine receptor: Evidence for a functionally distinct receptor on human lymphocytes. *Proc. Natl. Acad. Sci. USA*, 76:4632–4635.

Riley, V. (1975), Mouse mammary tumors: Alteration of incidence as apparent function of stress. *Science*, 189:465–467.

Roberts-Thomson, I. C., Whittingham, S., Youngchaiyud, U., & Mackay, I. R. (1974), Aging, immune response, and mortality. *Lancet*, 2:368–370.

Rogentine, G. N., van Kammen, D. P., Fox, B. H., Docherty, J. P., Rosenblatt, J. E., Boyd, S. C., & Bunney, W. E., Jr. (1979), Psychological factors in the prognosis of malignant melanoma: A prospective study. *Psychosom. Med.*, 41:647–655.

Rogers, M. P., Dubey, D., & Reich, P. (1979), The influence of the psyche and the brain on immunity and disease susceptibility: A critical review. *Psychosom. Med.*, 41:147–164.

———— Reich, P., Strom, T. B., & Carpenter, C. B. (1976), Behaviorally conditioned immunosuppression: Replication of a recent study. *Psychosom. Med.*, 38:447–451.

———— Trentham, D. E., Dynesius-Trentham, R., Daffner, K., & Reich, P. (1983), Exacerbation of collagen arthritis by noise stress. *J. Rheumatol.*, 10:651–654.

———— ———— McCune, W. J., Ginsberg, B., Rennke, H. G., Reich, P., & David, J. R. (1980), Effect of psychological stress on the induction of arthritis in rats. *Arthritis Rheum.*, 23:1337–1342.

Roitt, I. M. (1980), *Essential Immunology*, 4th ed. Boston: Blackwell.

Roszkowski, W., Plaut, M., & Lichtenstein, L. M. (1977), Selective display of histamine receptors on lymphocytes. *Science*, 195–685.

Roszman, T. L., & Brooks, W. J. (1980), Immunobiology of primary intracranial tumours: III. Demonstration of a qualitative lymphocyte abnormality in patients with primary brain tumours. *Clin. Exp. Immunol.*, 39:395–402.

Sachar, E. J. (1975), *Topics in Psychoendocrinology*. New York: Grune & Stratton.

Schleifer, S. J., Keller, S. E., Camerino, M., Thornton, J. C., & Stein, M. (1983), Suppression of lymphocyte stimulation following bereavement. *J. Amer. Med. Assn.*, 250:374–377.

Selye, H. (1955), Stress and disease. *Science*, 122:625–631.

Seville, R. H. (1978), Psoriasis and stress. II. *Brit. J. Dermatol.*, 98:151–153.

Shek, P. N., & Sabiston, B. H. (1983), Neuroendocrine regulation of immune processes. *Internat. J. Immunopharmacol.*, 5:23–33.

Shekelle, R. B., Raynor, W. J., Ostfeld, A., Garron, D. C., Bieliauskas, L. A., Liu, S. C., Maliza, C., & Paul, O. (1981), Psychological depression and 17-year risk of death from cancer. *Psychosom. Med.*, 43:117–125.

Siegal, F. P. (1975), Suppressors in the network of immunity. *New Engl. J. Med.*, 298:102–103.

Siegel, H. S., & Latimer, J. W. (1975), Interactions and antibody titres in young male chickens (gallus domesticus). *Anim. Behav.*, 23:323–330.

Singh, U., & Owen, J. J. T. (1976), Studies on the maturation of thymus stem cells: The effects of catecholamines, histamine and peptide hormones on the expression of T cell alloantigens. *Eur. J. Immunol.*, 6:59–62.

Sklar, L. S., & Anisman, H. (1979), Stress and coping factors influence tumor growth. *Science*, 205:513–515.

———— Bruto, V., & Anisman, H. (1981), Adaptation to the tumor-enhancing effects of stress. *Psychosom. Med.*, 43:331–341.

Smolensky, M. H., & Reinberg, A., eds. (1977), *Chronobiology in Allergy and Immunology*. Springfield, IL: Thomas.

Solomon, G. F. (1969), Stress and antibody response in rats. *Internat. Arch. Allergy*, 35:97–104.

———— Allansmith, M., McClellan, B., & Amkraut, A. (1969), Immunoglobulins in psychiatric patients. *Arch. Gen. Psychiat.*, 20:272–279.

———— Amkraut, A. A., & Kasper, P. (1974), Immunity, emotions and stress. *Ann. Clin. Res.*, 6:313–322.

———— Levine, S., & Kraft, J. K. (1968), Early experience and immunity. *Nature*, 220:821–822.

———— Moos, R. H. (1965), The relationship of personality to the presence of rheumatoid factor in asymptomatic relatives of patients with rheumatoid arthritis. *Psychosom. Med.*, 27:350–360.

Spry, C. J. (1972), Inhibition of lymphocyte recirculation by stress and corticotropin. *Cell Immunol.*, 4:86–96.

Stein, M., Schiavi, R. C., & Camerino, M. (1976), Influence of brain and behavior on the immune system. *Science*, 191:435–440.

———— Schleifer, S., & Keller, S. (1980), Psychological factors affecting physical conditions: Immune disorders. In: *Comprehensive Textbook of Psychiatry*,

3rd ed., Vol. 2, ed. H. I. Kaplan, A. M. Freedman, & B. J. Sadock. Baltimore: Williams & Wilkins, pp. 1961–1972.

Strom, T. B., Carpenter, C. B., Garovoy, M. R., Austen, K. F., Merrill, J. P., & Kaliner, M. (1973), The modulating influence of cyclic nucleotides upon lymphocyte mediated cytotoxicity. *J. Exp. Med.*, 138:381–393.

Stutman, O. (1975), Immunodepression and malignancy. *Adv. Cancer Res.*, 22:261–422.

Szentivanyi, A., & Filipp, G. (1958), Anaphylaxis and the nervous system. *Ann. Allergy*, 16:143–151.

Talal, N. (1979), Systemic lupus erythematosus, autoimmunity, sex and inheritance. *New Eng. J. Med.*, 301:838–839.

Thomas, C. B., Duszynski, K. R., & Shaffer, J. W. (1979), Family attitudes reported in youth as potential predictors of cancer. *Psychosom. Med.*, 41:287–301.

Vanderkamp, H., & Daly, R. (1968), The abnormal lymphocyte in schizophrenia. *Internat. J. Neuropsychiat.*, 4:4–5.

Vessey, S. H. (1960), Effects of grouping on levels of circulating antibodies in mice. *Proc. Soc. Exp. Biol. Med.*, 115:252–255.

Viederman, M. (1975), Psychogenic factors in kidney transplant rejection: A case study. *Amer. J. Psychiat.*, 132:957–959.

Visintainer, M. A., Volpicelli, J. R., & Seligman, M. E. (1982), Tumor rejection in rats after inescapable or escapable shock. *Science*, 216:437–439.

Walford, R. L. (1974), Immunologic theory of aging: Current status. *Fed. Proc.*, 33:2020.

—— Liu, R. K., Mathies, M., Gerbase-Delima, M., & Smith, G. S. (1973), Long-term dietary restriction and immune function in mice: Response to sheep red blood cells and to mitogenic agents. *Mech. Aging Dev.*, 2:447.

Wara, D. W. (1981), Thymic hormones and the immune system. In: *Advances in Pediatrics*, ed. L. A. Barness. Chicago: Yearbook Medical, 28:229–270.

Wayner, E. A., Flannery, G. R., & Singer, G. (1978), Effects of taste aversion conditioning on the primary antibody response to sheep red blood cells and *Brucella abortus* in the albino rat. *Physiol. Behav.*, 21:995–1000.

Weiner, H. (1972), Presidential address: Some comments on the trasduction of experience by the brain. Implications for our understanding of the relationship of mind to body. *Psychosom. Med.*, 34:355–380.

—— (1980), Psychological factors affecting physical conditions: Respiratory Disorders. In: *Comprehensive Textbook of Psychiatry*, 3rd ed., Vol. 2, ed. H. I. Kaplan, A. M. Freedman, & B. J. Sadock. Baltimore: Williams & Wilkins, pp. 1907–1917.

Whittingham, S., Mackay, I. F., Jones, I. H., & Davies, B. (1968), Absence of brain antibodies in patients with schizophrenia. *Brit. Med. J.*, 1:347–348.

Williams, J. M., Peterson, R. G., Shea, P. A., Schmedtje, J. F., Bauer, D. C., & Felten, D. L. (1981), Sympathetic innervation of murine thymus and spleen: Evidence for a functional link between the nervous and immune systems. *Brain Res. Bull.*, 6:38–94.

Williams, R. M., Kraus, L. J., & Dubey, P. P. (1979), Circadian bioperiodicity in natural killer cell activity of human blood. *Chronobiologia*, 6:1972–1975.

Wistar, R., & Hildemann, W. H. (1960), Effects of stress on skin transplantation immunity in mice. *Science*, 131:159–160.

10.
Endocrine Regulation

SEYMOUR LEVINE, PH.D., and
CHRISTOPHER L. COE, PH.D.

Traditionally, psychosomatic disease has been defined as "a bodily disorder whose nature can be appreciated only when emotional disturbances, that is, psychological happenings, are investigated in addition to physical disturbances, that is, somatic happenings" (Halliday, 1948, p. 45). Thus, some of the primary factors involved in the etiology of pathophysiological states, such as peptic ulcers, hypertension, and cardiovascular disease, have been assumed to be psychological in origin. In recent years there has also been a growing awareness of the importance of psychological processes in many other disease states that had originally been considered exclusively somatic in origin. As a consequence, there has emerged a broader, more encompassing definition of "psychosomatic" that is perhaps best exemplified by the development of a larger discipline called behavioral medicine. *Behavioral medicine* has been defined as "the field concerned with the development of behavioral science knowledge and techniques relevant to the understanding of physical health and illness and the application of this knowledge and techniques to prevention, diagnosis, treatment, and rehabilitation. Psychosis, neurosis, and substance abuse are included only insofar

This research was supported by HD-02881 from the National Institute of Child Health and Human Development (NICH&HD); MH-23645 from the National Institute of Mental Health (NIMH); and by Research Scientist Award MH-19936 from NIMH to Seymour Levine.

as they contribute to physical disorders as an end point" (Schwartz and Weiss, 1978, p. 7). A basic premise of behavioral medicine is that psychological factors play an important role in most pathophysiological processes and that, although specific viral and bacterial agents are the initial cause of somatic disorder, psychological factors can influence the course and ultimate outcome of the pathological condition.

Over the years, a number of models have been proposed which have integrated psychological and psychosocial variables as important components of the process that leads to disruption of normal function. Although some of these models have been related to specific diseases, such as hypertension (Page and McCubbin, 1965), other models have been more general and have attempted to examine the chain of events involved in psychological induction of disease (Kagan and Levi, 1974; Henry and Stephens, 1977; Ursin and Murison, 1983). The model presented by Henry and Stephens is prototypic and includes a number of factors that have consequences for disease outcomes. This model, presented in Figure 1, indicates that there are experiential, perceptual, and physiological factors which all interact to determine the ultimate pathophysiological effect on the organism.

It is notable that almost all of these models include stress as one of the major determinants of disease. Its importance has been emphasized by a recent publication from the Institute of Medicine, entitled *Research on Stress in Health and Disease* (Elliott and Eisdorfer, 1982). In fact, when one looks at current trends in research on psychological factors and disease outcomes, one would get the impression that stress is the twentieth century plague. Although epidemiological studies and experimental data clearly indicate that stress is intimately involved in disease processes, one wonders that there is not an even greater incidence of certain illnesses in view of the broad spectrum of events now subsumed under this rubric (Holmes and Rahe, 1967). For example, most major life changes, both personal and professional, appear to have effects on the physiological systems involved in the stress syndrome. This issue will be dealt with

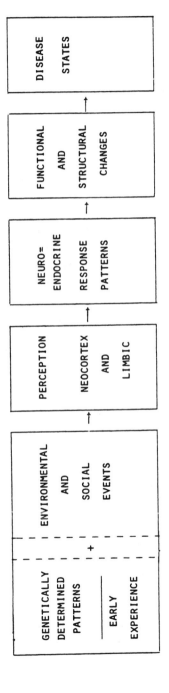

Figure 1. Psychobiological model of factors involved in the neuroendocrine mediation of disease. (After Henry and Stephens, 1977.)

in a later portion of this chapter, which is concerned with coping.

It is not the purpose of this chapter to dwell extensively on problems related to the definition of stress, but it is important to note that, historically, the conceptualization of stress has always involved changes in the endocrine system. Initially, the changes were specifically related either to increased secretion of catecholamines or to activation of the pituitary-adrenal system. The problems are best illustrated by examining the concept of stress beginning with Selye's (1936) early work in which he defined a general adaptation syndrome (GAS) in rodents. This nonspecific response occurred after diverse noxious agents, such as exposure to cold, surgical injury, spinal shock, and muscular exercise. The essential argument was that the response did not depend upon the type of agent that produced it; rather, like inflammation, it was deemed as nonspecific. GAS was divided into three stages: an alarm reaction, a stage of resistance, and a stage of exhaustion. The initial stage included activation of the pituitary-adrenal system and eventually resulted in adrenal hypertrophy, thymicolymphatic involution, and gastric ulceration if the noxious stimuli persisted. If the response to the aversive situation was sustained, physiological resistance ultimately developed and it was hypothesized that stressed subjects would enter a third stage—exhaustion—which occurred 1 to 3 months after the initial exposure.

Problems with this view have occurred at several levels. First, there was an early emphasis on the physical and chemical aspects of the stressful stimuli, and we now know that psychosocial stimuli are also potent elicitors of the stress response. Second, Selye has received much criticism for the "nonspecificity" view because, with modern hormone assays, it is now possible to detect differential endocrine responses to certain stimuli. Further, the importance of the final stage of exhaustion has been questioned. Diseases due to exhaustion of this syndrome are rare, and, with the exception of a few animal models (e.g., intruders in wild rat colonies), have not been demonstrated as a response to psychosocial stimuli (Allen, 1972). Moreover, a number of physicians have studied moribund patients and have found that adrenal exhaustion did not occur even at death. Rather, there is usually increased adrenal output immediately before and after death (Sandberg, Eik-nes, Migeon, and Samuels, 1956; Done, Ely, and Kelly, 1958).

The dramatic picture described by Selye is emphatically different from the present day concept of stress in the lay literature, which includes the daily troubles and anxieties of commuters and executives. The broader use of the term has resulted in an urgency to reduce or eliminate stress in both personal and professional arenas, even though Selye (1974) himself has minimized the significance of this type of stress and stated that its absence occurs only after death. This paradoxical situation reveals that we do not have a clear and generally accepted definition. As a consequence, there is a serious communication problem and increasing talk about a crisis in stress research (Wolf, Almy, Bachrach, Spiro, Sturdevant, and Weiner, 1979). At the very least, there is a growing impatience with the present state of vagueness in an area so vitally important for issues of health and quality of life. We believe that much of the controversy over stress theory can be eliminated through clarification of the "afferent limb," that is, by focusing on the nature of the stimuli that provoke physiological responses rather than on the physiological responses themselves. This type of investigation requires an unusual integration of physiology and psychology —disciplines which have traditionally been separated—and puts the major emphasis on psychological variables.

The purpose of this chapter is to examine the importance of psychological variables that have been determined to have profound endocrinological consequences both in animals and humans. In fact, the major conceptual framework pervading this chapter is that one of the primary aspects of stressful stimuli eliciting an endocrine response is psychological in nature. This perspective is derived from Mason's (1968, 1975a,b) review of psychoendocrine research, particularly involving the pituitary-adrenal cortical system. As mentioned above, much of the early stress research had emphasized the nonspecificity of the organism's response to a wide variety of physical stressors (Selye, 1950). However, even in the 1950s, it was becoming increasingly apparent that psychological factors were importantly involved. For example, in one study, Renold, Quingley, Kennard, and Thorn (1951) examined the physiological response of participants in the Harvard Boat Race. Utilizing a traditional measure of that period, the decline in eosinophils following stress, they found that eosinophils in the crew members were markedly lower 4 hours after the race. This decline could have been attributed solely to the exercise and physical strain, but the investigators also discovered that the coxswains and coaches had similar eosinophil drops, even though their stress was purely psychological. In Mason's major review of the stress literature in 1968, he pointed out that much of the prior work, including the experiments on physical stimuli, shared one important characteristic, namely, that a typical aspect of the stressful experience was exposure to novel, strange, or unfamiliar environments. Therefore, the common thread that may have explained the animals' response was the psychological dimension of the stimuli, rather than the particular physical trauma to which they had been exposed. In subsequent research, Mason (1975) was able to show that when animals are exposed to the stimuli in such a way that they do not experience distress or novelty, then typical stressors such as heat or fasting do not necessarily result in activation of the pituitary-adrenal system. The concept that psychological variables can activate, and inhibit, the endocrine system has subsequently received much support in experimental studies on both animals and humans.

PITUITARY-ADRENAL SYSTEM

Although the response to stress can best be defined as a syndrome, which includes many changes in neurochemical and metabolic processes, for the purposes of this chapter we will focus on the response of two hormone systems: pituitary-adrenal and pituitary-gonadal. It is important to remember, however, that we are utilizing these as model systems. There is abundant evidence indicating that the hormone function of other endocrine systems—including catecholamines, insulin, growth hormone, and prolactin—can also be influenced by psychological variables. In addition, it has been demonstrated recently that the endorphins are also extremely responsive to stress. In fact, it appears that almost all of the stimuli capable of eliciting an ACTH response from the pituitary are also capable of releasing beta endorphins (Guillemin, Vargo, Rossier, Minick, Ling, Rivier, Vale, and Bloom, 1977). There are two reasons for focusing on the pituitary-adrenal system in the context of psychosomatic illness. First, there is an extensive data base showing the effects of psychological variables on the pituitary-adrenal system. Second, and perhaps more important, is the profound influence that adrenal hormones have on many basic functions related to health.

The effects of stress and coping on health are based on an intimate interrelationship among the many functions of the brain. It begins with perception and the higher processes of cognition, emotions, and drives, and eventually results in effects on vital functions such as breathing, heart rate, blood pressure, and a variety of metabolic processes. Perhaps the best understood mechanisms involving the neuroregulation of endocrine function are concerned with the release of adrenal corticoids. Neurons in the median eminence of the brain discharge corticotropin-releasing factor (CRF) into the portal blood vessels, which causes the pituitary gland to release adrenocorticotropin (ACTH), which stimulates the cortex of the adrenal gland to secrete glucocorticoids into the bloodstream (Figure 2). There are neural mechanisms involved both in the activation and inhibition of the pituitary-adrenal system, in addition to a negative feedback control loop which inhibits the further release of CRF and ACTH. Corticoids have important and vital functions in adapting the body to stress (Cope, 1972; Miller, 1980). One of their most well-known effects is the reduction of inflammation, by increasing vasomotor tone and capillary permeability; and

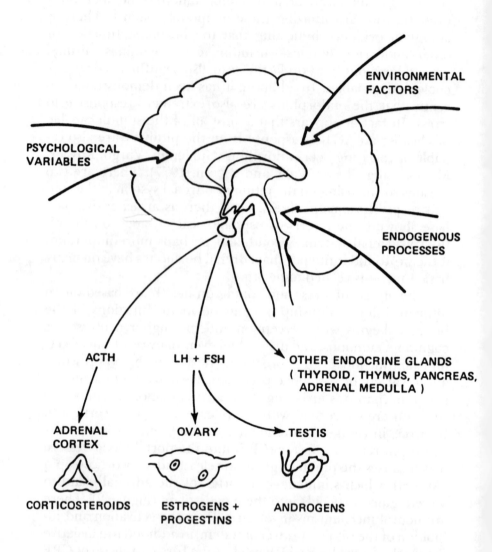

Figure 2. Neuroendocrine regulation of the pituitary-adrenal and gonadal systems.

thus, they are frequently used in the treatment of severe arthritis. Glucocorticoids also raise blood sugar levels, from whence their name is derived, and have a number of inhibitory or anti-anabolic effects that are important in mobilizing the body to deal with the stressful situation. At high levels, corticoids inhibit growth and result in osteoporosis, muscular atrophy, a reduction in the amount of lymphoid tissue, and an increase in the uptake and breakdown of amino acids in the liver. When corticoids are given therapeutically for their anti-inflammatory effects, they may, therefore, have a variety of adverse side effects. They can interfere with the action of insulin, and thus precipitate and exacerbate diabetes; contribute to peptic ulcers, cause loss of calcium from the bones, suppress growth, cause menstrual irregularities, and induce hypertension. However, a patient who is deficient in corticosteroids, when exposed to the physical stress of surgery or other severe trauma, will die in acute vascular collapse unless it is prevented by administration of glucocorticoids (see Figure 2).

One especially important action of the glucocorticoids is on the immune system. Glucocorticoids cause the involution of lymphoid tissue, suppress gamma globulin formation, reduce the eosinophil count, and interfere with the action of the white blood cells. The immunosuppressive effects of glucocorticoids are clinically valuable in reducing the body's tendency to reject organ transplants, but they greatly increase the susceptibility of infection. Furthermore, glucocorticoids are involved in mobilizing fatty acids from the adipose tissue and in other aspects of the basal metabolism. Given the numerous effects that glucocorticoids have on metabolic processes, it is not surprising that there should have been such an extensive investigation of the influence of psychological factors on pituitary-adrenal activity.

There have been many attempts in recent years to resolve the issue of the primary stimuli that elicit the endocrine response, in particular pituitary-adrenal responses, which occur under conditions of stress. As Mason (1975a) pointed out, when the psychologically threatening or arousing aspects of the situation were altered, classical stresses such as fasting and heat no longer activated the pituitary-adrenal system. In the case of heat, there was, in fact, a reduction in the corticoids when the mode of presentation was gradual. The importance of the rate of presentation of a particular stimulus was also demonstrated in another experiment that used a potent physiological insult to induce adrenocortical activity. Hemorrhage in the magnitude of 10 ml/kg at the rate of 6.6 ml/kg/min actively stimulates the adrenal cortex of the dog. In contrast, if the same ultimate volume of blood loss is achieved at a much slower rate of hemorrhage (i.e., 0.3 ml/kg/min), the pituitary-adrenal system does not activate (Gann, 1969). That rapid hemorrhaging induces adrenocortical activity, while slow rates of hemorrhaging do not, once again indicates that the rate of stimulus change is one important parameter for the induction of pituitary-adrenal activity. The fact that dexamethasone blocks the pituitary-adrenal response at a high rate of hemorrhaging clearly indicates that neuroendocrine systems are involved and that the effect was not mediated peripherally. Regardless of the specific explanation that accounts for these results, their general significance cannot be underestimated.

More recent studies on psychoendocrine responses have indicated further that it may be possible to use adrenal activity as a measure of specific emotional responses, rather than simply as a reflection of undifferentiated arousal (Mason, 1975a,b; Hennessy and Levine, 1979). In addition, studies on psychological stress bring out one point quite clearly: the great individual differences typically observed in response to a given stressor can best be explained in terms of cognitive mechanisms. For example, a subject's perception of a stressor as a threat, or the coping responses that are available to the subject, may well determine the physiological response. It may be insufficient, therefore, to merely describe the stimulus operations involved in producing a stressor. A psychobiological approach to understanding endocrine function cannot escape making reference to cognitive processes.

In his description of arousal theory, Berlyne (1960, 1967)

provides a framework for the description of the processes by which stimulators of arousal (and thus, activators of the pituitary-adrenal response) operate. Novelty, uncertainty, and conflict are considered primary determinants of arousal. These have been labeled by Berlyne as collative factors, because in order to evaluate them, it is necessary to compare similarities and differences between stimulus elements (novelty), or between stimulus-evoked expectations (uncertainty). The basic cognitive process involved in stimulation of the pituitary-adrenal system, then, is one of comparison. To a large extent, the cognitive processes of comparison can be best understood by adding the concept of uncertainty, although there are some differences between uncertainty and novelty.

Uncertainty seems to be a major factor underlying many psychological responses. The processes involving neuroendocrine activation under conditions of uncertainty are best explained by a model elaborated by Sokolov (1960) to account for the general process of habituation. The pattern of habituation is familiar to most people. A subject is presented with an unexpected stimulus and shows an alerting reaction. Physiological components of this orienting reaction are well known—general activation of the brain, decreased blood flow into the extremities, changes in electrical resistance of the skin, and increases in both adrenomedullary and cortical hormones. If the stimulus is frequently repeated, all of these reactions gradually diminish and eventually disappear, and the subject is said to be habituated. It does appear, however, that physiological responses may habituate more slowly than the observed behavioral reactions. Sokolov's model, in essence, is based on a matching system in which new stimuli or situations are compared with a representation in the central nervous system of prior events. This matching process results in the development of expectancies whereby the organism is either habituated or gives an alerting arousal reaction (Pribram and Melges, 1969). Thus, the habituated organism has an internal representation of prior events with which to deal with the environment—expectancies—and if the environment does not contain any new contingencies, the habituated organism no longer responds with the physiological responses related to the alerting reaction. Activation of the pituitary-adrenal system by any change in expectancy can also be accounted for by invoking the powerful explanatory capacity of the Sokolov model.

NOVELTY AND UNCERTAINTY

Exposure of an animal to *novelty* is one of the most potent experimental conditions leading to an increase in pituitary-adrenal activity. Novelty can be classified as a collative variable, since the recognition of any stimulus situation as being novel requires a comparison between present stimulus events and those experienced in the past. Increases in pituitary-adrenal activity in response to novelty have been demonstrated in humans as well as animals. For example, increased adrenocortical activity, as evidenced by elevated levels of circulating cortisol, are observed in individuals during their first exposure to procedures involved in drawing blood at a blood bank. However, if they have had prior blood bank experience, there are no such increases (Mendoza and Barchas, 1982). Further, in an experiment to be discussed in detail later, young adults experiencing their first jump off a tower during parachute training also show a dramatic elevation of adrenocortical activity, which is not observed on subsequent jumps from the tower (Levine, 1978). Studies on animals also indicate another important characteristic of the cognitive process which results in pituitary-adrenal activation, that is, the ability of the animal to discriminate similar versus unfamiliar stimulus elements (Figure 3).

In a series of experiments on rats and mice it was demonstrated that if novelty was varied along a continuum with increasing changes in the stimulus elements, there was a graded adrenocortical response according to the degree to which the environment represented a discrepancy from the normal cage living environment of the organism (Hennessy and Levine,

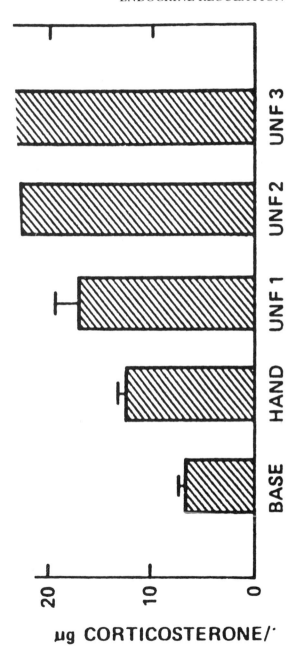

Figure 3. Adrenal response of rats to different degrees of novelty. Handling unfamiliar metal cage with new bedding (UNF1), unfamiliar metal cage with no bedding (UNF2), and novel plastic container (UNF3). (From Hennessy, Heybach, Vernikos, and Levine, 1979.)

1977; Hennessy, Heybach, Vernikos, and Levine, 1979). Thus, minor changes, such as placing the animal in a different cage, but one identical with its home cage, resulted in an elevation of plasma corticosterone, but one that was significantly less than when the animal was placed in a totally novel cage containing none of the elements of its familiar living conditions. This capacity to make fine discriminations resulting in graded elevations of pituitary-adrenal activity are clearly demonstrative of the remarkable capacity of the central nervous system to regulate the output of pituitary-adrenal response. Novelty, according to the theory presented by Sokolov, should indeed be one of the most potent variables that elicits increases in pituitary-adrenal activity. Insofar as an organism has no expectations about an unfamiliar environment, that environment should represent a degree of uncertainty that should lead to increases in neuroendocrine activity.

Although novelty can be subsumed under the general concept of uncertainty, not all conditions which create uncertainty are novel. Uncertainty can also be evoked by insufficient information concerning the nature of upcoming events. Uncertainty can be seen to vary along the continuum from highly certain, predictable events to highly uncertain, unpredictable events. The presentation of a novel stimulus is likely to lead to an increase in uncertainty because, by definition, there is little information the organism can use to predict forthcoming events. However, uncertainty can also be defined in terms of contingencies between environmental events. Experimentally, the dimension of uncertainty can be controlled by limiting the amount of information available to the organism to predict the occurrence of a specific event. Thus, one would hypothesize that if an organism is given information about the occurrence of either an appetitive or an aversive stimulus, such predictability should lead to a reduction in the pituitary-adrenal response. Further, situations in which there is an absence of predictability should lead to a dramatic increase.

There are many experiments that illustrate the value of predictability in modifying the pituitary-adrenal response to a variety of stimuli (Weinberg and Levine, 1980). One illustration of the effects of reducing uncertainty by providing predictability can be seen in a study by Dess, Linwick, Patterson, Overmier, and Levine (1983). Dogs were subjected to a series of electric shocks which were either controllable or predictable. The predictable condition involved presenting the animal with a tone prior to the onset of shock. In the unpredictable condition, no such tone was presented. The adrenocortical response observed on subsequent testing of these animals clearly indicated the importance of reducing uncertainty by predictability. Animals that did not have the signal preceding the shock showed an adrenocortical response which was two to three times that observed in animals with previous predictable shock experiences. It should be noted that the procedures used in this experiment are typical of those utilized in experiments examining learned helplessness (Seligman, 1975). Learned helplessness refers to the protracted effects resulting from prolonged exposure to unpredictable and uncontrollable stimuli of an aversive nature. It has been observed that organisms exposed to this type of an experimental regime show long-term deficits in terms of their inability to perform appropriately under subsequent testing conditions. Further, these animals show a much greater increase in adrenocortical response when exposed to novelty (Levine, Madden, Conner, Moskal, and Anderson, 1973) than do control animals. Thus, an organism exposed to an uncontrollable and unpredictable set of aversive stimuli not only shows a dramatic increase in adrenocortical activity while exposed to these conditions, but there is also a long-term effect in other unrelated test conditions. The concept of control is particularly important in understanding these long-term effects, and it will be dealt with later when the issue of coping is discussed.

There is yet another series of experiments related to the issue of uncertainty. These do not utilize aversive stimuli typical of stress research, but are more directly related to a psychological response commonly described as *frustration*. Frustration can be evoked when the organism fails to achieve a desired goal following a history of successful fulfillment of these goals. Experimentally, the operations utilized to produce frustration involve either preventing an animal from making the appropriate response to achieve a desired object, or not reinforcing the animal for a response that has had a prior history of reinforcement. In a broader sense, frustration involves the failure of an animal to fulfill expectancies developed in previous experiences and, thus, can be subsumed under the larger heading of uncertainty. For example, rats trained to press a lever for water, in which each lever-press delivered a small amount of water, showed a dramatic elevation of plasma corticosterone when the water was no longer available following the lever-press response (Coe, Stanton, and Levine, 1983; Coover, 1983). Elevations of plasma corticosterone have been shown to be a robust and reliable phenomenon occurring under many experimental conditions in which reinforcement contingencies are altered (Figure 4). Thus, not only is an elevation of plasma corticosterone observed when reinforcement is eliminated, but if the animal receives less reinforcement than it has previously become accustomed to, then elevations of plasma corticosterone also occur.

A similar phenomenon can be observed when using aversive stimuli. If an animal has learned to make an appropriate avoidance response that eliminates the occurrence of an electric shock, and this animal is then prevented from making the response, an increase in pituitary-adrenal activity occurs even when no electric shock is delivered (Coover, Ursin, and Levine, 1973). These experiments have led to the belief that one of the primary conditions to activate the neuroendocrine mechanisms leading to a subsequent adrenal response is a change in expectancies concerning well-established behaviors. In the case of the appetitive learning situation when reinforcement is eliminated, as well as in the avoidance experiment, activation of the pituitary-adrenal system occurred following disruption of ongoing behavior which had once led to a predictable set of outcomes. This can best be understood if one assumes that, under con-

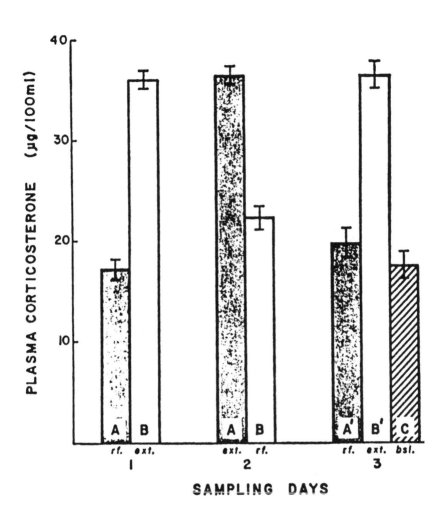

Figure 4. Adrenal response of rats to reinforcement and extinction sessions. Order of conditions was controlled by using two groups of subjects (A and B). (From Coover, Goldman, and Levine, 1971.)

ditions whereby frustration is evoked, the absence of reinforcement represents a condition in which uncertainties are introduced.

INHIBITION OF PITUITARY-ADRENAL ACTIVITY

To a very large extent, most of the research examining the influence of psychological factors on pituitary-adrenal hormones has been concerned with activation of this system. Recently, however, evidence has been accumulating which indicates that the pituitary-adrenal system is bidirectional. That is, psychological stimuli not only activate the system, but can also inhibit it. This inhibition is manifested by either reduced elevations of plasma corticoids during aversive stimulation, or by an actual decrease in pituitary-adrenal output resulting in lower levels of circulating corticoids (Goldman, Coover, and Levine, 1973; Hennessy, King, McClure, and Levine, 1977; Levine, Weinberg, and Brett, 1979). The rationale for introducing this particular set of data at this point is that if the absence of reinforcement leads to uncertainty resulting in activation of the pituitary-adrenal system, then it might be expected that the presence of predictable expected events could result in an inhibition or prevention of an elevation.

To summarize these experiments, it has been demonstrated that if access to food and water is restricted to the morning hours, the normal daily rhythm of adrenal hormones is reoriented to the period of consummatory behavior (i.e., the levels of plasma corticosteroids are elevated in the morning, whereas they are usually low during that period in a nocturnal rodent) (Johnson and Levine, 1973). Within five minutes of consuming food or water, however, there is a marked decline in plasma corticoids accompanied by a concomitant drop in ACTH (Gray, Bergfors, Levin, and Levine, 1978; Heybach and Vernikos-Danellis, 1979). These studies have shown that consummatory behavior initiates an inhibitory process which reduces both

ACTH and corticoid secretion at the levels of the CNS, the pituitary, and the adrenal. There is also evidence indicating that when reinforcement occurs in an operant conditioning experiment, there is a comparable drop in glucocorticoids following consummatory behavior (Goldman et al., 1973; Coe et al., 1983). It has further been demonstrated that the availability of a consummatory response can reduce an organism's pituitary-adrenal response to a normally stressful situation (Levine, et al., 1979). Thus, when exposed to novelty, rats usually show a striking elevation of plasma corticosterone, as has been discussed previously. However, if a consummatory response such as drinking is available in the novel environment, the response to this novelty is markedly reduced or absent.

The fact that drinking reduced the pituitary-adrenal response to novelty raised the possibility that it might similarly buffer the animal's response to a different type of psychological stressor—the thwarting of a previously reinforced response for obtaining food. The phenomenon of schedule-induced polydipsia was first described by Falk (1961). Schedule-induced drinking has been typically observed in a situation where the animal is substantially reduced in weight by partial food deprivation and then placed on an intermittent food reinforcement schedule. Under these circumstances the organism experiences repeated interruption of the operant response necessary to obtain food. Thus, while the situation is positive with respect to reduction in an important need (hunger), it does contain an aversive component as well (frustration induced by delays in a highly motivated, goal-directed behavior). When the periods between reinforcement exceed a particular time (for the rat, 30 seconds), there is a striking increase in other behaviors which are not usually reinforcing, such as excessive gnawing or water consumption. It was determined in a series of experiments (Levine et al., 1979) that such excessive drinking results in a reduction in plasma corticoids, which are normally high during intermittent food reinforcement if the animal is not permitted to drink. Thus, the drinking behavior does appear to serve a beneficial function in terms of reducing the physiological response to an aversive situation.

One of the most obvious implications of these data is related to the problem of obesity. Excessive food consumption can be viewed as behavior that may serve to reduce aversive levels of arousal. Just as excessive drinking has no obvious adaptive value with respect to the primary motivation of the animal in the case of schedule-induced polydipsia, so food consumption is usually unrelated to the emotional events that often precipitate eating binges in obese individuals. However, it is possible that both of these instances of "abnormal" consumption may be useful in maintaining a normal level of arousal.

Finally, it should be mentioned that the phenomenon of consummatory-induced inhibition of the pituitary-adrenal system does not require ingestion. It has been demonstrated that once an animal has been exposed to consummatory behavior for a period of time, presentation of stimuli paired with this consummatory behavior can also serve to inhibit the pituitary-adrenal system (Levine and Coover, 1976; Coover, Sutton, and Heybach, 1977). The phenomenon of pituitary-adrenal inhibition, thus, is conditionable. Whereas uncertain events can induce activation of the pituitary-adrenal system, it appears that events associated with reinforcement and which are highly predictable, are equally able to serve the opposite function—to reduce pituitary-adrenal activity.

COPING

Since the time of Bernard and Cannon, the importance of maintaining physiological homeostasis has been well known. The consequences of inappropriate adrenal secretion are evident from the effects of both hyper- and hypo-adrenal output. Organisms deprived of adrenal corticoids are clearly in jeopardy and unable to effectively deal with even minor stressors that are of little consequence to an intact organism, such as water or salt restriction. Conversely, excessive secretion of the pituitary-adrenal system is also maladaptive. As we have described previously, prolonged elevations of adrenocortical hormones can have high biological cost, leading to increased susceptibility to psychosomatic illnesses as well as other pathophysiological processes, through their effects on the immune system. It would follow, therefore, that there must have evolved a set of mechanisms available to the organism whereby it could regulate and modulate excessive output of adrenocorticoids. We believe that these mechanisms are predominantly psychological and should be classified under the general rubric of *coping*.

Coping differs from habituation in one profound sense. In the case of habituation, it is presumed that the organism has changed its evaluation of the stimulus through repeated experience and has developed a set of expectancies concerning the benign characteristics of the stimulus or environment. Coping, on the other hand, is a more active process and can be defined in terms of the absence of a physiological response even under conditions in which the aversive stimuli continues to be present. In the case of coping, cognitive and behavioral processes are actively involved in determining whether an individual does or does not respond to a specific stressful situation. It is not just the aversive nature of the stimuli *per se* that determines the physiological response, but rather the individual's evaluation of these stimuli. We can regard this as a filter or gating function. An organism can alter its evaluation of potentially threatening or aversive stimuli if it can avoid, alter, or master the stress-inducing aspects of the situation. In a previous context, we have discussed the importance of predictability. There are two other psychological processes also involved in the process of altering an organism's evaluation of stressful events: (1) control over aspects of the situation and (2) feedback about the efficacy of its actions.

Perhaps the most important single determinant of the ability of the organism to reduce its hormonal responses to aversive stimuli is control. *Control* can best be defined as the capacity to make active responses during the presence of an aversive stimulus. These responses are frequently effective in allowing the animal to avoid or escape from the stimulus, but they may also function by providing the animal with the opportunity to change from one set of stimulus conditions to another, rather than to escape the aversive stimulus entirely. Control, in and of itself, can reduce an organism's physiological response to such noxious stimuli as electric shock. It has been observed that rats able to press a lever to terminate shock show less severe physiological disturbances (e.g., weight loss and gastric lesions) than yoked controls which cannot respond, even though both animals receive the identical amount of shock. Similarly, animals able to escape from shock show a reduction in plasma corticosterone following repeated exposures of shock (Davis, Porter, Livingstone, Herrmann, MacFadden, and Levine, 1977). The effects of control have also been demonstrated in an experiment by Hanson, Larson, and Snowdon (1976). These investigators studied rhesus monkeys that were exposed to another noxious stimulus—a loud noise. One group of monkeys were permitted to control the duration of the noxious stimulus by making a lever-press response to terminate the noise. A comparable group of monkeys were given the identical amount of noise, but were not permitted to regulate the duration. The animals that were allowed control procedures showed identical levels of plasma cortisol as those which were not exposed to the noise at all, compared to the yoked controls that showed extremely high levels of plasma cortisol.

The effect of control on plasma cortisol levels was also demonstrated very clearly in a recent experiment on dogs (Dess et al., 1983). These animals were subjected to a standard procedure used to produce learned helplessness. They were placed in a hammock and given uncontrollable and unpredictable shock. Other dogs were allowed to control the shock and terminate it by making a panel-press response with their heads. We have previously discussed the role of predictability within the context of this experiment. The results further indicated that controllability also affected the magnitude of the cortisol response to the shock. Having neither control nor predictability elicited the maximum cortisol response; having both minimized the impact of the shock. However, the capacity to control the stimuli appeared to have a greater effect in reducing the cortisol response to shock.

Rodin (1980) has presented an elegant series of studies with profound implications for the importance of control in human situations. As others had previously suggested (Birren, 1958; Gould, 1972), Rodin hypothesized that the transition from adulthood to old age may represent a loss of control. She further argued that the ability to sustain a sense of personal control in old age may be greatly influenced by societal factors, and that this, in turn, could affect the physical well-being of an aged individual. In order to investigate this problem, she introduced a program of "coping skill training" in a nursing home population, which was intended to reintroduce control to a group of individuals who felt a high degree of helplessness about their situation as a function of being institutionalized. There were two impressive aspects of the cortisol data presented in this study. First, among the aged in institutions, cortisol levels appear to be chronically elevated, similar to those observed in depressed individuals. Perhaps more important, however, was that individuals who were trained in certain aspects of coping skills (including control) showed a marked and significant reduction of their elevated cortisol levels.

The concept of control in reducing stress in humans can be observed in other situations as well, such as the work environment. Rose and associates (Rose, Jenkins, Hurst, Herd, and Hall, 1982a; Rose, Jenkins, Hurst, Kreger, Barrett, and Hall, 1982b; Rose, Jenkins, Hurst, Livingston, and Hall, 1982c) investigated a variety of endocrine parameters, including growth hormone and cortisol, in a large group of air traffic controllers during and after the work day. The job demands placed upon air traffic controllers have been considered to be extremely stressful. Blood samples were obtained automatically at 20-minute intervals over a five-hour period from a large group of working air traffic controllers in their routine occupational environment. The data indicated that cortisol and growth hormone levels were not appreciably elevated, and that both hormones showed a lack of consistency across repeated studies in terms of average levels or measures of episodic secretory activity. Thus, there appeared to be little in the way of an increased stress physiology under working conditions which were presumed to be stressful. It is important to note, however, that the population selected for study was composed of highly experienced individuals who had been on the job an average of 11 years. One could conclude, therefore, that as a consequence of their extensive work experience these individuals had developed adequate coping mechanisms, particularly in their ability to exercise control over the environment, which enabled them to minimize the physiological consequences of their stressful occupation.

FEEDBACK

Although it is clear that control is a major factor involved in coping, the ability or efficiency with which an organism can cope is also dependent upon another factor—feedback. *Feedback* refers to stimuli or information occurring after a behavioral response has been made in reaction to an event. These stimuli may be used to convey information to the responding organism indicating that it has made the correct response to a noxious event, for example, or that the aversive event is terminated for at least some interval of time. According to Weiss (1971a,b,c), the amount of stress an animal actually experiences when exposed to noxious stimuli depends upon the number of coping attempts the animal makes (control) and the amount of relevant information the coping response produces (feedback). As the required number of coping responses increase and/or the amount of relevant feedback decreases, the amount of stress experienced increases. In an extensive series of studies, Weiss demonstrated that if two groups of rats were subjected to the same amount of electric shock, the severity of the ulceration was reduced if the animal could respond—avoid and escape—and if the situation had some feedback information, i.e., a signal following the termination of shock. Although feedback information usually occurs in the context of control, namely, information about the efficacy of a response, it has been reported that feedback information *per se*, even in the absence of control, can reduce the pituitary-adrenal response to noxious stimuli. Hennessy et al. (1977) reported that the presence of a signal following the delivery of shock resulted in a reduced adrenocortical response even in the absence of control. In contrast, the pituitary-adrenal response of animals given a random signal was not significantly different from those animals that had no signal at all.

Although the human data concerning the role of feedback are not abundant, there is one large study (Ursin, Baade, and Levine, 1978) that investigated the coping process in humans following repeated experience with parachute training (Figure 5). In this study, the hormonal and behavioral responses of a group of Norwegian paratroop trainees were examined following repeated exposure to jumping off a 10-meter tower on a guide wire. After the first jump experience, there was a dramatic elevation of plasma cortisol, but as early as the second jump, there was a significant drop to basal levels; thereafter basal levels persisted on subsequent jumps (Figure 6). It is also important to note that the fear ratings changed dramatically following the first and second jumps, so that there was very little fear expressed after the second jump, even though there had been a very high rating of fear prior to the first jump. We believe that both aspects of the coping model presented by Weiss (1971a,b,c) can be applied to this situation. The individuals were able to make appropriate responses; that is, after the first experience they had already improved their performance of the task. However, since the individuals were jumping on a guide wire, performance was probably not the critical factor. The second aspect of the coping model, feedback, may be more important in this context. Although the situation was potentially

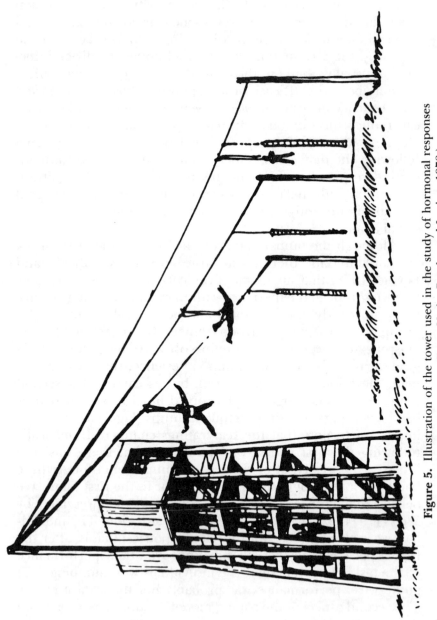

Figure 5. Illustration of the tower used in the study of hormonal responses of Norwegian paratroopers. (From Ursin, Baade, and Levine, 1978.)

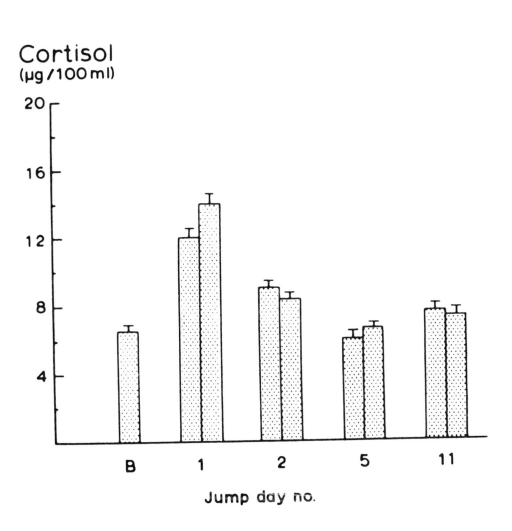

Figure 6. Plasma cortisol levels of Norwegian paratroopers immediately after and 20 minutes after successive training jumps. (From Levine, 1978.)

dangerous and threatening, the trainees had gone through the experience and suffered no bad consequences. Thus, a maximum amount of feedback about the absence of danger in a potentially threatening situation became quickly obvious.

When one closely examines the three factors—control, predictability, and feedback—that have been shown to be involved in the coping process, they all have common elements which can be viewed within the framework of the determinant of the stress response proposed earlier—uncertainty. Each of these factors, acting either alone or more probably in concert, appears to have the capacity to reduce uncertainty. Control provides the organism with the capacity to eliminate, or at least to regulate, the duration of the aversive stimuli. Thus, the uncertainty involved in unpredictable and uncontrollable situations is reduced. We have discussed predictability in a previous section of this chapter, and by definition, it serves to reduce uncertainty. Feedback can also be viewed in terms of reducing uncertainty, since feedback provides information to the organism about the efficacy and success of the response being emitted. We can therefore speculate that any set of operations that reduces uncertainty, whether they be passive such as habituation, or active such as the utilization of control, predictability, or feedback, can lead to an amelioration or elimination of adrenal activation.

SOCIAL SUPPORT

"Friends eventually forgive and come back together because people need people more than they need pride" (Prather, 1972). We turn to literature for a statement that captures the essence of an important process in social organisms, the role that social partners play in modifying and ameliorating the response to stressful events. There is now ample behavioral and physiological data which point to the importance of social relationships in determining an individual's ability to cope with

stress. Hamburg and Adams (1967) emphasized the great need
for the continuity of personal relationships when individuals
are involved in crisis. There have been several studies that have
pointed directly to social support as a major determinant in
specific health-related issues. Nuckolls, Cassel, and Kaplan
(1972) studied the relationship between social stress, as measured by the cumulative life-change scores of Holmes and Rahe
(1967), and psychological assets relating it to the prognosis of
pregnancy. These studies showed that women with high life-
change scores before and during pregnancy had an excessive
incidence of complications if their social support was low, while
a high level of social support appeared to be protective against
adverse outcomes. Cobb (1976) discussed further evidence
showing that social support affected the length of hospitalization and the rate of recovery from illness, minimized the effects
of retirement and bereavement, and helped one to endure the
threat of catastrophe. Cobb also studied the effects of social
support on the effects of job termination. One hundred men
whose jobs were abolished were visited by public health nurses
before and after their jobs had terminated, and periodically up
to 24 months after being unemployed. The results showed a
tenfold increase in arthritis (with two or more swollen joints)
in men who had low social support, as compared to men who
had a great deal of social support.

    The effects of social support on the pituitary-adrenal system
have been inferred in the now highly cited studies of Bourne
(1970, 1971) conducted during the Viet Nam war. There were
two studies that are relevant to this discussion. In the first study,
Bourne (1970) measured urinary levels of corticoids in helicopter medics who were involved in medical evacuation flights.
The striking finding was that when 17-OHCS levels on flight
days were compared to output on those days when the medics
remained on base, there were no significant differences. In fact,
their overall levels tended to be lower than comparable levels
of recruits and of the general population of men in the United
States. Although this study was not experimental, so that social
factors could not be manipulated, Bourne hypothesized that a

strong support group was an important social asset, and that one of the defenses being used by these helicopter medics was a deep belief that their task was worthwhile, as observed by the gratitude of the men they rescued. This feeling, combined with a sense of personal worth, was socially validated by the frequent medals and the additional merit pay they received.

In the second study (Bourne, 1971), a group of men in the Special Forces who had intercepted a message that their isolated camp was to be attacked by the Viet Cong in a few days, were evaluated. Again, 24-hour urine samples were obtained from the men in camp, both before the expected attack and several days following. Although the attack actually did not occur, anticipation of the attack resulted in different levels of urinary 17-OHCS excreted in some of the men. Most of the Special Forces enlisted personnel were enthusiastic about the impending attack and spent much of their time in task-oriented activities, such as bringing extra ammunition, fortifying their defenses, etc. Their behavior and attitude was in sharp contrast to the captain and the radio operator who spent much of their time communicating with the commanding officer at battalion headquarters, the captain under considerable pressure to perform well. Both the radio operator and the captain showed sharp increases in corticoid excretion on the day of the expected attack, compared to the days preceding and following this day. In contrast, most of the enlisted men actually showed a suppression of adrenocorticoids on the expected day of attack, which returned to basal levels in the following days. According to Bourne, the problem confronting the radio operator and the captain was that the orders being issued might not be relevant to the present situation, so that the officer had to compromise between satisfying his superiors and not disturbing the experienced soldiers with orders that they would regard as inappropriate. Bourne noted that the officer's duty did not permit him to keep busy with emotionally satisfying manual chores of the camp. In addition, the demands made upon the young officer to maintain his role as an authority figure over the older and experienced enlisted men was a tension-inducing influence that could have elevated his adrenal output. Once again, according to Bourne, the most important asset is the group consensus as to how a stimulus should be perceived. Although Bourne implicated social variables in the modulation of the adrenocortical response under these extremely stressful conditions, it is clear that the data are open to other interpretations. One could argue that in the case of both the helicopter medics and the enlisted men, they were able to exercise a large degree of control, and that this control may be the more important determinant of their low level of adrenal activity under these circumstances.

There is available experimental data that clearly implicate the role of social factors both in accentuating and modulating the pituitary-adrenal response. In order to study the influence of social behavior on hormonal systems, it is of course essential to investigate an animal whose predominant way of life is social. There are many forms of social organization and social behavior among animals, but it is in the primate species that the most striking feature of adaptation appears to be living in groups. Hans Kummer, a leading primatologist, has stated, "primates seem to have only one unusual asset in coping with their environments: a type of society which, through constant association of young and old and through a long life duration, exploits their large brains to produce adults of great experience. One may, therefore, expect to find some specific primate adaptations in the way primates do things as groups" (1971, pp. 37–38). In several experiments using a small South American primate, the squirrel monkey, we have found that group living can serve to reduce the individual's hormonal responses to events outside the group (Vogt, Coe, and Levine, 1981). Animals in groups communicate, and communication about available resources facilitates the survival of all group members. In addition, one of the primary adaptive functions served by groups is that gregarious animals are better at discovering, mobbing, and chasing a predator than single individuals. Further, by existing in a stable social situation in which it is possible to rely on the reactions of familiar social partners, the individuals may also show a reduced stress response.

Nonhuman primates generally exhibit strong behavioral reactions indicative of fear when exposed to a snake or snake-like objects (Vogt et al., 1981). In order to determine whether a group could serve as an effective modulator of stress responses, we exposed squirrel monkeys to a live boa constrictor, which was presented above their cage in a wire mesh box. Monkeys living in social groups consisting of males and females were exposed to the snake for 30 minutes while in a group, and also after being removed from the group and placed in an individual cage (Figure 7). An empty box, similar to the one containing the snake, was placed on top of the monkeys' cage on different days to control for the effects of general disturbance. All of the monkeys showed increased vigilance, agitated activity, and total avoidance of the stimulus box when the snake was presented in either the group or individual condition. However, while the presence of the snake consistently produced a behavioral response, it did not elicit adrenal activation in the monkeys when they remained in the group. Thus, it did appear that the social group could reduce the physiological response to a potentially threatening stimulus. Of equal importance was the fact that when the monkeys were separated from the group and placed in an unfamiliar cage, they showed striking elevations in plasma cortisol which were as great as those produced by exposure to the snake while alone. Whether these elevations in plasma cortisol following removal from the social group represent a response to loss of social partners or a response to novelty was difficult to specify in this experiment, but it is clear that the individual is much more prone to stress following disruption of group integrity. In additional experiments, we have subjected animals living in social groups to a variety of potentially stressful stimuli, such as a strange mobile robot, an unfamiliar nonspecific, loud noise, etc. In none of these conditions while the animals were living as a group in their home environment were we able to elicit a pituitary-adrenal response.

Conversely, the disruption of social relationships is, in fact,

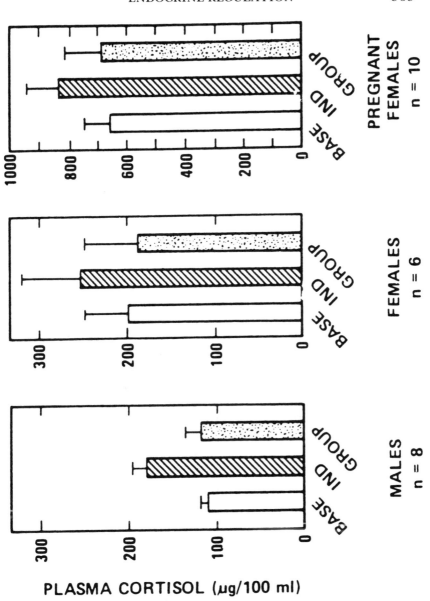

PLASMA CORTISOL (µg/100 ml)

Figure 7. Adrenal response of squirrel monkeys following 1-hour exposures to a snake while alone or in social groups. Note that the high cortisol levels are typical for this species and females characteristically have elevated levels during pregnancy. (From Vogt, Coe, and Levine, 1981.)

one of the most potent psychological stresses we have observed in monkeys (Coe and Levine, 1981; Coe, Wiener, and Levine, 1983). Stress responses to this specific social disruption emerge early in life. This is best exemplified by the mother-infant relationship, which, for the infant, is the basis of its early experiences with any kind of social interaction. In general, when one observes a mother and infant monkey in a social group, one finds that as the infant becomes older it spends more time away from its mother, increasingly investigating the physical environment and interacting with other members of the group. However, a common observation is that even relatively independent infants will immediately seek proximity and make contact with the mothers when a novel and fear-eliciting situation occurs. Soon after contact has been achieved, the infants begin to show reduced signs of behavioral agitation. We have now reported an extensive series of studies which have indicated that infants respond to loss of the mother with dramatic elevations of plasma cortisol (Coe et al., 1983). In the squirrel monkey, this response tends to increase according to the length of separation; and even following repeated separations, the response is elicited at the same magnitude on the last separation as the first. However, this intense adrenal response is in striking contrast to the effects of resumption of contact with the attachment figure. If the infant is permitted to resume contact with its mother after a brief separation, then the adrenal response typically observed after the disturbance appears to be suppressed. Mothers and infants that are separated but immediately reunited show no increases in pituitary-adrenal activity. The capacity of social contact to buffer the stress response of infants appears to be specific to the attachment figure.

When an infant monkey is separated from its mother, the context in which the separation occurs can also greatly affect the extent of the pituitary-adrenal response. In several experiments we have shown that if an infant is separated from its mother and permitted to remain in its home environment with familiar conspecifics, the pituitary-adrenal response, although still elicited, is reduced when compared to an infant who is totally isolated (Figure 8).

More recently, we have investigated the effects of separating the infant from its mother, placing it either alone in a novel environment, permitting it to remain in its home cage with familiar conspecifics, or placing it in an identical cage with unfamiliar mothers and infants. The results indicate that it is only the presence of familiar social figures which can reduce the pituitary-adrenal response to separation. Infants separated and placed with unfamiliar conspecifics do, in fact, show a striking elevation of plasma cortisol, which is actually somewhat higher than that seen in animals placed alone in a novel environment. These studies demonstrate both the potentially supportive role of the social group and the importance of familiarity in determining whether the beneficial effects will occur.

One of the important aspects of social support systems which differs from ordinary coping mechanisms is that these systems do not require the organism to deal directly with the aversive event *per se*. How then is it possible to fit the data on social support within the general context of the propositions that uncertainty leads to an activation of the pituitary-adrenal response, and that reduction of uncertainty reduces or eliminates this response? Cobb (1976) discusses social support as a moderator of life stress and sees it as providing information that falls into three categories. The first leads the subject to believe that he is loved and cared for. The second leads a person to have higher self-esteem as a result of public expression of approval. The third is the perception of social congruity derived from a shared network of information and mutual obligation in which each member participates, and the common knowledge is shared and accepted by all. It is possible to speculate that all three types of information derived from social support serve to minimize an individual's level of uncertainty about the situation. Thus, the availability of stable and familiar social relationships can provide a set of predictable outcomes due in part to the long history of previous interaction and experience.

These hypotheses would lead to the prediction that an un-

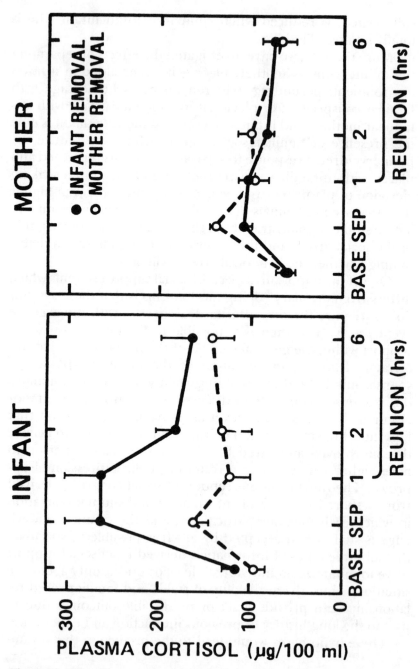

Figure 8. Adrenal responses of squirrel monkeys following separation of mothers and infants for 30 minutes. Note that the response is greater when the separated subject is isolated than when allowed to remain in the home environment. Infant recovery following reunion is also more protracted after isolation.

familiar social group would provide none of these beneficial features and, in fact, would constitute a condition of high uncertainty and therefore lead to an elevation of pituitary-adrenal activity. Thus, in the case of the infant separated from its mother and placed in an unfamiliar social group, we saw no amelioration of the stress response. In adult organisms, we have also found that one of the most reliable elicitors of increased pituitary-adrenal activity is the formation of new social groups. We have demonstrated in several experiments that there is a striking elevation of plasma cortisol when animals are placed in a new social group and, in fact, this elevation of cortisol can continue for several months (Gonzalez, Hennessy, and Levine, 1981; Coe, Smith, Mendoza, and Levine, 1983). Not only does the formation of a new social group have profound effects on the pituitary-adrenal system, but we have also determined that other endocrine systems are influenced by group formation—in particular, the pituitary-gonadal system.

PITUITARY-GONADAL SYSTEM

Whereas we have emphasized the importance of uncertainty and reduction of uncertainty as modifiers of the pituitary-adrenal system, the pituitary-gonadal system appears to be influenced not only by stressful events, but also by events related to reproductive activities and social interactions. The suppressive effects of stress on testicular and ovarian functions are probably the most well-known data, but it is apparent that gonadal hormone secretion can also be activated by certain types of external stimulation. Much of the latter research stems from studies on reproduction in animals that have shown the importance of environmental and physiological processes in stimulating sexual behavior (Desjardins, 1978). In particular, experiments on the hormone cycles of seasonally breeding species have demonstrated that these animals rely heavily on environmental cues for synchronizing the timing of the mating and birth periods

(Michael and Zumpe, 1976; Land, 1978). The seasonal recrudescences of testicular and ovarian activity in many of these species is also affected by psychological processes, such as territorial behavior and the presence of receptive mates (Rose, Bernstein, Gordon, and Lindsley, 1978; Rosenblatt, 1978). These findings have served to reshape our earlier view of gonadal hormone secretion as invariant and, in conjunction with the stress studies, have provided us with a large body of research on how psychological processes influence gonadal function.

The suppressive effect of stress on reproductive behavior and physiology has been known to breeders of domesticated animals for centuries. However, it was the conceptualization of the stress syndrome and the concurrent realization that the pituitary was regulated by the hypothalamus which provided a neuroendocrine explanation for the phenomena. As with ACTH, the secretion of gonadotrophins from the pituitary is controlled by releasing factors from the hypothalamus, and these hypothalamic areas are, in turn, influenced by higher brain centers and peripheral hormone levels. A wide variety of stimuli have been shown either to directly affect gonadotrophin secretion or to indirectly modulate the system by altering the feedback sensitivity of the hypothalamus to gonadal hormones. With regard to stress, some of the effects are corticoid-mediated, while others occur specifically at the gonads through alterations in secretion or local blood flow rates (Doerr and Pirke, 1976).

The effect of physical trauma can be best exemplified by the testosterone decline which a number of physicians have observed during surgery (Aono, Kurachi, Mizutani, Hamanaka, Uozumi, Nakasima, Koshiyama, and Matsumoto, 1972). Typically, following moderate surgery involving a blood loss of less than 300 ml and a duration of 1 to 2 hours, there are decreased levels of testosterone for 3 to 4 days with a rebound to normal or slightly above normal levels at the end of a week. Following major surgery, such as pulmonary lobectomy, heart surgery, or total gastrectomy, the decreased testosterone output persists for 2 to 3 weeks. While these testosterone decreases are associated with concomitant drops in LH levels, it is important to note that the gonadal decrease actually precedes the change at the pituitary level. Moreover, attempts to stimulate testicular secretion directly with HCG did not return the circulating levels of testosterone to normal, revealing that the inhibition occurred at both the pituitary and gonadal levels.

The evidence for a suppressive effect of physical trauma concurs with experimental studies on the effects of psychologically induced stress. Some of the earliest studies on this issue were conducted on the effects of overcrowding in both natural and captive animal populations (Christian, 1963). In addition to causing adrenal hypertrophy and higher mortality, overcrowding had a number of inhibitory effects on reproductive physiology and behavior. Subsequent studies have refined this analysis and have shown that overcrowding has differential effects depending upon the aggressivity and social rank of the animals. That is, only those animals that receive the most aggression and are low in the social hierarchy show the inhibitory effects. In fact, aggressive animals of higher social rank may actually show increases in testosterone levels.

Similar effects have also been observed in studies on the correlation between dominance, aggression, and testosterone levels in nonhuman primates. Although the correlation between social rank and testosterone is low in stable groups under normal conditions, during periods of aggression there is often a high correlation. One way of studying this phenomenon is to examine hormone levels in newly formed social groups, since there is usually a period of aggression before a social hierarchy is established between the previously unfamiliar animals. An example of the effect of establishing dominance relationships is shown in Figure 9, which illustrates the adrenal and gonadal responses observed in seven pairs of male squirrel monkeys (Coe, Franklin, Smith, and Levine, 1982).

As can be seen, both males showed increased adrenal secretion in response to the behavioral agitation, but the gonadal response was more selective. Males that become dominant showed a striking increase in testosterone levels at 24 hours

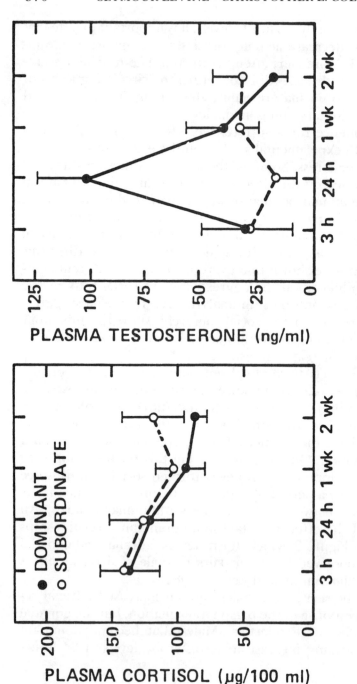

Figure 9. Adrenal and gonadal responses of male squirrel monkeys to pair formation. Both dominant and subordinate members of each pair showed increased cortisol levels, but only dominant males showed increased testosterone levels. (From Coe, Franklin, Smith, and Levine, 1982.)

after pair formation, whereas subordinate males tended to show a decline. In this study, the effect on hormone levels was transient, but in other experiments conducted during the mating period when hormone levels are higher, we have observed sustained effects for several weeks. Similar findings have been obtained in other primate species, such as the talapoin monkey and the rhesus macaque (Rose, Bernstein, and Gordon, 1975; Eberhart, Keverne, and Meller, 1980). In general, researchers have found that winners of fights show testosterone elevations, while losers of fights show lower levels of gonadal hormones. In time, as the aggression level subsides in stable groups, the correlation decreases and may be entirely absent unless wounding occurs, in which case the testosterone suppressions may be prolonged.

A legacy of this animal heritage can still be seen in humans. During periods of severe stress, such as in combat or in victims of torture, lowered levels of testosterone usually occur. Similarly, amenorrhea is a common symptom in women during highly stressful times, such as in war situations. Even in somewhat more benign environments, such as in military training school or during periods of extended school examinations, lower than normal levels of testosterone may occur (Kreuz, Rose, and Jennings, 1972). Moreover, the transient effect of aggression on testosterone titers has also been observed in men. Elevations in testosterone have been observed in winners of fights or contests in several situations including mock combat, collegiate wrestling, and competitive tennis matches (Mazur and Lamb, 1980). To alleviate any concerns on the part of casual weekend tennis players, however, this statement should be qualified; the tennis match must be highly competitive and the victory definitive.

Just as with the adrenal, then, we must be cognizant of the potential for bidirectional changes in testosterone secretion. While severe and prolonged stress is usually suppressive, acute stress can actually result in transient increases. Thus, moderate exercise on a treadmill can increase testosterone in men, but sustained running, such as in a marathon, will depress testosterone levels (Nieschlag, 1979). An example of transient increases and decreases following psychogenic stress was obtained in the study on Norwegian paratroopers described earlier in this chapter (Davidson, Smith, and Levine, 1978). As can be seen in Figure 10, testosterone levels were suppressed immediately before and 20 minutes after the first jump. However, on successive jumps, the decline was not observed, and following the fifth and eleventh jumps, significant increases occurred immediately after jumping. This finding of a transient elevation in testosterone immediately after acute stress concurs with a number of studies on LH and testosterone in other stressful situations (Gray, Smith, Damassa, Ehrenkranz, and Davidson, 1977; Coe, Mendoza, Davidson, Smith, Dallman, and Levine, 1978; Nieschlag, 1979).

Up to now we have emphasized the general effects of stress on adrenal and gonadal physiology, but the selective response of the gonadal hormones to social and sexual stimuli is equally important. It should not be too surprising that psychological processes related to reproduction have been shown to influence hormone secretion and other aspects of reproductive physiology. For example, in a wide variety of species, ranging from rodents to boars to primates, the presence of opposite-sex partners has been shown to raise testosterone levels in males. Conversely, the presence of same-sex animals has been shown to have an inhibitory effect in a number of species. In the case of female mice, the presence of only other female conspecifics will cause the females to become anestrus, while the introduction of a male will initiate synchronized estrus (Rosenblatt, 1978). Another example of this type of effect can be found in a number of monogamous primate species from South America. Only the dominant male and female in these family groups will reproduce, and it has been found that the inhibition in females is due to an alteration in feedback sensitivity at the hypothalamic level (Hearn, 1983).

To provide an example of this kind of psychological stimulation, we have included a figure from one of our studies on the response of male squirrel monkeys to females (Figure 11)

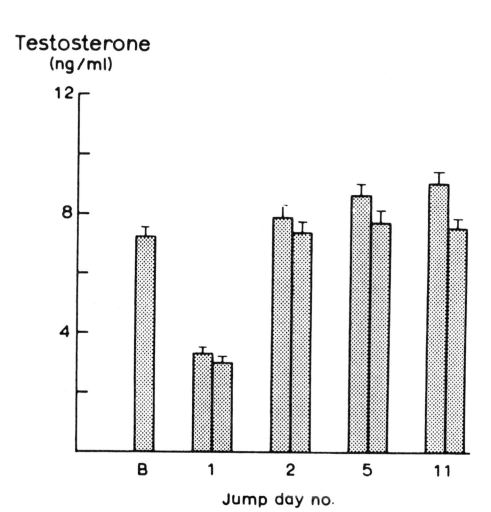

Figure 10. Testosterone response of Norwegian paratroopers immediately after and 20 minutes after successive training jumps. (From Davidson, Smith, and Levine, 1978.)

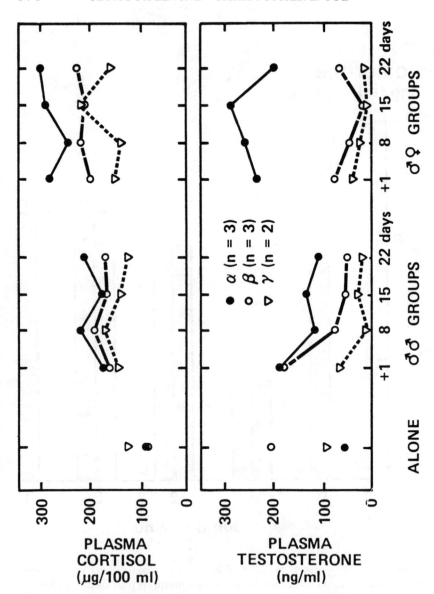

Figure 11. Adrenal and gonadal responses of male squirrel monkeys following formation of three male groups. Males that became dominant showed greater elevations in cortisol and testosterone, especially after females were introduced. (From Mendoza, Coe, Lowe, and Levine, 1979.)

(Mendoza, Coe, Lowe, and Levine, 1979). The study had three phases: males living alone, three all-male groups, and three male-female groups. As described before, when the male triads were housed together as a group, there was a differential effect of the resulting dominance ranks on both adrenal and gonadal hormones. All males showed increases in adrenocortical output following group formation, but dominant males showed the greatest increases. Moreover, there was a selective gonadal response. Dominant males had the highest levels of testosterone, and this effect became more pronounced after females were introduced. During the weeks with females, testosterone levels in dominant males increased further, whereas subordinate males showed decreased levels.

Although some of these effects could be attributed to the occurrence of reproductive behavior, since it is known that sexual activity can increase testosterone levels, several studies have now shown that mating is not a prerequisite for these hormone changes to occur. In rats, it has been shown that LH increases can be conditioned to cues previously associated with the presentation of females (Graham and Desjardins, 1980). An equivalent test of the psychogenic source in humans has been the assessment of the hormone response to viewing pornographic movies. Although not all men show testosterone increases after viewing pornographic movies, a certain percentage do, indicating the potential for psychological influence over gonadal activity (Pirke, Kockett, and Dittmar, 1974).

The question remains as to the medical significance of these findings on the gonadal system. In the case of severe stress and amenorrhea in women, it is clear that there are direct medical consequences. Similarly, following protracted changes in endocrine physiology, such as occur in anorexia nervosa, there may be persistent alterations in adrenal and ovarian physiology even after rehabilitation. In men, however, the medical significance of changes in testosterone are more difficult to specify, at least when the alterations remain within the normal physiological range. In humans, libidinal drive does not appear to be directly related to hormone level unless testosterone titers drop into the hypogonadal range (Nieschlag, 1979). A more probable outcome would be an influence on sexual proficiency, mediated by changes in androgen-dependent tissues. Effects on the prostate, seminal vesicles, and the other accessory sex glands could influence both spermatogenesis and semen production (Fujii, 1977). We would also anticipate a greater influence of these factors during development, since the effects of stress on pubertal maturation are well documented in animals.

Finally, just as adrenal hormones have a general effect on body tissues, gonadal hormones make an important contribution to the internal milieu. Testosterone has anabolic effects on certain tissues, such as muscle, whereas gonadal steroids tend to have an inhibitory influence on lymphocytes, similar to corticosteroids. The full significance of these psychologically induced hormone changes remains to be determined, but it is clear that sex hormones have an important role in the etiology of a number of diseases, such as rheumatoid arthritis, to name one. Moreover, a number of studies have now shown that testosterone can have a general influence on behavior by influencing attention span, persistence, and mood (Archer, 1977; Houser, 1979).

CONCLUSION

In 1933, the eminent British neurophysiologist, Lord Sherrington, wrote, "The question who turns the key, to use that metaphor, is soon answered, the outside world." This statement was used by Sherrington in a discussion attempting to describe the relationship between environmental factors and internal biological rhythms. What has become increasingly apparent since the time of Sherrington is that organisms live in concert with their environment and that many factors which occur in what is seemingly the outside world do indeed have profound consequences on endogenous processes. The secretion of hormones from many glands in the body is sensitive to a whole

variety of environmental changes. In this chapter, we have focused primarily on two hormone systems that result in the secretion of corticosteroids from the adrenal and androgens from
the testes. This is not to imply that these are the only hormone
systems in which environmental factors have a regulatory role.
It is clear that the peptide hormones emanating from the pituitary, including growth hormone, prolactin, LH, and beta
endorphins, are also responsive to environmental and psychological processes.

The field of neuroendocrinology has made tremendous advances in the past few decades in understanding those chemical
substances which qualify as hormones, not only in the pituitary
and peripheral organs, but in the central nervous system. Increasingly, the distinction between hormones and neurotransmitters has blurred as we have come to appreciate the
neuromodulatory role of many hormones. The way in which
these new CNS hormones respond to experiential factors has
not yet been thoroughly investigated. This is perhaps due to
the greater effort spent in attempting to isolate and identify
these hormones. However, when the methods of measuring
these particular substances become routine and readily available, there is no question that many of the issues dealt with in
this chapter will be investigated with regard to these new and
exciting substances. What is important for the purpose of this
discussion is that we believe that we have clearly demonstrated
the profound influence of psychological factors on the regulation of life-sustaining endocrine systems. A psychosomatic
approach to health and disease issues must, therefore, incorporate the fact that organisms actively respond to environmental information and that the psychological processing of this
information contributes to the regulation of peripheral systems
by modifying the ultimate regulator, the central nervous system.

REFERENCES

Allen, H. M. (1972), Gastrointestinal erosions in wild rats subjected to "social
stress." *Life Sci.*, 11:351–356.

Aono, T., Kurachi, K., Mizutani, S., Hamanaka, Y., Uozumi, T., Nakasima, A., Koshiyama, K., & Matsumoto, K. (1972), Influence of major surgical stress on plasma levels of testosterone, luteinizing hormone and follicle-stimulating hormone in male patients. *J. Clin. Endocrinol. Metab.*, 35:535–542.

Archer, J. (1977), Testosterone and persistence in mice. *Anim. Behav.*, 25:479–488.

Berlyne, D. E. (1960), *Conflict, Arousal and Curiosity.* New York: McGraw-Hill.

—— (1967), Arousal and reinforcement. In: *Nebraska Symposium on Motivation*, ed. D. Levine. Lincoln: University of Nebraska Press, pp. 1–110.

Birren, J. (1958), Aging and psychological adjustment. *Rev. Educ. Res.*, 28:475–490.

Bourne, P. G. (1970), *Men, Stress, and Viet Nam.* Boston: Little, Brown.

—— (1971), Altered adrenal function in two combat situations in Viet Nam. In: *The Physiology of Aggression and Defeat*, ed. B. E. Eleftheriou & J. P. Scott. New York: Plenum, pp. 265–290.

Christian, J. J. (1963), Endocrine adaptive mechanisms and the physiological regulation of population growth. In: *Physiological Mammalogy*, Vol. 1, ed. W. Mayer & R. van Gelder. New York: Academic Press, pp. 189–253.

Cobb, S. (1976), Social support as a moderator of life stress. (Presidential address.) *Psychosom. Med.*, 38:300–314.

Coe, C. L., Franklin, D., Smith, E. R., & Levine, S. (1982), Hormonal responses accompanying fear and agitation in the squirrel monkey. *Physiol. Behav.*, 29:1051–1057.

—— Levine, S. (1981), Normal responses to mother-infant separation in nonhuman primates. In: *Anxiety: New Research and Changing Concepts*, ed. D. F. Klein & J. G. Rabkin. New York: Raven Press, pp. 155–177.

—— Mendoza, S. P., Davidson, J. M., Smith, E. R., Dallman, M. F., & Levine, S. (1978), Hormonal response to stress in the squirrel monkey (*Saimiri sciureus*). *Neuroendocrinology*, 26:367–377.

—— Smith, E. R., Mendoza, S. P., & Levine, S. (1983), Varying influence of social status on hormone levels in male squirrel monkeys. In: *Hormones, Drugs, and Social Behavior*, ed. A. Kling & H. D. Steklis. New York: Spectrum, pp. 7–32.

—— Stanton, M. E., & Levine, S. (1983), Adrenal responses to reinforcement and extinction: Role of expectancy versus instrumental responding. *Behav. Neurosci.*, 97:654–657.

—— Wiener, S. G., & Levine, S. (1983), Psychoendocrine responses of mother and infant monkeys to disturbance and separation. In: *Symbiosis in Parent-Young Interactions*, ed. H. Moltz & L. A. Rosenblum. New York: Plenum, pp. 189–214.

Coover, G. D. (1983), Positive and negative expectancies: The rat's reward environment and pituitary-adrenal activity. In: *Biological and Psychological*

Basis of Psychosomatic Disease, ed. H. Ursin & R. Murison. Oxford: Pergamon Press, pp. 45–60.

―――― Goldman, L., & Levine, S. (1971), Plasma corticosterone increases produced by extinction of operant behavior in rats. *Physiol. Behav.*, 6:261–263.

―――― Sutton, B. R., & Heybach, J. P. (1977), Conditioning decreases in plasma corticosterone level in rats by pairing stimuli with daily feedings. *J. Comp. Physiol. Psychol.*, 91:716–726.

―――― Ursin, H., & Levine, S. (1973), Plasma corticosterone levels during active avoidance learning in rats. *J. Comp. Physiol. Psychol.*, 82:170–174.

Cope, C. L. (1972), Adrenal function and stress. In: *Adrenal Steroids and Disease*, ed. C. L. Cope. Philadelphia: Lippincott, pp. 199–225.

Davidson, J. M., Smith, E. R., & Levine, S. (1978), Testosterone. In: *Psychobiology of Stress: A Study of Coping Men*, ed. H. Ursin, E. Baade, & S. Levine. New York: Academic Press, pp. 57–62.

Davis, H., Porter, J. W., Livingstone, J., Herrmann, T., MacFadden, L., & Levine, S. (1977), Pituitary-adrenal activity and lever press shock escape behavior. *Physiol. Psychol.*, 5:280–284.

Desjardins, C. (1978), Potential sources of variation affecting studies on pituitary-gonadal function. In: *Symposium on Animal Models for Research on Contraception*, ed. N. J. Alexander. Hagerstown: Harper & Row, pp. 13–32.

Dess, N. K., Linwick, D., Patterson, J., Overmier, J. B., & Levine, S. (1983), Immediate and proactive effects on controllability and predictability on plasma cortisol responses to shocks in dogs. *Behav. Neurosci.*, 97:1005–1016.

Doerr, P., & Pirke, K. M. (1976), Cortisol-induced suppression of plasma testosterone in normal adult males. *J. Clin. Endocrinol. Metab.*, 43:622–629.

Done, A. K., Ely, R. S., & Kelly, V. C. (1958), Studies of 17-hydroxycorticosteroids. XIV. Plasma 17-hydroxycorticosteroid concentrations at death in human subjects. *Amer. J. Dis. Child.*, 96:655–665.

Eberhart, J. A., Keverne, E. B., & Meller, R. E. (1980), Social influences on plasma testosterone levels in male talapoin monkeys. *Horm. Behav.*, 14:247–265.

Elliott, G. R., & Eisdorfer, C., ed. (1982), *Stress and Human Health*. New York: Springer.

Falk, J. L. (1961), Production of polydipsia in normal rats by an intermittent food schedule. *Science*, 133:195–196.

Fujii, T. (1977), Role of age and androgen in the regulation of sex accessory organs. In: *Regulatory Mechanisms Affecting Gonadal Hormone Action: Advances in Sex Hormone Research*, Vol. 3, ed. J. A. Thomas & R. L. Singhal. Baltimore: University Park Press, pp. 103–137.

Gann, D. C. (1969), Parameters of the stimulus initiating the adrenocortical response to hemorrhage. *Ann. N.Y. Acad. Sci.*, 156:740–755.

Goldman, L., Coover, G. D., & Levine, S. (1973), Bidirectional effects of reinforcement shifts on pituitary-adrenal activity. *Physiol. Behav.*, 10:209–214.

Gonzalez, C. A., Hennessy, M. B., & Levine, S. (1981), Subspecies differences in hormonal and behavioral responses after group formation in squirrel monkeys. *Amer. J. Primatol.*, 1:439–452.

Gould, R. (1972), The phases of adult life: A study in developmental psychology. *Amer. J. Psychiat.*, 129:521–531.

Graham, J. M., & Desjardins, C. (1980), Classical conditioning: Induction of luteinizing hormone and testosterone secretion in anticipation of sexual activity. *Science*, 210:1039–1041.

Gray, G. D., Bergfors, A. M., Levin, R., & Levine, S. (1978), Comparison of the effects of restricted morning or evening water intake on adrenocortical activity in female rats. *Neuroendocrinol.*, 25:236–246.

——— Smith, E. R., Damassa, D. A., Ehrenkranz, J. R. L., & Davidson, J. M. (1977), Chronic suppression of pituitary-testicular function by stress in rats. *Fed. Proc.*, 36:322. (Abstract.)

Guillemin, R., Vargo, T., Rossier, J., Minick, S., Ling, N., Rivier, C., Vale, W., & Bloom, F. (1977), β-endorphin and adrenocorticotropin are secreted concomitantly by the pituitary gland. *Science*, 197:1368–1369.

Halliday, J. L. (1948), *Psychosocial Medicine: A Study of the Sick Society.* New York: Norton.

Hamburg, D. A., & Adams, J. E. (1967), A perspective on coping behavior: Seeking and utilizing information in major transitions. *Arch. Gen. Psychiat.*, 17:277–284.

Hanson, J. D., Larson, M. E., & Snowdon, C. T. (1976), The effects of control over high intensity noise on plasma cortisol levels in rhesus monkeys. *Behav. Biol.*, 16:333–340.

Hearn, J. (1983), *Reproduction in New World Primates.* Lancaster, PA: MTP Press.

Hennessy, J. W., King, M. G., McClure, T. A., & Levine, S. (1977), Uncertainty, as defined by the contingency between environmental events, and the adrenocortical response of the rat to electric shock. *J. Comp. Physiol. Psychol.*, 91:1447–1460.

——— Levine, S. (1979), Stress, arousal, and the pituitary-adrenal system: A psychoendocrine hypothesis. In: *Progress in Psychobiology and Physiological Psychology*, Vol. 8, ed. J. M. Sprague & A. N. Epstein. New York: Academic Press, pp. 133–178.

Hennessy, M. B., Heybach, J. P., Vernikos, J., & Levine, S. (1979), Plasma corticosterone concentrations sensitively reflect levels of stimulus intensity in the rat. *Physiol. Behav.*, 22:821–825.

——— Levine, S. (1977), Effects of various habituation procedures on pituitary-adrenal responsiveness in the mouse. *Physiol. Behav.*, 18:799–802.

Henry, J. P., & Stephens, P. M. (1977), *Stress, Health, and the Social Environment: A Sociobiologic Approach to Medicine.* New York: Springer-Verlag.

Heybach, J. P., & Vernikos-Danellis, J. (1979), Inhibition of adrenocorticotrophin secretion during deprivation-induced eating and drinking in rats. *Neuroendocrinol.,* 28:329–338.

Holmes, T. H., & Rahe, R. H. (1967), The social readjustment rating scale. *J. Psychosom. Res.,* 11:213–218.

Houser, B. B. (1979), An investigation of the correlation between hormonal levels in males and mood, behavior and physical discomfort. *Horm. Behav.,* 12:185–197.

Johnson, J. T., & Levine, S. (1973), Influence of water deprivation of adrenocortical rhythms. *Neuroendocrinol.,* 11:268–273.

Kagan, A. R., & Levi, L. (1974), Health and environment—psychosocial stimuli: A review. *Soc. Sci. Med.,* 8:225–241.

Kreuz, L. E., Rose, R. M., & Jennings, J. R. (1972), Suppression of plasma testosterone levels and psychological stress. *Arch. Gen. Psychiat.,* 26:479–482.

Kummer, H. (1971), *Primate Societies: Group Techniques of Ecological Adaptation.* Chicago: Aldine-Atherton.

Land, R. B. (1978), Reproduction in young sheep: Some genetic and environmental sources of variation. *J. Reprod. Fertil.,* 52:427–436.

Levine, S. (1978), Cortisol changes following repeated experiences with parachute training. In: *Psychobiology of Stress: A Study of Coping Men,* ed. H. Ursin, E. Baade & S. Levine. New York: Academic Press, pp. 51–56.

——— Coover, G. D. (1976), Environmental control of suppression of the pituitary-adrenal system. *Physiol. Behav.,* 17:35–37.

——— Madden IV, J., Conner, R. L., Moskal, J. R., & Anderson, D. C. (1973), Physiological and behavioral effects of prior aversive stimulation (preshock) in the rat. *Physiol. Behav.,* 10:467–471.

——— Weinberg, J., & Brett, L. P. (1979), Inhibition of pituitary-adrenal activity as a consequence of consummatory behavior. *Psychoneuroendocrinol.,* 4:275–286.

Mason, J. W. (1968), A review of psychoendocrine research on the pituitary-adrenal cortical system. *Psychosom. Med.,* 30:576–607.

——— (1975a), A historical view of the stress field. *J. Hum. Stress,* 1:6–12.

——— (1975b), A historical view of the stress field. *J. Hum. Stress,* 1:22–36.

Mazur, A., & Lamb, T. A. (1980), Testosterone, status and mood in human males. *Horm. Behav.,* 14:236–246.

Mendoza, S. P., & Barchas, P. (1982), Social mediation of stress: Human applications of a nonhuman primate model. Presented at the Symposium on Hormones and Behavior, Western Psychological Association, Sacramento, Cal., April.

——— Coe, C. L., Lowe, E. L., & Levine, S. (1979), The physiological response to group formation in adult male squirrel monkeys. *Psychoneuroendocrinol.*, 3:221–229.

Michael, R. P., & Zumpe, D. (1976), Environmental and endocrine factors influencing annual changes in sexual potency in primates. *Psychoneuroendocrinol.*, 1:303–313.

Miller, N. E. (1980), A perspective on the effects of stress and coping on disease and health. In: *Coping and Health*, ed. S. Levine & H. Ursin. New York: Plenum, pp. 323–353.

Nieschlag, E. (1979), The endocrine function of the human testis in regard to sexuality. In: *Sex Hormones and Behavior*, Ciba Foundation Symposium 62, 1978. Amsterdam: Excerpta Medica, pp. 183–197.

Nuckolls, K. B., Cassel, J., & Kaplan, B. H. (1972), Psychosocial assets, life crisis and the prognosis of pregnancy. *Amer. J. Epidemiol.*, 95:431–441.

Page, I. H., & McCubbin, J. W. (1965), The physiology of arterial hypertension. In: *Handbook of Physiology*, Sect. 2, Circ. 3, ed. W. F. Hamilton. Washington, DC: American Physiological Society, pp. 2163–2208.

Pirke, K. M., Kockett, G., & Dittmar, F. (1974), Psychosexual stimulation and plasma testosterone in man. *Arch. Sex. Behav.*, 3:577–584.

Prather, H. (1972), *I Touch the Earth and the Earth Touches Me*. New York: Doubleday.

Pribram, K. H., & Melges, F. T. (1969), Psychophysiological basis of emotion. *Handbook of Clinical Neurology*, Vol. 3, ed. P. J. Vinken & G. W. Bruyn. Amsterdam: North-Holland, pp. 316–342.

Renold, A. E., Quingley, T. B., Kennard, H. E., & Thorn, G. W. (1951), Reaction of the adrenal cortex to physical and emotional stress in college oarsmen. *New Eng. J. Med.*, 244:754–757.

Rodin, J. (1980), Managing the stress of aging: The role of control and coping. In: *Coping and Health*, ed. S. Levine & H. Ursin. New York: Plenum, pp. 171–202.

Rose, R. M., Bernstein, I. S., & Gordon, T. P. (1975), Consequences of social conflict on plasma testosterone levels in rhesus monkeys. *Psychosom. Med.*, 37:50–61.

—— —— —— Lindsley, J. G. (1978), Changes in testosterone and behavior during adolescence in the male rhesus monkey. *Psychosom. Med.*, 40:60–70.

—— Jenkins, C. D., Hurst, M., Herd, J. A., & Hall, R. P. (1982a), Endocrine activity in air traffic controllers at work. II. Biological, psychological and work correlates. *Psychoneuroendocrinol.*, 7:113–123.

—— —— —— Kreger, B. E., Barrett, J., & Hall R. P. (1982b), Endocrine activity in air traffic controllers at work. III. Relationship to physical and psychiatric morbidity. *Psychoneuroendocrinol.*, 7:125–134.

—— —— —— Livingston, L., & Hall, R. P. (1982c), Endocrine activity in air traffic controllers at work. I. Characterization of cortisol and growth hormone levels during the day. *Psychoneuroendocrinol.*, 7:101–111.

Rosenblatt, J. S. (1978), Behavioral regulation of reproductive physiology: A selected review. In: *Comparative Endocrinology*, ed. P. J. Galliard & H. H. Boer. Amsterdam: Elsevier, pp. 177–188.

Sandberg, A. A., Eik-nes, K., Migeon, C. J., & Samuels, L. T. (1956), Metabolism of adrenal steroids in dying patients. *J. Clin. Endocrinol.*, 16:1001–1016.

Schwartz, G. E., & Weiss, S. M. (1978), Yale conference on behavioral medicine: A proposed definition and statement of goals. *J. Behav. Med.*, 1:3–12.

Seligman, M. E. P. (1975), *Learned Helplessness: On Depression, Development and Death.* San Francisco: W. H. Freeman.

Selye, H. (1936), A syndrome produced by diverse nocuous agents. *Nature* (London), 138:32.

────── (1950), *Stress.* Montreal: Acta.

────── (1974), *Stress Without Distress.* London: Hodder & Stoughton.

Sherrington, C. S. (1933), *The Brain and Its Mechanisms.* Cambridge, UK: Cambridge University Press.

Sokolov, E. N. (1960), Neuronal models and the orienting reflex. In: *The Central Nervous System and Behavior*, ed. M. A. B. Brazier. New York: Josiah Macy, Jr., Foundation, pp. 187–276.

Ursin, H., Baade, E., & Levine, S., eds. (1978), *Psychobiology of Stress: A Study of Coping Men.* New York: Academic Press.

────── Murison, R. C. (1983), The stress concept. In: *Biological and Psychological Basis of Psychosomatic Disease*, ed. H. Ursin & R. Murison. New York: Pergamon Press, pp. 7–13.

Vogt, J. L., Coe, C. L., & Levine, S. (1981), Behavioral and adrenocorticoid responsiveness of squirrel monkeys to a live snake: Is flight necessarily stressful? *Behav. Neur. Biol.*, 32:391–405.

Weinberg, J., & Levine, S. (1980), Psychobiology of coping in animals: The effects of predictability. In: *Coping and Health*, ed. S. Levine & H. Ursin. New York: Plenum, pp. 39–59.

Weiss, J. M. (1971a), Effects of coping behavior in different warning signal conditions on stress pathology in rats. *J. Comp. Physiol. Psychol.*, 77:1–13.

────── (1971b), Effects of coping behavior with and without a feedback signal on stress pathology in rats. *J. Comp. Physiol. Psychol.*, 77:22–30.

────── (1971c), Effects of punishing the coping response (conflict) on stress pathology in rats. *J. Comp. Physiol. Psychol.*, 77:14–21.

Wolf, S., Almy, T. P., Bachrach, W. H., Spiro, H. M., Sturdevant, R. A., & Weiner, H. (1979), The role of stress in peptic ulcer disease. *J. Hum. Stress*, 5:27–37.

11.
The Genetics of Psychosomatic Disorders

KENNETH K. KIDD, PH.D., and
LOIS A. MORTON, M.D., PH.D.

INTRODUCTION

Most of the disorders studied by investigators in the field of psychosomatic medicine have not received the attention of human geneticists. This can be explained by the fact that psychosomatic disorders, in general, are not determined by genetic factors alone but also have significant nongenetic contributions. As such, these disorders are complex—although they often concentrate in families and appear to have a significant genetic contribution, they do not follow the simple Mendelian patterns of inheritance predicted for traits that are nearly 100 percent genetically determined. Until recently, complex traits have received little attention in the entire field of genetics because there are very few models available for predicting transmission patterns that are influenced by a combination of genetic and nongenetic factors. Indeed, although this is an area of genetic research that has witnessed great progress, it still "has a long way to go." Even the most sophisticated models available at the present time must make many simplified assumptions in order for their solutions to be mathematically tractable. At least some of these assumptions are probably not valid for many complex disorders; yet the robustness of the methods used has not been tested systematically.

Nevertheless, these models offer the best available means for sorting out genetic and nongenetic factors. The models have been applied, for the most part, to complex *behavioral* disorders, such as stuttering, Tourette syndrome, schizophrenia, depression, and anxiety disorders, by researchers in the field of behavior genetics. These investigators, most often geneticists collaborating with psychologists or psychiatrists, attempt to identify and validate the contribution of one or more genetic components in the etiology of disorders of human behavior. Investigators in the field of psychosomatic medicine, on the other hand, generally seek to identify and confirm the role of specific nongenetic components in the determination of complex somatic disorders. The disorders studied in behavior genetics and psychosomatic medicine almost never overlap. Yet many of the general research goals are the same in both fields. Nature-nurture arguments are not the issue. Rather, the question is which specific inherited factors interact with which specific nongenetic factors to result in the phenotype, i.e., the observable trait or disorder? It is only the *approach* to this question that differs: behavior geneticists most often look for genetic factor(s), while investigators studying psychosomatic disorders most often look for nongenetic factor(s). These two approaches are based on different convictions about the relative importance of various etiologic factors and about the methods that will most efficiently identify specific factors. However, both have suffered from oversimplified assumptions required by their respective models in the search for relevant contributory factors.

Investigators in both behavior genetics and psychosomatic medicine have called for a reevaluation of the methods used to study complex disorders (Kidd and Matthysse, 1978; Weiner, 1982). Many researchers in both fields feel that the assumption of etiologic homogeneity in such disorders greatly hinders progress. Weiner (1982) has argued persuasively that the study of the effects of nongenetic factors in psychosomatic disorders is warranted only within etiologically homogeneous subgroups of patients. Looking for the effect of a nongenetic factor in an etiologically heterogeneous group of patients assumes that the factor will be important in most, if not all, etiologic subgroups. For a disorder such as peptic ulcer disease, which is known to be heterogeneous with respect to etiology and pathophysiology, the premise that a nongenetic factor would have the same effect on all susceptible individuals is not reasonable. In this case, as with other psychosomatic disorders, it becomes important to develop and utilize models that do not assume etiologic homogeneity. This is the same problem of heterogeneity that confronts behavior geneticists, who have attempted to circumvent the problem by developing methodologic strategies and mathematical models that are appropriate for the study of complex traits. We will examine these methods in detail, discussing particularly how they might be applied to psychosomatic disorders. First, however, it is wise to consider the specific methodologic problems posed by complex disorders, both behavioral and psychosomatic, in order to identify inappropriate assumptions implicit in simpler models.

METHODOLOGIC ISSUES

As mentioned earlier, there are several complexities that arise in the development of methods for the study of psychosomatic and behavioral disorders. One commonly encountered problem is the contribution of multiple factors, no one of which is sufficient to cause the disorder. Geneticists label a trait "complex" when both genetic and nongenetic factors contribute to its development. This is certainly the case with several psychosomatic disorders, such as ischemic heart disease, rheumatoid arthritis, and peptic ulcer disease, and with several behavioral disorders such as stuttering, Tourette syndrome, schizophrenia, and depression. All of these disorders have been demonstrated to cluster in families—suggesting although not proving a genetic component—and all have been shown to have significant nongenetic contributions as well. In general the evidence for a genetic component takes the form of increased risk to relatives, greater concordance for illness among monozygotic twin pairs than among dizygotic twin pairs, or cosegregation of the trait with a known genetic marker within families. Evidence for a nongenetic component is provided by monozygotic twin concordances of less than 100 percent.

When a trait has been shown to be complex, i.e., when both genetic and nongenetic factors are known to contribute to etiology and pathogenesis, many simple methods for the identification of etiologic factors are no longer appropriate. Specifically, observed frequencies of genetic segregation of the trait will not agree with the frequencies predicted by simple genetic hypotheses such as autosomal dominant, autosomal recessive, X-linked, polygenic, or other simple models of inheritance. Likewise, comparison of a measurable variable or factor in groups of affected versus unaffected individuals may fail to show a significant difference simply because no single factor (genetic or nongenetic) is necessary for the development of the disorder. Prospective studies that search for the importance of environmental factors are handicapped by an inability to identify genetically vulnerable individuals, thus making it impossible to control for genetic predisposition. Even high-risk studies, such as those that focus on the offspring of affected individuals, employ a heterogeneous sample. For example, only 50 percent of the offspring of one affected parent will be vulnerable if vulnerability is inherited as a rare autosomal dominant trait. However, identifying those unaffected siblings who have inherited the vulnerability may be impossible. Thus the measurement of variables presumed to reflect vulnerability in affected versus unaffected individuals may fail to find a significant difference between the groups because the unaffected individuals included both susceptible and nonsusceptible members. Note that this problem does not arise when genetic vulnerability alone is sufficient for the development of the trait, as in simple Mendelian disorders.

A second problem that arises in the study of complex traits is variable expressivity of the disorder. For many behavioral traits, most notably depression, assignment of affected versus unaffected status is especially difficult because it is hard to evaluate whether etiologic heterogeneity or variable expressivity is responsible for the variation within a disorder. Situations involving many etiologically distinct but phenotypically similar disorders must be distinguished from conditions in which a spectrum of phenotypes reflects a single underlying genetic vulnerability. Without a reliable index of genetic vulnerability, decisions about which phenotypes should be included in the affected spectrum will be imprecise at best and biased at worst. Misclassification of individuals into affected and unaffected categories makes the search for etiologic factors, whether genetic or nongenetic, quite difficult.

This is a difficulty encountered with the study of many psychosomatic disorders as well. Certainly definition of rheumatoid arthritis (RA) suffers from variable expression of the underlying vulnerability. Patients can be divided into groups based on the presence or absence of serum rheumatoid factor, but some patients from both groups will meet the American Rheumatologic Association's criteria for "definite" rheumatoid arthritis and others will fail to meet them. Indeed some patients who are seropositive for rheumatoid factor will have no clinical manifestations of rheumatoid arthritis whatsoever. Distinction of RA from other chronic types of polyarthritis becomes increasingly difficult as milder cases are included in the diagnostic spectrum. Yet some mildly affected patients almost certainly have less classical presentations of the same underlying disease. Severity may be controlled by factors other than those conferring vulnerability to RA. These "severity factors" may be genetically determined (Panayi, Wooley, and Batchelor, 1978) or nongenetically determined. Ultimately, for complex disorders with variable expression, a method for reliably identifying genetically vulnerable individuals is necessary. Only then can investigators begin to evaluate the roles of other factors, both genetic and nongenetic, in the development of severely affected, mildly affected, and unaffected phenotypes.

A third obstacle to understanding the etiology of many complex disorders is their variable age of onset. This problem is related to that of variable expressivity. Because many of these disorders have a broad range of ages at onset extending well into adulthood, it is impossible to know whether an unaffected individual will remain so throughout his lifetime or will later contract the disease. Certainly the likelihood of having subsequent onset of the disease decreases with age. Thus, the probability that an unaffected individual is not susceptible is a function of the age of that individual. This is an important consideration for the study of genetic and nongenetic factors in both psychosomatic and behavioral disorders. Once again, affected/unaffected dichotomies may not correspond to susceptible/nonsusceptible dichotomies, so that the search for mean differences between affected and unaffected groups will be biased toward negative results.

For geneticists, who are attempting to determine the mode of inheritance of a complex trait, variable age of onset presents additional problems. Misclassification of individuals as "unaffected," who will later become affected, may lead to incorrect parameter estimates for genetic models. Variable age of onset may also bias analyses against finding evidence for genetic linkage of the complex trait to known genetic markers, an important means of proving genetic contribution to a disorder. Although it is possible to incorporate correction for variable age of onset into genetic segregation and linkage analyses, the mathematics are quite complex (Heimbuch, Matthysse, and Kidd, 1980; Thompson and Weissman, 1981). Nevertheless, the effects of even crude correction have been quite dramatic for bipolar affective disorder (Morton and Kidd, 1981) and Huntington's disease (Hodge, Spence, Crandall, Sparkes, Sparkes, Crist, and Tideman, 1980). We can expect that genetic studies of many other behavioral and psychosomatic disorders with variable age of onset would benefit by employing a similar approach. This tactic may be especially fruitful in those disorders reported to have a population association with alleles at HLA loci, such as rheumatoid arthritis, inflammatory bowel disease, and peptic ulcer disease (Mallas, MacKintosh, Asquith, and Cooke, 1976; Rotter, Rimoin, Gursky, Terasaki, and Sturdevant, 1977; Panayi et al., 1978). Demonstration of cosegregation of HLA haplotypes with the illness in families would constitute compelling evidence for a genetic component to the disorder and might aid in determining the nature of that genetic component and in distinguishing possible etiologic subtypes.

Finally, the most important obstacle to any etiologic study of a complex trait is the presence of etiologic heterogeneity. It is quite likely to be present in many of these disorders, given the variability in phenotypic expression and the complex nature of their pathophysiologies. Certainly for many behavioral and psychosomatic disorders, most notably ischemic heart disease (IHD) and peptic ulcer disease (PUD), there is good evidence for heterogeneity. Among the known etiologies for peptic ulcer disease, as described by Rotter and Rimoin (1977), are the Zollinger-Ellison syndrome, characterized by gastrin-secreting tumors of the pancreas or duodenum (Isenberg, Walsh, and Grossman, 1973) and the familial multiple endocrine adenoma-peptic ulcer disease complex, or MEN Type 1 (Ballard, Frame, and Hartsock, 1964). In addition, cases of peptic ulcer disease not associated with a particular syndrome are characterized by heterogeneity with respect to several physiological variables, such as pepsinogen concentration, acid secretion, rate of gastric emptying, and glucose tolerance test measurements (see Rotter and Rimoin, 1977, for a review). Genetic heterogeneity has also been implicated within those cases of PUD that are not part of the known syndromes. Doll and Kellock (1951) originally speculated that gastric and duodenal ulcers were inherited by separate mechanisms. More recently, Rotter, Sones, Samloff, Richardson, Gursky, Walsh, and Rimoin (1979b) have reported two PUD families with elevated serum pepsinogen I in which patterns of concentration are consistent with autosomal dominant inheritance, although patterns in most families are not consistent with Mendelian transmission.

For ischemic heart disease as well, a variety of risk factors have been implicated in pathogenesis, most notably diabetes mellitus (an etiologically and genetically heterogeneous entity in itself), hypertension, smoking, obesity, and positive family history of the disorder. At least some degree of genetic heterogeneity is present: the genetic hyperlipidemias are a family of inherited disorders leading to early, severe ischemic heart disease, but there appear to be independent genetic contributions as well. Even in those cases not attributable to hyperlipidemias, there is a familial concentration of the disorder. It is not clear whether this can be totally explained by the genetic contribution to known risk factors such as diabetes and hypertension or whether other genetically determined factors are also present.

In addition, familial clustering might simply reflect various social and cultural factors shared within families. Known nongenetic risk factors for ischemic heart disease include smoking (a proven independent risk factor), obesity (which appears to influence risk primarily through its association with hypertension and diabetes), and personality type (a risk factor of disputed importance). Once again, the search for nongenetic factors, such as personality variables, in genetically heterogeneous groups of patients may be biased against positive findings, if the nongenetic factor makes a significant contribution in only a single genetic subgroup. For example, factors such as stress that may affect circulating lipid levels (Dimsdale and Herd, 1982) are probably not significant factors determining the degree of atherosclerotic disease in patients with genetic hyperlipidemias, although these same factors *may* play a significant role in the precipitation of myocardial infarctions or other sudden events through another mechanism.

ANALYTIC METHODS

In this section we will focus on several examples illustrating the application of the methods of behavior genetics to two disorders complicated by gene-environment interactions, i.e., ankylosing spondylitis and stuttering. Neither of these disorders poses all of the problems of complex disorders that were discussed in the previous section. Yet each presents significant obstacles to analysis. Ankylosing spondylitis has both genetic and nongenetic etiologic components, as well as a variable age of onset and variable expressivity. We will discuss how a genetic approach to this disorder has partially solved some etiologic questions and has provided an opportunity to better address unsolved questions about how nongenetic factors may operate. Stuttering is a complex disorder with both nongenetic and genetic components and with possible genetic heterogeneity in its etiology. A major source of variability in the expression of stuttering is the question of recovery versus persistence into adulthood. Both genetic and cultural transmission hypotheses have been suggested to explain the familial clustering, but no clear explanation has emerged. A discussion of completed analyses of both disorders and of analyses in progress on stuttering should contribute to a general understanding of the strengths and limitations of many genetic/analytic methods for complex disorders.

Ankylosing Spondylitis

Ankylosing spondylitis (AS) is a chronic progressive arthritis of the spine that typically begins in early adulthood and frequently leads to a fusion of vertebrae, severely limiting the range of motion of the back. For many years it was believed to be a disorder nearly limited to males, but genetic and immunologic studies have led to the recognition of a milder form of the disorder in females.

Early studies of the HLA system (the major histocompatibility locus system in humans) led to many reports of associations between specific HLA alleles and specific diseases. One such report suggested an association between HLA B-27 and AS. Further studies of the HLA system that corrected for multiple statistical tests and demographic stratification have failed to confirm most of the initially reported associations. The association between AS and B-27 is an exception: it represents the strongest association known to date between a single HLA antigen and a disease. Specifically, 88 to 96 percent of AS patients have the B-27 antigen, whereas 7 percent of unaffected whites and even fewer unaffected blacks have the allele for B-27 (Brewerton, Caffrey, Hart, James, Nicholls, and Sturrock, 1973; Schlosstein, Terasaki, Bluestone, and Pearson, 1973).

This finding suggests several hypotheses for the role of B-27 in the etiology of AS. Since it is known that HLA alleles follow Mendelian patterns of inheritance, the simplest hypothesis is that B-27 plays a causal role in the development of AS. This hypothesis has been viewed skeptically because the pathogenesis of AS is not consistent with any known functions of the serologically determined antigens. A favored hypothesis is that an allele at a closely linked immune response locus confers susceptibility to AS. However, this second hypothesis does not in itself predict an association at the population level between the disease and any single HLA allele. Rather, one generally expects only the association of HLA alleles and disease within families, as a result of cotransmission of adjacent linked alleles. This within-family association, incidentally, is the type of HLA association reported for many other diseases such as Type 1 diabetes.

In order to explain the population association of B-27 and AS without invoking a causal role for B-27, one must hypothesize that an immune response allele conferring increased susceptibility to AS and the B-27 allele are in linkage disequilibrium. Linkage disequilibrium means that the two alleles co-occur on the same chromosomes more often than expected, implying that the combination is somehow favored in the population. This is not an unreasonable hypothesis: linkage disequilibrium exists within the HLA complex of loci. Unfortunately, without a more precise knowledge of the hypothetical gene products of the immune response locus, this explanation cannot be tested.

Family studies of AS, with special attention to the within-family association of HLA B-27 and the disease, have changed some widely held beliefs about ankylosing spondylitis. Most surprisingly, the sex difference in prevalence was not apparent when complete family studies of an affected individual were undertaken: equal proportions of susceptible male and female relatives of probands were affected. Of those relatives with the B-27 allele, about 40 percent of both males and females were found to be affected, although females certainly tended to have milder forms of the disorder. Kidd (1982) hypothesized that several factors were probably responsible for previously reported sex differences: (1) males appear to be afflicted with a more severe form of the disorder, increasing the probability that they would seek help; (2) in the past, limitation of spine motion was probably a greater economic hardship for many males than for females, again increasing the probability of help-seeking by males; and (3) the widely held belief that AS is almost exclusively a disease of males was self-fulfilling in that physicians were more likely to ascribe the symptoms of AS in females to other chronic arthritides, e.g., rheumatoid arthritis. Interestingly, it is unlikely that the data on the sex ratio in AS would have come to attention except through this type of family study.

Finally, because an easily determined genetic marker is closely linked to the susceptibility locus for AS, it is possible to identify genetically susceptible individuals with reasonable certainty. This offers an important opportunity for the study of nongenetic factors that either precipitate or offer protection against ankylosing spondylitis in vulnerable individuals. By controlling for genetic predisposition, the likelihood of identifying important nongenetic factors is greatly increased. AS, therefore, demonstrates how genetic studies can both increase understanding about pathogenesis and suggest avenues for etiologic research.

STUTTERING

Stuttering is a disorder of speech characterized by interruptions or blocks in the normally smooth transition from the production of one sound to the production of another. Blocks are recognized as repetitions, prolongations, or silent gaps. Stuttering is quite common in the general population—approximately 5 percent of males and 2 percent of females have stuttered at some point during their lives. In addition, stuttering has long been observed to cluster in families though Mendelian patterns are not recognized. Unlike the case of AS, neither a transmissible index of susceptibility nor a closely linked genetic marker has been identified.

Much of the initial work on stuttering has consisted of fitting transmission models, both genetic and cultural, to family data obtained by history from the proband. Kidd, Heimbuch, and Records (1981) analyzed data on 2035 relatives of 397 adult stutterers, most of whom were ascertained by referral from speech pathologists in New Haven area speech clinics or intensive therapy programs in California, New York, and Virginia. The remainder were contacted through local chapters of the Council of Adult Stutterers and through various third-party referrals. The method of ascertainment, as will be seen shortly, is an important variable that can influence the outcome of many genetic analyses. The probands, or index cases, were interviewed directly whenever possible. However, for about 50 percent of the sample, probands answered the interview questions through a self-report questionnaire. Because a layman's recognition of the symptoms and judgment about the presence or absence of stuttering correspond well with those of a speech pathologist, the self-report questionnaire is an acceptable alternative to direct interview.

A variety of approaches have been applied to these data. Kidd et al. (1981) used the logistic model described by Cox (1970) to predict the frequencies in siblings and children of affected ("ever stuttered") and unaffected ("never stuttered") classes using a variety of independent variables. These analyses demonstrated an increased risk of stuttering over that in the general population in these relatives of stutterers. A further increase occurred when a parent was also a stutterer, a finding suggestive of vertical transmission of susceptibility. It was also shown that males have a risk of stuttering twice as high as the risk to females; this observation is consistent with the higher prevalence in males in the general population. In addition, these analyses demonstrated that the risk to relatives of a female stutterer is higher than that to relatives of a male stutterer. This finding offers support for the hypothesis that susceptibility is transmitted within families *and* that sex-specific thresholds are involved, with females requiring a greater susceptibility than males in order to become affected. Under this hypothesis, female stutterers would have more susceptibility factors segregating in their families, and thus more of their relatives would be likely to be affected as compared with the families of male stutterers.

The demonstration of vertical transmission alone, however, does not distinguish between genetic and cultural modes of transmission. Indeed, some genetic hypotheses clearly cannot explain the data. For example, X-linked inheritance is incompatible with so many father-son pairs of stutterers. In addition, simple genetic hypotheses that fail to incorporate environmental factors will not fit the available data. Any single-gene model must incorporate incomplete penetrance in order to explain non-Mendelian frequencies in sibships. Models of entirely nongenetic transmission also deserve consideration; many nongenetic hypotheses for the precipitation of stuttering, such as imitation of other stutterers within the family, an association with general anxiety levels characteristic of the family, and forcing an unnatural hand preference on children have been suggested in the past. All such nongenetic factors are compatible with vertical transmission as well.

The testing of hypotheses on these data has been limited to several simple cultural and genetic models. The genetic models tested fall into two major categories: multifactorial-polygenic (MFP) and single-major-locus (SML). Both assume a continuous underlying distribution of liability with a threshold that determines the liability necessary to become affected. The MFP model assumes that liability is determined by a large number of genetic loci, with equal and additive effects. The SML model assumes a single locus with two alleles; each of the three genotypes has a normally distributed liability associated with it. Both models incorporate random, nontransmitted environmental effects. For a trait like stuttering with significantly different prevalences in males and females, these models must be modified to incorporate two thresholds, one for each sex. These sex-specific threshold versions of single-major-locus and multifactorial-polygenic models have both given acceptable fits to the family data (Kidd, Kidd, and Records, 1978). Thus, while very different genetic models cannot be distinguished from each other, genetic hypotheses are indeed compatible with the data.

Several simple models of cultural transmission can be excluded by the data. For example, direct imitation of a parental model could potentially explain the occurrence of stuttering in only a small minority of the child probands ascertained as part of this study (Kidd et al., 1978), since the vast majority of parents who ever stuttered had recovered long before the birth of the proband. In addition, other analyses have shown both that stutterers are randomly distributed with respect to birth order and that age of the proband at the time of separation from older siblings is unrelated to stuttering. These findings argue against the hypothesis that the object of imitation is an older sibling. The old idea that stuttering results from the thwarting of a natural preference for the left hand was not supported by these data, which showed a distribution of handedness among stutterers that was not significantly different from the distribution in an age- and sex-matched control group (Records, Heimbuch, and Kidd, 1977). Thus this study has failed as yet to identify cultural factors or models of cultural transmission that adequately explain the data. Of course, this lack of significant findings does not exclude a variety of alternative cultural hypotheses. Likewise, the adequate fit of several genetic models to these data does not prove a genetic component. Indeed the finding that two very different genetic hypotheses can both give acceptable fits to the data is rather discouraging. Proof of genetic transmission awaits actual identification of the gene product(s) conferring susceptibility or demonstration of cosegregation of stuttering with a closely linked genetic marker within families. Cox and Kidd (1979) have developed more complex single-major-locus and multifactorial-polygenic models that incorporate severity thresholds in addition to the sex thresholds mentioned earlier. These models again assume an underlying continuous distribution of liability; the form of the distribution is a function of both the model and the specific parameter estimates assumed. Four different thresholds are defined along the liability scale, corresponding to thresholds for mildly affected males, mildly affected females, severely affected males, and severely affected females. Cox and Kidd (1983) applied these sex and severity threshold models to the data on 397 adult persistent stutterers, with relatives who were persistent stutterers assigned to the severely affected categories and relatives who were recovered stutterers assigned to the mildly affected categories. The models did not adequately fit the data. Thus, recovery from stuttering is unlikely to be transmitted as a milder expression of the susceptibility genotype. Cox (1982) points out that several explanations for this finding are plausible. First, severity, as defined by recovery versus persistence, may be determined either by nongenetic factors or by genetic factors transmitted independently of susceptibility. Second, the method of ascertainment alone, which resulted in an aberrant sex ratio among the siblings of probands, could account for the heterogeneous pattern of recovery observed in the relatives of probands. This suggests the need for collection of another sample of both recovered and persistent probands utilizing a different ascertainment strategy.

Pedigree and linkage analyses of selected high-density pedigrees of stuttering have failed to prove either a particular mode of transmission or linkage to a known marker (Morton and Kidd, 1979; Cox, 1982). Pedigree analyses of a small subset of seven high-density pedigrees, after correction for the bias introduced by high-density selection, suggested some starting parameters sets that may be used for subsequent pedigree analysis of the entire dataset. Linkage analyses of stuttering in 14 high-density families did not show statistically significant co-transmission with any of 17 tested markers. However, when parameter estimates were varied to maximize the lod score (the statistic used to express the degree of cosegregation within specific families) for complete linkage (i.e., no recombination) between Gc and stuttering, a suggestive lod score of 1.104 (corresponding to an odds ratio of 2.7) was obtained.

Finally, in an attempt to get a level closer to the basic defect in stuttering, Cox (1982) studied measures of dichotic listening, a test thought likely to reflect cerebral lateralization. Twenty-four persistent stutterers, 24 recovered stutterers, 64 nonstuttering members of families with a stuttering proband, and 43 nonstuttering controls were tested. Recovered stutterers in families with multiple stutterers showed differences on some measures when compared to persistent stutterers or nonstutterers. This finding raises the question that perhaps atypical lateralization is related to recovery from stuttering, rather than susceptibility to stuttering. Under such a hypothesis, recovery could be either transmitted independently of susceptibility or not transmitted at all. However, prospective studies are necessary to validate the hypothesis that measures of dichotic listening do indeed correlate with recovery from stuttering and to determine whether atypical lateralization precedes or follows recovery.

Thus, stuttering represents a complex behavioral trait that has been approached from many viewpoints, using a variety of very different methods. A clear understanding of the genetic and nongenetic factors involved in its etiology has not yet emerged. Nevertheless, it does not seem unreasonable to expect that continued efforts in genetic research will be helpful in clarifying its etiology, as in the case of ankylosing spondylitis.

APPLICATIONS TO PSYCHOSOMATIC DISORDERS

In this section we will discuss three psychosomatic disorders in some detail, specifically mentioning the evidence for a genetic contribution, the current state of knowledge concerning the mode of inheritance of these genetic components, and the most reasonable approaches for further study. We have chosen to examine rheumatoid arthritis (RA), peptic ulcer disease (PUD), and ischemic heart disease (IHD) because each merits further genetic study.

RHEUMATOID ARTHRITIS (RA)

Rheumatoid arthritis is a chronic, generally symmetric polyarthritis primarily affecting the peripheral joints. Its etiology is unknown. Onset is most frequently between the third and seventh decades, and women are affected more often than men. Basically, the arthritis is the result of synovial proliferation that gradually destroys underlying cartilage and bone, eventually leading to the characteristic bony erosive changes seen on x-ray. The inflammatory process that ensues leads to increasing destruction and weakness of both the joint capsule and supporting structures. RA is associated with a variety of extraarticular manifestations, most notably the occurrence of so-called rheumatoid nodules in subcutaneous tissue, lung parenchyma, pleura, and myocardium, the development of vasculitis in both small- and medium-sized vessels, and atrophy of skeletal muscles. The relationship of these extraarticular manifestations to the predominant polyarthritis is not understood.

Apparently, immunologic factors play an important role in the early pathogenesis of the disease. Most patients with RA have antibodies specific for the Fc fragment of IgG in their sera and joint fluids. These antibodies are called rheumatoid factors, but do not occur solely in patients with RA. Patients with many forms of chronic infection and other connective tissue diseases, as well as many healthy elderly individuals, also have serum rheumatoid factors. Immune complexes, some from the self-association of the IgG rheumatoid factor molecules, are found in the synovial fluid of many patients. It has been speculated that some infectious agent initiates the immunologic and subsequent inflammatory processes, but no such agent has been identified.

A genetic predisposition to attack by an infectious agent or some other etiologic factor has been suggested as well. There has been much disagreement over the meaning of observed familial clustering. Lewis-Fanning (1950) reported an increased incidence of RA in the fathers, mothers, and siblings of RA probands, based on information given by the proband. A variety of other studies, using clinical data derived from examination of relatives, reported an increased incidence of RA in relatives (see Lawrence, 1970, for a review). However, studies employing the American Rheumatologic Association (ARA) criteria for probable or definite RA showed little, if any, increased incidence among relatives of RA probands (Bennett and Burch, 1968; Lawrence, 1970). Interestingly, Lawrence (1970) showed that the degree of familial aggregation was dependent on the criteria used to diagnose both probands and relatives, with severe forms of the disease showing a greater tendency to cluster in families.

As has been stated previously, familial aggregation does not prove genetic transmission. However, there is additional evidence supportive of a genetic contribution to RA. The hypothesis of a genetically transmitted susceptibility to RA is consistent with the finding of an association with the HLA antigen DR4. Family studies of cosegregation are necessary, however, to prove the importance of such a finding. Twin studies have shown concordance rates of 25 to 40 percent among monozygotic pairs and 5 to 11 percent among dizygotic pairs, again depending upon the inclusion of milder cases. These figures argue strongly for the presence of both genetic and nongenetic factors, but give little further information on the nature of those factors. Lawrence (1970) has argued that the data are consistent with polygenic inheritance, but we know of no studies testing single-major-locus models that incorporate environmental factors. Thus we cannot exclude this set of hypotheses.

In summary, the evidence for a genetic contribution to at least severe forms of RA is quite good. Familial clustering, monozygotic greater than dizygotic twin concordance, and the association of the disease with a genetically transmitted HLA antigen all support the hypothesis of a genetic contribution to RA. On the other hand, monozygotic twin concordances of less than 100 percent and non-Mendelian patterns of familial concentration argue for a significant contribution of environmental factors as well.

A variety of additional approaches to the data are appropriate. The most promising approach, however, is to look further at the association between HLA DR4 and RA by extending the HLA studies to families. The identification of cosegregation between HLA haplotypes and RA in families would prove a significant major-gene effect in the etiology of at least a subset of RA. In addition, it would contribute important information concerning the mode of genetic transmission and would permit the identification of vulnerable individuals prior to manifestation of the disorder, at least within families where a significant number of unique alleles were segregating. Once a marker of genetic vulnerability has been identified, it is possible to classify unaffected individuals as either susceptible or nonsusceptible with a high degree of certainty. Given this capability, etiologic studies of both genetic and nongenetic factors are much more likely to uncover real associations.

To date, most family studies of HLA and RA have not used the more powerful techniques of multigenerational genetic linkage analysis. Rather, they have looked only at the frequencies of specific haplotypes in affected and unaffected relatives, with special attention paid to DR4, the allele that is associated with RA at the population level. Several investigators have reported preliminary evidence consistent with cosegregation of RA and an HLA haplotype (Nunez, Moore, and Ball, 1980; Brackertz and Wernet, 1980), whereas other groups have found no increased sharing of HLA haplotypes among affected siblings (Strom and Moller, 1981). Consistent with the known population association, there is a high frequency of DR4 in families with more than one affected individual. Interestingly, Michalski, McCombs, DeJesus, and Anderson (1982) and Brackertz and Wernet (1980) reported that individuals homozygous for DR4 appear to have a more severe and progressive form of the disease. However, all of these preliminary family studies have failed to prove cosegregation of RA and HLA haplotypes. One alternative hypothesis is that DR4 confers increased susceptibility to some infectious agent, but that further transmission within a family is nearly HLA-independent because the presence of the infectious agent alone is the predominant factor. A second alternative is that RA is genetically transmitted by a locus that is not linked to HLA but that an HLA-linked locus controls the severity, perhaps by influencing the level of the immune response. This hypothesis is consistent with the observations that DR4 homozygotes have a more severe form of the disease.

However, Rossen, Brewer, Sharp, Yunis, Schanfield, Birdsall, Ferrell, and Templeton (1982), in one of the rare studies to use multigenerational linkage analysis, observed cosegregation of HLA haplotypes and RA in the families of four juvenile rheumatoid arthritis (JRA) probands. They found evidence highly suggestive of very close linkage when dominant inheritance and a penetrance of 80 percent were assumed. In addition, the phenotypes of unaffected individuals less than 30 years of age were considered unknown in order to incorporate, at least crudely, the variable age of onset. This result is most interesting because many of the affected relatives in these families had onset of the disease in adulthood. This suggests that at least some adult-onset RA patients are manifesting a disease that is an alternate expression of the genotype conferring susceptibility to JRA, which many investigators have considered a distinct disease entity. Further studies may prove extremely helpful in understanding the relationships among the rheumatoid arthritides, including the role of genetic factor(s).

Peptic Ulcer Disease

The term peptic ulcer disease (PUD) is used to describe a variety of erosive lesions found in the upper gastrointestinal tract, principally in the stomach and the duodenum. The etiology in most cases is not understood, although the common final pathway appears to involve an imbalance between the quantity of acid-pepsin produced and the resistance of the mucosa to corrosion. Acid is secreted by the parietal cells of the gastric mucosa in response to a variety of stimuli, both hormonal and neural. The acid cleaves inactive pepsinogen molecules, which are present in specific cells of the gastric and duodenal mucosa, thereby generating active pepsins. The secretion of acid also provides the proper pH environment for the activity of the pepsin. Pepsin is a proteolytic enzyme that functions in the digestion of proteins. In addition, pepsin appears to play a role, along with acid, in damaging the mucosal barrier in peptic ulcer disease.

Thus a variety of mechanisms can facilitate the development of peptic ulcers. Any factor that increases acid secretion can be expected to increase mucosal damage, both through the direct corrosive effect of the acid and through increased levels of active pepsin. This is the mechanism whereby patients with the Zollinger-Ellison syndrome develop peptic ulcer: gastrinomas secrete enormous amounts of gastrin, which, in turn, increases acid secretion. Coffee is also known to stimulate acid secretion. An alternative mechanism for peptic ulcer development is an increase in inactive pepsinogen molecules. Maximal gastric acid secretion is positively correlated with serum levels of pepsinogen I. Thus, the presence of increased numbers of precursor molecules would be expected to lead to increased pepsin concentrations and, therefore, an increased tendency to ulceration. Likewise, any factors known to damage the mucosal epithelium, thereby interrupting the barrier to back-diffusion of hydrogen ions, could be expected to increase the frequency of ulceration. Certainly salicylates, alcohol, and bile acids appear to interrupt this barrier.

PUD occurs in two principal locations, the antrum of the stomach (gastric ulcers) and the first portion of the duodenum (duodenal ulcers). Ulcers present at these two different locations often appear to be distinguishable clinically and indeed may be etiologically and physiologically different. Duodenal ulcer (DU) patients, on average, have rates of acid secretion that are higher than normal but normal serum gastrin levels. As a group, these patients also have a greater gastrin response to a protein-containing meal and a greater acid secretory response to gastrin itself. In addition, DU patients are somewhat more likely to have blood group O, to be nonsecretors with respect to ABH antigens and to have the HLA B5 allele than the general population. Environmental factors that may increase either susceptibility to duodenal ulcer or ulcer activity include cigarette smoking and chronic anxiety.

Gastric ulcer (GU) patients often have normal or even reduced levels of acid secretion. Indeed, a defective mucosal barrier is thought to be the most important factor in many patients. Because GU patients have been shown to have increased duodenal-gastric reflux of bile and higher concentrations of bile in the stomach when compared to patients without ulcers, it has been hypothesized that reflux of bile is an important mechanism for gastric ulcer development. Observations that the enzymes cholecystokinin and secretin fail to increase pyloric sphincter tone in GU patients, as they do in normal individuals, are consistent with hypotheses of decreased pyloric sphincter competence leading to reflux.

Thus, physiologic data suggest differences between duodenal and gastric ulcer patients. Consistent with the idea of separate etiologies, Doll and Kellock (1951) observed that gastric ulcer tends to cluster in the families of gastric ulcer probands, and duodenal ulcer tends to cluster in the families of duodenal ulcer probands. Nevertheless, distinct etiologies, modes of inheritance, and nongenetic risk factors have not been proven. Understandably, some controversy over the true separateness of these two disease entities remains.

It is precisely this area that could be better defined by more extensive genetic studies. For example, proof of cosegregation within one clinically defined subgroup of the disorder and a known genetic marker would validate the clinical subtyping. Likewise, genetic studies of the families of outliers, i.e., individuals with values outside the normal range for a particular physiologic variable such as increased basal acid secretion, may prove fruitful in terms of identifying either Mendelian modes of inheritance or linkage to known genetic markers where studies of more heterogeneous groups of patients often fail. This is essentially the strategy employed by Rotter et al. (1979b) in their studies of the inheritance of elevated serum pepsinogen I and DU. By selecting for study only the families of a subgroup of patients who had elevated serum pepsinogen, they found evidence consistent with cotransmission of the abnormally high pepsinogen level and PUD. Further studies, using multigenerational pedigree analysis of all sequentially ascertained families of high pepsinogen I probands, may validate the existence of that biochemically defined subgroup. Furthermore, the correct identification of one etiologic subgroup may help in the discovery of other etiologies as well.

As with most other psychosomatic disorders, peptic ulcer disease has long been observed to cluster in families, but no simple Mendelian patterns have been observed when heterogeneous samples of patients are studied. Frequencies of the disease in first-degree relatives of peptic ulcer disease patients have been observed to be as high as 24.5 percent, depending on the sex and type of relative (Monson, 1970). In general, frequencies in fathers and brothers of probands have been reported as 10 to 25 percent and those in mothers and sisters as lower, about 3 to 10 percent (Doll and Buch, 1950; Monson, 1970; Jirasek, 1971). These rates are increased over the general population's lifetime prevalence of 2 to 10 percent (Rotter, 1980). However, it should be stressed that the prevalence rates in relatives reported in most of the PUD studies were based on history from the proband rather than direct interview and examination of relatives. Tarpila, Samloff, Pikkarainen, Vuoristo, and Ihamaki (1982), however, interviewed and examined through endoscopy 154 first-degree relatives of PUD patients and 154 age- and sex-matched first-degree relatives of normal controls. They found that 13 percent of the relatives of PUD patients had endoscopic evidence of disease compared to 3.9

percent of the relatives of controls. This difference in relatives' morbidity, based on objective findings, offers much more compelling evidence for familial aggregation of disease than studies based only on history from the proband. Obviously, it is desirable to have family data obtained by direct clinical examination of the relatives in order to better estimate segregation ratios of the disease. For these studies, large multigenerational families provide much more information than small nuclear families.

A second type of genetic data comes from twin studies of PUD. One of the best such studies is that of Eberhard (1968), who examined x-rays of many cotwins. Eberhard reported that 11 of 78 (14.1 percent) dizygotic pairs were concordant for PUD and 17 of 34 (50 percent) monozygotic pairs were concordant. These data suggest that both genetic and nongenetic factors are likely to be important in the etiology of peptic ulcer. Although genetic and etiologic heterogeneity could account for the observed non-Mendelian segregation patterns, genetic heterogeneity alone cannot explain a monozygotic twin concordance of 50 percent. We are forced to conclude that nongenetic factors are important as well, among which may be those personality traits, such as chronic anxiety or increased sensitivity to criticism, that are often thought to be associated with PUD.

A final line of genetic evidence, though very limited to date, comes from the animal studies summarized by Rotter (1980). For example, Williams, Howie, Helyer, and Simpson (1967) reported a high frequency of peptic ulcer disease (over 50 percent) in NZB mice who lived to terminal stages of illness. NZB is an inbred strain that is highly susceptible to autoimmune diseases, suggesting to some that PUD may have an autoimmune etiology.

Extensive multigenerational analyses of transmission patterns have not been undertaken on any large scale. Mendelian patterns of inheritance have been observed, however, in subsets of PUD patients. For example, patients with Zollinger-Ellison syndrome have a tumor of the pancreas or duodenum that secretes excessive amounts of gastrin. Ten to 40 percent of Zollinger-Ellison patients also have tumors of nonpancreatic endocrine tissue, most often of the pituitary, adrenals, ovaries, and thyroid (Isenberg et al., 1973). This combined syndrome of Zollinger-Ellison and nonpancreatic, endocrine tumors is known as multiple endocrine neoplasia type I (MEN I). Patterns of transmission within families are consistent with autosomal dominant inheritance of a highly penetrant gene (Lamers, Stadil, and Van Tongeren, 1978). Other Mendelian disorders with PUD as a prominent component have been reported as well. Neuhauser, Daly, Magnelli, Barreras, Donaldson, and Opitz (1976) described a syndrome characterized by essential tremor, nystagmus, and duodenal ulceration; this syndrome was inherited in an autosomal dominant fashion in a large multigenerational family of Swedish-Finnish ancestry. More recently, Halal, Gervais, Baillargeon, and Lesage (1982) observed a gastrocutaneous syndrome of peptic ulcer/hiatal hernia, multiple lentigines/cafe-au-lait spots, hypertelorism, and severe myopia segregating in a single large family. However, patients with these genetic syndromes comprise a very small minority of patients with PUD.

In the absence of identification of the actual gene product(s) conferring susceptibility to a complex disorder, a demonstration of cosegregation with a known genetic marker is also convincing proof of a genetic contribution. Linkage to a known genetic marker has not been proven for PUD. However, many interesting, although weak, population associations have been reported. An increased frequency of PUD among individuals with blood group O, with a relative risk of 1.3, was first reported by Aird, Bentall, Mehiger, and Roberts (1954). This finding has been subsequently confirmed by several investigators (see Langman, 1973, for a review). Duodenal ulcer has been reported to be associated with nonsecretor status for ABH antigens, with 35.3 percent of DU patients being nonsecretors as compared to 24.2 percent of control probands (Clarke, Edwards, Haddock, Howell-Evans, McConnell, and Sheppard, 1956). In addition, investigators have reported associations with Rh positivity, alpha-l-antitrypsin deficiency, HLA B5, and G-6PD deficiency, but none of these associations has been consistently observed.

Rotter (1980) has argued convincingly that common peptic ulcer disease, i.e., that which is not known to be part of a Mendelian syndrome, is actually a heterogeneous group of disorders. For example, Rotter et al. (1979b) identified a group of PUD probands with elevated serum levels of pepsinogen I and studied the families of several of these probands in detail. These families showed not only transmission of PUD in a pattern consistent with autosomal dominant inheritance but also cosegregation of elevated serum pepsinogen I with the PUD. However, proof that patients with hyperpepsinogenemia constitute a homogeneous subgroup, with a large genetic contribution to etiology, awaits further pedigree analyses of sequentially ascertained hyperpepsinogenemic probands. In the meantime, the data of Rotter et al. (1979b) are very intriguing. A second preliminary report by Rotter et al. (1979a) describes a family with multiple-affected members in which the peak rate of gastric emptying in three of three family members with unoperated ulcer disease is higher than one of two unaffected relatives and six of six unaffected, unrelated controls. As with many other physiologic variables, rapid gastric emptying has not been found uniformly in all PUD patients (Rotter and Rimoin, 1977). Although this finding suggests another variable that may be useful in future large-scale studies of PUD patients and their families, it hardly constitutes proof of an etiologic subtype. Nevertheless, the hypothesis that genetic heterogeneity is partially responsible for non-Mendelian familial clustering is quite plausible. Some of the physiologic variables that may provide clues to etiologic subtypes include both elevated serum pepsinogen I and rapid gastric emptying as well as acid hypersecretion and gastrin response to a standard meal (Byrnes, Lam, and Sircus, 1976). A screen for patients who are outliers with respect to one or more of these physiologic variables may provide family data that will help clarify both etiologic and genetic questions.

ISCHEMIC HEART DISEASE

Ischemic heart disease (IHD) is a worldwide major cause of morbidity and mortality. Primary manifestations of IHD are angina, myocardial infarction, and sudden death. Ischemia of the myocardium, resulting from a decreased basal level of coronary blood flow and/or an inability to increase coronary blood flow in response to an increased demand for oxygen, is most often the result of atherosclerotic lesions in the coronary arteries. The causes of coronary atherosclerosis are multiple. To some degree, the accumulation of atherosclerotic lesions, or plaques, is a normal result of aging. However, a variety of risk factors has been implicated in the accelerated accumulation of plaques, leading to premature ischemic heart disease. Most notable among these factors is the serum cholesterol level, which was demonstrated by the Framingham heart study (Kannel, Castelli, Gordon, and McNamara, 1971) to be positively correlated with the risk of IHD, most significantly in younger age groups and in males. Risk appeared to increase continuously with serum level; there was no evidence that a "critical" level dramatically increased risk. Moreover, serum cholesterol level had significant predictive value even after excluding patients with hypertension, diabetes, current smoking history, and EKG abnormalities, all of which represent additional known risk factors. Thus, the cholesterol level itself appeared to be an important contributory factor.

Coronary disease is of interest to investigators in both genetics and psychosomatic medicine. First, IHD has captured the attention of geneticists because it is known to cluster in families; indeed, the genetics of a subset of IHD, which associated with the Mendelian hyperlipidemias, is well understood. Second, IHD has long been of interest to individuals in psychosomatic medicine for two reasons: (1) certain behavior patterns have been reported to be associated with increased risk (Rosenman, Jenkins, Brand, Friedman, Straus, and Wurm, 1975); and (2) there have been many reports of variation in lipid levels, both cholesterol and triglycerides, in response to a variety of emotional stimuli (see Dimsdale and Herd, 1982, for a review).

Genetic studies of IHD have been confined to the hyperlipidemias (see Motulsky, 1976; Frederickson, Goldstein, and Brown, 1978; or Brown and Goldstein, 1980, for reviews). Frederickson et al. (1978) discussed in detail the six well-defined familial hyperlipoproteinemias, which are associated with premature IHD to varying degrees. Familial hypercholesterolemia (type IIA hyperlipoproteinemia) is probably the best understood of the hyperlipoproteinemias. The condition is inherited as a simple autosomal dominant with nearly complete expression of the elevated serum cholesterol phenotype. The disorder is quite strongly associated with the premature development of ischemic heart disease. Stone, Levy, Frederickson, and Verter (1974) reported that 52 percent of male type IIA heterozygotes have fatal or nonfatal IHD by age 60 compared to 12.7 percent of normal male controls. The same study reported that female type IIA heterozygotes had a 32.8 percent risk of IHD by age 60 compared to a 9.1 percent risk for female controls. Other studies have reported similar risk figures (Gagne, Moorjam, Brun, Toussant, and Lupien, 1979; Hirobe, Matsuzawa, Ishikawa, Tarui, Yamamoto, Namta, and Fujimoto, 1982). Homozygotes have a greatly accelerated course of IHD, with death from myocradial infarction usually occurring before age 30 (Frederickson et al., 1978). This is consistent with the dramatically increased levels of serum cholesterol observed in homozygotes.

In both homozygotes and heterozygotes with type IIA hyperlipoproteinemia, the elevation in cholesterol content is in the low-density lipoprotein, or LDL, fraction. The LDL appears to be increased in amount, but normal in composition. The actual defect in familial hypercholesterolemia is in the membrane receptor for LDL, which is necessary for the intracellular transfer and subsequent metabolism of cholesterol (Goldstein and Brown, 1975). Homozygotes generally possess between 0 and 10 percent of the normal number of LDL receptors while known heterozygotes possess on average 50 percent of the normal number of LDL receptors. The resultant decreased binding of LDL to its receptor leads to decreased transfer of cholesterol into the cells and subsequent decreased formation of cholesterol esters, which are necessary for suppression of cholesterol synthesis. The normal negative-feedback process is therefore interrupted, leading to uncontrolled or, in the case of heterozygotes, inadequately controlled, serum cholesterol levels.

Familial dysbetalipoproteinemia (type III hyperlipoproteinemia) is much rarer than familial hypercholesterolemia. Elevation of serum cholesterol is due to the circulation of particles derived from the catabolism of very low density lipoprotein, or VLDL. These particles contain both cholesterol esters and triglycerides and are normally taken up by the liver. In familial dysbetalipoproteinemia, however, there is a block in that normal uptake process, resulting in an abnormal accumulation of the particles. Defective uptake is due to the genetically determined deficiency of a component of apoprotein E, EIII (Uterman, Vogelberg, Steinmetz, Schoenborn, Pruin, Jaeschko, Hess, and Canzler, 1979). The disease is inherited as an autosomal recessive with very low penetrance; only about 1 percent of homozygotes with complete EIII deficiency manifest the familial dysbetalipoproteinemia syndrome. Hypothyroidism, obesity, and diabetes mellitus are known to increase the likelihood of disease expression. Familial dysbetalipoproteinemia, like familial hypercholesterolemia, is strongly associated with premature IHD. Both diseases are known to result from single-gene mutations, but the primary biochemical defects are unknown. Familial hypertriglyceridemia, associated with elevated serum triglyceride but normal serum cholesterol, is transmitted in an autosomal dominant fashion. The disease is generally not expressed until the individual reaches the late 20s. Both obesity and diabetes mellitus further increase the risk of IHD.

Familial-combined hyperlipidemia is also inherited in an autosomal dominant pattern. Affected individuals may have either elevated serum cholesterol or triglycerides. Lipid elevation varies substantially over time.

It is important to realize that the Mendelian hyperlipidemias account for only a small fraction of individuals with elevated lipid levels. For example, familial hypercholesterolemia has a population prevalence of about 0.2 percent and familial combined hyperlipidemia a prevalence of about 1.5 percent. As

Brown and Goldstein (1980) note, this means that only three in 20 individuals with a serum cholesterol level in the upper 5 percent of the population actually have one of the known genetic hyperlipidemias. Other causes of hypercholesterolemia are clearly important. Interestingly, even in those cases not known to be due to a single-gene defect, familial clustering does occur, with about 10 percent of the first-degree relatives of these hyperlipidemic probands also having hyperlipidemia. However, this familial clustering may simply reflect the familial clustering of some causes of secondary hyperlipidemia, such as diabetes mellitus and alcohol consumption.

Psychosomatic studies of IHD have concentrated on the increased risk that appears to be associated with type A behavior (Rosenman et al., 1975; Brand, Rosenman, Sholtz, and Friedman, 1976; Jenkins, Zyzanski, and Rosenman, 1976). Some investigators have reported that type A behavior correlates well with objective findings at coronary angiography (Zyzanski, Jenkins, Ryan, Flessas, and Everisti, 1976), whereas other investigators have found no significant correlation (Dimsdale and Herd, 1980). Consistent with the hypothesis that type A behavior is at least a marker for increased risk of ischemic events, Kahn, Kornfeld, Frank, Heller, and Hoar (1980) and Krantz, Arabian, Davia, and Parker (1982) reported that individuals classified as type A were more likely to have operative and perioperative complications of coronary artery bypass surgery. Many hypotheses have been proposed in an attempt to explain the observed associations, but no consensus has emerged. It remains unclear whether type A behavior is simply a marker for increased risk or truly a causal factor, and whether, if it is a causal factor, it can be causal in all individuals or only in some individuals who also have a predisposing genotype.

In a separate but related group of studies reviewed by Dimsdale and Herd (1982), many investigators have found evidence for an association of changes in circulating plasma lipid levels with emotional arousal or highly stressful situations. Few of these studies have been longitudinal in design, although Francis (1979) reported on changes in cholesterol and other serum lipid levels in 20 students followed for two and a half months during an academic quarter. Francis (1979) found cholesterol levels peaked 10 to 12 days after stressful period corresponding to the beginning of the semester and the midterm examinations. The demonstration that transient changes in serum lipid levels are associated with stress suggests that lipid elevation may be the mechanism whereby the response to stress increases the risk of IHD. However, it is not clear that transient elevations in lipids actually affect the process of atherogenesis significantly. Perhaps the most interesting question, posed by Dimsdale and Herd (1982), is whether certain individuals might be prone to an exaggerated lipemic response to stress. If that is true, one would then like to know whether these individuals are also at greater risk for IHD.

This is the type of question that might be approached by an initial large sample survey followed by further study of individuals who are among the most extreme responders. The identification of these "outliers," if present, may form the basis for a homogeneous subgroup that can then be better characterized by family studies and longitudinal prospective studies. In this way, it would be possible to discover whether the lipemic response to stress is in part genetically determined, whether abnormal responders have a positive family history for IHD and, finally, whether these individuals themselves are at greater risk for IHD than a control group matched for other known IHD risk factors. Obviously, such a study is a tremendous undertaking, requiring at least preliminary evidence to suggest either an abnormal response to stress in a subgroup of individuals or an association between a sustained lipemic response to continual stress and increased risk for IHD.

DIRECTIONS FOR FUTURE RESEARCH

In the previous section, we have discussed in some detail the current state of genetic information in three psychosomatic disorders and have made some specific recommendations for further research. However, in suggesting approaches and strategies for the entire field, we must be more general. We believe it is most sensible to concentrate on the problem of genetic and etiologic heterogeneity in psychosomatic disorders. The potential effects of heterogeneity on the study of a disorder's etiology are tremendous. Weiner (1982) has discussed the implications of heterogeneity for psychosomatic studies, stressing the need to define homogeneous subgroups using biological markers. Within such subgroups, the chances of identifying precipitating and ameliorating factors, both psychological and environmental, are greatly increased. Psychosomatic research is much more likely to yield specific efficacious therapies by examining etiologically homogeneous subgroups.

From a genetic perspective, we would like to make an additional point. We would argue that the search for etiologically homogeneous subgroups is benefited by the tools of genetic analysis, in conjunction with biological information. An apparently homogeneous biological subgroup may prove to be genetically and etiologically heterogeneous upon closer inspection. Such heterogeneity is likely to be meaningful in planning appropriate therapies. In this context, we would like to discuss briefly three analytic strategies that may prove useful in the study of disorders with known or potential genetic heterogeneity.

SEARCH FOR OUTLIERS

One of the most widely employed methods in etiologic studies of complex disorders is the search for mean differences in biochemical variables between groups of affected and unaffected individuals. However, if etiologic heterogeneity exists, this method may fail to recognize significant associations present in only a subset of patients. In this type of situation, case-control studies may serve a useful purpose in screening large groups of affected individuals for those who are *outliers*, i.e., those who lie outside the normal range of values for a given variable or variables. These patients may represent a more etiologically homogeneous group appropriate for further studies of both genetic and nongenetic risk factors. For example, this method may represent an important tool in the study of peptic ulcer disease. The studies of Rotter et al. (1979b) are certainly consistent with autosomal dominant inheritance of a physiologically distinguishable subtype of PUD. This hypothesis could be tested by screening a large group of PUD patients for elevated serum levels of pepsinogen. The families of all patients with sufficiently increased levels can then be studied. Genetic segregation analyses can be used to discern the mode of inheritance and linkage analyses performed in order to identify linked genetic markers. This subset of patients also represents an important group for further study of nongenetic factors that may contribute to the development of PUD.

High-Risk Studies

As mentioned earlier, many prospective studies of individuals at increased risk for developing a disorder suffer from the inability to identify vulnerable individuals. However, some investigators have used prospective studies to search for an index of genetic vulnerability, i.e., some variable or measure that reflects an inherited susceptibility. By looking at an array of variables that may potentially reflect genetic susceptibility and noting which of these variables, if any, are predictive of later contracting the disease, one may be successful in identifying such an index. One cannot expect the correlation between index and disease to be a perfect one in complex disorders, however, since nongenetic factors are also known to be operating. In addition, this method is sensitive to the presence of significant genetic heterogeneity, because different genetic subtypes probably correspond to different indices of vulnerability. Certainly, once an index of vulnerability is identified, it can be used to ascertain individuals at high-risk for the disorder, providing an excellent opportunity for prospective studies of nongenetic factors that act to either precipitate or protect against contraction of the disease.

Thus, high-risk studies are most useful either with those disorders for which there is little or no genetic heterogeneity suspected or with disorders for which homogeneous subsets have been identified by some other means. High-risk studies might be useful, for example, in IHD, by selecting for follow-up the offspring of patients with no known transmissible risk factors. A prospective study of these individuals might permit the identification of new indexes of inherited susceptibility. Alternatively, one could choose to study the offspring of patients with a specific genetic hyperlipidemia, a disorder for which vulnerable individuals can be identified, and look prospectively at environmental and psychological factors that both increase and decrease the probability of ischemic events in vulnerable individuals.

Linkage Analyses

Finally, one genetic method that is almost uniquely suited to the detection of genetic heterogeneity is linkage analysis. Morton (1956) felt that this was an important use of the methodology developed to look for cosegregation of traits and markers. He described a test for heterogeneity among lod scores, and applying this method, he and his colleagues have elucidated the mode of inheritance of limb-girdle muscular dystrophy, severe mental defect, and deaf-mutism (Chung, Robison, and Morton, 1959; Morton and Chung, 1959; Dewey, Barrai, Morton, and Mi, 1965). Linkage analysis may be useful in the study of disorders for which either genetic linkage or population association between the disorder and one or more alleles at a marker locus has been reported. Genetic linkage analyses of such disorders may be helpful in elucidating the mode of inheritance or in detecting the presence of genetic heterogeneity. For example, this technique permitted Kravitz, Skolnick, Cannings, Carmelli, Baty, Amos, Johnson, Mendell, Edwards, and Cartwright (1979) to clarify the mode of inheritance for hem-